Software Development, Design and Coding

With Pat   ng,

Seco

John F. Dooley

Apress®

Software Development, Design and Coding

John F. Dooley
Galesburg, Illinois, USA

ISBN-13 (pbk): 978-1-4842-3152-4   ISBN-13 (electronic): 978-1-4842-3153-1
https://doi.org/10.1007/978-1-4842-3153-1

Library of Congress Control Number: 2017961306

Cover image designed by Vexels.com

Managing Director: Welmoed Spahr
Editorial Director: Todd Green
Acquisitions Editor: Todd Green
Development Editor: James Markham
Technical Reviewer: Michael Thomas
Coordinating Editor: Jill Balzano
Copy Editor: Corbin Collins
Compositor: SPi Global
Indexer: SPi Global
Artist: SPi Global

Distributed to the book trade worldwide by Springer Science+Business Media New York, 233 Spring Street, 6th Floor, New York, NY 10013. Phone 1-800-SPRINGER, fax (201) 348-4505, e-mail orders-ny@springer-sbm.com, or visit www.springeronline.com. Apress Media, LLC is a California LLC and the sole member (owner) is Springer Science + Business Media Finance Inc (SSBM Finance Inc). SSBM Finance Inc is a **Delaware** corporation.

For information on translations, please e-mail rights@apress.com, or visit www.apress.com/rights-permissions.

Apress titles may be purchased in bulk for academic, corporate, or promotional use. eBook versions and licenses are also available for most titles. For more information, reference our Print and eBook Bulk Sales web page at www.apress.com/bulk-sales.

Any source code or other supplementary material referenced by the author in this book is available to readers on GitHub via the book's product page, located at www.apress.com/9781484231524. For more detailed information, please visit www.apress.com/source-code.

Printed on acid-free paper

For Diane, who is always there, and for Patrick,
the best son a guy could have.

Contents

About the Author

John F. Dooley is the William and Marilyn Ingersoll Emeritus Professor of Computer Science at Knox College in Galesburg, Illinois. Before returning to teaching in 2001, Professor Dooley spent nearly 18 years in the software industry as a developer, designer, and manager working for companies such as Bell Telephone Laboratories, McDonnell Douglas, IBM, and Motorola, along with an obligatory stint as head of development at a software startup. He has more than two dozen professional journal and conference publications and four books to his credit, along with numerous presentations. He has been a reviewer for the Association for Computing Machinery Special Interest Group on Computer Science Education (SIGCSE) Technical Symposium for the last 36 years and reviews papers for the IEEE Transactions on Education, the ACM Innovation and Technology in Computer Science Education (ITiCSE) Conference, and other professional conferences. He has developed short courses in software development and created three separate software engineering courses at the advanced undergraduate level.

About the Technical Reviewer

Michael Thomas has worked in software development for more than 20 years as an individual contributor, team lead, program manager, and vice president of engineering. Michael has more than ten years experience working with mobile devices. His current focus is in the medical sector using mobile devices to accelerate information transfer between patients and healthcare providers.

Acknowledgments

I'd like to thank Todd Green of Apress for encouraging me and making this book possible. The staff at Apress, especially Jill Balzano and Michael Thomas, have been very helpful and gracious. The book is much better for their reviews, comments, and edits.

Thanks also to all my students in CS 292 over the last 12 years, who have put up with successive versions of the course notes that became this book, and to my CS department colleagues David Bunde and Jaime Spacco, who put up with me for all these years. And my thanks also go to Knox College for giving me the time and resources to finish both editions of this book.

Finally, I owe everything to Diane, who hates that I work nights, but loves that I can work at home.

Preface

What's this book all about? Well, it's about how to develop software from a personal perspective. We'll look at what it means for you to take a problem and produce a program to solve it from beginning to end. That said, this book focuses a lot on design. How do you design software? What things do you take into account? What makes a good design? What methods and processes are there to help you design software? Is designing small programs different from designing large ones? How can you tell a good design from a bad one? What general patterns can you use to help make your design more readable and understandable?

It's also about code construction. How do you write programs and make them work? "What?" you say. "I've already written eight gazillion programs! Of course I know how to write code!" Well, in this book, we'll explore what you already do and investigate ways to improve on that. We'll spend some time on coding standards, debugging, unit testing, modularity, and characteristics of good programs. We'll also talk about reading code, what makes a program readable, and how to review code that others have written with an eye to making it better. Can good, readable code replace documentation? How much documentation do you really need?

And it's about software engineering, which is usually defined as "the application of engineering principles to the development of software." What are *engineering principles*? Well, first, all engineering efforts follow a defined *process*. So we'll be spending a bit of time talking about how you run a software development project and what phases there are to a project. We'll talk a lot about agile methodologies, how they apply to small development teams and how their project management techniques work for small- to medium-sized projects. All engineering work has a basis in the application of science and mathematics to real-world problems. So does software development. As I've said already, we'll be spending *a lot* of time examining how to design and implement programs that solve specific problems.

By the way, there's at least one other person (besides me) who thinks software development is not an engineering discipline. I'm referring to Alistair Cockburn, and you can read his paper, "The End of Software Engineering and the Start of Economic-Cooperative Gaming," at http://alistair.cockburn.us/The+end+of+software+engineering+and+the+start+of+economic-cooperative+gaming.

Finally, this book is about professional practice, the ethics and the responsibilities of being a software developer, social issues, privacy, how to write secure and robust code, and the like. In short, those fuzzy other things that one needs in order to be a *professional* software developer.

This book covers many of the topics described for the ACM/IEEE Computer Society *Curriculum Guidelines for Undergraduate Degree Programs in Computer Science* (known as CS2013).[1] In particular, it covers topics in a number of the Knowledge Areas of the Guidelines, including Software Development Fundamentals, Software Engineering, Systems Fundamentals, Parallel and Distributed Computing, Programming Languages, and Social Issues and Professional Practice. It's designed to be both a textbook

---

[1]The Joint Task Force on Computing Education. 2013. "Computer Science Curricula 2013: Curriculum Guidelines for Undergraduate Degree Programs in Computer Science." New York, NY: ACM/IEEE Computer Society. www.acm.org/education/CS2013-final-report.pdf.

for a junior-level undergraduate course in software design and development and a manual for the working professional. Although the chapter order generally follows the standard software development sequence, one can read the chapters independently and out of order. I'm assuming that you already know how to program and that you're conversant with at least one of these languages: Java, C, or C++. I'm also assuming you're familiar with basic data structures, including lists, queues, stacks, maps, and trees, along with the algorithms to manipulate them.

In this second edition, most of the chapters have been updated, some new examples have been added, and the book discusses modern software development processes and techniques. Much of the plan-driven process and project-management discussions from the first edition have been removed or shortened, and longer and new discussions of agile methodologies, including Scrum, Lean Software Development, and Kanban have taken their place. There are new chapters on parallel programming and parallel design patterns, and a new chapter on ethics and professional practice.

I use this book in a junior-level course in software development. It's grown out of the notes I've developed for that class over the past 12 years. I developed my own notes because I couldn't find a book that covered all the topics I thought were necessary for a course in software development, as opposed to one in software engineering. Software engineering books tend to focus more on process and project management than on design and actual development. I wanted to focus on the design and writing of real code rather than on how to run a large project. Before beginning to teach, I spent nearly 18 years in the computer industry, working for large and small companies, writing software, and managing other people who wrote software. This book is my perspective on what it takes to be a software developer on a small- to medium-sized team and help develop great software.

I hope that by the end of the book you'll have a much better idea of what the design of good programs is like, what makes an effective and productive developer, and how to develop larger pieces of software. You'll know a lot more about design issues. You'll have thought about working in a team to deliver a product to a written schedule. You'll begin to understand project management, know some metrics and how to review work products, and understand configuration management. I'll not cover everything in software development—not by a long stretch—and we'll only be giving a cursory look at the management side of software engineering, but you'll be in a much better position to visualize, design, implement, and test software of many sizes, either by yourself or in a team.

CHAPTER 1

Introduction to Software Development

"Not only are there no silver bullets now in view, the very nature of software makes it unlikely that there will be any—no inventions that will do for software productivity, reliability, and simplicity what electronics, transistors, and large-scale integration did for computer hardware. We cannot expect ever to see twofold gains every two years."

— Frederick J. Brooks, Jr.[1]

So, you're asking yourself, why is this book called *Software Development, Design and Coding*? Why isn't it called *All About Programming* or *Software Engineering*? After all, isn't that what software development is? Well, no. Programming is a part of software development, but it's certainly not all of it. Likewise, software development is a part of software engineering, but it's not all of it.

Here's the definition of software development that we'll use in this book: *software development* is the process of taking a set of requirements from a user (a problem statement), analyzing them, designing a solution to the problem, and then implementing that solution on a computer.

Isn't that programming, you ask? No. *Programming* is really the implementation part, or possibly the design and implementation part, of software development. Programming is central to software development, but it's not the whole thing.

Well, then, isn't it software engineering? Again, no. *Software engineering* also involves a process and includes software development, but it also includes the entire management side of creating a computer program that people will use, including project management, configuration management, scheduling and estimation, baseline building and scheduling, managing people, and several other things. Software development is the fun part of software engineering.

So, software development is a narrowing of the focus of software engineering to just that part concerned with the creation of the actual software. And it's a broadening of the focus of programming to include analysis, design, and release issues.

---

[1]Brooks, Frederick. "No Silver Bullet." *IEEE Computer* (1987). 20(4): 10-19.

© John F. Dooley 2017

J. F. Dooley, *Software Development, Design and Coding*, https://doi.org/10.1007/978-1-4842-3153-1_1

What We're Doing

It turns out that, after 70 or so years of using computers, we've discovered that developing software is hard. Learning how to develop software correctly, efficiently, and beautifully is also hard. You're not born knowing how to do it, and many people, even those who take programming courses and work in the industry for years, don't do it particularly well. It's a skill you need to pick up and practice—a lot. You don't learn programming and development by reading books—not even this one. You learn it by doing it. That, of course, is the attraction: to work on interesting and difficult problems. The challenge is to work on something you've never done before, something you might not even know if you can solve. That's what has you coming back to create new programs again and again.

There are probably several ways to learn software development. But I think that all of them involve reading excellent designs, reading a lot of code, writing a lot of code, and thinking deeply about how you approach a problem and design a solution for it. Reading a lot of code, especially really beautiful and efficient code, gives you lots of good examples about how to think about problems and approach their solution in a particular style. Writing a lot of code lets you experiment with the styles and examples you've seen in your reading. Thinking deeply about problem solving lets you examine how you work and how you do design, and lets you extract from your labors those patterns that work for you; it makes your programming more intentional.

So, How to Develop Software?

The first thing you should do is read this book. It certainly won't tell you everything, but it will give you a good introduction into what software development is all about and what you need to do to write great code. It has its own perspective, but that's a perspective based on 20 years writing code professionally and another 22 years trying to figure out how to teach others to do it.

Despite the fact that software development is only part of software engineering, software development is the heart of every software project. After all, at the end of the day what you deliver to the user is working code. A team of developers working in concert usually creates that code. So, to start, maybe we should look at a software project from the outside and ask what does that team need to do to make that project a success?

In order to do software development well, you need the following:

- *A small, well-integrated team*: Small teams have fewer lines of communication than larger ones. It's easier to get to know your teammates on a small team. You can get to know their strengths and weaknesses, who knows what, and who is the "go-to" person for particular problems or particular tools. Well-integrated teams have usually worked on several projects together. Keeping a team together across several projects is a major job of the team's manager. Well-integrated teams are more productive, are better at holding to a schedule, and produce code with fewer defects at release. The key to keeping a team together is to give them interesting work to do and then leave them alone.

- *Good communication among team members*: Constant communication among team members is critical to day-to-day progress and successful project completion. Teams that are co-located are better at communicating and communicate more than teams that are distributed geographically (even if they're just on different floors or wings of a building). This is a major issue with larger companies that have software development sites scattered across the globe.

- *Good communication between the team and the customer*: Communication with the customer is essential to controlling requirements and requirements churn during a project. On-site or close-by customers allow for constant interaction with the development team. Customers can give immediate feedback on new releases and be involved in creating system and acceptance tests for the product. Agile development methodologies strongly encourage customers to be part of the development team and, even better, to be on site daily. See Chapter 2 for a quick introduction to a couple of agile methodologies.

- *A process that everyone buys into*: Every project, no matter how big or small, follows a process. Larger projects and larger teams tend to be more plan-driven and follow processes with more rules and documentation required. Larger projects require more coordination and tighter controls on communication and configuration management. Smaller projects and smaller teams will, these days, tend to follow more agile development processes, with more flexibility and less documentation required. This certainly doesn't mean there is *no* process in an agile project; it just means you do what makes sense for the project you're writing so that you can satisfy all the requirements, meet the schedule, and produce a quality product. See Chapter 2 for more details on process and software life cycles.

- *The ability to be flexible about that process*: No project ever proceeds as you think it will on the first day. Requirements change, people come and go, tools don't work out or get updated, and so on. This point is all about handling risk in your project. If you identify risks, plan to mitigate them, and then have a contingency plan to address the event where the risk actually occurs, you'll be in much better shape. Chapter 4 talks about requirements and risk.

- *A plan that every one buys into*: You wouldn't write a sorting program without an algorithm to start with, so you shouldn't launch a software development project without a plan. The *project plan* encapsulates what you're going to do to implement your project. It talks about process, risks, resources, tools, requirements management, estimates, schedules, configuration management, and delivery. It doesn't have to be long and it doesn't need to contain all the minute details of the everyday life of the project, but everyone on the team needs to have input into it, they need to understand it, and they need to agree with it. Unless everyone buys into the plan, you're doomed. See Chapter 3 for more details on project plans.

- *To know where you are at all times*: It's that communication thing again. Most projects have regular status meetings so that the developers can "sync up" on their current status and get a feel for the status of the entire project. This works very well for smaller teams (say, up to about 20 developers). Many small teams will have daily meetings to sync up at the beginning of each day. Different process models handle this "stand-up" meeting differently. Many plan-driven models don't require these meetings, depending on the team managers to communicate with each other. Agile processes often require daily meetings to improve communications among team members and to create a sense of camaraderie within the team.

- *To be brave enough to say, "Hey, we're behind!"*: Nearly all software projects have schedules that are too optimistic at the start. It's just the way we developers are. Software developers are an optimistic bunch, generally, and it shows in their estimates of work. "Sure, I can get that done in a week!" "I'll have it to you by the end of the day." "Tomorrow? Not a problem." No, no, no, no, no. Just face it. At some point you'll be behind. And the best thing to do about it is tell your manager right away. Sure, she might be angry—but she'll be angrier when you end up a month behind and she didn't know it. Fred Brooks's famous answer to the question of how software projects get so far behind is "one day at a time." The good news, though, is that the earlier you figure out you're behind, the more options you have. These include lengthening the schedule (unlikely, but it does happen), moving some requirements to a future release, getting additional help, and so on. The important part is to keep your manager informed.

- *The right tools and the right practices for this project*: One of the best things about software development is that every project is different. Even if you're doing version 8.0 of an existing product, things change. One implication of this is that for every project, one needs to examine and pick the right set of development tools for this particular project. Picking tools that are inappropriate is like trying to hammer nails with a screwdriver; you might be able to do it eventually, but is sure isn't easy or pretty or fun, and you can drive a lot more nails in a shorter period of time with a hammer. The three most important factors in choosing tools are the application type you are writing, the target platform, and the development platform. You usually can't do anything about any of these three things, so once you know what they are, you can pick tools that improve your productivity. A fourth and nearly as important factor in tool choice is the composition and experience of the development team. If your team is composed of all experienced developers with facility on multiple platforms, tool choice is pretty easy. If, on the other hand, you have a bunch of fresh-outs and your target platform is new to all of you, you'll need to be careful about tool choice and fold in time for training and practice with the new tools.

- *To realize that you don't know everything you need to know at the beginning of the project*: Software development projects just don't work this way. You'll always uncover new requirements. Other requirements will be discovered to be not nearly as important as the customer thought, and still others that were targeted for the next release are all of a sudden requirement number 1. Managing *requirements churn* during a project is one of the single most important skills a software developer can have. If you're using new development tools—say, that new web development framework—you'll uncover limitations you weren't aware of and side-effects that cause you to have to learn, for example, three other tools to understand them—for example, that that web development tool is Ruby based, requires a specific relational database system to run, and needs a particular configuration of Apache to work correctly.

Conclusion

Software development is the heart of every software project and is the heart of software engineering. Its objective is to deliver excellent, defect-free code to users on time and within budget—all in the face of constantly changing requirements. That makes development a particularly hard job to do. But finding a solution to a difficult problem and getting your code to work correctly is just about the coolest feeling in the world.

> *"[Programming is] the only job I can think of where I get to be both an engineer and an artist. There's an incredible, rigorous, technical element to it, which I like because you have to do very precise thinking. On the other hand, it has a wildly creative side where the boundaries of imagination are the only real limitation. The marriage of those two elements is what makes programming unique. You get to be both an artist and a scientist. I like that. I love creating the magic trick at the center that is the real foundation for writing the program. Seeing that magic trick, that essence of your program, working correctly for the first time, is the most thrilling part of writing a program."*

> —Andy Hertzfeld (designer of the first Mac OS)[2]

---

[2]Lammers, Susan. *Programmers at Work*. (Redmond, WA: Microsoft Press, 1986).

References

Brooks, Frederick. "No Silver Bullet." *IEEE Computer* (1987). 20(4): 10-19.

Lammers, Susan. *Programmers at Work.* (Redmond, WA: Microsoft Press, 1986).

CHAPTER 2

Software Process Models

If you don't know where you're going, any road will do.

If you don't know where you are, a map won't help.

—Watts Humphrey

Every program has a life cycle. It doesn't matter how large or small the program is, or how many people are working on the project—all programs go through the same steps:

1. Conception

2. Requirements gathering/exploration/modeling

3. Design

4. Coding and debugging

5. Testing

6. Release

7. Maintenance/software evolution

8. Retirement

Your program may compress some of these steps, or combine two or more steps into a single piece of work, but all programs go through all steps of the life cycle.

Although every program has a life cycle, many different process variations encompass these steps. Every development process, however, is a variation on two fundamental types. In the first type, the project team will generally do a complete life cycle—at least steps 2 through 7—before they go back and start on the next version of the product. In the second type, which is more prevalent now, the project team will generally do a partial life cycle—usually steps 3 through 5—and iterate through those steps several times before proceeding to the release step.

These two general process types can be implemented using two classes of project management models. These are traditional *plan-driven models*,[1] and the newer *agile development* models.[2] In plan-driven models, the methodology tends to be stricter in terms of process steps and when releases happen. Plan-driven models have more clearly defined phases, and more requirements for sign-off on completion of a phase

---

[1]Paulk, M. C. *The Capability Maturity Model: Guidelines for Improving the Software Process*. (Reading, MA: Addison-Wesley, 1995.)

[2]Martin, R. C. *Agile Software Development, Principles, Patterns, and Practices*. (Upper Saddle River, NJ: Prentice Hall, 2003.)

© John F. Dooley 2017

J. F. Dooley, *Software Development, Design and Coding*, https://doi.org/10.1007/978-1-4842-3153-1_2

7

before moving on to the next phase. Plan-driven models require more documentation at each phase and verification of completion of each work product. These tend to work well for large contracts for new software with well-defined deliverables. The agile models are inherently incremental and make the assumption that small, frequent releases produce a more robust product than larger, less frequent ones. Phases in agile models tend to blur together more than in plan-driven models, and there tends to be less documentation of work products required, the basic idea being that code is what is being produced, so developer efforts should focus there. See the Agile Manifesto web page at `http://agilemanifesto.org` to get a good feel for the agile development model and goals.

This chapter takes a look at several software life cycle models, both plan driven and agile, and compares them. There is no one best process for developing software. Each project must decide on the model that works best for its particular application and base that decision on the project domain, the size of the project, the experience of the team, and the timeline of the project. But first we have to look at the four factors, or variables, that all software development projects have in common.

The Four Variables

The four variables of software development projects are as follows:

- *Cost* is probably the most constrained; you can't spend your way to quality or being on schedule, and as a developer you have very limited control over cost. Cost can influence the size of the team or, less often, the types of tools available to the team. For small companies and startups, cost also influences the environment where the developers will work.

- *Time* is your delivery schedule and is unfortunately many times imposed on you from the outside. For example, most consumer products (be they hardware or software) will have a delivery date somewhere between August and October in order to hit the holiday buying season. You can't move Christmas. If you're late, the only way to fix your problem is to drop features or lessen quality, neither of which is pretty. Time is also where Brooks's law gets invoked (adding programmers to a late project just makes it later).

- *Quality* is the number and severity of defects you're willing to release with. You can make short-term gains in delivery schedules by sacrificing quality, but the cost is enormous: it will take more time to fix the next release, and your credibility is pretty well shot.

- *Features* (also called *scope*) are what the product actually does. This is what developers should always focus on. It's the most important of the variables from the customer's perspective and is also the one you as a developer have the most control over. Controlling scope allows you to provide managers and customers control over quality, time, and cost. If the developers don't have control over the feature set for each release, then they are likely to blow the schedule. This is why developers should do the estimates for software work products.

A Model That's not a Model At All: Code and Fix

The first model of software development we'll talk about isn't really a model at all. But it is what most of us do when we're working on small projects by ourselves, or maybe with a single partner. It's the *code and fix model*.

The code and fix model, shown in Figure 2-1, is often used in lieu of actual project management. In this model there are no formal requirements, no required documentation, and no quality assurance or formal testing, and release is haphazard at best. Don't even think about effort estimates or schedules when using this model.

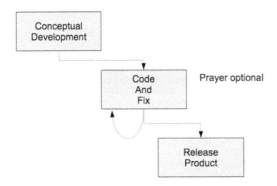

Figure 2-1. *The code and fix process model*

Code and fix says take a minimal amount of time to understand the problem and then start coding. Compile your code and try it out. If it doesn't work, fix the first problem you see and try it again. Continue this cycle of type-compile-run-fix until the program does what you want with no fatal errors and then ship it.

Every programmer knows this model. We've all used it way more than once, and it actually works in certain circumstances: for quick, disposable tasks. For example, it works well for proof-of-concept programs. There's no maintenance involved, and the model works well for small, single-person programs. It is, however, a *very dangerous* model for any other kind of program.

With no real mention of configuration management, little in the way of testing, no architectural planning, and probably little more than a desk check of the program for a code review, this model is good for quick and dirty prototypes and really nothing more. Software created using this model will be small, short on user interface niceties, and idiosyncratic.

That said, code and fix is a terrific way to do quick and dirty prototypes and short, one-off programs. It's useful to validate architectural decisions and to show a quick version of a user interface design. Use it to understand the larger problem you're working on.

Cruising over the Waterfall

The first and most traditional of the plan-driven process models is the *waterfall* model. Illustrated in Figure 2-2, it was created in 1970 by Winston Royce,[3] and addresses all of the standard life cycle phases. It progresses nicely through requirements gathering and analysis, to architectural design, detailed design, coding, debugging, integration and system testing, release, and maintenance. It requires detailed documentation at each stage, along with reviews, archiving of the documents, sign-offs at each process phase, configuration management, and close management of the entire project. It's an exemplar of the plan-driven process.

---

[3]Royce, W. W. *Managing the Development of Large Software Systems*. Proceedings of IEEE WESCON. (Piscataway, NJ, IEEE Press. 1970.)

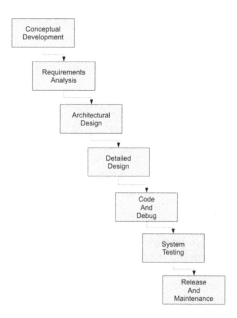

Figure 2-2. *The waterfall process model*

It also doesn't work.

There are two fundamental and related problems with the waterfall model that hamper its acceptance and make it very difficult to implement. First, it generally requires that you finish phase N before you continue on to phase N+1. In the simplest example, this means you must nail down *all* your requirements before you start your architectural design, and finish your coding and debugging before you start anything but unit testing. In theory, this is great. You'll have a complete set of requirements, you'll understand exactly what the customer wants and everything the customer wants, so you can then confidently move on to designing the system.

In practice, though, this never happens. I've never worked on a project where all the requirements were nailed down at the beginning of the work. I've never seen a project where big things didn't change somewhere during development. So, finishing one phase before the other begins is problematic.

The second problem with the waterfall is that, as stated, it has no provision for backing up. It is fundamentally based on an assembly-line mentality for developing software. The nice little diagram shows no way to go back and rework your design if you find a problem during implementation. This is similar to the first problem above. The implications are that you really have to nail down one phase and review everything in detail before you move on. In practice this is just not practical. The world doesn't work this way. You never know everything you need to know at exactly the time you need to know it. This is why software is a wicked problem. Most organizations that implement the waterfall model modify it to have the ability to back up one or more phases so that missed requirements or bad design decisions can be fixed. This helps and generally makes the waterfall model usable, but the requirement to update all the involved documentation when you do back up makes even this version problematic.

All this being said, the waterfall is a terrific theoretical model. It isolates the different phases of the life cycle and forces you to think about what you really do need to know before you move on. It's also a good way to start thinking about very large projects; it gives managers a warm fuzzy because it lets them think they know what's going on (they don't, but that's another story). It's also a good model for inexperienced teams working on a well-defined, new project because it leads them through the life cycle.

Iterative Models

The best practice is to iterate and deliver incrementally, treating each iteration as a closed-end "mini-project," including complete requirements, design, coding, integration, testing, and internal delivery. On the iteration deadline, deliver the (fully-tested, fully-integrated) system thus far to internal stakeholders. Solicit their feedback on that work, and fold that feedback into the plan for the next iteration.

(From "How Agile Projects Succeed"[4])

Although the waterfall model is a great theoretical model, it fails to recognize that all the requirements aren't typically known in advance, and that mistakes will be made in architectural design, detailed design, and coding. Iterative process models make this required change in process steps more explicit and create process models that build products a piece at a time.

In most iterative process models, you'll take the known requirements—a snapshot of the requirements at some time early in the process—and prioritize them, typically based on the customer's ranking of what features are most important to deliver first. Notice also that this is the first time we've got the customer involved except at the beginning of the whole development cycle.

You then pick the highest priority requirements and plan a series of iterations, where each iteration is a complete project. For each iteration, you'll add a set of the next highest priority requirements (including some you or the customer may have discovered during the previous iteration) and repeat the project. By doing a complete project with a subset of the requirements every time at the end of each iteration, you end up with a complete, working, and robust product, albeit with fewer features than the final product will have.

According to Tom DeMarco, these iterative processes follow one basic rule:

Your project, the whole project, has a binary deliverable. On the scheduled completion day, the project has either delivered a system that is accepted by the user, or it hasn't. Everyone knows the result on that day. The object of building a project model is to divide the project into component pieces, each of which has this same characteristic: each activity must be defined by a deliverable with objective completion criteria. The deliverables are demonstrably done or not done." [5]

So, what happens if you estimate wrong? What if you decide to include too many new features in an iteration? What if there are unexpected delays?

Well, if it looks as if you won't make your iteration deadline, there are only two realistic alternatives: move the deadline or remove features. We'll come back to this problem later when we talk about estimation and scheduling.

The key to iterative development is "live a balanced life—learn some and think some and draw and paint and sing and dance and play and work every day some,"[6] or in the software development world, *analyze* some and *design* some and *code* some and *test* some every day. We'll revisit this idea when we talk about the agile development models later in this chapter.

---

[4]www.adaptionsoft.com/on_time.html
[5]DeMarco, T. *Controlling Software Projects: Management, Measurement and Estimation.* (Upper Saddle River, NJ: Yourdon Press, 1983.)
[6]Fulghum, Robert. *All I Really Need to Know I Learned in Kindergarten.* (New York, NY: Ivy Books. 1986.)

Evolving the Iterative Model

A traditional way of implementing the iterative model is known as evolutionary prototyping.[7] In *evolutionary prototyping*, illustrated in Figure 2-3, one prioritizes requirements as they are received and produces a succession of increasingly feature-rich versions of the product. Each version is refined using customer feedback and the results of integration and system testing. This is an excellent model for an environment of changing or ambiguous requirements, or a poorly understood application domain. This is the model that evolved into the modern agile development processes.

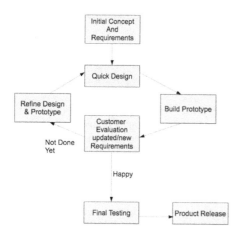

Figure 2-3. *Evolutionary prototyping process model*

Evolutionary prototyping recognizes that it's very hard to plan the full project from the start and that feedback is a critical element of good analysis and design. It's somewhat risky from a scheduling point of view, but when compared to any variation of the waterfall model, it has a very good track record. Evolutionary prototyping provides improved progress visibility for both the customer and project management. It also provides good customer and end user input to product requirements and does a good job of prioritizing those requirements.

On the downside, evolutionary prototyping leads to the danger of unrealistic schedules, budget overruns, and overly optimistic progress expectations. These can happen because the limited number of requirements implemented in a prototype can give the impression of real progress for a small amount of work. On the flip side, putting too many requirements in a single prototype can result is schedule slippages because of overly optimistic estimation. This is a tricky balance to maintain. Because the design evolves over time as the requirements change, there is the possibility of a bad design, unless there's the provision of re-designing—something that becomes harder and harder to do as the project progresses and your customer is more heavily invested in a particular version of the product. There is also the possibility of low maintainability, again because the design and code evolve as requirements change. This may lead to lots of re-work, a broken schedule, and increased difficulty in fixing bugs post-release.

Evolutionary prototyping works best with tight, experienced teams who have worked on several projects together. This type of cohesive team is productive and dexterous, able to focus on each iteration and usually producing the coherent, extensible designs that a series of prototypes requires. This model is not generally recommended for inexperienced teams.

---

[7]McConnell, S. *Rapid Development: Taming Wild Software Schedules*. (Redmond, WA: Microsoft Press, 1996.)

Risk: The Problem with Plan-Driven Models

Risk is the most basic problem in software. *Risk* manifests itself in many ways: schedule slips, project cancelation, increased defect rates, misunderstanding of the business problem, false feature richness (you've added features the customer really doesn't want or need), and staff turnover. Managing risk is a very difficult and time-consuming management problem. Minimizing and handling risk are the key areas of risk management. Agile methodologies seek to minimize risk by controlling the four variables of software development.

Agile methods recognize that to minimize risk, developers need to control as many of the variables as possible, but they especially need to control the scope of the project. Agile uses the metaphor of "learning to drive." Learning to drive is not pointing the car in the right direction. It's pointing the car, constantly paying attention, and making the constant minor corrections necessary to keep the car on the road. In programming, the only constant is change. If you pay attention and cope with change as it occurs, you can keep the cost of change manageable.

Agile Methodologies

Starting in the mid 1990s, a group of process mavens began advocating a new model for software development. As opposed to the heavyweight plan-driven models mentioned earlier and espoused by groups like the Software Engineering Institute (SEI) at Carnegie Mellon University,[8] this new process model was lightweight. It required less documentation and fewer process controls. It was targeted at small- to medium-sized software projects and smaller teams of developers. It was intended to allow these teams of developers to quickly adjust to changing requirements and customer demands, and it proposed to release completed software much more quickly than the plan-driven models. It was, in a word, agile.[9]

Agile development works from the proposition that the goal of any software development project is working code. And because the focus is on working software, then the development team should spend most of their time writing code, not writing documents. This gives these processes the name *lightweight*.

Lightweight methodologies have several characteristics: they tend to emphasize writing tests before code, frequent product releases, significant customer involvement in development, common code ownership, and *refactoring*—rewriting code to make it simpler and easier to maintain. Lightweight methodologies also suffer from several myths. The two most pernicious are probably that lightweight processes are only good for very small projects, and that you don't have any process discipline in a lightweight project. Both of these are incorrect.

The truth is that lightweight methodologies have been successfully used in many small- and medium-sized projects—say, up to about 500,000 lines of code. They have also been used in very large projects. These types of projects can nearly always be organized as a set of smaller projects that hang together and provide services to the single large product at the end. Lightweight processes can be used on the smaller projects quite easily. Lightweight methodologies also require process discipline, especially at the beginning of a project when initial requirements and an iteration cycle are created, and in the test-driven-development used as the heart of the coding process.

The rest of this chapter describes the agile values and principles, then looks at two lightweight/agile methodologies, eXtreme Programming (XP) and Scrum, and finally talks about an interesting variant: lean software development.

---

[8]Paulk, M. C. (1995.)
[9]Cockburn, A. *Agile Software Development.* (Boston, MA: Addison-Wesley, 2002.)

Agile Values and Principles

In early 2001 a group of experienced and innovative developers met in Snowbird, Utah to talk about the state of the software development process. All of them were dissatisfied with traditional plan-driven models and had been experimenting with new lightweight development techniques. Out of this meeting came the Agile Manifesto.[10] The original description proposed by the group included two parts: values (the manifesto itself) and principles. The values are as follows:

- Individuals and interactions over processes and tools

- Working software over comprehensive documentation

- Customer collaboration over contract negotiation

- Responding to change over following a plan

The idea behind the manifesto is that although the authors understood the value of the latter items in each value, they preferred to think and work on the former items. Those things—individuals, working software, collaboration, and responding to change—are the most important and valuable ideas in getting a software product out the door.

The principles run as follows:

1. Our highest priority is to satisfy the customer through early and continuous delivery of valuable software.

2. Welcome changing requirements, even late in development. Agile processes harness change for the customer's competitive advantage.

3. Deliver working software frequently, from a couple of weeks to a couple of months, with a preference to the shorter timescale.

4. Business people and developers must work together daily throughout the project.

5. Build projects around motivated individuals. Give them the environment and support they need, and trust them to get the job done.

6. The most efficient and effective method of conveying information to and within a development team is face-to-face conversation.

7. Working software is the primary way to measure progress.

8. Agile processes promote sustainable development. The sponsors, developers, and users should be able to maintain a constant pace indefinitely.

9. Continuous attention to technical excellence and good design enhances agility.

10. Simplicity—the art of maximizing the amount of work not done—is essential.

11. The best architectures, requirements, and designs emerge from self-organizing teams.

12. At regular intervals, the team reflects on how to become more effective and then tunes and adjusts its behavior accordingly.

---

[10]www.agilealliance.org/agile101/

eXtreme Programming (XP)

Kent Beck and Ward Cunningham created XP around 1995. XP is a "lightweight, efficient, low-risk, flexible, predictable, scientific, and fun way to develop software."[11]

XP Overview

XP relies on the following four fundamental ideas:

- *Heavy customer involvement*: XP requires that a customer representative be part of the development team and be on site at all times. The customer representative works with the team to define the content of each iteration of the product. They also create all the acceptance tests for each interim release.

- *Continuous unit testing (also known as test-driven development, or TDD)*: XP calls for developers to write the unit tests for any new features before any of the code is written. In this way the tests will, of course, initially all fail, but it gives a developer a clear metric for success. When all the unit tests pass, you've finished implementing the feature.

- *Pair programming*: XP requires that pairs of developers write all code. In a nutshell, pair programming requires two programmers—a driver and a navigator—who share a single computer. The *driver* is actually writing the code while the *navigator* watches, catching typos, making suggestions, thinking about design and testing, and so on. The pair switches places periodically (every 30 minutes or so, or when one of them thinks he has a better way of implementing a piece of code). Pair programming works on the "two heads are better than one" theory. Although a pair of programmers isn't quite as productive as two individual programmers when it comes to number of lines of code written per unit of time, their code usually contains fewer defects, and they have a set of unit tests to show that it works. This makes them more productive overall. Pair programming also provides the team an opportunity to refactor existing code—to re-design it to make it as simple as possible while still meeting the customer's requirements. Pair programming is not exclusive to XP, but XP was the first discipline to use it exclusively. In fact, XP uses pair programming so exclusively that no code written by just a single person is typically allowed into the product.

- *Short iteration cycles and frequent releases*: XP typically uses release cycles in the range of just a few weeks or months, and each release is composed of several iterations, each on the order of three to five weeks. The combination of frequent releases and an on-site customer representative allows the XP team to get immediate feedback on new features and to uncover design and requirements issues early. XP also requires constant integration and building of the product. Whenever a programming pair finishes a feature or task and it passes all their unit tests, they immediately integrate and build the entire product. They then use all the unit tests as a regression test suite to make sure the new feature hasn't broken anything already checked in. If it does break something, they fix it immediately. So, in an XP project, integrations and builds can happen several times a day. This process gives the team a good feel for where they are in the release cycle every day and gives the customer a completed build on which to run the acceptance tests.

---

[11]This is a very short description of how XP works; for a much more eloquent and detailed explanation see the bible of XP: Beck, K. *Extreme Programming Explained: Embrace Change*. (Boston, MA: Addison-Wesley, 2000.)

The Four Basic Activities

XP describes four activities that are the bedrock of the discipline:

- *Designing*: Design while you code. "Designing is creating a structure that organizes the logic in the system. Good design organizes the logic so that a change in one part of the system doesn't always require a change in another part of the system. Good design ensures that every piece of logic in the system has one and only one home. Good design puts the logic near the data it operates on. Good design allows the extension of the system with changes in only one place."[12]

- *Coding*: The code is where the knowledge of the system resides, so it's your main activity. The fundamental difference between plan-driven models and agile models is this emphasis on the code. In a plan-driven model, the emphasis is on producing a set of work products that together represent the entire work of the project, with code being just one of the work products. In agile methodologies, the code is the sole deliverable and so the emphasis is placed squarely there; in addition, by structuring the code properly and keeping comments up to date, the code becomes documentation for the project.

- *Testing*: The tests tell you when you're done coding. Test-driven development is crucial to the idea of managing change. XP depends heavily on writing unit tests before writing the code that they test and on using an automated testing framework to run all the unit tests whenever changes are integrated.

- *Listening*: To your partner and to the customer. In any given software development project, there are two types of knowledge. The customer has knowledge of the business application being written and what it is supposed to do. This is the domain knowledge of the project. The developers have knowledge about the target platform, the programming language(s), and the implementation issues. This is the technical knowledge of the project. The customer doesn't know the technical side, and the developers don't have the domain knowledge, so listening—on both sides—is a key activity in developing the product.

Implementing XP: The 12 Practices

We (finally) get to the implementation of XP. Here are the rules that every XP team follows during their project. The rules may vary depending on the team and the project, but in order to call yourselves an XP team, you need to do some form of these things. The practices described here draw on everything previously described: the four values, the 12 principles, and the four activities. This is really XP:

- *The planning game*: Develop the scope of the next release by combining business priorities and technical estimates. The customer and the development team need to decide on the *stories* (read: *features*) that will be included in the next release, the priority of each story, and when the release needs to be done. The developers are responsible for breaking the stories up into a set of tasks and for estimating the duration of each task. The sum of the durations tells the team what they really think they can get done before the release delivery date. If necessary, stories are moved out of a release if the numbers don't add up. Notice that estimation is the responsibility of the developers and not the customer or the manager. In XP *only* the developers do estimation.

---

[12]Beck, (2000).

- *Small releases*: Put a simple system into production quickly and then release new versions on a very short cycle. Each release has to make sense from a business perspective, so release size will vary. It's far better to plan releases in durations of a month or two rather than 6 or 12 months. The longer a release is, the harder it is to estimate.

- *Metaphor*: "A simple shared story of how the whole system works." The metaphor replaces your architecture. It needs to be a coherent explanation of the system that is decomposable into smaller bits—stories. Stories should always be expressed in the vocabulary of the metaphor, and the language of the metaphor should be common to both the customer and the developers.

- *Simple design*: Keep the design as simple as you can each day and re-design often to keep it simple. According to Beck, a simple design (1) runs all the unit tests, (2) has no duplicated code, (3) expresses what each story means in the code, and (4) has the fewest number of classes and methods that make sense to implement the stories so far.[13]

- *Testing*: Programmers constantly write unit tests. Tests must all pass before integration. Beck takes the hard line that "any program feature without an automated test simply doesn't exist."[14] Although this works for most acceptance tests and should certainly work for all unit tests, this analogy breaks down in some instances, notably in testing the user interface in a GUI. Even this can be made to work automatically if your test framework can handle the events generated by a GUI interaction. Beyond this, having a good set of written instructions will normally fill the bill.

- *Refactoring*: Restructure the system "without changing its behavior" to make it simpler—removing redundancy, eliminating unnecessary layers of code, or adding flexibility. The key to refactoring is to identify areas of code that can be made simpler and to do it while you're there. Refactoring is closely related to collective ownership and simple design. Collective ownership gives you permission to change the code, and simple design imposes on you the responsibility to make the change when you see it needs to be made.

- *Pair programming*: Two programmers at one machine must write all production code in an XP project. Any code written alone is thrown away. Pair programming is a dynamic process. You may change partners as often as you change tasks to implement. This has the effect of reinforcing collective ownership by spreading the knowledge of the entire system around the entire team. And it avoids the "beer truck problem," where the person who knows everything gets hit by a beer truck and thus sets the project schedule back months.

- *Collective ownership*: The team owns everything, implying that anyone can change anything at any time. In some places this is known as "ego-less programming." Programmers need to buy into the idea that anyone can change their code and that collective ownership extends from code to the entire project; it's a team project, not an individual one.

- *Continuous integration*: Integrate and build every time a task is finished, possibly several times a day (as long as the tests all pass). This helps to isolate problems in the code base; if you're integrating a single task change, then the most likely place to look for a problem is right there.

---

[13]Beck, (2000)
[14]Beck, (2000)

- *40-hour week*: Work a regular 40-hour week. Never work a second week in a row with overtime. The XP philosophy has a lot in common with many of Tom DeMarco's *Peopleware* arguments. People are less productive if they're working 60 or 70 hours a week than if they're working 40 hours. When you're working excessive amounts of overtime, several things happen. Because you don't have time to do chores and things related to your "life," you do them during the workday. Constantly being under deadline pressure and never getting a sustained break also means you get tired and then make more mistakes, which somebody then needs to fix. But being in control of the project and working 40 hours a week (give or take a few) leaves you with time for a life, time to relax and recharge, and time to focus on your work during the workday—making you more productive, not less.

- *On-site customer*: A customer is part of the team, is on-site, writes and executes functional tests, and helps clarify requirements. The customer's ability to give immediate feedback to changes in the system also increases team confidence that they're building the right system every day.

- *Coding standards*: The team has them, follows them, and uses them to improve communication. Because of collective code ownership, the team must have coding standards and everyone must adhere to them. Without a sensible set of coding guidelines, it would take much, much longer to do refactoring and it would decrease the desire of developers to change code. Notice that I said *sensible*. Your coding standards should make your code easier to read and maintain: they shouldn't constrict creativity.

Scrum

The second agile methodology we'll look at is Scrum. *Scrum* derives its name from rugby, where a *Scrum* is a means of restarting play after a rules infraction. The Scrum uses the 8 forwards on a rugby team (out of 15 players in the rugby union form of the game) to attempt to (re)gain control of the ball and move it forward towards the opposing goal line. The idea in the agile Scrum methodology is that a small team is unified around a single goal and gets together for sprints of development that move them towards that goal.

Scrum is, in fact, older than XP, with the original process management idea coming from Takeuchi and Nonaka's 1986 paper, "The New New Product Development Game."[15] The first use of the term *Scrum* is attributed to DeGrace and Stahl's 1990 book *Wicked Problems, Righteous Solutions*.[16] Scrum is a variation on the iterative development approach and incorporates many of the features of XP. Scrum is more of a management approach than XP and doesn't define many of the detailed development practices (like pair programming or test-driven development) that XP does, although most Scrum projects will use these practices.

Scrum uses teams of typically no more than ten developers. Just like other agile methodologies, Scrum emphasizes the efficacy of small teams and collective ownership.

---

[15]Takeuchi, H. and I. Nonaka. "The New New Product Development Game." *Harvard Business Review* **64**(1): 137-146 (1986).
[16]DeGrace, P. and L. H. Stahl. *Wicked Problems, Righteous Solutions: A Catalogue of Modern Software Engineering Paradigms*. (Englewood Cliffs, NJ: Yourdon Press, 1990.)

Scrum Roles

Scrum defines three roles in a development project. The first is the *product owner*, the person who generates the requirements for the product and prioritizes them. The requirements normally take the form of *user stories*—features that can be summarized by sentences like "As a <type of user>, I want to <do or create something>, so that <some value is created>." These user stories turn into one or more tasks that suggest how to create the feature. The product owner adds the user stories to the product backlog and prioritizes them. This points the development team towards the most valuable work. The product owner is also charged with making sure that the team understands the requirements behind the user stories. Once the team completes a user story, they have added value to the end product.

Scrum projects are facilitated by a *Scrum master* whose job it is to manage the backlogs, run the daily Scrum meetings, coach the team, and protect the team from outside influences during the sprint. The Scrum master may or may not be a developer but they are an expert in the Scrum process and are the go-to person for questions on Scrum. The Scrum master is emphatically *not* the manager of the team. Scrum teams are teams of equals and arrive at decisions by consensus.

Besides the product owner and the Scrum master, everyone else involved in the project is on the development team. The *development team* itself is self-organizing; the members of the Scrum team decide among themselves who will work on what user stories and tasks, assume collective ownership of the project, and decide on the development process they'll use during the sprint. The entire team is dedicated to the goal of delivering a working product at the end of every sprint. This organization is reinforced every day at the Scrum meeting.

The Sprint

Scrum is characterized by the *sprint*, an iteration of between one and four weeks. Sprints are time-boxed in that they are of a fixed duration and the output of a sprint is what work the team can accomplish during the sprint. The delivery date for the sprint does not move out. This means that sometimes a sprint can finish early, and sometimes a sprint will finish with less functionality than was proposed. A sprint always delivers a usable product.

Scrum Artifacts

Scrum requirements are encapsulated in two backlogs. The *product backlog* is the prioritized list of all the requirements for the project; the product owner creates it. The product owner prioritizes the product backlog, and the development team breaks the high-priority user stories into tasks and estimates them. This list of tasks becomes the *sprint backlog*. The *sprint backlog* is the prioritized list of user stories for the current sprint. Once the sprint starts, only the development team may add tasks to the sprint backlog—these are usually bugs found during testing. No outside entity may add items to the sprint backlog, only to the product backlog.

One important thing about the Scrum process is that in most Scrum teams, the sprint backlog is *visual*. It's represented on a board using either Post-It notes or index cards, with one note or card per task; it may also be an online virtual board. For example, see Jira or Pivotal Tracker. This *task board* always has at least three columns: ToDo, InProgress, and Done. The task board provides a visual representation of where the team is during the sprint. At a glance, any team member can see what tasks are currently available to be picked up, which are actively being worked on, and which are finished and integrated into the product baseline. This visual task board is similar to the Kanban board that we'll talk about later.

Sprint Flow

Before the first sprint starts, Scrum has an initial planning phase that creates the product list of the initial requirements, decides on an architecture for implementing the requirements, divides the user stories into prioritized groups for the sprints, and breaks the first set of user stories into tasks to be estimated and assigned. They stop when their estimates occupy all the time allowed for the sprint. Tasks in a sprint should not be longer than one day of effort. If a task is estimated to take more than one day of effort, it is successively divided into two or more tasks until each task's effort is the appropriate length. This rule comes from the observation that humans are terrible at doing exact estimations of large tasks and that estimating task efforts in weeks or months is basically just a guess. So, breaking tasks down into smaller pieces gives the team a more reliable estimate for each.

Sprints have a daily Scrum meeting, which is a stand-up meeting of 15–30 minutes duration (the shorter, the better) where the entire team discusses sprint progress. The daily Scrum meeting allows the team to share information and track sprint progress. By having daily Scrum meetings, any slip in the schedule or any problems in implementation are immediately obvious and can then be addressed by the team at once. "The Scrum master ensures that everyone makes progress, records the decisions made at the meeting and tracks action items, and keeps the Scrum meetings short and focused."[17]

At the Scrum meeting, each team member answers the following three questions in turn:

- What tasks have you finished since the last Scrum meeting?

- Is anything getting in the way of your finishing your tasks?

- What tasks are you planning to do between now and the next Scrum meeting?

Discussions other than responses to these three questions are deferred to other meetings. This meeting type has several effects. It allows the entire team to visualize progress towards the sprint and project completion every day. It reinforces team spirit by sharing progress—everyone can feel good about tasks completed. And finally, the Scrum meeting verbalizes problems, which can then be solved by the entire team.

Some Scrum teams have a meeting in the middle of the sprint called story time. In *story time* the team and the product owner take a look at the product backlog and begin the process of prioritizing the user stories in the backlog and breaking the high priority stories into tasks that will become part of the next sprint's backlog. Story time is optional, but has the advantage of preparing for the planning meeting for the next sprint.

At the end of the sprint two things happen. First, the current version of the product is released to the product owner, who may perform acceptance testing on it. This usually takes the form of a demo of the product near the end of the last day of the sprint. This meeting and demo is called the *sprint review*. After the sprint review, the team will wrap up the sprint with a sprint retrospective meeting. In the *sprint retrospective*, the team looks back on the just completed sprint, congratulates themselves on jobs well done, and looks for areas in which they can improve performance for the next sprint. These meetings typically don't last long (an hour or so) but are a valuable idea that brings closure to and marks the end of the current sprint.

At the start of the next sprint, another planning meeting is held where the Scrum master and the team re-prioritize the product backlog and create a backlog for the new sprint. With most Scrum teams, estimates of tasks become better as the project progresses, primarily because the team now has data on how they've done estimating on previous sprints. This effect in Scrum is called *velocity*; the productivity of the team can actually increase during the project as they gel as a team and get better at estimating tasks. This planning meeting is also where the organization can decide whether the project is finished—or whether to finish the project at all.

---

[17]Rising, L. and N. S. Janoff. "The Scrum Software Development Process for Small Teams." *IEEE Software* **17**(4): 26-32 (2000).

After the last scheduled development sprint, a final sprint may be done to bring further closure to the project. This sprint implements no new functionality, but prepares the final deliverable for product release. It fixes any remaining bugs, finishes documentation, and generally productizes the code. Any requirements left in the product backlog are transferred to the next release. A Scrum retrospective is held before the next sprint begins to ponder the previous sprint and see whether any process improvements can be made. Scrum is a project-management methodology and is typically silent on development processes. Despite this, Scrum teams typically use many of the practices described earlier in the XP practices section. Common code ownership, pair programming, small releases, simple design, test-driven development, continuous integration, and coding standards are all common practices in Scrum projects.

Lean Software Development

Lean software development is not really an agile methodology. It's more of a philosophy that most agile methodologies, like XP and Scrum, draw from and from which they seek guidance and inspiration. Lean software development comes from the just-in-time manufacturing processes (also known as the Toyota Production System, among other names) that were introduced in Japan in the 1970s and then made their way around the world in the 1980s and 1990s, encouraged by the publication in 1990 of *The Machine That Changed The World* by Womack, et. al.[18] Just-in-time manufacturing evolved into first *lean manufacturing* and then into *lean product management systems* throughout the 1990s. The publication of Poppendieck & Poppendieck's *Lean Software Development: An Agile Toolkit*[19] in 2003 marked the movement of lean into the agile development community.

Lean software development is a set of principles designed to improve productivity, quality, and customer satisfaction. Lean wants to eliminate from your process anything that doesn't add value to the product. These non-value-adding parts of your process are called *waste*. Lean also emphasizes that the team should only be working on activities that add value to the product right now.

The Poppendiecks transformed the lean principles that started at Toyota into seven key principles for software development:

1. Eliminate Waste

2. Build Quality In

3. Create Knowledge

4. Defer Commitment

5. Deliver Fast

6. Respect People

7. Optimize the Whole

We'll go through each of these principles briefly to illustrate how they apply to software development and how agile methodologies make use of them.

---

[18]Womack, James P., Daniel T. Jones, and Daniel Roos. *The Machine That Changed the World: The Story of Lean Production -- Toyota's Secret Weapon in the Global Car Wars That Is Now Revolutionizing World Industry*. (New York, NY: Simon & Schuster, 1990.)

[19]Poppendieck, Mary, and Tom Poppendieck. *Lean Software Development: An Agile Toolkit*. (Upper Saddle River, NJ: Addison-Wesley Professional, 2003.)

Principle 1: Eliminate Waste

Lean software development wants you to eliminate anything that doesn't add value to the product. Things that don't add value are, as mentioned, waste. Obviously in any kind of production or development environment you want to eliminate waste. Waste costs you money and time. The question here, in a software development project, is: "What is waste?" Some things may be obviously wasteful: too many meetings (some will say meetings of any kind), too much documentation, unnecessary features, and unclear or rapidly changing requirements. But there are others, such as partially written code, code for "future features" that the customer may never use, defects in your code and other quality issues, excessive task switching (you as a developer are assigned several tasks and you have to keep switching between them), and too many features or tasks for a given iteration or release.

All these things constitute waste, and in a lean environment the team's job is to minimize waste in all forms. Only by doing that can the team increase productivity and deliver working code fast.

The next question is: "How do we eliminate waste?" A general way to focus on waste in a project and work towards eliminating all forms of it is to consider the team's development process and how it's working. In Scrum this is the end of sprint retrospective. During the retrospective, the team looks back on the just-finished sprint and asks "What can we improve?" A lean team will turn that question into "What was wasteful and how can we change to be less wasteful next time?" Teams that make these little improvements in their process at the end of every sprint, focusing on one or two items to change each time, will learn more and more about what works and what doesn't in their process and are on the way to continuous process improvement.

Principle 2: Build Quality In

Quality issues are the bane of every software developer. Defects in code, testing your code more than once, logging defects, fixing defects, re-testing, all result in waste you'd like to eliminate. It turns out that agile processes are on top of removing this type of waste in order to build quality software. Nearly all agile teams will implement two techniques that improve code quality at the source: pair programming and test-driven development (TDD). Both of these techniques allow developers to write, test, and fix code quickly and before the code is integrated into the product code base, where defects become harder to find and fix. Integrating new features as soon as they're done gives the testing team a new version of the product to test as quickly as possible and shortens the amount of time between code creation and testing. Another technique to improve quality in XP teams is *constant feedback*. In XP, because the customer is part of the team, they can evaluate new iterations of the product constantly, giving the developers instant feedback on what's working and what's not.

There is one other relatively painless, but probably heretical thing you as a developer can do that will add to the quality of your code: don't log defects in a defect tracking system. But wait! How are you going to document that there's a defect to be fixed later? The answer is *you don't*. You fix it—*now*. As soon as you find it. That builds quality in and eliminates waste at the same time.[20]

Principle 3: Create Knowledge

It seems obvious that, as your team works through requirements, creates a design, and implements the code that will become a product, that you are creating knowledge. However, another way to describe this lean principle is to say, "The team must learn new things constantly." Learning new things is what's happening as you work through a project. You learn by working to understand requirements. You learn by beginning with an initial design and realizing that the design will change as the requirements do. You learn that the detailed

---

[20]Poppendieck and Poppendieck (2003. pp. 25-26).

design evolves and isn't truly finished until you have code written. And you learn that by implementing new requirements and fixing defects that you can make the code simpler by refactoring as often as you can. Thus you're creating knowledge that's embodied in the code you produce and ship.

Principle 4: Defer Commitment

This lean principle really dates back to the early 1970s and the advent of top-down structured design. What *Defer Commitment* means is *put off decisions* (particularly irreversible ones) as long as you can and only make them when you must. In top-down design you start with a general formulation of the problem solution and push decisions about implementation down as you make the design and the code more detailed. This gives you more flexibility at the upper levels and pushes the commitment to a particular design or piece of code down until you have no alternative but to write it. This is why you write libraries and APIs, so at any particular level of the code you can use something at a lower level without needing to know the implementation details. At that lower level you'll hopefully know more about what needs to be done, and the code will write itself.

This principle also means that you shouldn't put decisions off too late. That has the possibility of delaying the rest of the team and making your design less flexible. Also try to make as few irreversible decisions as you can to give yourself as much flexibility at all levels of your code.

Principle 5: Deliver Fast

Well, this seems obvious too. Particularly in the age of the Internet, mobile applications, and the Internet of Things, it seems that faster must be better. And that's true. Companies that can bring quality products to market faster will have a competitive edge. "First to market" players will gain a larger market share initially and if they continue to release products quickly can maintain that edge over time. Additionally, if your team minimizes the amount of time between when the customer or product owner generates the requirements and when you deliver a product that meets those requirements, there is less time for the requirements—and the market—to change.

How do you deliver fast? Well, first you should adhere to other lean principles, especially Eliminate Waste and Build Quality In. Both of these will improve productivity and allow you to deliver product iterations faster. But there is more. You should keep things simple. This means keep the requirements simple. Don't add too many features and don't spend time planning on future features. Don't over-engineer the solution. Find a reasonable solution, a reasonable set of data structures, and reasonable algorithms to implement your solution. Remember that the perfect is the enemy of the good—and the fast. Finally, the best way to Deliver Fast is to have an experienced, well-integrated, cooperative, self-organizing, loyal-to-each-other team with the right skill set for your product. Nothing will help more than a good team.

Principle 6: Respect People

Respecting people is all about building strong, productive teams. It's based on the idea that the people doing the work should make the decisions. Process and product-creation decisions shouldn't be imposed from above—they should be generated from the trenches. From the manager's perspective, respecting your team means empowering the team to make their own decisions, including about task time estimates and decomposition, processes, tools, and design. This empowerment means that the manager must learn to listen to their team and take their ideas and concerns into consideration. It means that the manager must act as a shield for their team so that they can get the job done. Everyone on the team is enjoined to create an environment where everyone is able to speak their mind and disagreements are resolved with respect for each other. This creates a team with open communication and decision-making transparency.

Principle 7: Optimize the Whole

"A lean organization optimizes the whole value stream, from the time it receives an order to address a customer need until software is deployed and the need is addressed. If an organization focuses on optimizing something less than the entire value stream, we can just about guarantee that the overall value stream will suffer."[21]

The main idea behind Optimize the Whole is to keep the entire product picture in sight as you develop. Agile organizations do this by having strong, multi-disciplinary teams that are co-located and that contain all the skills and product creation functions they need to deliver a product that meets the customer's needs with little reference to another team.

Kanban

The Kanban method is a practice derived from lean manufacturing (the Toyota Production System) and other change-management systems; it draws most of its original ideas from the just-in-time manufacturing processes. Just like lean software development, Kanban isn't really a process. Rather it's an objective and a set of principles and practices to meet that objective.

Kanban uses three ideas to influence a development process: work-in-progress (WIP), flow, and lead time. *Work-in-progress* is the total number of tasks the team is currently working on, including all the states in which a task may find itself (in-progress, done, testing, review, and so on). *Flow* is the passage of tasks from one state to another on the way to completion. *Lead time* is the amount of time it takes a task to move from its initial state to its completed state.

The Kanban board, WIP, and Flow

Work-in-progress and flow are illustrated visually in Kanban via the use of a *Kanban board*. A Kanban board will look familiar to most agile practitioners because it's a variant on the Scrum *task board*. Figure 2-4 shows a generic task/Kanban board. These boards are often physical white boards that occupy one wall of a common space for the team. On this board the team will either write in tasks or use (in Scrum) index cards or post-it notes to identify tasks. This makes the tasks easy to move from column to column (state to state) on the board.

ToDo	Doing	DONE

Figure 2-4. *A generic task/Kanban board*

---

[21]Poppendieck & Poppendieck (2003. p. 39).

With this type of board, the user has the option of changing the number and headings of the columns in order to make the board fit their process. When Scrum and Kanban are applied to software development, the board might start out looking more like Figure 2-5.

ToDo	Develop	Review	Test	DONE

Figure 2-5. A task/Kanban board applied to a software development project

If the team is using a Kanban board, they'll add the maximum number of tasks that are allowed in each of the first four columns. This maximum work-in-progress is used to control the flow of work through the team. The Kanban board will then look like Figure 2-6.

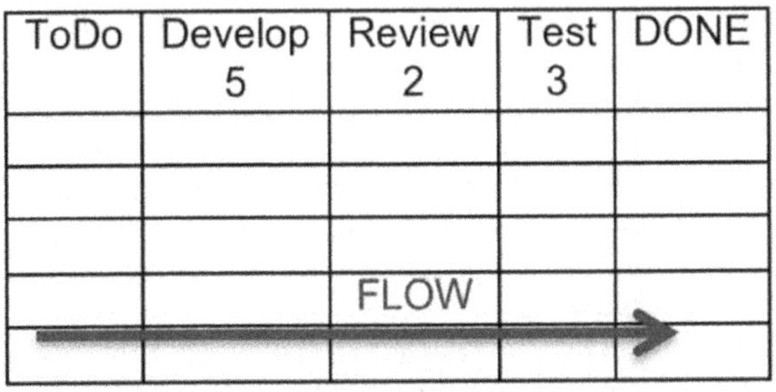

ToDo	Develop 5	Review 2	Test 3	DONE
		FLOW		

Figure 2-6. A Kanban board illustrating Work-in-Progress maxima and Flow

In Figure 2-6 the maximum number of Work-in-Progress tasks is ten. This means the team can't work on more than ten tasks at a time, as denoted in each column. So, for example, say that every state on the Kanban board is maxed-out (there are five tasks in development, two in review, and three in testing) and a developer finishes a task in the Develop state. That task cannot move to the Review state until one of the two currently under review tasks is finished. We've just exposed a bottleneck in the Flow. In Kanban, what the developer would do is jump in to help either review one of the two tasks in that state, or help test a task in the Task state. No new tasks can be pulled into the Develop state until there is room for the finished task downstream.

Let's further say that at some time later on that there are only three tasks in Develop, one in Review, and three in Test, so the team isn't working at maximum. If a developer is available, that developer will select a task from the ToDo state, pull it into Develop, and begin working. If a developer finishes a task in Develop, that task can then flow into Review, and the developer can then pull a task from the ToDo list into Develop and begin work.

Thus, with Kanban the objective is to maximize Work-in-Progress within the constraint of the maximum number of tasks allowable at any time. There is no time-boxing as in Scrum; the goal is to move tasks through as quickly as possible—have the shortest lead time—while maximizing productivity and working up to the maximum number of tasks allowable.

You can note that when I say *maximizing Work-in-Progress*, I don't mean giving the team more work. In fact, the goal in keeping the maximum number of tasks in each state low is to reduce the team's workload and allow them to focus on a smaller number of tasks (to avoid multi-tasking). The idea is that this will reduce stress and increase quality *and* productivity.

Kanban also works by using a *pull system*. Instead of pushing items out to other teams, Kanban tells developers to pull items from their ToDo state as they have the capacity to handle them. You'll notice that there are some things missing here, notably how things get on the ToDo list, and what Done means. That's because Kanban isn't really a project-management technique. In order to use Kanban, you need to have some process in place already and you need to manage it.

Lead Time

Probably the biggest difference between using Kanban and Scrum is time-boxing. Scrum uses time-boxed sprints and measures the team's productivity by using *velocity* (the number of task points finished per sprint) as its metric. This works well for Scrum and gives the team an idea of how well they're performing at the end of every sprint. Over time the team's average velocity is used as a predictor to decide how many tasks to include in each sprint.

Because Kanban isn't time-boxed, it uses a different productivity metric: lead time. *Lead time* is the amount of time it takes for the team to get one task from the initial ToDo (or Waiting, or Queued) state to the Done (or Integrated, or Released) state. Lead time can be measured in hours or days; it answers the question: "From this point, how long will it take this task to get to Done?" When a task enters the ToDo state, that date—called the *entry date*—is marked on the index card. As the task moves from state to state, the date the move happens is also marked on the card until finally the task is complete and it moves to the Done state. That final date is the *done date*. The difference between the done date and the entry date is the lead time for that task. Over time, as the team finishes more and more tasks, you can compute the average lead time for the team and answer the question just posed. Note that the lead time is realistic because it also includes time when the task is in some queue waiting to be worked on.

Kanban is not so different from Scrum, and elements of Kanban are typically used in projects that implement Scrum. In Scrum, at the end of every sprint you have working software with a particular set of features available. In Kanban, at the end of every task completion you have working software with a new feature added.

Conclusion

As can be seen from the methodologies described in this chapter, iteration is the key, whether you're using an evolutionary, plan-driven process or an agile development one. Recognize that the best way to build a complex piece of software is incrementally. Learn that designing, writing, testing, and delivering incrementally better code is your first step to writing great software.

References

Anderson, David J. Kanban: *Successful Evolutionary Change for Your Technology Business*. (Sequin, WA: Blue Hole Press, 2010.)

Beck, K. *Extreme Programming Explained: Embrace Change*. (Boston, MA: Addison-Wesley, 2000.)

Cockburn, A. *Agile Software Development*. (Boston, MA: Addison-Wesley, 2002.)

DeGrace, P. and L. H. Stahl. *Wicked Problems, Righteous Solutions: A Catalogue of Modern Software Engineering Paradigms*. (Englewood Cliffs, NJ: Yourdon Press, 1990.)

DeMarco, T. Controlling Software Projects: Management, Measurement and Estimation. (Upper Saddle River, NJ: Yourdon Press, 1983.)

Fulghum, Robert. *All I Really Need to Know I Learned in Kindergarten*. (New York, NY: Ivy Books. 1986.)

Martin, R. C. Agile Software Development, Principles, Patterns, and Practices. (Upper Saddle River, NJ: Prentice Hall, 2003.)

McConnell, S. *Rapid Development: Taming Wild Software Schedules*. (Redmond, WA: Microsoft Press, 1996.)

Paulk, M. C. *The Capability Maturity Model: Guidelines for Improving the Software Process*. (Reading, MA: Addison-Wesley, 1995.)

Poppendieck, Mary, and Tom Poppendieck. *Lean Software Development: An Agile Toolkit*. (Upper Saddle River, NJ: Addison-Wesley Professional, 2003.)

Rising, L. and N. S. Janoff. "The Scrum Software Development Process for Small Teams." *IEEE Software* 17(4): 26-32 (2000).

Royce, W. W. *Managing the Development of Large Software Systems*. Proceedings of IEEE WESCON, (Piscataway, NJ, IEEE Press, 1970.)

Takeuchi, H. and I. Nonaka. "The New New Product Development Game." *Harvard Business Review* 64(1): 137-146 (1986).

Waters, Kelly. *Seven Key Principles of Lean Software Development*. Retrieved on 12 June 2017. `www.101ways.com/7-key-principles-of-lean-software-development-2/` (2010).

Womack, James P., Daniel T. Jones, and Daniel Roos. *The Machine That Changed the World: The Story of Lean Production -- Toyota's Secret Weapon in the Global Car Wars That Is Now Revolutionizing World Industry*. (New York, NY: Simon & Schuster, 1990.)

CHAPTER 3

■ ■ ■

Project Management Essentials

Quality, features, schedule—pick two.

Project management? Isn't this a software development book?

Yes, but working on a larger-than-one-person development project means working on a team; and working on a team means being managed. So learning something about project management from both sides is an essential part of learning software development.

Project management is an involved and complicated set of tasks. We'll restrict ourselves to several tasks that will impact you as a developer the most:

- Project planning

- Estimation and scheduling

- Resource management

- Project oversight

- Project reviews and presentations

- The project retrospective

Traditional project managers usually take on a great deal of responsibility. They are responsible for managing scope, cost, estimation, schedule, quality, personnel, communication, risk, and more. However, in an agile project, the entire team is usually responsible for managing the project. If there is a separate project manager, that person is largely responsible for the following:

- Making sure the team has the resources it needs

- Ensuring that the team adheres to the agile values and principles

- Facilitating communications

- Shielding the team from outside interruptions

In particular, the agile project manager doesn't manage the day-to-day operations of the team. That's up to the team itself. The objective is to make sure there is no delay in management decision-making.

© John F. Dooley 2017
J. F. Dooley, *Software Development, Design and Coding*, https://doi.org/10.1007/978-1-4842-3153-1_3

Project Planning

Project planning is *forever*. By that I mean that project planning continues throughout the entire duration of the project. "The Plan" is never really set in stone, because things in a typical software project are usually in constant flux. In those projects that are using a plan-driven process model, a *project plan* is an actual document, written by the project manager, that is approved and signed off on by the development team and by upper management. It is, in effect, a *contract*, albeit a rolling one, of what the team is going to do and how they're going to do it. It says how the project will be managed, and in the most extreme plan-driven projects, even states how and when the document itself will be modified.

What's in the project plan? Generally a project plan consists of the following seven parts:

- Introduction and explanation of the project

- Team organization

- Risk analysis

- Hardware, software, and human resource requirements

- Task list and size and effort estimates

- Project schedule

- Project monitoring and reporting mechanisms, collectively known as project oversight

Not all of these are necessary for all projects or project methodologies. In particular, plan-driven projects will use all of them, whereas agile projects may use a few on a single page.

A project plan is a great tool for setting down what you think you're doing, an outline of how it will be done, and how you plan on executing the outline. The problem with a project plan is that it's static. Once it's written and signed off on, upper management thinks the project will run exactly as stated in the plan. But the reality of the project often thwarts the plan.

As with many other parts of project management, agile methodologies do project planning differently. An agile project plan

- is feature-based (remember it's built around getting production code running quickly).

- is organized into iterations.

- is multi-layered (because it knows that things will change and that the initial set of requirements are not complete or detailed enough).

- is owned by the team, not the project manager.

Project Organization

The project organization section of the plan contains the following three things:

- How you're going to organize the team

- What process model the project will be using

- How will the project be run on a day-to-day basis

If you're working with an experienced team, all this is already known to everyone, so your project organization section can be "We'll do what we usually do." However, this section is a necessity for brand-new projects and inexperienced teams, because the organization section gives you something to hang your hat on when you start the actual project work.

Agile projects simplify the three items just mentioned. Nearly all agile teams are self-organizing. Because they're small and because one of the agile principles is the idea of common code ownership, agile developers don't segregate themselves based on what part of the code they're working on or on a particular skill set. Agile developers share code, share testing, and share expertise. Like all software developers, those on an agile project are constantly learning new things and improving their skills.

No matter what agile process model is being used—XP, Scrum, Crystal, feature-driven, and so on—all agile projects are iterative, use short development cycles, and produce running code with more features at the end of each iteration. Simple.

Different agile projects will run differently on a day-to-day basis. But pretty much all of them include daily stand-up meetings, at least daily integrations, and some form of shared programming—for example, pair programming. Whether the project is using a time-boxed methodology or not, iterations are typically short, and developers spend quite a bit of time writing and executing unit tests.

Risk Analysis

In the risk analysis section, you need to think about the bad things.[1] What can possibly go wrong with this project? What's the worst that could happen? What will we do if it does?

Some risks to watch out for include the following:

- *Schedule slips*: That task that you estimated would take three days has just taken three weeks. In a plan-driven project, this can be an issue if you don't have regular status meetings. Waiting three weeks to tell your boss that you're late is always worse than telling them that you'll be late as soon as you know it. Don't put off delivering bad news. In an agile project this is unlikely, because most agile projects have a daily status meeting (see the Scrum meeting section in Chapter 2). That way, schedule slips are noticed almost immediately, and corrective action can take place quickly.

- *Defect rate is excessive*: Your testing is finding lots of bugs. What do you do—continue to add new features or stop to fix the bugs? Again, this can be a real issue in a project where integration builds happen according to a fixed schedule—say, once a week. In a project where integrations happen every day, or every time a new feature is added, you can keep up with defects more easily. In either case, if you're experiencing a high defect rate, the best thing to do is to stop, take a look around, and find the root cause of the defects before adding more functionality. This can be very hard to do from a project-management standpoint, but you'll thank yourself in the end.

- *Requirements misunderstood*: What you're doing isn't what the customer wanted. This classic problem is the result of the fact that customers and developers live in two different worlds. The customer lives in the application domain where they understand from a user's perspective what they want the product to do. The developer understands from a technical perspective how the product will work. Occasionally, these worlds intersect and that's good; but lots of times they don't and that's where you get a misunderstanding of requirements. The best ways to avoid this situation are to have the customer on site as often as possible and to produce deliverable products as often as possible.

---

[1]McConnell, S. *Rapid Development: Taming Wild Software Schedules*. (Redmond, WA: Microsoft Press, 1996.)

- *Requirements churn*: New features, altered features, deleted features . . . will the misery never end? Requirements churn is probably the largest single reason for missed delivery dates, high defect rates, and project failure. Churn happens when the customer (or your own marketing folks, or the development team itself) continues to change requirements while development is underway. It leads to massive amounts of rework in the code, retesting of baselines, and delay after delay. Managing requirements is the single most important job of the project manager. In a plan-driven process, a change control board (CCB) examines each new requirement and decides whether to add it to the list of features to be implemented. There may be a member of the development team on the CCB, but that's not required, so the danger here is that the CCB adds new features without understanding all the scheduling and effort ramifications. In agile processes, the development team keeps control of the prioritized requirements list (called the product backlog in Scrum), and only adjusts the list at set points in the project—after iterations in XP, and after each sprint in Scrum.

- *Turnover*: Your most experienced developer decides to join a startup three weeks before product delivery. The best way to reduce turnover is to (1) give your developers interesting work, (2) have them work in a pleasant environment, and (3) give them control over their own schedules. Oddly enough, money is not one of the top motivators for software developers. This doesn't mean they don't want to get paid well, but it does mean that throwing more money at them in order to get them to work harder or to keep them from leaving doesn't generally work. And if, despite your best efforts, your best developer does leave, you just have to move on. Trust me, it won't be the end of the world. The best way to mitigate the effect of turnover is to spread the knowledge of the project around all the members of the development team. Principles like *common code ownership* and techniques like *pair programming* work to invest all the team members in the product and spread the knowledge of the code across the entire team. One of the best books on managing and keeping software developers is *Peopleware* by Tom DeMarco.[2]

Once you've got a list of the risks to your project, you need to address each one and talk about two things: *avoidance* and *mitigation*. For each risk, think about how you can avoid it. Build slack into your schedule, do constant code reviews, freeze requirements early, do frequent releases, require pair programming so you spread around the knowledge of the code, and the like. Then you need to think about what you'll do if the worst-case scenario does happen; this is *mitigation*. Remove features from a release, stop work on new features and do a bug hunt, negotiate new features into a future release, and so on. If a risk becomes a reality, you'll have to do *something* about it; it's better to have planned what you'll do beforehand.

Once you address avoidance and mitigation, you'll have a plan on how to handle your identifiable risks. This doesn't completely let you off the hook, because you're bound to miss risks; but the experience of addressing the risks you do come up with will enable you to better handle new ones that surprise you during the project. If your project is using an iterative process model, it's a good idea to revisit your risks after every iteration and see which ones have changed, identify any new ones, and remove any that can no longer happen.

---

[2]DeMarco, T. and T. Lister. *Peopleware: Productive Projects and Teams, Second Edition.* (New York, NY: Dorset House Publishing Company, 1999.)

Resource Requirements

This section is a piece of cake. How many people do you need for the project? Do they all need to start at once, or can their starting dates on the project be staggered as phases are initiated? How many computers do you need? What software will you be using for development? What development environment do you need? Is everyone trained in that environment? What support software and hardware do you need? Yes, you do need a configuration management system and a stand-alone build machine, no matter which process model you're using.

The platform you're targeting and the application domain you're working in answer many of these resource questions for you. That's the easy part. Questions about team size, start dates, and phases of the project will likely not be able to be answered until you do a first cut at effort estimation and scheduling.

Task Estimates

The first step toward a project schedule is seeing what you'll be doing and figuring out how long each step will take. This is the classic chicken-egg problem. You can't really do estimation until you have a fairly detailed decomposition of the features or user stories into tasks. But your manager always wants effort estimates and schedule data before you start doing the design. Resist this. Make design your top priority once you've got some idea of the requirements. If you select a small set of high priority requirements and then design a solution for that feature set, then you can do an effort estimation of that iteration. Don't worry that the requirements might change—they will. You need a detailed decomposition of features into implementable tasks before you can do effort estimation.

Don't *ever* believe anyone who tells you, "That feature will take six months to do." That is a wild-assed guess (WAG) and bears little to no relation to reality. You just *can't* estimate something that big. The best you can do is to say, "I was once on a team that implemented a feature like that in six months." And even that only helps a little.

You've got to get your work broken down into tasks that are no more than about a week in duration. One or two days is a much better bet. Even better, never do estimation in any unit except *person-hours*. That way you'll be more tempted to work with small increments of hours, and you'll break your larger tasks down into smaller ones that you may actually know how to do. Once you have a believable list of tasks, you can start doing size and then effort estimation. Size always needs to come first, because you just can't figure out how long something will take until you have an idea of how big it is.

Size can be several things, depending on your work breakdown and your development model; functional modules, number of classes, number of methods, number of function points, number of object points, or that old standby, uncommented lines of code. Actually, no matter what you initially measure size in, you'll end up with estimates in terms of KLOC—thousands of uncommented lines of code.

There are several techniques for getting effort estimates: COCOMO II,[3] function point analysis, and the Delphi method are just three. All, however, depend on being able to count things in your design. The estimation mantra is: *size first, then effort and cost estimates, finally schedule.*

All other things being equal, the Delphi method is a quick and relatively efficient estimation technique. Here's one way it can work: find three of your most senior developers. These are the folks who've got the most experience and who should therefore be able to give you a good guess. Then give them the task breakdown (assuming they weren't already involved in doing the initial breakdown—the ideal situation). Then ask them to give you three numbers for each task: the shortest amount of time it should take, the longest amount of time it should take, and the "normal" amount of time it should take, all in person-hours. Once you have these numbers, add them all up, the shortest together, the longest together, and the "normal" together and take the mean. Those are your estimates for each task—the averages of the best guess by your best developers for each task. You then use those average values for each task as the official (for now) effort estimate and proceed to create a schedule.

---

[3]Boehm, 2000.

Finally, you should have the right people—the developers who will do the work—do all the estimates for the project. Managers should *never* do development estimates. Even if a manager has been a developer in the past, unless they're deeply involved in the actual development work, they shouldn't be in the business of doing development estimates.

Project Schedule

Once you have estimates of the tasks in your first release or iteration and have people resource estimates, you can create a schedule. There are several things to take into account before you can look at that spiffy Gantt chart with the nice black diamond that marks the release date. Here's one possible list:

- Get your developers to tell you the *dependencies* between tasks. There will be some tasks that can't start before others finish. There may be tasks that can start once others are half-finished. There will be some that can all start together. You need to know because the task dependencies will push out your delivery date.

- Figure out what your *duty cycle* is. Out of each eight-hour day, how many hours do your developers actually *do* development? You need to remember that reading mail, attending meetings, doing code reviews, taking breaks, going to the bathroom, and lunch all eat up time. You can't assume that an eight-hour task will be done in a single day. Realistically, out of each eight-hour day, two to four hours are eaten up with other stuff, so your duty cycle can be as low as 50%—four hours a day. Duty cycles can also vary based on corporate culture, so you need to figure out what yours is before you start to schedule.

- Take weekends, vacations, sick days, training, and slack into account when you're making the schedule. If your senior developer has a task on the critical path of your project, you probably need to know that they're taking that three-week vacation in May.

- You can't schedule a developer to work on two tasks at the same time. Most project-scheduling software won't let you do this by default, but most of them will let you override that. Don't. You'll be tempted to do this so that your schedule doesn't push out past whatever deadline your manager or marketing team wants, but resist the temptation. You'll only have to change the schedule when you miss the date anyway.

Finally, use project-scheduling software to make your schedule. You don't have to do this—just using a simple spreadsheet technique like the one proposed in Chapter 9 of *Joel on Software* by Joel Spolsky[4] can work for small projects. But using real project-management software like Microsoft Project, Fast Track Scheduling, Basecamp, or Merlin for plan-driven projects and web applications like Jira, Pivotal Tracker, or Trello for agile projects provides lots of features that make keeping the schedule up to date much easier. The big thing that project-management software can do that your spreadsheet can't is track dependencies. Joel doesn't understand how Microsoft Project is useful in this; in fact, he says, "I've found that with software, the dependencies are so obvious that it's just not worth the effort to formally keep track of them."[5] This might be true for small projects, but when your team gets to be 10 developers or larger and you're working on 100 or more tasks, knowing *something* about the dependencies of your project can help manage who's working on what, and when. This knowledge is even more critical for agile methodologies like Scrum. In Scrum projects—where you're using short time-boxed sprints and you need to know the priorities of each user story in the product backlog and how they relate to each other and you must have good estimates for how long each task will take and you need to track the progress of a number of tasks in the sprint backlog every day—knowing dependencies can be the difference between making your sprint and not.

---

[4]Spolsky, J. *Joel on Software*. (Berkeley, CA: Apress, 2004.)
[5]Spolsky, 2004.

Joel is right that tools like Microsoft Project are overkill for many projects, so for those, you can use a spreadsheet approach that just lists the features and tasks you can see right now (see Table 3-1); but project-management software sure is handy to have around when you need it.

Table 3-1. *Spolsky's Painless Schedule (with the Velocity Addition)*

1	2	3	4	5	6	7	8	9
Feature	Task	Priority	Orig Est	Curr Est	Elapsed	Remaining	Developer	Velocity

Spolsky's painless schedule lists the following seven columns that should be in every schedule:

- *Feature* name

- *Tasks* within the feature

- The *Priority* of the task

- The *Original Estimate* (in person-hours)

- The *Current Estimate* (in person-hours)

- The *Elapsed Time* worked on the task (in person-hours)

- The *Remaining Time* on the task (also in person-hours)

Joel correctly emphasizes that tasks need to be fine-grained and small in terms of effort. Otherwise, as noted previously, your estimates will most likely be wildly off. He also suggests that each developer either have a separate spreadsheet or, as shown here, you add an eighth column with the developer assigned to the task. Having all the tasks on the same sheet makes it more crowded, but easier to see all the tasks at once. Though not exactly "painless," this method of keeping a schedule is useful for smaller projects with a fairly limited number of tasks.

Velocity

I suggest adding a ninth column to measure the *velocity* of each task. Velocity is a term from XP[6] and is defined as *the estimated effort of a task, divided by the actual effort*. In our case, we'd use the Original Estimate of the task and the Elapsed Time. If you overestimate your task, your velocity will be greater than one (your task took less time than you originally thought); if you underestimate, it will be less than one (the task took you longer than you originally thought). Ideally, velocity should be 1.0, but that hardly ever happens.

It's worth noting that humans are really bad at estimating time. To get around this problem, some project-management tools have you create an estimate using *magnitude* instead. The simplest type lets you do small, medium, or large for estimates, whereas others (for example, Pivotal Tracker and Trello) let you give each task some number of points on a scale—say, 1, 2, 4, or 8 points for each task. This makes it easy to total up the number of points the team is trying to implement in each time-boxed iteration and over time gives you the average numbers of points a team can implement per iteration.

---

[6]Beck, K. *Extreme Programming Explained: Embrace Change*. (Boston, MA: Addison-Wesley 2000.)

The reason for using velocity is to give each developer and the project manager an idea of how accurate the developer's estimates are and to help do a better job of estimating next time. Ideally, as a developer gains experience, their velocity will approach 1.0 on each task. Alternatively, if a developer's velocity jumps around a lot (one task is 0.6, another is 1.8, a third is 1.2), then a crash course in estimation techniques might be appropriate. In my experience, a new developer's velocity will start out gyrating wildly, with most values well under 1.0; the new developer is overly optimistic. But as time goes along velocities will settle into a range centered on 1.0, maybe from 0.85 to 1.15. As a developer gains a history, the project manager can then start to depend more on their estimates, and the schedules will be more accurate.

Project Oversight

Project oversight is what happens once you've got a schedule and your project is underway. It will typically include a number of review meetings for things like the overall architecture, design, and code. Once your project begins, the work needs to be managed. How this happens depends on the process you're using. But regardless of the process, you need to manage the schedule, manage the developers, manage the process itself, and above all, manage your manager.

A manager's technique is critical to keeping a project on schedule. Fear is not a motivator. Appealing to professional pride is, though. If your boss doesn't support you, you're doomed.

Without creative, supportive management, you're doomed. If your people aren't happy, you don't have a hope. Treat your developers as humans, not resources. Supporting your team and keeping them insulated from distractions is your number one job. Remember, projects are cooperative, social events.[7]

Status Reviews and Presentations

Status reviews and presentations are an inescapable part of any project. The bigger the project, the more formal the review. Remember that reporting status doesn't fix problems, and that generally upper management doesn't like hearing about problems. Tough. When you give a project status report, just tell them where your project is and where it's going during the period before the next status report. Don't embellish and don't make excuses; be honest about problems and where you are in the schedule. Just providing good news is usually bad for your reputation; something will go wrong at some point, so it's best to report it and get it out of the way right away. You must communicate bad news about the project as soon as possible. That's the best way to mitigate the problem and get others involved in helping to find a solution.

When giving a presentation, be it a status review or a technical presentation, make sure you know your audience. Set your presentation to the level of the audience and keep the purpose of your presentation in front of you and them at all times. PowerPoint is ubiquitous in the industry, so learn to use it effectively. Keep your PowerPoint presentations short and to the point. Avoid cramming your slides with lots of bullet points. Don't make your bullet points complete sentences, mostly because you'll be tempted to read them. This is the kiss of death for two reasons: it takes too long and takes attention away from what you're actually saying. And it insults the audience. Surely they know how to read? Your bullet points should be talking points that you can then expand upon. This lets your audience focus on you, the speaker, rather than the slides. When you're constructing a PowerPoint presentation, use as few words as you can.

---

[7]Cockburn, A. "The End of Software Engineering and The Start of Economic-Cooperative Gaming." *Computer Science and Information Systems* **1**(1): 1 - 32 (2004).

Defects

Inevitably, you'll introduce defects (errors) into your program. Defects don't just appear; developers put them there. As a developer, your aim is twofold:

- Introduce as few defects as possible into the code you write.

- Find as many of them as you can before releasing the code.

■ **Note**   By the way, I'm deliberately not using the word *bug* here, because it sounds both inoffensive and cute. Defects are neither. They are errors in your code that *you* put there. See Chapter 13 for a more detailed discussion on errors.

Despite your best efforts, though, you *will* release code with defects in it. It's just inevitable. For a program of any size, there are just too many possible paths through the program (called a *combinatorial explosion*) and too many different ways to introduce bad data for there not to be defects. Your objective is to release with as few defects as possible and to make those defects ones that don't really impact the product or its performance. To make this a reality, most development organizations have a set of defect levels they use to characterize just how bad a defect really is. These defect levels are generally built into a *defect tracking system* that allows developers and project managers to see how many and how severe the current defects are. One set of levels looks like the following:

1. *Fatal*: Either this defect causes the product to crash, or a fundamental piece of functionality doesn't work (for example, you can't save files in your new word processor).

2. *Severe*: A major piece of functionality doesn't work, and there's no workaround for it that the user can perform (such as Cut and Paste don't work at all).

3. *Serious*: A piece of functionality doesn't work, but there is a workaround for it that the customer can perform (for example, the keyboard shortcuts for Cut and Paste don't work, but the pull-down menus do).

4. *Annoying*: There's a minor defect or error in the documentation that may annoy the user, but doesn't affect how the program works (say, Paste is always spelled Patse).

5. *New feature request*: This isn't a defect, but a request for the product to do something new (as in, the word processor should have a speech-to-text feature built in).

Whenever you find a defect in a piece of code, you'll file a defect report in the defect tracking system (to keep track of how many defects you're finding, what types they are, and how severe they are) and you'll characterize the defect by severity level. When the developers are fixing defects, they start at level 1 and work their way down.

In nearly all organizations, no product can release with known level 1 or level 2 defects in it. Most organizations also try their best to remove all the level 3 defects as well.

The Retrospective

Most development teams will do a retrospective after every project. A *retrospective*, as the name implies, is an opportunity to reflect on the project just completed and answer a few questions. Typically, the questions will be like the following:

- What went right? Did our process work the way we anticipated? Did we meet our schedule? Did we implement all the features required by the customer?

- What went wrong? Why did we have so many defects? Why did we need to work 60-hour weeks for the last month of the project?

- What process issues came up? Did we follow our process? If not, what parts were problematic?

- What do we need to fix for next time? Given the answers to the preceding questions, what do we need to fix in our process, work habits, or environment for the next project?

- Who's responsible for the fixes? Someone has to be responsible for the changes to our process—who is it? (Don't make it a manager; the development team should own the process).

In a plan-driven project, the retrospective is typically held either after the product release or after each major iteration of the product. In an agile project, a retrospective is always held after every iteration. So, for example, in Scrum a retrospective is held after every sprint.

Conclusion

So where do we end up? We've gone through the general parts of managing projects, and I've presented some alternative ways of doing project management. The most important ideas to consider are that *the developers should own the process* and *management should be supportive and listen to the developers*—particularly where schedules and estimates are concerned—and be the buffer between the developers and the world. If you can work in an organization where those things are true, be a happy camper, because you'll be able to write great code.

References

Beck, K. *Extreme Programming Explained: Embrace Change.* (Boston, MA: Addison-Wesley 2000.)

Boehm, B., C. Abts, et. al. *Software Cost Estimation with COCOMO II.* (Englewood Cliffs, NJ: Prentice-Hall, 2000).

Cockburn, A. "The End of Software Engineering and The Start of Economic-Cooperative Gaming." *Computer Science and Information Systems* 1(1): 1 - 32 (2004).

DeMarco, T. and T. Lister. *Peopleware: Productive Projects and Teams, Second Edition.* (New York, NY: Dorset House Publishing Company, 1999).

McConnell, S. *Rapid Development: Taming Wild Software Schedules.* (Redmond, WA: Microsoft Press, 1996.)

Spolsky, J. *Joel on Software.* (Berkeley, CA: Apress, 2004).

CHAPTER 4

▪ ▪ ▪

Requirements

The hardest single part of building a software system is deciding what to build. No other part of the conceptual work is as difficult in establishing the detailed technical requirements, including the interfaces to people, to machines, and to other software systems. No other part of the work so cripples the results if done wrong. No other part is more difficult to rectify later. Therefore, the most important function that the software builder performs for the client is the iterative extraction and refinement of the product requirements.

—Fred Brooks[1]

Before you start coding –— yes, *before* you start coding—you need to know what it is you're going to build. That's what requirements are: a list of stuff you have to implement in order to create your terrific program. Most developers hate requirements. Really, all we'd like to do is sit down and start coding. All of us have that super-programmer mentality: "Just give me the problem and I can sit down and design and code it on the fly."

Not! If you want to be a productive developer, make fewer errors, and come up with a good, clean design, you need requirements. And the more detailed they are, the better. A good set of requirements tells you just what the program is supposed to do. It gives you the scaffolding around which you'll hang your design. You'll do requirements anyway—it's one of those steps in a standard development life cycle that you can't avoid—but if you don't make room for it in your project, you won't create a great program. Being intentional about requirements forces you to think about the details of the program and lets you listen to the users so you have a better idea of what they really want. So let's talk about requirements.

What Types of Requirements Are We Talking About?

We're really talking about *functional requirements*, the list of features the user will see and be able to use when they fire up your program. These are the "black box" requirements that show the external behavior of your program. As far as the user is concerned these are the only requirements that matter. In a plan-driven process the output of this activity of identifying requirements is a *functional specification* of what the software system is supposed to do. For an agile process the output is a set of *user stories* that define the *product backlog*.

During the course of uncovering requirements for your project you'll usually see four different types: user requirements, domain requirements, non-functional requirements, and non-requirements.

---

[1]Brooks, F. P. The Mythical Man-Month : Essays on Software Engineering, Silver Anniversary Edition. (Boston, MA: Addison-Wesley, 1995.)

© John F. Dooley 2017
J. F. Dooley, *Software Development, Design and Coding*, https://doi.org/10.1007/978-1-4842-3153-1_4

User Requirements

User requirements are nearly always expressed in natural language. They are the details of what the user expects to see as they use the program. They also include descriptions of screen layouts, dialog boxes, and menus. Any interaction element in the program should be described in the user requirements. For example:

> Logging into the system: When Gloria clicks the Login button on the main page, a Login dialog box appears in the middle of the screen. The Login dialog must contain two text boxes, labeled "Username" and "Password." There must also be two buttons in the dialog box, labeled "Submit" and "Cancel." If at any time Gloria clicks the Cancel button, the dialog box shall disappear and she will be taken back to the previous screen. In normal usage, she will click in the Username text box and type in her username, and then click in (or tab to) the Password text box and type in her password. The text typed in the Password text box must be hidden. Once Gloria is finished typing in her username and password she must click the Submit button. If she has entered a correct user name/password combination she will then be taken to the main menu page. If Gloria's user name/password combination is incorrect, an "Invalid username or password, please try again" message shall appear in the dialog box, the text boxes shall be cleared, and she will be given the opportunity to login again.

As seen in this section, you can express user requirements as scenarios, and as detailed screen-by-screen descriptions. Remember to use pictures as much as you can when you're doing user requirements. If your program is web-based, you can create lots of quick and dirty HTML pages to show the user. If it's not web-based, use a drawing program to create pictures of what the user will see, or just draw them by hand on paper.

Domain Requirements

These are requirements that are imposed on you by the application domain of the program. If you're writing a new version of an income tax program, you will be constrained by the latest IRS regulations. A general ledger program will have to abide by the latest edition of the Generally Accepted Accounting Principles (GAAP), and a smartphone will need to implement the latest Global System for Mobile communication (GSM) protocols. You don't need to write down all these requirements, just refer to them. A set of detailed domain requirements gives the developers information they will need during the design of the program. Domain requirements are usually considered "middle layer" software because they are the heart of the application, below the user interface and above the operating system, networking, or database software. A lot of domain requirements will get implemented as separate classes and libraries with their own APIs. Users are concerned with domain requirements only insofar as they affect the user requirements.

Non-Functional Requirements

Non-functional requirements are constraints on the services and functions of the program and also expectations about performance. They can include target platform specifications, timing constraints, performance requirements, memory usage requirements, file access privileges, security requirements, response times, minimum number of transactions per second, and so on. These are usually requirements that may not be visible to the user, but that do effect the user experience. An example of this type of requirement is that your web page must load and display within three seconds.

Non-Requirements

These are the things you're not going to do. You will need to communicate this to the customer because after laying out what the program will do, the most important thing to do in the requirements phase is *manage expectations*. One of the worst phrases a customer can utter at that final demo before you release is, "But I thought it was going to do . . ." You need to tell all the stakeholders in a project what the program is going to do and also what it's not going to do. In particular you need to let them know that there are requirements that won't be implemented—at least not in the current release. "Only one countdown timer may run at a time." "There will not be a defrost cycle that allows defrost modes to be selected by food type." It's likely that your customer won't read this section, but at least you can point to it when they ask. Be careful, though, because the number of things that your program will not do is nearly infinite.

Requirements Gathering in a Plan-Driven Project

A *functional specification* describes what the program will do entirely from the user's perspective. It doesn't care how the software is implemented. It talks about the features of the program and specifies screens, menus, dialogs, and the like. Think of it as a badly written user manual. A second kind of spec can be called a *technical specification*. The technical specification describes the internal implementation details of the program. That is, it talks about data structures, algorithms used, database models, choice of programming language, and so on. We're not going to talk about technical specs, just functional specs.

"Wait," you say. "What about all those agile methodologies we talked about in Chapter 2? *They* don't write functional specs. So there! I'm off the hook." Well, in fact, agile methodologies *do* write functional specifications. They're just in a different format from the 300-page single-spaced requirements document that some plan-driven methodologies require. XP requires that, together with the customer representative or product owner, you write *user stories* that lay out what the program will do. That's a spec. We will discuss how agile methodologies do requirements later in this chapter. The important part and the idea behind this entire chapter is to *write down what your program is supposed to do before you start coding*.

But I Don't Like Writing!

A standard argument made by software developers is that they can't write. Nonsense! Everyone can learn to write functional specs. But writing is work. You have to get in there and practice writing before you'll be any good at it. If you're still in school (be it undergrad or graduate school), take a course in writing, one where you've got to write essays or journal entries or stories or poetry every single week. You should also have to read other works critically; reading other people's writing, whether good or bad, is a great way to learn how to write better.

Functional requirements should always be written in a natural language. Why? Well, it's the Sapir-Whorf linguistic relativity hypothesis, don't you know?[2] In a nutshell, language not only determines what you *do* say, it determines what you *can* say (and think). That is, the language you use determines what kinds of thoughts you are able to have; it tends to constrain your thinking processes, and thus what you can think about and how you express your thoughts. If the language doesn't have room for certain kinds of thoughts, you are much less likely to think them. Natural languages are much more expressive and varied than programming languages, so you want to write requirements and do your designs in natural languages and save the programming languages for implementation later. Whether you believe the Sapir-Whorf hypothesis or not, it's nearly always a good idea to develop your functional requirements in a natural language so you

---

[2]http://en.wikipedia.org/wiki/Linguistic_relativity (retrieved September 15, 2009).

don't get bogged down in the syntactic and semantic details of a programming language before you need to. This doesn't mean you can't think about implementation while you're doing the functional requirements (you will, trust me), but just shunt those thoughts over into a "technical note" sidebar of your specification or a completely separate document.[3] You might also look at Kenneth Iverson's Turing Award lecture, "Notation as a Tool of Thought," for a similar discussion.[4]

Outline of a Functional Specification

Every functional specification is different, just as every software development project is different. So take this outline with a grain of salt and just use the parts that apply to your project. Lots of the ideas here are from Spolsky.[5] Every function specification should have the elements discussed in the following sections.

Overview

This is your executive summary. A paragraph or at most two of what the program is supposed to do. "This program runs your microwave oven. It interfaces to a keypad and an LCD display that provides user input and output functionality. Its functions are limited to those that a standard microwave would have, with the addition of single buttons for pizza and coffee reheating. It also will run a time of day clock and a stand-alone countdown timer. It doesn't control the light. It has a safety interlock that will prevent the microwave from starting if the door is open."

Disclaimer

You should always put in a statement right at the beginning that "This specification isn't done yet. If you think something is missing or wrong, just sent me an email." That helps keep all the marketing guys off your back and lets you file new feature requests in your mail trash bin. Lots of people will put a big, black DRAFT in the header or footer of the document. That can work as well, but folks tend to ignore it. Some people will use a big DRAFT watermark on their specs, so that every page has the word embedded behind the text. That doesn't stop people from yelling at you either. At some point your disclaimer should change to something like "This specification is as complete as it will be for this release. If you think something is missing or wrong, just sent an email to the author and we'll consider it for the next release."

Author's Name

Somebody needs to be responsible for the functional specification. Not a committee, not the development team, *one person*. This is usually either the development manager or the project manager, depending on how your company sets up development projects. There are pros and cons to all the different organizational arrangements.

If the development manager (the person to whom the developers report) is in charge of the functional spec, then that person is usually up to speed on all the technical aspects of the project. That's good. On the other hand, if your boss writes the functional spec, it might be harder to tell them that there's something wrong with the specification, or that you don't agree with the design. Also, development managers were probably developers at one time and so they may not have the people skills (read: charm and schmoozing skills) necessary to talk to marketing, the customer, documentation, testing, and so on.

---

[3]Spolsky, J., *Joel on Software*. (Berkeley, CA: Apress, 2004.)
[4]Iverson, K. E. "Notation as a Tool of Thought." *Communications of the ACM* **23**(8): 444–465 (1980).
[5]Spolsky, 2004.

If your company uses project managers that are in charge of the specification, design, and schedule, but don't have developers directly reporting to them, then you run the risk of getting someone that isn't as technically astute as a former developer. On the other hand, these folks can usually charm the socks off the other teams, so negotiations are a lot smoother. Project managers need to have some technical skills and to be very good at getting all the stakeholders to reach consensus on the contents of the functional specification.

Scenarios of Typical Usage

These are the actual requirements. A great way to get customers to respond to your requirements list is to present several scenarios of typical usage of the program to them as part of the specification. This has a couple of advantages:

- First, if you write the scenarios as if they're user stories, the customer is more likely to read them.

- Second, customers are more likely to understand what you're doing and come up with ideas for things you've missed or gotten wrong. This is always a good thing, because the more customer input you get early in the process, the more likely you'll actually create something they want.

In many agile methodologies, including XP, user stories are often written like scenarios. In XP, the customer is part of the project team, so you get constant feedback on user stories and daily program builds. In Scrum, the customer isn't required to be part of the project team, but they are strongly encouraged to keep in close contact with the team. Also in Scrum, shorter sprint lengths allow the customer to see working versions of the product more often. In the Unified Modeling Language (UML, see www.uml.org), there is an entire notation used to create *use cases* (another word for scenarios). But as already discussed, nothing beats natural language for describing usage scenarios. We'll come back to use cases later, in Chapter 8.

Once you've written a couple of scenarios, you'll have a much better idea of how your program will flow, and what screens, dialog boxes, menus, and so on you'll need. This lets you go through each one of those screens and flesh out the details of how they're laid out, what buttons, text boxes, icons, graphics, and so on they'll have, and what other screens they connect to. Use pictures! A picture of a screen or a dialog box is worth way more than a thousand words. It gives the reader something to react to and it gets them thinking about program flow and user interface issues.

Open Issues

When you first write the functional specification, there will be one or two things you don't know. That's okay. Just put them in the "Open Issues" section. Then every time you meet with the customer, point to this section and try to get answers. Some of these questions will move to requirements sections and some will end up in the "Non-requirements" section, after you get those answers. By the end of the project, though, this section should be empty. If it's not, well, you've got issues that will haunt you.

Design and New Feature Ideas

If you're like most developers, you'll be trying to design and code the program in your head all the time you're doing your requirements gathering and analysis. That's just what developers do. The two types of notes developers and project managers typically create are technical notes containing design or coding ideas for developers, and marketing notes containing feature ideas for the marketing folks and the customer. So, to keep from forgetting the design and implementation ideas you have during the requirements phase, write a separate notebook. This notebook is just a separate document that contains a note for later. Ideally it's a document that's shared with the entire team.

Finally, as your project proceeds through development, new requirements and features will surface. This always happens. But if you want to keep to a schedule and deliver a working product, you just *can't* implement everything that will come up. If you want your requirements to be up to date, you need a place to put all the tasks you will do later. That's what a "Backlog" document is for—all the requirements you're going to consider for the next release of the product. This does a couple of good things for you. It tells the customer you haven't forgotten these features, and that by moving them to the next release you are committed to delivering the current release as close to the published schedule as possible. And it tells the developers that you're not out of control and that the project has a good shot at being done with high quality and on time. For more information on backlogs, take a look any of the Scrum agile methodology descriptions.[6]

One More Thing

One more thing about the functional specification: don't obsess. Chances are, you'll do a good job of picking out requirements and writing them down in the functional spec, but it won't be as detailed as you like and it won't be complete. Don't worry. The only time a functional specification is complete is when you ship the release. Don't spend time trying to get every single detail correct; don't spend time trying to tease every requirement out of your customer. It just won't happen. Set a time limit, do your best, and let it go. You don't want to have a bunch of developers sitting around twiddling their thumbs with nothing to do, waiting for the spec, do you?

Requirements Gathering in an Agile Project

First things first. In an agile development project there is no functional specification. That's because agile developers recognize from the beginning that the requirements will change and so they should embrace change and defer making decisions about requirements and design as long as possible. Also, because in an agile project the customer is an integral part of the team, the agile developers also know that they can get immediate feedback on feature implementations and they can get timely updates on requirements from the customer. This doesn't necessarily make the process of gathering requirements any easier, but it gives everyone more confidence that the current set of requirements is the right set.

For most agile methodologies the key idea in requirements gathering is the *user story*. The user story is just that—a description of some feature or scenario that the customer wants to execute in order to get some type of work done. The classic way to describe the contents of a user story is to say, "*As a <role>, I want to do <action>, so that <reason/benefit>.*" By expressing a user story this way, you get to the *who, what*, and *why* of the requirement.

The Three Cs

A user story has three fundamental components, expressed by Ron Jeffries in 2001: the card, the conversation, and the confirmation.[7]

---

[6]Schwaber, K. and M. Beedle. *Agile software development with Scrum.* (Upper Saddle River, NJ: Prentice Hall, 1980.)
[7]http://ronjeffries.com/xprog/articles/expcardconversationconfirmation/

Card

All user stories are written on *cards*. A card can be a Post-It note, an index card, or a larger piece of paper. But it's nearly always a physical thing. Although the card contains the text of the story "As a <role> I want to <action> so that <benefit/result>," it's really an invitation to a collaborative conversation about what the story really means and what the user really wants. Note that the card isn't very detailed. It usually just contains an outline of the story. It's a placeholder for the real requirement that will be subsequently hashed out. Stakeholders can write on the card, put estimates on it, questions, and so forth.

Conversation

The *conversation* about a user story takes place between all the important stakeholders in the project, the product owner or user, the development team, the testers, marketing folks, and maybe others. This is a substantive discussion about what the product owner really wants from the story. The conversation is ideally held in person, and the discussion will include more details about the story, possibly estimates of size, and an estimate of the relative priority of the story. The conversation may include breaking the original story into two or more smaller stories if the initial estimates indicate the effort to implement the story may be too large.

Confirmation

The last component of a user story is *confirmation*. The user or product owner provides this information in the form of *acceptance criteria* for the story. The acceptance criteria are usually written on the back of the card as a short bullet list. These criteria will end up being *acceptance tests* that the product owner will use to confirm that the implementation of the story is acceptable to the user. The best way to create acceptance tests is for the product owner to generate examples of the story in use and then for the development team to automate the examples. That way, the product owner can execute the acceptance tests on the delivered feature and confirm whether the implementation works or not.

INVEST in Stories

Note that the three components of a user story just mentioned don't tell us all about the story. A lot of the details will come out of the conversation and the confirmation. They also don't tell us anything about the *quality* of the story and what makes a good user story. Bill Wake, in a classic blog post, laid out the characteristics of a good user story using the acronym INVEST.[8]

Independent

The idea here is that your user stories should be *independent of each other*. That way a single user story (which, depending on the agile process you're using, may take several iterations to fully implement) can be scheduled and implemented separately from any other user story. Wake gives the example of a multi-layered cake. If you take a slice out of the cake, you can eat (implement) just that one slice, independently of any other. This may not be completely possible—think of things like the radio software in a mobile phone. In order to fully test part of the user interface embodied in a user story, you may have to have all the radio software working first. We'll see this same idea later on as loose coupling in object-oriented design.

---

[8]http://xp123.com/articles/invest-in-good-stories-and-smart-tasks/

Negotiable

A good story leaves room for the parties involved to *negotiate the details* of its implementation; it provides the essence of the requirement. The story is not so specific that it reads like a contract. Rather it provides the developer with a goal and allows the owner and the developer room to create an interesting and workable implementation.

Valuable

A good user story must be *valuable to the customer*. It must describe a feature or a service that the customer wants. Because user stories will be scheduled and implemented in a development iteration, they must add value to the product when the iteration is complete. In addition, if the team decides a user story is too large and must be split into two or more stories, each of them must provide value to the customer. This idea gives the development team guidance on how to split stories—based on value to the customer, not on technology.

Estimable

User stories must be able to be *estimated*. Estimation is critical to the product owner so that they can assign a relative priority to the story. This characteristic also allows the team to focus on the size of the story. Stories that are too large can't really be estimated and so should be candidates for splitting. Estimation is part of the negotiation in the conversation. It means to look at both the size of the story and the possible effort involved in implementing it. If a team is having trouble estimating the size or the effort of a particular story, it may be that the story is too large and needs to be split. Estimation is also the first step in decomposing the story into implementable tasks.

Small

As implied above, good user stories should be *small*. Ideally, a user story should be implementable in a single sprint or iteration. That will allow the development team to decompose the story into a number of small tasks—ideally of eight person-hours or less worth of effort. It also speaks to the Value characteristic because if it's small, the story will add value for the customer at the end of a single iteration. One way to manage story sizes is to not care about them if the story is low priority. As the story moves up in the product backlog, it will become more important, and at some point it will be important enough to do a detailed estimate of its effort. If large enough, (longer than a single iteration), you should consider splitting it into smaller stories.

Testable

Good stories must be *testable*. This harkens back to the plan-driven idea of *traceability*. Once implemented, one should be able to trace a feature back through the implementation and design and into the original requirements. In agile, this practice is usually implemented using test-driven development (TDD) and acceptance criteria. The product owner writes the acceptance criteria, and the developers will implement the unit tests that will confirm that a task is correct. The acceptance tests the product owner will use confirm that the user story is correctly implemented. This is typically the definition of *Done* in an agile environment.

If a user story is written and the product owner is unsure or unclear about how to write the acceptance criteria, this may mean that the story details are unclear and the story conversation should be restarted to clear up any confusion.

The Testable characteristic is also a way for the development team to include non-functional requirements (performance, response time, usability, and so on) as things to be tested.

Product Backlog

At this point, the total number of user stories generated by the product owner and agreed upon by the development team is added to a list of the total number of things that need to be done to create the product. This is known as the *product backlog*. Where a plan-driven process team will have a long, detailed document—the functional specification—an agile product team will have a stack of cards that ends up defining the product. This stack of cards is only preliminary, though. As the development process moves along, an agile product team will be adding, removing, and dividing user story cards constantly. The product owner will be the primary person doing this job, and it's the product owner's job to decide when the product is done and should be released. There may still be cards left in the stack when a product is released. Those cards are destined for the next product effort.

SMART Tasks

Once the team agrees on a set of user stories and adds them to the product backlog, the developers must then plan for the next iteration or sprint. This planning includes taking each user story and breaking it down into a set of implementable tasks, each of which is easy to estimate with effort requiring a relatively short amount of developer time. In short, *tasks* are the work to be done in order to implement user stories.

This work of decomposing stories into tasks is the work of the development team, not the product owner. Generally the entire team will do this exercise as part of planning the next iteration or sprint. The estimates for the tasks are added up until the amount of effort reaches the amount of time available to the team in the next iteration. In Scrum, tasks can be assigned point values based on their perceived difficulty. The more difficult the task, the more points are assigned. The team will add up the points for the high-priority tasks until the point value reaches the team's average velocity. These tasks are then presented to the product owner, who either approves the list of work to be done or suggests changes by changing the priorities of stories in the product backlog. Eventually everyone agrees on the stories, and tasks for the iteration and work can begin.

In order to perform this decomposition and effort estimation, the team must be able to identify tasks within stories and write them out on cards so they can be put on a task or kanban board. Each task must meet certain goals, characterized by the acronym SMART.

Specific

Where user stories can be general and leave room for interpretation and negotiation, the tasks created from them need to be specific so they can be implemented. This will likely uncover hidden requirements in the stories. These requirements can be incorporated into the tasks or they may require the creation of a new user story that will then get put in the product backlog. In any event, tasks should be as specific as possible, including details about data structures and user interfaces if necessary.

Measurable

The key idea here is that the team needs to know when all the requirements for the task have been completed. That is, when is the task *done*? Each team will have a different definition of *done*, but it should include things like "the feature works as listed on the task," "all the unit tests pass," and "the code has been reviewed and integrated."

Achievable

The task must be something that a developer can do within the timeframe of the iteration or sprint. The developer must also have the skill set necessary to achieve the task. This doesn't mean the developer can't ask for help. This goal can also integrate well with the idea of *pair programming*, which will spread the required skill set across two developers.

Relevant

This goal ties in with the Valuable story component discussed earlier. With respect to tasks, this means that the task must do something that makes progress towards the creation of the user story implementation. It should add value to the iteration for the customer.

Time-Boxed

This goal means that the task, as estimated, can be finished within the iteration or sprint. If the task turns out to be harder than expected, the team is expected to divide it into two or more tasks and estimate them separately. The other goal implied here is that the total number of points assigned to the tasks included in the iteration is doable within the team's average velocity.

Sprint/Iteration Backlog

As the tasks are created from user stories and estimated, they're added to the sprint/iteration backlog as things to do in the next sprint or iteration. Depending on the agile methodology being used, once an agreed-upon number of tasks are added to the backlog, the number of tasks in the backlog may or may not be changed while the sprint or iteration is underway. In Scrum, no more tasks may be added, except by the developers themselves, for the duration of the sprint. Any new work that's discovered must be added to the product backlog instead.

Requirements Digging

Most software engineering texts use the phrase *requirements elicitation* to talk about the process of getting your users to tell you what they want. Hunt and Thomas, in their book *The Pragmatic Programmer*, use the much more descriptive phrase *requirements digging* to emphasize the point that what you're really doing is digging for all those requirements that your customer doesn't know they want yet.[9] Hunt and Thomas also make the terrific distinction between requirements, policies, and implementations as a way to illustrate the requirements digging process.

For example, "The system must let the user choose a loan term" is a nice succinct requirement. It says that there's something you have to do. It isn't specific enough for implementation yet, but it tells the developer something concrete that must be built.

"Loan terms must be between 6 months and 30 years" isn't a requirement, although it kind of looks like one. This statement is an example of a *business policy*. When statements like this are presented to developers as requirements, they have a tendency to hard-code the statement in the program. Wrong, wrong, wrong. Policies like this can change, so you need to be very careful about putting business policies in your

---

[9]Hunt, A. and D. Thomas. *The Pragmatic Programmer: From Journeyman to Master*. (Boston, MA: Addison-Wesley, 2000.)

requirements. It's almost always the case that you need to implement a more general version of the business policy than is stated. The real requirement is probably something like "Loan terms are of finite length but the length of the loan will vary by type of loan." This tells you that you probably need to build a table-driven subsystem to handle this feature. That way, the loan term for a particular type of loan can be changed by making a single change in a data table, and the code doesn't need to change at all.

"The user must be able to select a loan term using a drop-down list box" isn't a requirement either, although, again, it may look like one. This is only a requirement if the customer absolutely must have a drop-down menu to choose their loan term. Otherwise, this is an example of the implementation that the customer would like to see, and it may not be a requirement. As Hunt and Thomas state in their book, "It's important to discover the underlying reason *why* users do a particular thing, rather than just *the way* they currently do it. At the end of the day, your development has to solve their *business problem*, not just meet their stated requirements. Documenting the reasons behind requirements will give your team invaluable information when making daily implementation decisions."

Why Requirements Digging Is Hard

There are several reasons why pulling requirements out of your customer is a really hard exercise. We'll look at a few of these.

Problems of Scope

Lots of times the boundaries of what your program is supposed to do are fuzzy. This can be because of several things. The program may be part of a larger system, and the integration of the parts is ill-defined. The customer may not have thought through exactly what they want the program to do, so they start throwing out all sorts of ideas, many of which may not even apply to the problem at hand. Finally, the customer may have dropped into implementation-land and be providing unnecessary levels of detail.

It takes lots of patience, discipline, repeatedly saying the word *no*, and repeatedly asking, "Why does this need to be part of the program?" in order to overcome problems of scope. Scope is directly related to requirements creep, so beware.

Problems of Understanding

Let's face it: the customer and you as the developer speak different languages. Your customer is the domain expert and they speak the domain language (accounts receivable, accounts payable, reconciliation, general ledger, and so on). You speak the design and implementation language (class, object, method, use case, recursion, activation record, and the like). This is usually worse than an American in Paris; at least there, both sides can pantomime their needs and figure things out. With problems of domain understanding, the best you can usually do is order drinks together.

There are usually two ways to overcome problems of understanding. The first is to have someone in the middle who has lived in both worlds and who can translate between the two. Some companies have folks called *system engineers* or *technical marketers* who fulfill this role. These folks have done development and have also worked the customer side of things, so they can speak both languages. Good system engineers are worth their weight in user stories.

The second way to promote understanding is to have the customer as part of the development team. This is the approach taken by some agile methodologies, notably XP. When the customer is part of the development team, you get to talk to them every day, ask them questions, and teach them technical stuff. Both sides benefit. And because the on-site customer sees intermediate product builds as soon as they pop out of your build machine, you get immediate feedback. Win, win, and win.

Problems of Volatility

Things change. This is by far the hardest part of requirements gathering and analysis and the biggest reason why schedules slip. You can't do anything about it. Get used to it. As Kent Beck says, "Embrace change." What you can do is *manage* change. Create a backlog of new features that get added as they arrive. In the Scrum methodology, new requirements are always added to the product backlog—they're not added to the current sprint backlog. This allows the current sprint to proceed normally, and the requirements are all reviewed at the end of the sprint. Another way to manage change is to push the decision onto the user. Give the user a choice: "If we implement this new feature it will add six weeks to the schedule. Do you still want it?" Alternatively: "If you want to keep to the original schedule, we can only implement and test one of A, B, or C. You pick the one you want most." This is one of the things that the agile folks mean by *courage*[10]; sometimes you have to take a stand and choose what's best for the project as a whole.

Non-Technical Problems

From a developer's perspective, non-technical problems with requirements are the worst ones you will see. In fact, these are problems developers should never see; their managers should shield them from non-technical problems. Non-technical requirements problems are fundamentally political. Examples abound. One group of customers in an organization has a different view of the program requirements than another group. Or worse, one manager has a different view than another manager. The program being developed will reduce the influence of one department by automating a function where they used to be the sole source of expertise. The program will distribute data processing across several departments where it was once centralized in a single department. The list goes on and on. The best advice for non-technical problems is to run away—quickly. Let your vice-president deal with it; that's why they're paid the big bucks.

Analyzing the Requirements

Once you've written down a set of requirements, you need to make sure that these are the right requirements for the program; you need to *analyze* them. Analysis has three basic parts.

First, you must *categorize* the requirements and organize them into related areas. This will help the designers a lot.

Second, you—or better yet, the customer—need to *prioritize* them. This is critical because you won't be able to implement all the requirements in the first product release (trust me, you won't). So, this prioritized list will be what you'll use to set the contents of each interim release.

Lastly, you need to *examine* each requirement in relation to all the others to make sure they fit into a coherent whole. Ask yourself a series of questions:

1. Is each requirement *consistent* with the overall project objective? If your program is supposed to sell your users books, it doesn't also have to compute their golf handicap.

2. Is this requirement *really necessary*? Have you added something that can be removed without impairing the essential functionality of the program? If your first release is supposed to allow users to buy books, you probably don't need to also allow them to buy sailboats.

---

[10]Beck, K. *Extreme Programming Explained: Embrace Change.* (Boston, qwo21iwqswMA: Addison-Wesley, 2000.)

3. Is this requirement *testable*? This is probably the most important question when you're doing requirements analysis. If you can't figure out how to test a requirement, then you can't know that you've implemented it correctly or that you're finished. All requirements *must* be testable, or else they're not requirements. In most agile methodologies, the rule is to write the test first, then write the code.

4. Is this requirement *doable* in the technical environment you've got to work in? This question normally applies to those non-functional requirements mentioned previously. Are your requirements feasible given the particular target platform or set of hardware constraints you must work under for this project? For example, if your target platform is a Macintosh running macOS, a requirement that the DirectX graphics library be used is not doable because DirectX is a Windows-only library.

5. Is this requirement *unambiguous*? Your requirements need to be as precise as possible (so that they are testable), because as sure as you're sitting here reading this, someone will misinterpret an ambiguous requirement, and you'll discover the error the day after you ship. Your requirements should never contain the words *or* or *may*.

Conclusion

Once you're done with your functional specification or set of user stories and the analysis of your requirements, you're done with the requirements phase. Right? Well, of course not. As we've said before: requirements change. So relax, don't obsess about the requirements. Do the best you can to get an initial list of clear, testable requirements and then move on to design. You'll always come back here later.

References

Beck, K. *Extreme Programming Explained: Embrace Change*. (Boston, MA: Addison-Wesley, 2000.)

Brooks, F. P. *The Mythical Man-Month : Essays on Software Engineering*, Silver Anniversary Edition. (Boston, MA: Addison-Wesley, 1995.)

Hunt, A. and D. Thomas. *The Pragmatic Programmer: From Journeyman to Master*. (Boston, MA: Addison-Wesley, 2000.)

Iverson, K. E. "Notation as a Tool of Thought." *Communications of the ACM* 23(8): 444–465 (1980).

Jeffries, Ron. "Essential XP: Cards, Conversation, and Confirmation." http://ronjeffries.com/xprog/articles/expcardconversationconfirmation/. Retrieved June 30, 2017. (August 30, 2001.)

Schwaber, K. and M. Beedle. *Agile Software Development with Scrum*. (Upper Saddle River, NJ: Prentice Hall, 1980.)

Spolsky, J., *Joel on Software*. (Berkeley, CA: Apress, 2004.)

Wake, William., "INVEST in Good Stories and SMART Tasks." *Agile Advice*. August 17. http://xp123.com/articles/invest-in-good-stories-and-smart-tasks/. Retrieved June 26, 2017. (2003.)

Wikipedia, Sapir-Whorf Linguistic Relativity Hypothesis, http://en.wikipedia.org/wiki/Linguistic_relativity. Retrieved September 15, 2009.

CHAPTER 5

▪ ▪ ▪

Software Architecture

> *What do we mean by a software architecture? To me the term architecture conveys a notion of the core elements of the system, the pieces that are difficult to change. A foundation on which the rest must be built.*
>
> —Martin Fowler[1]

Once you have an idea of *what* you're going to build, then you can start thinking about *how* you're going to build it. Of course, you've already been thinking about this from the very first requirement, but now you have permission to do it. Here we begin to delve into design.

There are really two levels of software design. The level we normally think of when we're writing programs is called *detailed design*. What operations do we need? What data structures? What algorithms are we using? How is the database going to be organized? What does the user interface look like? What are the calling sequences? These are all very detailed questions that need to be answered before you can really get on with the detailed work of coding (well, sort of—we'll get to that later).

But there's another level of design. This kind of design is all about *style*. If you were building a house, this design level asks questions like ranch or multi-story? Tudor or Cape Cod? Which direction do the bedroom windows face? Forced-air or hot-water heat? Three bedrooms or four? Open concept floor plan or closed? These questions focus somewhat on details, but they're much more about the style of the house and how you'll be using it, rather than things like 12- or 14-gauge wire for the electrical system or the dimensions of the air conditioning ductwork. This emphasis on style is what software architecture is all about. As Fowler says in this chapter's opening quote, you need the foundation before you can build the rest of the structure. Software architecture is a set of ideas that tells you which foundation is the right one for your program.

The idea of software architecture began as a response to the increasing size and complexity of programs. As Garlan and Shaw put it in the seminal document on software architecture: "As the size and complexity of software systems increases, the design problem goes beyond the algorithms and data structures of the computation: designing and specifying the overall system structure emerges as a new kind of problem. . . . This is the software architecture level of design."[2] Actually, *all* programs of any size and complexity have an architecture. It's just that for larger programs you need to be more intentional about your thinking about the architecture to make sure you have the right set of architectural patterns incorporated in your system design. You need to do this. It's so much harder to change things at the architectural level once the program has been written, because architectural features are so fundamental to the structure of the program.

---

[1]"Is Design Dead?" Retrieved from http://martinfowler.com/articles/designDead.html on July 3, 2017.
[2]Garlan, D. and M. Shaw. *An Introduction to Software Architecture*. Pittsburgh, PA: Carnegie Mellon University: 49. CMU/SEI-94-TR-21 (1994).

© John F. Dooley 2017
J. F. Dooley, *Software Development, Design and Coding*, https://doi.org/10.1007/978-1-4842-3153-1_5

There are many different styles of software architecture, and in any given project you'll probably use more than one. The architectural style used for a program depends on what it is you're doing. As we'll see, different types of programs in different domains will lead us to different architectural styles; we can also call these *architectural patterns* since they have many characteristics of the *design patterns* we'll see shortly. First, let's get some general vocabulary under our belts.

General Architectural Patterns

Whenever a software architect starts thinking about an architecture for a program, they usually start by drawing pictures. Diagrams of the architecture allow people to see the structure and framework of the program much more easily than text allows. Software architectures are normally represented as black box *graphs* where graph nodes are *computational structures* and the graph edges are *communication conduits* between the structures. The conduits can represent data flow, object message passing, or procedure calls. Notations of this type vary, and there are several standard notations, the most popular being the Unified Modeling Language (UML). Visual descriptions of architectures are generally easier to understand. A particular architectural style is a pattern that can represent a set of similar structures. Let's looks at several different common architectural styles.

The Main Program—Subroutine Architectural Pattern

The most traditional and oldest architectural pattern is the *main program—subroutine pattern*. It descends from Niklaus Wirth's 1971 paper "Program Development by Stepwise Refinement,"[3] although Wirth was just the first to formally define the top-down problem decomposition methodology that naturally leads to the main program—subroutine pattern.

The idea is simple. You start with a big problem and then try to decompose the problem into several smaller, semi-independent problems or pieces of the original problem. For example, nearly every problem that is amenable to solution by top-down decomposition can be divided into three parts immediately: input processing, computation of the solution, and output processing.

Once you have a problem divided into several pieces, you look at each piece individually and continue dividing, ignoring all the other pieces as you go. Eventually, you'll have a very small problem where the solution is obvious; now is the time to write code. So, you generally solve the problem from the top down, and write the code from the bottom up. There are many variations, however.

To quote from the conclusion to Wirth's paper:

1. Program construction consists of a sequence of refinement steps. In each step a given task is broken up into a number of subtasks. Each refinement in the description of a task may be accompanied by a refinement of the description of the data, which constitute the means of communication between the subtasks . . .

2. The degree of modularity obtained in this way will determine the ease or difficulty with which a program can be adapted to changes or extensions of the purpose . . .

3. During the process of stepwise refinement, a notation which is natural to the problem in hand should be used as long as possible . . . Each refinement implies a number of design decisions based upon a set of design criteria . . .

4. The detailed elaborations on the development of even a short program form a long story, indicating that careful programming is not a trivial subject.

---

[3]Wirth, N. "Program Development by Stepwise Refinement." *Communications of the ACM* **14**(4): 221-227 (1971).

Figure 5-1 gives an impression about how the main program—subroutine architecture works. We'll discuss top-down decomposition of problems much more in Chapter 7.

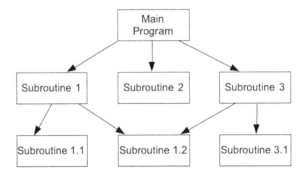

Figure 5-1. *A main program—subroutine architecture*

Pipe-and-Filter Architecture

In a pipe-and-filter style architecture, the computational components are called *filters* and they act as transducers that take input, transform it according to one or more algorithms, and then output the result to a communications conduit. The input and outputs conduits are called *pipes*.

A typical pipe-and-filter architecture is linear, as shown in Figure 5-2.

Figure 5-2. *The pipe-and-filter architecture*

The filters must be independent components. That's one of the beauties of a pipe-and-filter architecture. You can join different filters in the set in different orders to get different results. The classic example of a pipe-and-filter architectural style is the Unix shell, where there are a large number of small programs that typically do a single thing and that can be chained together using the Unix pipe mechanism. Here's an example that shows how a pipe-and-filter can work. This problem is from Jon Bentley's book *Programming Pearls*[4]:

> *The Problem: Given a dictionary of words in English, find all the anagrams in the dictionary. That is, find all the words that are permutations of each other. For example, pots, stop, and spot are anagrams of each other.*

So, what do we know? Well, first of all, all the anagrams have the same letters and the same number of letters in each word. That gives us the clue to the method you'll use to find the anagrams. Got it yet? Don't worry. I'll wait.

Yes! If you sort each word by individual letters, you'll end up with a string of characters that has all the letters in the word in alphabetical order. We call this creating a *sign* for the word. If you then sort the resulting list, all the anagrams will end up together in the sorted list because their sorted letters will be identical. If you then keep track of which words you sorted, you can then simplify the list and create a new list with, say, each set of anagrams on the same line of the output file. This is exactly how Bentley does it.

---

[4]Bentley, J. *Programming Pearls*, Second Edition. (Boston, MA: Addison-Wesley, 2000.)

But how does this relate to a pipe-and-filter architecture, you ask? Good question. Let's break down the solution again.

1. Create a sign for each word in the list by sorting the letters in each word; keep the sign and the word together.

2. Sort the resulting list by the signs; all the anagrams should now be together.

3. Squash the list by putting each set of anagrams on the same line, removing the signs as you do.

See the pipe-and-filter now? In Unix-speak it looks like this:

```
sign <dictionary.txt | sort | squash >anagrams.txt
```

sign is the filter we use to do step 1, with input file dictionary.txt. sign outputs a list of signs and their associated words, which is piped to the Unix sort utility (we didn't need to write that one). Sort then sorts the list by the first field on each line (its default behavior), which happens to be the sign of each word. It then outputs the sorted list to the next pipe. Squash takes the sorted list from the incoming pipe and compresses it by putting all the words with the same sign on the same line, eliminating the signs as it does so. This final list is sent via one last pipe (this time a Unix I/O redirection) to the output file anagrams.txt.

Note that this example has all the features of a standard pipe-and-filter architecture: independent computational components that perform a transformation on their input data and communication conduits that transmit the data from the output of one component to the input of the next. Note also that not all applications should use the pipe-and-filter architecture. For example, it won't work so well for interactive applications or applications that respond to events or interrupts. That's why we're going to look at more architectural styles.

An Object-Oriented Architectural Pattern

The advent of object-oriented analysis, design, and programming in the early 1980s (well, it really started in the 1960s, but no one was paying attention) brought with it a number of architectural and design patterns. We'll just focus on one object-oriented architectural pattern here and save discussions of the rest to Chapter 11, which covers design patterns.

The *Model-View-Controller* (MVC) architectural pattern is a way of breaking an application, or even just a piece of an application's interface, into three parts: the model, the view, and the controller. MVC was originally developed to map the traditional input, processing, and output roles of many programs into the GUI realm:

Input ➤ Processing ➤ Output

Controller ➤ Model ➤ View

The user input, the modeling of the external world, and the visual feedback to the user are separated and handled by model, view, and controller *objects,* as shown in Figure 5-3.

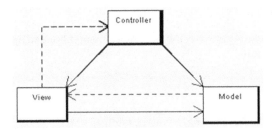

Figure 5-3. *The Model-View-Controller architecture*

- The *controller* interprets mouse and keyboard inputs from the user and maps these user actions into commands that are sent to the model and/or view to effect the appropriate change. The controller handles input.

- The *model* manages one or more data elements, responds to queries about its state, and responds to instructions to change state. The model knows what the application is supposed to do and is the main computational structure of the architecture—it *models* the problem you're trying to solve. The model knows the rules.

- The *view* or *viewport* manages a rectangular area of the display and is responsible for presenting data to the user through a combination of graphics and text. The view doesn't know anything about what the program is actually doing; all it does is take instructions from the controller and data from the model and display them. It communicates back to the model and controller to report status. The view handles the output.

The flow of an MVC program typically looks like this:

- The *user* interacts with the user interface (for example, the user clicks a button) and the controller handles the input event from the user interface, often via a registered handler or callback. The user interface is displayed by the view but controlled by the controller. Oddly enough, the controller has no direct knowledge of the view as an object; it just sends messages when it needs something on the screen updated.

- The *controller* accesses the model, possibly updating it in a way appropriate to the user's action (for example, the controller causes the user's shopping cart to be updated by the model). This usually causes a change in the model's state as well as in its data.

- A *view* uses the model to generate an appropriate user interface (for example, the view produces a screen listing the shopping cart contents). The view gets its own data from the model. The model has no direct knowledge of the view. It just responds to requests for data from whomever and to requests for transforming data from the controller.

- The controller, as the user interface manager, waits for further user interactions, which begins the cycle anew.

The main idea here is separation of concerns—and code. The objective is to separate how your program works from what it is displaying and how it gets its input data. This is classic object-oriented programming: create objects that hide their data and hide how they manipulate their data and then just present a simple interface to the world to interact with other objects. We'll see this again in Chapter 9.

An MVC Example: Let's Hunt!

A classic example of a program that uses the MVC architectural pattern is the Nifty Assignment presented by Dr. David Matuszek at the 2004 SIGCSE Technical Symposium.[5]

The Problem

The program is a simple simulation of a fox and a rabbit. The fox is trying to find the rabbit in a grid environment, and the rabbit is trying to get away. There are bushes that the rabbit can hide behind, and there are some restrictions on movement.

Figure 5-4 shows a typical picture of the game in action.

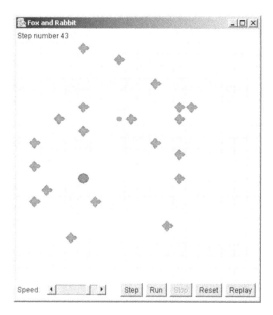

Figure 5-4. *A typical fox and rabbit hunt instance*

The fox is the large dot, the rabbit is the small dot, and the bushes are the fat crosses.

The objective of the programming assignment is to make the rabbit smarter so it can escape from the fox. We don't really care about this—we want to look at how the program is organized. Figure 5-5 shows the organization of the program. It's a UML object diagram taken from the BlueJ IDE. The key parts of the program are the three classes: Model, View, and Controller.

[5]Matuszek, David. "Rabbit Hunt," SIGCSE 2004 Technical Symposium, Nifty Assignments Session. Retrieved August 17, 2009, http://nifty.stanford.edu/2004/RabbitHunt/ (2004).

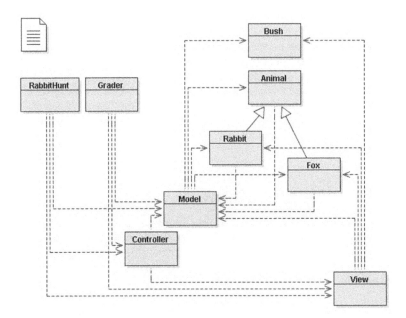

Figure 5-5. *The fox and rabbit hunt class structure*

Model

The model represents the rules of the game. It does all the computation and all the work of deciding whose turn it is, what happens during each turn, and whether anyone has won. The model is strictly internal and has practically nothing to do with the other parts of the program.

The model part of this program is actually composed of five classes: model (the "main" model class), animal, rabbit, fox, and bush. Rabbit and Fox are subclasses of Animal (as you can see from the solid arrows in the UML diagram). This is the part of the program that you really need to understand.

The RabbitHunt class just creates model, view, and controller objects and turns control over to the controller object. The controller object starts the model object and then just waits for the user to click a button. When a button is clicked, a message is sent to the model object, which decides what to do.

The model object

- places the fox, rabbit, and bushes in the field.

- gives the rabbit and the fox each a chance to move (one moves, then the other—they don't both move at the same time).

- tells the view to display the result of these two moves.

- determines which animal won.

View

The view displays what is going on. It puts an image on the screen so the user can see what's happening. The view is completely passive; it doesn't affect the hunt in any way, it's just a news reporter that gives you a (partial) picture of what is happening inside the model.

Controller

The controller is the part of the program that displays the controls (the five buttons and the speed controls at the bottom of the window). It knows as little as possible about the model and view; it basically tells the model when to go and when to stop.

The advantages of breaking the program up into these separate parts are many. We can safely rewrite the GUI in the `Controller` object or the display in the `view` object without changing the `model`. We can make the fox and/or the rabbit smarter (or dumber!) without changing the GUI or the display. We can reuse the GUI for a different application with very little effort. The list just goes on.

In short, MVC is your friend; use it wisely and often.

The Client-Server Architectural Pattern

Moving back to a more traditional architecture, we once again go back in time. Back in the day, all programs ran on big iron, and your entire program ran on a single machine. If you were lucky enough to be using a time-shared operating system, several people could be using the same program—albeit usually different copies—simultaneously. Then came personal computers and networks. And someone had the bright idea of dividing the work up between that big iron and your puny desktop machine. Thus was born the *client-server architecture*.

In a client-server architecture, your program is broken up into two different pieces that typically run on two separate computers. A server does most of the heavy lifting and computation; it provides services to its clients across a high-bandwidth network. Clients, on the other hand, mostly just handle user input, display output, and provide communication to the server. In short, the client program sends requests for services to the server program. The server program then evaluates the request, does whatever computation is necessary (including accessing a database, if needed), and responds to the client's request with an answer. The most common example of a client-server architecture today is the World Wide Web.

In the web model, your browser is the client. It presents a user interface to you, communicates with a web server, and renders the resulting web pages to your screen. The web server does a number of things. It serves web pages in HTML, but it also can serve as a database server, file server, and computational server—think about everything that Amazon.com does when you access that website in order to make a purchase.

Clients and servers don't have to be on different computers, though. Two examples of programs written using a client-server architecture where both sides can reside on the same computer are *print spoolers* and the *X Windows graphical system*.

In a print spooler application, the program you're running—a word processor, spreadsheet program, web browser—runs as a client that makes a request to a printing service that is implemented as a part of the computer's operating system. This service is typically known as a print spooler because it keeps a spool of print jobs and controls which jobs get printed and the order of their printing. So, from your word processor, you'll select Print from a menu, set certain attributes and often pick a printer, and then click OK in a dialog box. This sends a print request to the print spooler on your system. The print spooler adds your file to a queue of print jobs that it manages and then contacts the printer driver and makes requests for printing to occur. The difference here is that once you've clicked the OK button, your client program (the word processor) typically doesn't have any more contact with the print spooler; the print *service* runs unattended.

The X Window System (see `www.x.org/wiki/`) is a graphical windowing system used on all Unix- and Linux-based systems; it's also available for Apple's macOS and Microsoft Windows systems as an add-on windowing system. The X system uses a client-server architecture where the client programs and the server typically both reside on the same computer. The X system server receives requests from client programs, processes them for the hardware that's attached to the current system, and provides an output service that displays the resulting data in bitmapped displays. Client program examples include xterm—a windowed terminal program that provides a command line interface to Unix, xclock—you guessed it—a clock, and xdm, the X Window display manager. The X system allows hierarchical and overlapping windows and provides the ability to configure menus, scroll bars, open and close buttons, background and foreground colors, and graphics. X can also manage a mouse and keyboards. These days the main use of the X system is as a springboard to build more sophisticated window managers, graphical environments, graphical widgets, and desktop management windowing systems like GNOME and KDE.

The Layered Approach

The layered architectural approach suggests that programs can be structured as a series of layers, much like geologic strata, with a sequence of well-defined interfaces between the layers. This has the effect of isolating each layer from the ones above and below it so that one can change the internals of any layer without having to change any of the other layers in the program—that is, as long as your changes don't involve any changes to the interface. In a layered approach, interfaces are sacred. Two classic examples of a layered approach to programming are operating systems (OSes) and communications protocols.

An operating system's architecture has several objectives, among them to centralize control of the limited hardware resources and to protect users from each other. A layered approach to the operating system architecture does both of these things. Figure 5-6 shows a pretty standard picture of an OS architecture.

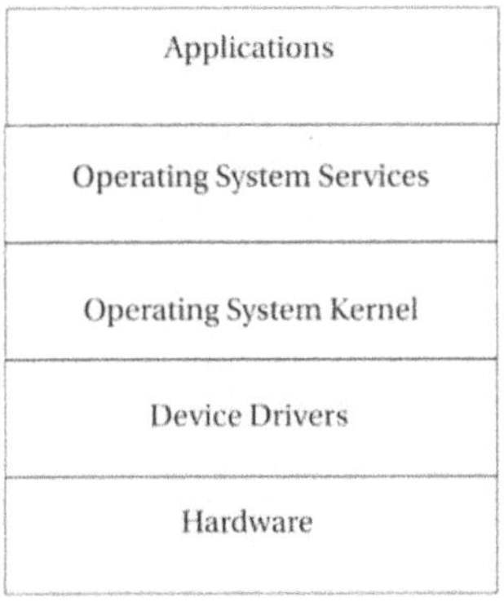

Figure 5-6. A layered architecture

In this layered model, user applications request OS services via a system call interface. This is normally the only way for applications to access the computer's hardware. Most OS services must make requests through the kernel, and all hardware requests must go through device drivers that talk directly to the hardware devices. Each of these layers has a well-defined interface, so that, for example, a developer may add a new device driver for a new disk drive without changing any other part of the OS. This is a nice example of information hiding.

The same type of interface happens in a communications protocol. The most famous of these layered protocols is the International Standards Organization (ISO) Open Systems Interconnection (OSI) seven-layer model This model looks like Figure 5-7.

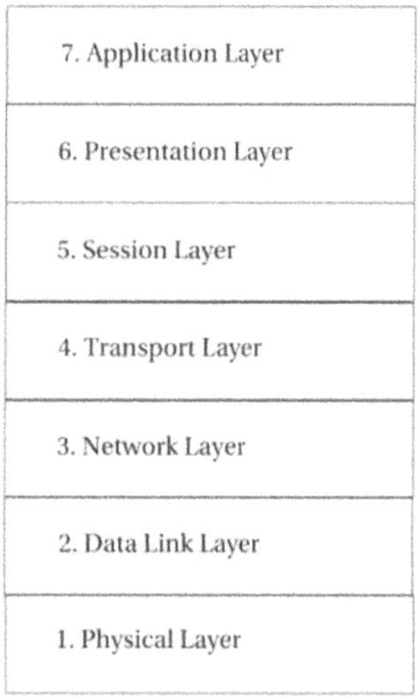

7. Application Layer
6. Presentation Layer
5. Session Layer
4. Transport Layer
3. Network Layer
2. Data Link Layer
1. Physical Layer

Figure 5-7. *The ISO-OSI layered architecture*

In this model, each layer contains functions or services that are logically similar and are grouped together. An interface is defined between each layer, and communication between layers is only allowed via the interfaces. A particular implementation need not contain all seven layers, and sometimes two or more layers are combined to make a smaller protocol stack. The OSI model defines both the seven-layer approach and all the interface protocols. The model can be downloaded as a PDF file from `www.itu.int/rec/T-REC-X.200/en`. (The ITU or International Telecommunications Union is the new name for the ISO.)

Examples of protocols that are implemented at each layer are shown in Table 5-1.

Table 5-1. *Layered Protocols Using the ISO-OSI Architecture*

Layer	Protocol
7. Application	HTTP, FTP, telnet
6. Presentation	MIME, SSL
5. Session	Sockets
4. Transport	TCP, UDP
3. Network	IP, IPsec
2. Data Link	PPP, Ethernet, SLIP, 802.11
1. Physical	

Conclusion

The software architecture is the core of your application. It is the foundation on which you build the rest of the program. It drives the rest of your design. There are many different styles of software architecture, and in any given project you'll probably use more than one. The architectural style used for a program depends on what you're doing. That's the beauty of these styles—it may not always be true that form follows function, but for software, design follows architecture. These foundational patterns lead you down the path of design, shaping how your program will be constructed and lived in. Go out there and build a great program.

References

Bentley, J. *Programming Pearls, Second Edition*. (Boston, MA: Addison-Wesley, 2000.)

Garlan, D. and M. Shaw (1994). *An Introduction to Software Architecture*. Pittsburgh, PA: Carnegie Mellon University: 49. CMU/SEI-94-TR-21 (1994).

Kernighan, B. W. and R. Pike. *The Practice of Programming*. (Boston, MA: Addison-Wesley, 1999.)

Matuszek, David. "Rabbit Hunt," SIGCSE 2004 Technical Symposium, Nifty Assignments Session. Retrieved August 17, 2009, `http://nifty.stanford.edu/2004/RabbitHunt/` (2004).

McConnell, S. *Code Complete 2*. (Redmond, WA: Microsoft Press, 2004.)

Wirth, N. "Program Development by Stepwise Refinement." *Communications of the ACM* **14**(4): 221-227 (1971).

CHAPTER 6

Design Principles

There are two ways of constructing a software design. One way is to make it so simple that there are obviously no deficiencies. And the other way is to make it so complicated that there are no obvious deficiencies.

—C. A. R. Hoare

One way to look at software problems is with a model that divides the problems into two different layers:

- *"Wicked" problems fall in the upper layer*: These are problems that typically come from domains outside of computer science (such as biology, business, meteorology, sociology, political science, and so on). These types of problems tend to be open ended, ill defined, and large in the sense that they require much work. For example, pretty much any kind of a web commerce application is a wicked problem. Horst W. J. Rittel and Melvin M. Webber, in a 1973 paper on social policy,[1] gave a definition for and a set of characteristics used to recognize a wicked problem that we'll look at later in this chapter.

- *"Tame" problems fall in the lower layer*: These problems tend to cut across other problem domains and tend to be better defined and small. Sorting and searching are great examples of tame problems. Small and well defined don't mean "easy," however. Tame problems can be very complicated and difficult to solve. It's just that they're clearly defined and you know when you have a solution. These are the kinds of problems that provide computer scientists with foundations in terms of data structures and algorithms for the wicked problems we solve from other problem domains.

According to Rittel and Webber, a wicked problem is one for which the requirements are completely known only after the problem is solved, or for which the requirements and solution evolve over time. It turns out this describes most of the "interesting" problems in software development. Recently, Jeff Conklin has revised Rittel and Webber's description of a wicked problem and provided a more succinct list of the characteristics of wicked problems.[2] To paraphrase:

1. *A wicked problem is not understood until after the creation of a solution*: Another way of saying this is that the problem is defined and solved at the same time.[3]

---

[1]Rittel, H. W. J. and M. M. Webber. "Dilemmas in a General Theory of Planning." *Policy Sciences* **4**(2): 155-169 (1973).
[2]Conklin, J. *Dialogue Mapping: Building Shared Understanding of Wicked Problems*. (New York, NY: John Wiley & Sons, 2005.)
[3]DeGrace, P. and L. H. Stahl *Wicked Problems, Righteous Solutions: A Catalogue of Modern Software Engineering Paradigms*. (Englewood Cliffs, NJ: Yourdon Press, 1990.)

© John F. Dooley 2017
J. F. Dooley, *Software Development, Design and Coding*, https://doi.org/10.1007/978-1-4842-3153-1_6

2. *Wicked problems have no stopping rule*: You can create incremental solutions to the problem, but there's nothing that tells you that you've found the correct and final solution.

3. *Solutions to wicked problems are not right or wrong*: They are better or worse, or good-enough or not-good-enough.

4. *Every wicked problem is essentially novel and unique*: Because of the "wickedness" of the problem, even if you have a similar problem next week, you basically have to start over again because the requirements will be different enough and the solution will still be elusive.

5. *Every solution to a wicked problem is a one-shot operation*: See the preceding bullet point.

6. *Wicked problems have no given alternative solutions*: There is no small, finite set of solutions to choose from.

Wicked problems crop up all over the place. For example, creating a word processing program is a wicked problem. You may think you know what a word processor needs to do—insert text, cut and paste, handle paragraphs, print, and so forth. But this list of features is only one person's list. As soon as you "finish" your word processor and release it, you'll be inundated with new feature requests: spell checking, footnotes, multiple columns, support for different fonts, colors, styles, and the list goes on. The word processing program is essentially never done—at least not until you release the last version and end-of-life the product.

Word processing is actually a pretty obvious wicked problem. Others might include problems where you don't really know if you can solve the problem at the start. Expert systems require a user interface, an inference engine, a set of rules, and a database of domain information. For a particular domain, it's not at all certain at the beginning that you can create the rules that the inference engine will use to reach conclusions and recommendations. So you have to iterate through different rule sets, send out the next version, and see how well it performs. Then you do it again, adding and modifying rules. You don't really know whether the solution is correct until you're done. Now that's a wicked problem.

Conklin, Rittel, and Webber say that traditional cognitive studies indicate that when faced with a large, complicated (wicked) problem, most people will follow a linear problem-solving approach, working top-down from the problem to the solution. This is equivalent to the traditional waterfall model described in Chapter 2.[4] Figure 6-1 shows this linear approach.

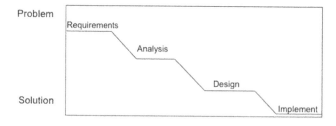

Figure 6-1. *Linear problem-solving approach*

---

[4]Conklin, J. *Wicked Problems and Social Complexity*. Retrieved from http://cognexus.org/wpf/wickedproblems.pdf on 8 September 2009. Paper last updated October 2008.

Instead of this linear, waterfall approach, real wicked problem solvers tend to use an approach that swings from requirements analysis to solution modeling and back until the problem solution is good enough. Conklin calls this an *opportunity-driven* or *opportunistic* approach because the designers are looking for any opportunity to make progress toward the solution.[5] Instead of the traditional waterfall picture in Figure 6-1, the opportunity-driven approach looks like Figure 6-2.

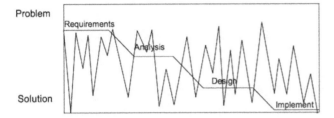

Figure 6-2. *The opportunity-driven development approach*

In this figure, the jagged line indicates the designer's work moving from the problem to a solution prototype and back again, slowly evolving both the requirements understanding and the solution iteration and converging on an implementation that's good enough to release. As an example, let's take a quick look at a web application.

Say a nonprofit organization keeps a list of activities for youth in your home county. The list is updated regularly and is distributed to libraries around the county. Currently, the list is kept on a spreadsheet and is distributed in hard copy in a three-ring binder. The nonprofit wants to put all its data online and make it accessible over the web. It also wants to be able to update the data via the same website. Simple, you say. It's just a web application with an HTML front end, a database, and middleware code to update and query the database as the back end. Not a problem.

Ah, but this is really a wicked problem in disguise. First of all, the customer has no idea what they want the web page(s) to look like. So whatever you give them the first time will not be precisely what they want; the problem won't be understood completely until you are done. Secondly, as you develop prototypes, they will want more features—so the problem has no stopping rule. And finally, as time goes on, the nonprofit will want new features. So there is no "right" answer; there is only a "good enough" answer. Very wicked.

Conklin also provides a list of characteristics of tame problems, ones for which you can easily and reliably find a solution. "A tame problem:

1. has a well-defined and stable problem statement;

2. has a definite stopping point, i.e., when the solution is reached;

3. has a solution which can be objectively evaluated as right or wrong;

4. belongs to a class of similar problems which are all solved in the same similar way;

5. has solutions which can be easily tried and abandoned; and

6. comes with a limited set of alternative solutions."

---

[5]Conklin, J. (2008)

A terrific example of a tame problem is sorting a list of data values:

- The problem is easily and clearly stated—sort this list into ascending order using this function to compare data elements.

- Sorting has a definite stopping point: the list is sorted.

- The result of a sort can be objectively evaluated (the list is either sorted correctly or it isn't).

- Sorting belongs to a class of similar problems that are all solved in the same way. Sorting integers is similar to sorting strings is similar to sorting database records using a key and so on.

- Sorting has solutions that can easily be tried and abandoned.

- Finally, sorting has a limited set of alternative solutions; sorting by comparison has a set of known algorithms and a theoretical lower bound.

What does this have to do with design principles, you ask? Well, realizing that most of the larger software problems we'll encounter have a certain amount of "wickedness" built into them influences how we think about design issues, how we approach the design of a solution to a large, ill-formed problem, and gives us some insight into the design process. It also lets us abandon the waterfall model with a clear conscience and pushes us to look for unifying heuristics that we can apply to design problems. In this chapter we'll discuss overall principles for design that I'll then expand upon in the chapters ahead.

The Design Process

Design is messy. Even if you completely understand the problem requirements (meaning it's a tame problem), you typically have many alternatives to consider when you're designing a software solution. You'll also usually make lots of mistakes before you come up with a solution that works. As we saw in Figure 6-2, your design will change as you understand the problem better over time. This gives the *appearance* of messiness and disorganization, but really, you're making progress.

Design is about tradeoffs and priorities. Most software projects are time-limited, so you usually won't be able to implement all the features that the customer wants. You have to figure out the subset that will give the customer the most high-priority features in the time you have available. So, you have to prioritize the requirements and trade off one subset for another.

Design is heuristic. For the overwhelming majority of projects, there is no set of cut-and-dried rules that say, "First we design component X using technique Y. Then we design component Z using technique W." Software just doesn't work that way. Software design is done using a set of ever-changing heuristics (rules of thumb) that each designer acquires over the course of a career. Over time, good designers learn more heuristics and patterns (see Chapter 11) that allow them to quickly move through the easy bits of a design and get to the heart of the wickedness of the problem. The best thing you can do is to sit at the feet of a master designer and learn the heuristics.

Designs evolve. Good designers recognize that for any problem, tame or wicked, the requirements will change over time. This will then cascade into changes in your design, so your design will evolve over time. This is particularly true across product releases and new feature additions. The trick here is to create a software architecture (see Chapter 5) that is amenable to change with limited effect on the downstream design and code.

Desirable Design Characteristics (Things Your Design Should Favor)

Regardless of the size of your project or what process you use to do your design, there are a number of desirable characteristics that every software design should have. These are the principles you should adhere to as you consider your design. Your design doesn't necessarily need to exhibit all of these characteristics, but having a majority of them will certainly make your software easier to write, understand, and use:

- *Fitness of purpose*: Your design must work, and it must work *correctly* in the sense that it must satisfy the requirements you've been given within the constraints of the platform on which your software will be running. Don't add new requirements as you go—the customer will do that for you.

- *Separation of concerns*: Related closely to modularity, this principle says you should separate out functional pieces of your design cleanly in order to facilitate ease of maintenance and simplicity. Modularity is good.

- *Simplicity*: Keep your design as simple as possible. This will let others understand what you're up to. If you find a place that can be simplified, do it! If simplifying your design means adding more modules or classes to your design, that's okay. Simplicity also applies to interfaces between modules or classes. Simple interfaces allow others to see the data and control flow in your design. In agile methodologies, this idea of simplicity is kept in front of you all the time. Most agile techniques have a rule that says if you're working on part of a program and you have an opportunity to simplify it (called *refactoring* in agile-speak), do it right then. Keep your design and your code as simple as possible at all times.

- *Ease of maintenance*: A simple, understandable design is amenable to change. The first kind of change you'll encounter is fixing errors. Errors occur at all phases of the development process: requirements, analysis, design, coding, and testing. The more coherent and easy to understand your design is, the easier it will be to isolate and fix errors.

- *Loose coupling*: When you're separating your design into *modules*—or in object-oriented design, into *classes*—the degree to which the classes depend on each other is called *coupling*. Tightly coupled modules may share data or procedures. This means that a change in one module is much more likely to lead to a required change in the other module. This increases the maintenance burden and makes the modules more likely to contain errors. Loosely coupled modules, on the other hand, are connected solely by their interfaces. Any data they both need must be passed between procedures or methods via an interface. Loosely coupled modules hide the details of how they perform operations from other modules, sharing only their interfaces. This lightens the maintenance burden because a change to how one class is implemented will not likely affect how another class operates as long as the interface is invariant. So, changes are isolated and errors are much less likely to propagate.

- *High cohesion*: The complement of loose coupling is high cohesion. *Cohesion* within a module is the degree to which the module is self-contained with regard both to the data it holds and the operations that act on the data. A class that has high cohesion pretty much has all the data it needs defined within the class template, and all the operations that are allowed on the data are defined within the class as well. So, any object that's instantiated from the class template is very independent and just communicates with other objects via its published interface.

- *Extensibility*: An outgrowth of simplicity and loose coupling is the ability to add new features to the design easily. This is extensibility. One of the features of wicked software problems is that they're never really finished. So, after every release of a product, the next thing that happens is the customer asks for new features. The easier it is to add new features, the cleaner your design is.

- *Portability*: Though not high on the list, keeping in mind that your software may need to be ported to another platform (or two or three) is a desirable characteristic. There are a lot of issues involved with porting software, including operating system issues, hardware architecture, and user interface issues. This is particularly true for web applications.

Design Heuristics

Speaking of heuristics, here's a short list of good, time-tested heuristics. The list is clearly not exhaustive and it's pretty idiosyncratic, but it's a list you can use time and again. Think about these heuristics and try some of them during your next design exercise. We will come back to all of these heuristics in much more detail in later chapters:

- *Find real-world objects to model*: Alan Davis[6] and Richard Fairley[7] call this *intellectual distance*. It's how far your design is from a real-world object. The heuristic here is to try to find real-world objects that are close to things you want to model in your program. Keeping the real-world object in mind as you're designing your program helps keep your design closer to the problem. Fairley's advice is to minimize the intellectual distance between the real-world object and your model of it.

- *Abstraction is key*: Whether you're doing object-oriented design and you're creating interfaces and abstract classes, or you're doing a more traditional layered design, you want to use abstraction. *Abstraction* means being lazy. You put off what you need to do by pushing it higher in the design hierarchy (more abstraction) or pushing it further down (more details). Abstraction is a key element of managing the complexity of a large problem. By abstracting away the details you can see the kernel of the real problem.

- *Information hiding is your friend*: Information hiding is the concept that you isolate information—both data and behavior—in your program so that you can isolate errors and isolate changes; you also only allow access to the information via a well-defined interface. A fundamental part of object-oriented design is *encapsulation*, a concept that derives from information hiding. You hide the details of a class away and only allow communication and modification of data via a public interface. This means that your implementation can change, but as long as the interface is consistent and constant, nothing else in your program need change. If you're not doing object-oriented design, think about using libraries for hiding behavior and using separate data structures (structs in C and C++) for hiding state.

- *Keep your design modular*: Breaking your design up into semi-independent pieces has many advantages. It keeps the design manageable in your head; you can just think about one part at a time and leave the others as black boxes. It takes advantage of information hiding and encapsulation. It isolates changes. It helps with extensibility and maintainability. Modularity is just a good thing. Do it.

---

[6]Davis, A. M. *201 Principles of Software Development*. (New York, NY: McGraw-Hill, 1995.)
[7]Fairley, R. E. *Software Engineering Concepts*. (New York, NY: McGraw-Hill, 1985.)

- *Identify the parts of your design that are likely to change*: If you make the assumption that there will be changes in your requirements, then there will likely be changes in your design as well. If you identify those areas of your design that are likely to change, you can separate them, thus mitigating the impact of any changes you need to make. What things are likely to change? Well, it depends on your application, doesn't it? Business rules can change (think tax rules or accounting practices), user interfaces can change, hardware can change, and so on. The point here is to anticipate the change and to divide up your design so that the necessary changes are contained.

- *Use loose coupling, interfaces, and abstract classes*: Along with modularity, information hiding, and change, using loose coupling will make your design easier to understand and to change as time goes along. *Loose coupling* says that you should minimize the dependencies of one class (or module) on another. This is so that a change in one module won't cause changes in other modules. If the implementation of a module is hidden and only the interface exposed, you can swap out implementations as long as you keep the interface constant. So you implement loose coupling by using well defined interfaces between modules, and in an object-oriented design, using abstract classes and interfaces to connect classes.

- *Use your knapsack full of common design patterns*: Robert Glass[8] describes great software designers as having "a large set of standard patterns" that they carry around with them and apply to their designs. This is what design experience is all about—doing design over and over again and learning from the experience. In Susan Lammer's book *Programmers at Work,*[9] Butler Lampson says, "Most of the time, a new program is a refinement, extension, generalization, or improvement of an existing program. It's really unusual to do something that's completely new. . . ." That's what design patterns are: they're descriptions of things you've already done that you can apply to a new problem.

- *Adhere to the Principle of One Right Place*: In his book *Programming on Purpose: Essays on Software Design*, P. J. Plauger says, "My major concern here is the Principle of One Right Place—there should be One Right Place to look for any nontrivial piece of code, and One Right Place to make a likely maintenance change.[10] " Your design should adhere to the Principle of One Right Place; debugging and maintenance will be much easier.

- *Use diagrams as a design language*: I'm a visual learner. For me, a picture really is worth a thousand or so words. As I design and code, I'm constantly drawing diagrams so I can visualize how my program is going to hang together, which classes or modules will be talking to each other, what data is dependent on what function, where do the return values go, what is the sequence of events. This type of visualization can settle the design in your head and can point out errors or possible complications in the design. Whiteboards or paper are cheap; enjoy!

---

[8]Glass, R. L. *Software Creativity 2.0*. Atlanta, GA, developer* (2006).
[9]Lammers, S. *Programmers At Work*. (Redmond, WA: Microsoft Press, 1986.)
[10]Plauger, P. J. *Programming on Purpose: Essays on Software Design*. (Englewood Cliffs, NJ: PTR Prentice Hall, 1993.)

Designers and Creativity

Don't think that design is cut and dried or that formal processes rules can be imposed to crank out software designs. It's not like that at all. Although there are formal restrictions and constraints on your design that are imposed by the problem, the problem domain, and the target platform, the process of reaching the design itself need not be formal. It's at bottom a creative activity. Bill Curtis, in a 1987 empirical study of software designers, came up with a process that seems to be what most of the designers followed[11]:

1.   Understand the problem.

2.   Decompose the problem into goals and objects.

3.   Select and compose plans to solve the problem.

4.   Implement the plans.

5.   Reflect on the design product and process.

Frankly, this is a pretty general list and doesn't really tell us all we'd need for software design. Curtis, however, then went deeper into step 3 on his list, "select and compose plans," and found that his designers used the following steps:

1.   Build a mental model of a proposed solution.

2.   Mentally execute the model to see if it solves the problem—make up input and simulate the model in your head.

3.   If what you get isn't correct, change the model to remove the errors and go back to step 2 to simulate again.

4.   When your sample input produces the correct output, select some more input values and go back and do steps 2 and 3 again.

5.   When you've done this enough times (you'll know because you're experienced) then you've got a good model and you can stop.[12]

This deeper technique makes the cognitive and the iterative aspects of design clear and obvious. We see that design is fundamentally a function of the mind, and is idiosyncratic and depends on things about the designer that are outside the process itself.

John Nestor, in a report to the Software Engineering Institute, came up with a list of what are some common characteristics of great designers.

Great designers

- have a large set of standard patterns.

- have experienced failing projects.

- have mastery of development tools.

- have an impulse towards simplicity.

- can anticipate change.

- can view things from the user's perspective.

- can deal with complexity.[13]

---

[11]Curtis, B., R. Guindon, et al. *Empirical Studies of the Design Process: Papers for the Second Workshop on Empirical Studies of Programmers.* Austin, TX, MCC (1987).
[12]Glass, R. L. *Software Creativity 2.0.* Atlanta, GA, developer* (2006).
[13]Glass, R. L. (2006)

Conclusion

So at the end of the chapter, what have we learned about software design?

- *Design is ad hoc, heuristic, and messy*: It fundamentally uses a trial-and-error and heuristic process, and that process is the natural one to use for software design. There are a number of well-known heuristics that any good designer should employ.

- *Design depends on understanding of prior design problems and solutions*: Designers need some knowledge of the problem domain. More importantly, they need knowledge of design and patterns of good designs. They need to have a knapsack of these design patterns that they can use to approach new problems. The solutions are tried and true. The problems are new but they contain elements of problems that have already been solved. The patterns are *malleable templates* that can be applied to those elements of the new problem that match the pattern's requirements.

- *Design is iterative*: Requirements change, and so must your design. Even if you have a stable set of requirements, your *understanding* of the requirements changes as you progress through the design activity, so you'll go back and change the design to reflect this deeper, better understanding. The iterative process clarifies and simplifies your design at each step.

- *Design is a cognitive activity*: You're not writing code at this point, so you don't need a machine. Your head and maybe a pencil and paper or a whiteboard are all you need to do design. As Dijkstra says, "We must not forget that it is not our business to make programs; it is our business to design classes of computations that will display a desired behavior.[14] "

- *Design is opportunistic*. Glass sums up his discussion of design with this: "The unperturbed design process is opportunistic—that is, rather than proceed in an orderly process, good designers follow an erratic pattern dictated by their minds, pursuing opportunities rather than an orderly progression.[15] "

All these characteristics argue against a rigid, plan-driven design process and for a creative, flexible way of doing design. This brings us back to the first topic in this chapter: design is just wicked.

And finally:

A designer can mull over complicated designs for months. Then suddenly the simple, elegant, beautiful solution occurs to him. When it happens to you, it feels as if God is talking! And maybe He is.

—Leo Frankowski (in *The Cross-Time Engineer*)

---

[14]Dijkstra, E. "The Humble Programmer." CACM 15(10): 859-866. (1972)
[15]Glass, R. L. (2006)

References

Conklin, J. *Dialogue Mapping: Building Shared Understanding of Wicked Problems.* (New York, NY: John Wiley & Sons, 2005.)

Conklin, J. *Wicked Problems and Social Complexity.* Retrieved from `http://cognexus.org/wpf/wickedproblems.pdf` on 8 September 2009. Paper last updated October 2008.

Curtis, B., R. Guindon, et al. *Empirical Studies of the Design Process: Papers for the Second Workshop on Empirical Studies of Programmers.* Austin, TX, MCC (1987).

Davis, A. M. *201 Principles of Software Development.* (New York, NY: McGraw-Hill, 1995.)

DeGrace, P. and L. H. Stahl. *Wicked Problems, Righteous Solutions: A Catalogue of Modern Software Engineering Paradigms.* (Englewood Cliffs, NJ: Yourdon Press, 1990.)

Dijkstra, E. "The Humble Programmer." CACM 15(10): 859-866 (1972).

Fairley, R. E. *Software Engineering Concepts.* (New York, NY: McGraw-Hill, 1985.)

Glass, R. L. *Software Creativity 2.0.* Atlanta, GA, developer* (2006).

Lammers, S. *Programmers At Work.* (Redmond, WA: Microsoft Press, 1986.)

McConnell, S. *Code Complete 2.* (Redmond, WA: Microsoft Press, 2004.)

Parnas, D. "On the Criteria to be Used in Decomposing Systems into Modules." CACM 15(12): 1053-1058 (1972).

Plauger, P. J. *Programming on Purpose: Essays on Software Design.* (Englewood Cliffs, NJ: PTR Prentice Hall, 1993.)

Rittel, H. W. J. and M. M. Webber. "Dilemmas in a General Theory of Planning." Policy Sciences 4(2): 155-169 (1973).

CHAPTER 7

Structured Design

Invest in the abstraction, not the implementation. Abstractions can survive the barrage of changes from different implementations and new technologies."

—Andy Hunt and Dave Thomas[1]

Structured Programming

Structured design has its genesis in Edsger Dijkstra's famous 1968 letter to the *Communications of the ACM*, "Go To Statement Considered Harmful." Dijkstra's paper concludes like this:

> *The go to statement as it stands is just too primitive; it is too much an invitation to make a mess of one's program. One can regard and appreciate the clauses considered (ed. if-then-else, switch, while-do, and do-while) as bridling its use. I do not claim that the clauses mentioned are exhaustive in the sense that they will satisfy all needs, but whatever clauses are suggested (e.g. abortion clauses) they should satisfy the requirement that a programmer independent coordinate system can be maintained to describe the process in a helpful and manageable way.[2]*

Programming languages created from this point onward, while not eliminating the goto statement (except for Java, which has none), certainly downplayed its use, and courses that taught programming encouraged students to avoid it. Instead, problem solving was taught in a top-down structured manner, where one begins with the problem statement and attempts to break the problem down into a set of solvable sub-problems. The process continues until each sub-problem is small enough to be either trivial or very easy to solve. This technique is called *structured programming*. Before the advent and acceptance of object-oriented programming in the mid 1980s, this was the standard approach to problem solving and programming. It's still one of the best ways to approach a large class of problems.

---

[1]Hunt, A. and D. Thomas. *The Pragmatic Programmer: From Journeyman to Master*. (Boston, MA: Addison-Wesley, 2000.)
[2]Dijkstra, E. "GoTo Statement Considered Harmful." *Communications of the ACM* **11**(3): 147-148 (1968).

© John F. Dooley 2017
J. F. Dooley, *Software Development, Design and Coding*, https://doi.org/10.1007/978-1-4842-3153-1_7

Stepwise Refinement

Niklaus Wirth formalized the structured design technique in his 1971 paper, "Program Development by Stepwise Refinement.[3] " *Stepwise refinement* contends that designing programs consists of a set of refinement steps. In each step, a given task is broken up into a number of subtasks. Each refinement of a task must be accompanied by a refinement of the data description and the interface. The degree of modularity obtained will determine the ease or difficulty with which a program can be adapted to changes in requirements or environment.

During refinement, you use a notation that's natural to the problem space. Avoid using a programming language for description as long as possible. Each refinement implies a number of design decisions based on a set of design criteria. These criteria include efficiency of time and space, clarity, and regularity of structure (simplicity).

Refinement can proceed in two ways: top-down or bottom-up. Top-down refinement is characterized by moving from a general description of the problem to detailed statements of what individual modules or routines do. The guiding principle behind stepwise refinement is that humans can concentrate on only a few things at a time—Miller's famous 7 +/- 2 chunks of data rule.[4] One works by

- Analyzing the problem and trying to identify the outlines of a solution and the pros and cons of each possibility.

- Designing the top levels first.

- Steering clear of language-specific details.

- Pushing down the details until you get to the lower levels.

- Formalizing each level.

- Verifying each level.

- Moving to the next lower level to make the next set of refinements (that is, repeat).

One continues to refine the solution until it seems as if it would be easier to code than to decompose; we'll see an example of this process later in this chapter.

That is, you work until you become impatient at how obvious and easy the design becomes. The downside here is that you really have no good metric on "when to stop." It just takes practice.

If you can't get started at the top, start at the bottom:

- Ask yourself, "What do I know that the system needs to do?" This usually involves lower level I/O operations, other low-level operations on data structures, and so on.

- Identify as many low-level functions and components as you can from that question.

- Identify common aspects of the low-level components and group them together.

- Continue with the next level up, or go back to the top and try again to work down.

Bottom-up assessment usually results in early identification of utility routines, which can lead to a more compact design. It also helps promote reuse—because you're reusing the lower-level routines. On the downside, bottom-up assessment is hard to use exclusively: you nearly always end up switching to a top-down approach at some point, and sometimes you find you just can't put a larger piece together from the bottom-up. This isn't really stepwise refinement, but it can help get you started. Most real step-wise refinements involve alternating between top-down and bottom-up design elements. Fortunately, top-down and bottom-up design methodologies can be very complementary.

---

[3]Wirth, N. "Program Development by Stepwise Refinement." *CACM* **14**(4): 221-227 (1971).
[4]Miller, G. A. "The magical number seven, plus or minus two: Some limits on our capacity for processing information." *Psychological Review* **63**: 81-97 (1956).

Example of Stepwise Refinement: The Eight-Queens Problem

The eight queens problem is familiar to most students. The problem is to find a placement of eight queens on a standard 8 × 8 chessboard in such a way that no queen can be attacked by any other. One possible solution to the eight-queens problem is shown in Figure 7-1.

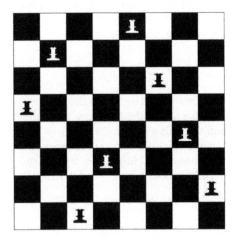

Figure 7-1. *One solution to the eight-queens problem*

Remember that queens can move any number of spaces horizontally, vertically, or diagonally. It turns out that no one has yet found an analytical solution to this problem, and it's likely one does not exist. So, how would you approach this problem? Go ahead, think about it. I'll wait.

. . .

. . .

Done? Okay. Let's see one way to decompose this problem.

Proposed Solution 1

The first thing we need to do is to look at the problem and tease out the requirements and the outline of a solution. This will start us down the road of answering the question of what the top-level decomposition should be.

First, you could think of solving the problem using brute force; just try all the possible arrangements of queens and pick the ones that work. With 8 queens and 64 possible squares there are

$$\frac{n!}{k!\,(n-k)!} = \frac{64!}{56!\,8!} = 2^{32}$$

possible board configurations, where n is the number of squares on the board and k is the number of queens, which is only 4,294,967,296 (a bit over 4 billion configurations). These days, that's not very many, so brute force might be the way to go.

So, if we generate a set A of all the possible board combinations, we can create a test called $q(x)$ that returns a *true* if the board configuration x is a solution, and returns *false* if x isn't a solution. Then we can create a program that looks like the following:

```
Generate the set A of all board configurations;
while there are still untested configurations in A do
```

```
x = the next configuration from A
if (q(x) == true) then print the solution x and stop
go back to the top and do it again.
```

Notice that all the work is getting done in two steps: generating the set A and performing the test $q(x)$. The generation of A only happens once, but performing the test $q(x)$ happens once for every configuration in A until you find a solution. Although this decomposition will surely work, it's not terribly efficient. Let's just say that we'd rather reduce the number of combinations. Efficiency is a good thing, after all.

Proposed Solution 2

Again, we need to start at the top level. But this time we've done some analysis, so we have a clearer idea of what has to happen. We've eliminated brute force, but we see that we can think in terms of board configurations. In order to reduce the number of total possible configurations and then come up with a more efficient algorithm, we need to think about the problem. The first thing to notice is that you can never have more than one queen in a column; in fact, you must have exactly one queen per column. That reduces the number of possible combinations to 2^{24} or just 16 million. Although this is good, it doesn't really change the algorithm. Our proposed solution would now look like this:

```
Generate the set B of restricted board configurations;
while there are still untested configurations in B do
            x = the next configuration from B
            if (q(x) == true) then print the solution x and stop
            go back to the top and do it again.
```

This version requires generating the set B of board positions, with one queen in each column, and still requires visiting up to 16 million possible board positions. Generating B is now more complicated than generating A because we now have to test to see whether a proposed board position meets the one queen per column restriction. There must be a better way.

Proposed Solution 3

Of course there is. We just need to be more intelligent about generating board configurations and evaluate board positions while we're generating them. Instead of generating a complete board configuration and then testing it, why not generate and test partial solutions? If we can stop as soon as we know we don't have a valid solution, things should go faster. Also, if we can back up from a bad solution to the last good partial solution, we can eliminate bad configurations more quickly.

Now we're at the point where we can do that top-level design, formalize it, and move down to the next refinement level.

Refinement 1

Here's the idea:

1. Put down a queen on the next row in the next available column.

2. Test the queen to see if she can attack any other queen. (That's a variation on the $q(x)$ test above.)

3. If she can attack, pick her back up, back up to the previous trial solution, and try again.

4. If she can't attack, leave her alone and go back to the top and try the next queen.

With this method, we're guaranteed that the trial solution at column j is correct. We then attempt to generate a new solution by adding a queen in column j + 1. If this fails, we just need to back up to our previous correct trial solution at column j and try again. Wirth calls this technique of creating and testing partial solutions a *stepwise construction of trial solutions*. And the backing-up technique is, of course, called *backtracking*. Here's more formal pseudo-code to find a single solution:

```
do {
            while ((row < 8) && (col < 8))  {
                if (the current queen is safe) then
                    advance: keep the queen on the board and advance to the next column
                else
                    the queen is not safe, so move up to the next row.
            }
            if (we've exhausted all the rows in this column) then
                regress: retreat a column, move its queen up a row, and start again.

    } while ((col < 8) && (col >= 0));
        if (we've reached column 8) then
            we have a solution, print it.
```

This solution tests only a single queen at a time. One implication of this is that, at any given time, there are only j queens on the board and so only j queens need to be tested each time through the outer loop. (One only needs to test the queens up through column j.) That reduces the amount of work in the testing routine.

This algorithm is our first formal view of the solution. Notice in the method described that we're using pseudo-code rather than a real programming language. That's because we want to push language details further down the refinement levels. Also, though we've got a general outline of the method, there are a lot of details still to be considered. These details have been pushed down in the hierarchy of control we're creating, and we'll get to them in the next refinement iteration. This is also a function of the stepwise refinement.

Now that we have a description of the algorithm, we can also work to verify it. The final verification will, of course, be watching the program produce a correct solution, but we're not at that point yet. However, we can surely take a chessboard (or a piece of paper) and walk through this algorithm by hand to verify that we can generate a placement of queens on the board that is a solution to the problem.

At this point we've got a more formal top-level description, we've done what verification we can, and we're ready to expand those fuzzy steps we saw earlier.

Refinement 2

Now that we've got a first cut at the program, we need to examine each of the steps in the program and see what they're made of. The steps we're interested in are as follows:

1. Check to see if the current queen is safe.

2. Keep a safe queen on the board and advance to the next column.

3. Advance an unsafe queen up a row.

4. Retreat a column and reset the queen in that column.

Checking to see if the current queen is safe means we need to check that there are no other queens on either of the diagonals (the up or down diagonals) or the row that the current queen is on. The row check is easy; one just checks all the other squares in the same row. To check the up and down diagonals, remember that if the current queen is at column j, we only need to check columns 1 through j – 1. If you think about it for a minute, you'll see that the difference between the row and column indexes of all the squares on the up diagonal (those that go from lower left to upper right) are a constant. Similarly, the sum of the row and column indexes of all the squares on the down diagonal (those that go from upper left to lower right) is also a constant. This makes it easier to figure out which cells are on the diagonal of a queen and how to check them.

Now we're ready to start considering data structures. Where did this come from, you ask? Well, stepwise refinement is mostly about describing the control flow of the program. But at some point you need to decide on exactly what the data will look like. For each problem you try to solve, this will happen at a different place in your refinement process. For this problem we're at a place where in the next refinement we should be writing more detailed pseudo-code. That's pretty much forcing us to think about data structures now, so we can do the pseudo-code.

In particular, now we need to ask ourselves how we're going to represent the board and the queens on the board. How are we going to represent the empty cells? We need a data structure that will allow us to efficiently represent queens and check whether they can be attacked. A first cut at this might be an 8 × 8 two-dimensional array where we place queens at the appropriate row and column intersections. Because we don't need to do any computation on this matrix—all we need is to indicate the presence or absence of a queen—we can save space by making it a Boolean array. This data structure also allows us to quickly check the rows, and the up and down diagonals for queens that can attack the current queen. So, we should use a 2D Boolean array, right?

Not so fast. This isn't the only way to think about the data representation for queens. In fact, if we think about the data structure and the operations we need to perform during the safety check, we might be able to simplify things a bit.

First of all, since we know that there can only be one queen in each column and one queen in each row, why not combine that information? Instead of a 2D array, why not just use a 1D Boolean array like the following:

```
boolean column[8];
```

`column[i]` = **true** means that the ith column is still free. For the diagonals, we can use the property about the constant difference or sum of up and down diagonals to create two other arrays

```
boolean up[-7..+7], down[0..14];
```

that will indicate which diagonal squares are free. With this arrangement, the test for a queen being safe looks like this:

```
(column[i] and up[row-col] and down[row+col])
```[5]

All right. That seems simple enough. We're finally done with this, right?

Well, no. There's yet another way to think about this: going back to using a 1D array, but this time using an integer array

```
int board[8];
```

[5]Dahl, O. J., E. Dijkstra, et al. (1972). *Structured Programming*. (London, UK: Academic Press, 1972.)

where each *index* into the array represents a column (0 through 7 in the eight queens case), and each *value* stored in the array represents the row on which a queen is deposited (also 0 through 7 in the eight queens case). Because we now have data on the exact location (rows and columns) of each queen, we don't need separate arrays for the up and down diagonals. The test for safety is a bit more difficult, but still simple. This might be the time for some more code. At this point it seems appropriate to move from pseudo-code to a real language. You'll have to make that move at some point in the refinement process. Just like deciding when to define your data structures, exactly when to insert language-specific features depends on the problem and what how detailed the refinement is at this point. A Java method to test for safety might look like this:

```java
public boolean isSafe (int[ ] board) {
        boolean safe = true;
        for (int i = 0; i < col; i++) {
                if ( ( ( board[i] + i) == (row + col) ) ||      // down diagonal test
                      ( ( board[i] - i) == (row - col) ) ||      // up diagonal test
                      ( board[i]    == row) )                    // row test
                        safe = false;
        }
        return safe;
}
```

Remember that because we're creating partial solutions by adding one queen to a column at a time, we only need to test the first col columns each time.

Now that we have the safety procedure out of the way and we've decided on a simple data structure to represent the current board configuration, we can proceed to the remaining procedures in the decomposition:

1. Keep a safe queen on the board and advance to the next column.

2. Advance an unsafe queen up a row.

3. Retreat a column and reset the queen in that column.

These are all simple enough to just write without further decomposition. That's a key point of structured programming: keep doing the decompositions until a procedure becomes obvious, and then you can code. These three methods then look like the following when written in code:

```java
/*
 * keep a safe queen on the board and advance to the next column
 * the queen at (row, col) is safe, so we have a partial solution.
 * advance to the next column
 */
public void advance (int[] board) {
    board[col] = row;           // put the queen at (row, col) on the board
    col++;                      // move to the next column
    row = 0;                    // and start at the beginning of the column
}
```

For *advance an unsafe queen up a row* we don't even need a method. The test in the main program for safety moves the queen up a row if the isSafe() method determines that the current (row, col) position is unsafe. The code for this is shown here:

```java
if (isSafe(board))
    advance(board);
else
    row++;
```

Finally, we have the following:

```
/**
 *  retreat a column and reset the queen in that column
 *  we could not find a safe row in current col
 *  so back up one col and move that queen
 *  up a row so we can start looking again
 */
public void retreat (int[] board) {
    col--;
    row = board[col] + 1;
}
```

The complete Java program is shown in Listing 7-1.

Listing 7-1. The Complete Non-Recursive Eight-Queens Program

```
/*
 *  NQueens.java
 *  8-Queens Program
 *  A non-recursive version for a single solution
 */

import java.util.*;

public class NQueens
{

        static int totalcount = 0;
        static int row = 0;
        static int col = 0;

    /*
     *  the queen at (row, col) is safe,
     *  so we have a partial solution.
     *  advance to the next column
     */
    public void advance (int[] board) {
        board[col] = row;
        col++;
        row = 0;
    }

    /*
     *  could not find a safe row in current col
     *  so back up one col and move that queen
     *  up a row
     */
    public void retreat (int[] board) {
        col--;
        row = board[col] + 1;
    }
```

```
/*
 *   check to see if queen at (row, col)  can be
 *   attacked
 */
public boolean isSafe (int[] board) {
    boolean safe = true;
    totalcount++;
    /*
     *  check diagonals and row for attacks
     *  since we're just checking partial solutions
     *  only need to go up to current col
     */
    for (int i=0; i<col; i++)  {
       if (( (board[i] + i) == (row + col) ) ||   // up diagonal
           ( (board[i] - i) == (row - col) ) ||   // down diagonal
           (board[i]  == row) ) {
           safe = false;
             }
    }
    return safe;
}

public static void main(String args[]) {
    int N = 8;       // default board size

    System.out.print("Enter the size of the board: ");
    Scanner stdin = new Scanner(System.in);
    N = stdin.nextInt();
    System.out.println();

    NQueens queen = new NQueens();
    /*
     *   index into board is a column number
     *   value stored in board is a row number
     *   so board[2] = 3; says put a queen on col 2, row 3
     */
    int[] board = new int [N];
    /*
     *   simple algorithm to build partial solutions
     *   for N-queens problem. Place a queen in the
     *   next available column, test to see if it
     *   can be attacked. If not, then move to the next
     *   column. If it can be attacked, move the queen
     *   up a row and try again.
     *   If we exhaust all the rows in a column, back up
     *   reset the previous column and try again.
     */
    do {
        while ((row < N) && (col < N))  {
            if (queen.isSafe(board)) {
                queen.advance(board);
            } else {
                row++;
```

83

```
            }
        }
        if (row == N) {
            queen.retreat(board);
        }

    } while ((col < N) && (col >= 0));

    /* If we've placed all N queens, we've got a solution */
    if (col == N) {
        for (int i = 0; i < N; i++) {
            System.out.print(board[i] + " ");
        }
    } else {
        System.out.println("No solution. ");
    }

    System.out.println();

    System.out.println("after trying " + totalcount +
                    " board positions.");
    }
}
```

Modular Decomposition

In 1972, David Parnas published a paper titled "On the Criteria to Be Used in Decomposing Systems into Modules" that proposed that one could design programs using a technique called *modularity*.[6] Parnas's paper was also one of the first papers to describe a decomposition based on *information hiding*, one of the key techniques in object-oriented programming. In his paper, Parnas highlighted the differences between a top-down decomposition of a problem based on the flow of control of a problem solution and a decomposition of the problem that used encapsulation and information hiding to isolate data definitions and their operations from each other. His paper is a clear precursor to object-oriented analysis and design (OOA&D), which we'll look at in the next chapter.

Although Parnas's paper pre-dates the idea, he was really talking about a concept called *separation of concerns*. "In computer science, *separation of concerns* is the process of separating a computer program into distinct features that overlap in functionality as little as possible. A concern is any piece of interest or focus in a program. Typically, concerns are synonymous with features or behaviors. Progress towards separation of concerns is traditionally achieved through modularity of programming and encapsulation (or "transparency" of operation), with the help of information hiding."[7] Traditionally, separation of concerns was all about separating functionality of the program. Parnas added the idea of separating the data as well, so that individual modules would control data as well as the operations that acted on the data and the data would be visible only through well-defined interfaces.

---

[6]Parnas, D. "On the Criteria to be Used in Decomposing Systems into Modules." *Communications of the ACM* **15**(12): 1053-1058 (1972).

[7]Wikipedia. "Separation of Concerns" 2009. http://en.wikipedia.org/wiki/. Retrieved December 7, 2009.

There are three characteristics of modularity that are key to creating modular programs:

- Encapsulation

- Loose coupling (how closely do modules relate to each other)

- Information hiding

In a nutshell, *encapsulation* means to bundle a group of services defined by their data and behaviors together as a module, and keep them together. This group of services should be coherent and should clearly belong together. (Like a function, a module should do just one thing.) The module then presents an *interface* to the user, and that interface is ideally the only way to access the services and data in the module. An objective of encapsulating services and data is *high cohesion*. This means that your module should do one thing and all the functions inside the module should work towards making that one thing happen. The closer you are to this goal, the higher the cohesion in your module. This is a good thing.

The complement of encapsulation is loose coupling. *Loose coupling* describes how strongly two modules are related to each other. This means we want to minimize the dependence any one module has on another. We separate modules to minimize interactions and make all interactions between modules through the module interface. The goal is to create modules with internal integrity (strong cohesion) and small, few, direct, visible, and flexible connections to other modules (loose coupling). Good coupling between modules is loose enough that one module can easily be called by others.

Loose coupling falls into four broad categories that go from good to awful:

- *Simple data coupling*: Where non-structured data is passed via parameter lists. This is the best kind of coupling, because it lets the receiving module structure the data as it sees fit and allows the receiving module to decide what to do with the data.

- *Structured data coupling*: Where structured data is passed via parameter lists. This is also a good kind of coupling, because the sending module keeps control of the data formats and the receiving module gets to do what it wants to with the data.

- *Control coupling*: Where data from module A is passed to module B and the content of the data tells module B what to do. This is not a good form of coupling; A and B are too closely coupled in this case because module A is controlling how functions in module B will execute.

- *Global-data coupling*: Where the two modules make use of the same global data. This is just awful. It violates a basic tenet of encapsulation by having the modules share data. This invites unwanted side-effects and ensures that at any given moment during the execution of the program neither module A nor module B will know precisely what is in the globally shared data. And what the heck are you doing using global variables anyway? Bad programmer!

Information hiding is often confused with encapsulation, but they're not the same thing. Encapsulation describes a process of wrapping both data and behaviors into a single entity—in our case, a module. Data can be publicly visible from within a module, and thus not hidden. Information hiding, on the other hand, says that the data and behaviors in a module should be controlled and visible only to the operations that act on the data within the module, so it's invisible to other, external modules. This is an important feature of modules (and later of objects as well) because it leaves control of data in the module that understands best how to manipulate the data and it protects the data from side-effects that can arise from other modules reaching in and tweaking the data.

Parnas was not just talking about hiding data in modules. His definition of information hiding was even more concerned with hiding design decisions in the module definition. "We propose . . . that one begins with a list of difficult design decisions or design decisions which are likely to change. Each module is then designed to hide such a decision from the others.[8]" Hiding information in this manner allows clients of a module to use the module successfully without needing to know any of the design decisions that went into constructing the module. It also allows developers to change the implementation of the module without affecting how the client uses the module.

Example: Keyword in Context

Back in the day, when Unix was young and the world was new, the Unix documentation was divided into eight different sections and the entire manual started with a *permuted index*. The problem with Unix is not the command line interface, and it's not the inverted tree file system structure. No, the problem with Unix is that the three guys who developed it, Kernighan, Ritchie, and Thompson, are the three laziest guys on the planet. How do I know? Where's my proof? Well, the proof is in practically every Unix command: `ls`, `cat`, `cp`, `mv`, `mkdir`, `ps`, `cc`, `as`, `ld`, `m4` . . . I could go on. Unix has to have the most cryptic command line set of any operating system on the planet. The cardinal rule for creating Unix command line tools was apparently, "Why use three characters when two will do?"

So, finding anything in any of the eight sections of Unix documentation could have been a real trial. Enter the permuted index. Every Unix man page starts with a header line that contains the name of the command and a short description of what the command does. For example, the `cat(1)` man page begins like this:

```
cat -- concatenate and print files
```

What if I don't know the name of a command, but I do know what it does? The permuted index solves this problem by making most of the words in the description (the articles were ignored) of the command part of the index itself. So that *cat* could be found under *cat* and also *concatenate*, *print*, and *files*. This is known as a *Keyword in Context* (KWIC) index. It works just dandy.

Our problem is to take as input two files, the first of which contains words to ignore, the second of which contains lines of text to index, and create a KWIC index for them. For example, say that we're ignoring the articles for, the, and, and so forth, and the second file looks like this:

```
The Sun also Rises
For Whom the Bell Tolls
The Old Man and the Sea
```

Our KWIC index would look like this:

```
            The Sun ALSO Rises
        For Whom the BELL Tolls
            The Old MAN and the Sea
                The OLD Man and the Sea
        The Sun also RISES
The Old Man and the SEA
                The SUN also Rises
    For Whom the Bell TOLLS
                For WHOM the Bell Tolls
```

---

[8]Parnas, 1972.

Note that each keyword is in all caps, each input line appears once for every index word in the line, and the keywords are sorted alphabetically. Each line of text has its keywords made visible by circularly shifting the words in the line. In the case of a tie (two lines of text have the same index word and so should appear together in the output), the lines of text should appear in the same order in which they appeared in the text input file. The question we have to answer is this: how do we create the KWIC index? A secondary question we'll need to answer almost immediately is: how do we store the data?

Top-Down Decomposition

We'll start by designing the problem solution using a top-down decomposition. *Top-down decompositions*, as we've seen with the eight queens problem earlier in this chapter, are all about control flow. We want to figure out how to sequentially solve the problem, making progress with each step we take. It's assumed that the data is stored separately from the routines and each subroutine in the control flow can access the data it needs. The alternative is to pass the data along to each subroutine as we call it; this can be cumbersome and time consuming because the data usually has to be copied each time you pass it to a routine. A first decomposition of this problem might look like the following:

1. Input the words to ignore and the text.

2. Create a data structure containing the circularly shifted lines of text, keeping track of which word in the line is the index word for this line.

3. Sort the circularly shifted lines of text by the index words.

4. Format the output lines.

5. Output the text.

Note that these five steps can easily become five subroutines that are all called in sequence from a main program. The data structure used for the input text could be an array of characters for each line, a String for each line, or an array of Strings for the entire input file. One could also use a map data structure that uses each index word as the key and a String containing the input text line as the value of the map element. There are certainly other possible data structures to be used. Sorting can be done by any of the stable sorting algorithms, and which algorithm to use would depend on the data structure chosen and on the expected size of the input text. Your sort must be stable because of the requirement that identical index words sort their respective lines in the same order in which they appear in the input text file. Depending on the programming language you use and the data structure you choose, sorting might be done automatically for you. The data structure you choose will affect how the circular shifts are done and how the output routine does the work of formatting each output line.

Now that we've got a feel for how a top-down decomposition might proceed, let's move on and consider a modular decomposition.

Modular Decomposition of KWIC

A modular decomposition of the KWIC problem can be based on information hiding in the sense that we will hide both data structures and design decisions. The modules we create won't necessarily be the sequential list we've just seen, but will be modules that can cooperate with each other and are called when needed. One list of modules for KWIC looks like this:

- A Line module (for lines of input text)

- A Keyword-Line pair module

- A KWICIndex module to create the indexed list itself

- A Circular Shift module

- A module to format and print the output

- A master control module—the main program

The Line module will use the Keyword-Line module to create a map data structure where each Line is a keyword and a list of lines that contain that keyword. The KWICIndex module will use the Line module to create the indexed list. The Circular Shift module will use the KWICIndex module (and recursively, the Line and Keyword-Line modules) and create the circularly shifted set of keyword-line pairs. Sorting will be taken care of internally in the KWICIndex module; ideally the index will be created as a sorted list, and any additions to the list will maintain the ordering of the index. The format and print module will organize the keyword-lines so that the keywords are printed in all caps and centered on the output line. Finally, the master control module will read the input, create the KWICIndex, and cause it to print correctly.

The key of these modules is that one can describe the modules and their interactions without needing the details of how each module is implemented and how the data is stored. That's hidden in the module description itself. Other designs are also possible. For example, it might be better to subsume the circular shift operations inside the Line module, allowing it to store the input lines and their shifts. Regardless, the next step in the design is to create the interface for each module and to coordinate the interfaces so that each module can communicate with every other module regardless of the internal implementation.

Listing 7-2 shows an implementation of the KWIC index program written in Java that somewhat closely follows the earlier discussion.

Listing 7-2. A Modular Version of the KWIC Solution

```java
/**
 * CLASS Line
 * Handle the storage of 3 key pieces of information.
 * the current line, the keyword, and the index of the
 * keyword in the line.
 *
 * Basically just like a struct in C.
 *
 */

public class Line implements Comparable<Line> {
    public String line;
    public String keyword;
    public int indexOf;

    public Line(String line, String keyword, int indexOf) {
        this.keyword = keyword;
        this.indexOf = indexOf;

        // capitalize the keyword in the line
        // grab the first part of the line
        String first = line.substring(0, indexOf);
        // capitalize the entire keyword
        String middle = keyword.toUpperCase();
        // grab the rest of the line after the keyword
        String last = line.substring(indexOf + keyword.length());
        // put it all back together
        this.line = first + middle + last;
    }
```

```
    /**
     * We want to sort lines based on keyword alone.
     * This will do a lexicographical comparison of the keywords
     * Remember that keyword is a String
     */
    @Override
    public int compareTo(Line other) {
        return this.keyword.compareToIgnoreCase(other.keyword);
    }
}

import java.util.Scanner;
import java.util.*;

/**
 * CLASS KwicIndex
 * A KwicIndex object contains a collection of Lines
 * and the words we are ignoring as keywords.
 *
 * We use a HashSet for the words to ignore because
 * we only ever want one of each of these words.
 *
 * We use a PriorityQueue for the lines because we
 * want to store them sorted by keywords and the PQ
 * does that for us automatically.
 *
 */

public class KwicIndex {
    public HashSet<String> wordsToIgnore;
    public PriorityQueue<Line> lines;

    /**
     * Constructor that initializes the lists and
     * reads all the words to ignore
     */
    public KwicIndex(Scanner ignore) {
        this.wordsToIgnore = new HashSet<String>();
        this.lines = new PriorityQueue<Line>();

        while (ignore.hasNext()) {
            this.wordsToIgnore.add(ignore.next());
        }
    }

    /**
     * Create an entry in the index for the given line.
     * @param str; a string to examine
     * @return
     */
    public void add(String str) {
        Scanner scan = new Scanner(str);
```

```
        int offset = 0;
        int words = -1;
        while (scan.hasNext()) {
            // grab the next word
            String temp = scan.next();
            words++;
            /** if this word is not to be ignored create a new line
              *  with the line shifted with the new word removed
              *  then add it to the list of lines
              */
            if (!wordsToIgnore.contains(temp.toLowerCase())) {
                Line version = new Line(str, temp, offset + words);
                this.lines.add(version);
            }
            offset += temp.length();
        }
    }

    /**
      * return the index so we can print it
      */
    public PriorityQueue<Line> getLines() {
        return lines;
    }
}

import java.util.*;

/**
  * CLASS Print
  * Print the resulting KWIC index
  *
  */

public class Print {
    public PriorityQueue<Line> lines;

    public Print(PriorityQueue<Line> lines) {
        this.lines = lines;
    }

    /**
      * Print to System.out the contents of the index
      * lines formatting adjusted so
      * keywords are in the same column
      */
    public void printIndex() {
        // make a new PriorityQueue
        PriorityQueue<Line> newLines = new PriorityQueue<Line>();
```

```java
            // lets figure out the length of the longest line
            int longest = 0;
            for (Line l : lines) {
                if (l.indexOf > longest) {
                    longest = l.indexOf;
                }
            }

            /**
             * do the printing
             */
            while (!lines.isEmpty()) {
                /** grab the line with smallest keyword */
                Line l = lines.poll();

                /** save the line */
                newLines.add(l);

                /**
                 * figure out the whitespace
                 * Here we figure out how far over to print
                 * the keyword based on putting the longest line
                 * right in the middle
                 */
                String retval = "";
                for (int i = 0; i < (longest - l.indexOf); i++) {
                    retval += " ";
                }

                /**
                 * construct the line
                 */
                retval += l.line;

                // output
                System.out.println(retval);
            }
            /** Save the lines from all that polling */
            this.lines = newLines;
        }
    }

import java.io.File;
import java.io.FileNotFoundException;
import java.util.Scanner;

/**
 * CLASS Main
 * Manage the KWIC indexing system.
 *
 * @author jfdooley
```

```
     *
     */

public class Main {

    public static void main(String[] args) {
        /**
         * declare the Scanners to read the files
         */
        Scanner scan = null;
        Scanner ignore = null;
        /**
         * usage and file opening
         *
         * if we have the correct number of input args
         * we try to open the input files
         */
        if (args.length == 2) {
            try {
                scan = new Scanner(new File(args[0]));
                ignore = new Scanner(new File(args[1]));
            } catch (FileNotFoundException ex) {
                System.out.println(ex.getMessage());
                System.exit(1);
            }
            /**
             * wrong number of input args. Give user a usage
             * message and leave
             */
        } else {
            System.out.println("Usage: java Main <inputFile> <wordsToIgnore>");
            System.exit(1);
        }

        /**
         * first we create an KwicIndex object & add
         * the words to ignore to it
         */
        KwicIndex index = new KwicIndex(ignore);

        /**
         * Now we add all the lines to the index
         *   the add() method does the work of the circular shift
         *   and adding the shifted lines to the priority queue
         */
        while (scan.hasNextLine()) {
            index.add(scan.nextLine());
        }

        /**
         * Finally we print the index we just created
         */
```

```
        Print prt = new Print(index.getLines());
        prt.printIndex();
    }
}
```

We create four Java classes:

- Line: Creates the data structure for the lines that are input from a text file.

- KwicIndex: Takes the words to ignore and the input lines and creates a sorted permuted index. Lines are shifted and added to the index based on the keyword.

- Print: Takes the KwicIndex object and prints the permuted index in the right order and shifted accordingly.

- Main: Checks that the command line arguments are correct, creates the initial KwicIndex object, and calls the methods to add new lines and to do the printing.

Giving this program a file called input.txt with the following input

```
Descent of Man
The Ascent of Man
The Old Man and The Sea
A Portrait of the Artist As a Young Man
A Man is a Man but Bubblesort is a dog
this is dumb
```

produces the following output:

```
                                A Portrait of the Artist As a Young Man
                        A Man is A Man but Bubblesort is a dog
  A Man is a Man but Bubblesort is A dog
         A Portrait of the Artist As A Young Man
                                A Man is a Man but Bubblesort is a dog
                A Portrait of the ARTIST As a Young Man
          A Portrait of the Artist AS a Young Man
                           The ASCENT of Man
              A Man is a Man but BUBBLESORT is a dog
                           DESCENT of Man
      something i do not know how to DO
                     something i DO not know how to do
  A Man is a Man but Bubblesort is a DOG
                          this is DUMB
          something i do not know HOW to do
                     something I do not know how to do
                        A Man IS a Man but Bubblesort is a dog
  A Man is a Man but Bubblesort IS a dog
                        this IS dumb
          something i do not KNOW how to do
                           A MAN is a Man but Bubblesort is a dog
               Descent of MAN
          A Man is a MAN but Bubblesort is a dog
               The Old MAN and The Sea
          The Ascent of MAN
```

```
A Portrait of the Artist As a Young MAN
                    something i do NOT know how to do
                              The OLD Man and The Sea
                              A PORTRAIT of the Artist As a Young Man
            The Old Man and The SEA
                              SOMETHING i do not know how to do
                              THIS is dumb
        something i do not know how TO do
     A Portrait of the Artist As a YOUNG Man
```

We'll continue this discussion on modular decomposition in much more detail in Chapter 8, in a discussion of object-oriented design.

Conclusion

Structured design describes a set of classic design methodologies. These design ideas work for a large class of problems. The original structured design idea, stepwise refinement, has you decompose the problem from the top down, focusing on the control flow of the solution. It also relates closely to some of the architectures mentioned in Chapter 5, particularly the main program-subroutine and pipe-and-filter architectures. Modular decomposition is the immediate precursor to the modern object-oriented methodologies and introduced the ideas of encapsulation and information hiding. These ideas are the fundamentals of your design toolbox.

References

Dahl, O. J., E. Dijkstra, et al. (1972). *Structured Programming.* (London, UK: Academic Press, 1972.)

Dijkstra, E. "GoTo Statement Considered Harmful." Communications of the ACM 11(3): 147-148 (1968).

Hunt, A. and D. Thomas. *The Pragmatic Programmer: From Journeyman to Master.* (Boston, MA: Addison-Wesley, 2000.)

McConnell, S. *Code Complete 2.* (Redmond, WA: Microsoft Press, 2004.)

Miller, G. A. "The magical number seven, plus or minus two: Some limits on our capacity for processing information." *Psychological Review* 63: 81-97 (1956).

Parnas, D. "On the Criteria to be Used in Decomposing Systems into Modules." Communications of the ACM 15(12): 1053–1058 (1972).

Wikipedia. "Separation of Concerns" (2009). http://en.wikipedia.org/wiki/ Separation_of_concerns. Retrieved December 7, 2009.

Wirth, N. "Program Development by Stepwise Refinement." CACM 14(4): 221-227 (1971).

CHAPTER 8

Object-Oriented Overview

Object-oriented programming is an exceptionally bad idea, which could only have originated in California.

—Edsger Dijkstra

The object has three properties, which makes it a simple, yet powerful model building block. It has state so it can model memory. It has behavior, so that it can model dynamic processes. And it is encapsulated, so that it can hide complexity.

—Trygve Reenskaug, *Working With Objects*

Well, yes, we've all learned about the object-oriented programming (OOP) paradigm before. But it never hurts to go over some basic definitions so we're all on the same page for our discussion about object-oriented analysis and design.

First of all, objects are *things*. They have an *identity* (a name), a *state* (a set of attributes that describes the current data stored inside the object), and a defined set of *behaviors* that operate on that state. A *stack* is an object, as is an automobile, a bank account, a window, or a button in a graphical user interface. In an object-oriented program, a set of cooperating objects pass messages among themselves. The messages make requests of the destination objects to invoke methods that either perform operations on their data (thus changing the state of the object), or to report on the current state of the object. Eventually work gets done. Objects use *encapsulation* and *information hiding* (remember, they're different) to isolate data and operations from other objects in the program. Shared data areas are (usually) eliminated. Objects are members of *classes* that define attribute types and operations.

Classes are *templates* for objects. Classes can also be thought of as factories that generate objects. So an Automobile class will generate instances of autos, a Stack class will create a new stack object, and a Queue class will create a new queue. Classes may inherit attributes and behaviors from other classes. Classes may be arranged in a class hierarchy where one class (a *super class* or *base class*) is a generalization of one or more other classes (*sub-classes*). A sub-class inherits the attributes and operations from its super class and may add new methods or attributes of its own. In this sense a sub-class is more specific and detailed than its super class; hence, we say that a sub-class extends a super class. For example, a BankAccount object may include the customer's name, address, balance, and a unique BankAccount ID number; it will also allow deposits and withdrawals and the current balance can be queried. A CheckingAccount is a more specific version of a BankAccount; it has all the attributes and operations of a BankAccount, but it adds data and behaviors that are specific to checking accounts, like check numbers and a per-check charge. In Java this feature is called *inheritance*, whereas in UML it's called *generalization*.[1]

---

[1]Fowler, M. *UML Distilled.* (Boston, MA: Addison-Wesley, 2000.)

J. F. Dooley, *Software Development, Design and Coding*, https://doi.org/10.1007/978-1-4842-3153-1_8

There are a number of advantages to inheritance. It's an *abstraction mechanism* that may be used to classify entities. It's a *reuse mechanism* at both the design and the programming level. The inheritance graph is a source of organizational knowledge about domains and systems.

And, of course, there are problems with inheritance as well. It makes object classes that aren't self-contained; sub-classes can't be understood without reference to their super classes. Inheritance introduces complexity, and this is undesirable, especially in critical systems. Inheritance also usually allows overloading of operators (*methods* in Java), which can be good (polymorphism) or bad (screening useful methods in the superclass).

OOP has a number of advantages, among them easier maintenance, because objects can be understood as stand-alone entities. Objects are also appropriate as reusable components. But for some problems, there may be no mapping from real-world objects to system objects, meaning that OOP is not appropriate for all problems.

An Object-Oriented Analysis and Design Process

Object-oriented analysis (OOA), design (OOD), and programming (OOP) are related but distinct. OOA is concerned with developing an *object model of the application domain*. So, for example, you take the problem statement, generate a set of features and (possibly) use cases,[2] tease out the objects and some of the methods within those objects that you'll need to satisfy the use case, and you put together an architecture of how the solution will hang together. That's object-oriented analysis.

OOD is concerned with developing an *object-oriented system model* to satisfy requirements. You take the objects generated from your OOA, figure out whether to use inheritance, aggregation, composition, abstract classes, interfaces, and so on, in order to create a coherent and efficient model, draw the class diagrams, flesh out the details of what each attribute is and what each method does, and describe the interfaces. That's the design.

Some people like object-oriented analysis, design, and programming[3] and some people don't.[4]

OOA allows you to take a problem model and re-cast it in terms of objects and classes, and OOD allows you to take your analyzed requirements and connect the dots between the objects you've proposed and fill in the details with respect to object attributes and methods. But how do you really do all this?

Well, here is a proposed process from that starts to fill in some of the details.[5] We'll figure out the rest as we go along:

1. *Write (or receive) the problem statement*: Use this to generate an initial set of features.

2. *Create the feature list*: The feature list is the set of program features that you derive from the problem statement; it contains your initial set of requirements. The feature list may be a set of user stories. To help generate the feature list, you can put together a set of *scenarios*, narrative descriptions of how the user will walk through using the program to accomplish a task. A scenario should be technology agnostic and should be explicitly from the user's perspective. It's not how the program works; it's about what the user wants to accomplish and how the user gets the task done. It can also talk about what the user knows. User stories are very brief and high level. Scenarios are longer and provide more detail. A user story might generate several scenarios.

---

[2]Cockburn, A. *Writing Effective Use Cases*. (Boston, MA: Addison-Wesley, 2000.)
[3]Beck, K., and B. Boehm. "Agility through Discipline: A Debate." *IEEE Computer* 36 (6):44-46 (2003).
[4]Graham, Paul. "Why Arc isn't Especially Object Oriented," retrieved from `www.paulgraham.com/noop.html`on October 12, 2009.
[5]McLaughlin, Brett D., et. al. *Head First Object-Oriented Analysis & Design*. (O'Reilly Media, Inc. Sebastopol, CA: 2007.)

3. *Write up use cases*[6]: This helps refine the features, dig out new requirements, and expose problems with the features you just created. Use cases are more specific descriptions of how a user accomplishes a task using the program; they describe how the user interacts with the system. Use cases ". . . capture the goal of an action, the trigger event that starts a process, and then describe each step of the process including inputs, outputs, errors and exceptions. Use cases are often written in the form of an actor or user performing an action followed by the expected system response and alternative outcomes.[7] " Each scenario or user story might create several use cases.

4. Break the problem into subsystems or modules or whatever you want to call them as long as they're smaller, self-contained bits usually related to functionality.

5. Map your features, subsystems, and use cases to domain objects; create abstractions.

6. Identify the program's objects, methods, and algorithms.

7. Implement this iteration.

8. Test the iteration.

9. If you've not finished the feature list and you still have time and/or money left, go back to step 4 and do another iteration, otherwise . . .

10. Do final acceptance testing and release.

Note that this process leaves out a lot of details, like the length of an iteration. How many features end up in an iteration? How and when do we add new features to the feature list? How exactly do we identify objects and operations? How do we abstract objects into classes? Where do we fix bugs that are found in testing? Do we do reviews of code and other project work products?

Leaving out steps here is okay. We're mostly concerned with the analysis and design elements of the process. We'll discuss ideas on the rest of the process in this chapter, and some of the answers are also in Chapter 3 on project management.

How do the preceding process steps fit into the software development life cycle? Well, I'm glad you asked. Recall that the basic development life cycle has four steps:

1. Requirements gathering and analysis

2. Design

3. Implementation and testing

4. Release, maintenance, and evolution

---

[6]N.B. In some of the literature on requirements gathering, the definitions of *scenario* and *use case* used here are reversed. That is, the use case is a general description of accomplishing a goal, and the scenario is the list of explicit steps used to accomplish the task. I prefer the definitions given here. A lively discussion of the differences between user stories and use cases can be found at http://wiki.c2.com/?UserStoryAndUseCaseComparison.

[7]Schaeffer, Nadine. "User Stories, Scenarios, and Use Cases," retrieved from http://cloudforestdesign.com/2011/04/25/introduction-user-stories-user-personas-use-cases-whats-the-difference/ on July 10, 2017.

We can easily assign the previous ten steps into four buckets, as follows:

Requirements Gathering and Analysis

1. Problem statement

2. Feature list creation

3. Use case generation

Design

1. Break up the problem.

2. Map features and use cases to domain objects.

3. Identify objects, methods, and algorithms.

Implementation and Testing

1. Implement this iteration.

2. Test the iteration.

3. If you've not finished with the feature list or out of time, go back to step 4, otherwise . . .

Release/Maintenance/Evolution

1. Do final acceptance testing and release.

Once again we can ignore the details of each process step for now. These details really depend on the process methodology you choose for your development project. The description of the process just given uses an iterative methodology and can easily be fitted into an agile process or a more traditional staged release process.

Note also that you'll need to revisit the requirements whenever you get to step 4, because you're likely to have uncovered or generated new requirements during each iteration. And whenever your customer sees a new iteration, they'll ask for more stuff (yes, they will—trust me). This means you'll be updating the feature list (and re-prioritizing) at the beginning of each new iteration.

Doing the Process

Let's continue by working through an extended example, seeing where the problem statement leads us and how we can tease out requirements and begin our object-oriented analysis.

The Problem Statement

Burt, the proud owner of Birds by Burt, has created the ultimate in bird feeders. Burt's Bird Buffet and Bath (B⁴), is an integrated bird feeder and birdbath. It comes in 12 different colors (including camo) and 1, 3, and 5 lb. capacities. It will hold up to one gallon of water in the attached bird bath and has a built-in hanger so you can hang it from a tree branch or from a pole. The B⁴ is just flying off the shelves. Alice and Bob are desperate for a B⁴, but they'd like a few changes. Alice is a techno-nerd and a fanatic songbird watcher. She knows that her favorite songbirds only feed during the day, so she wants a custom B⁴ that allows the feeding doors to open automatically at sunrise and close automatically at sunset. Burt, ever the accommodating owner, has agreed and the hardware division of Birds by Burt is hard at work designing the B⁴++ for Alice. Your job is to write the software to make the hardware work.

The Feature List

The first thing we need to do is figure out what the B⁴++ will actually *do*. This version seems simple enough. We can almost immediately write down three requirements:

- The feeding doors must all open and close simultaneously.

- The feeding doors should open automatically at sunrise.

- The feeding doors should close automatically at sunset.

That doesn't seem so bad. The requirements are simple, and no user interaction is required. The next step is to create a use case so we can see just what the bird feeder is really going to do.

Use Cases

A *use case* is a description of what a program does in a particular situation. It's the detailed set of steps that the program executes when a user asks for something. Use cases always have an *actor*—some outside agent that gets the ball rolling, and a *goal*—what the use case is supposed to have done by the end. The use case describes what it takes to get from some initial state to the goal from the user's perspective.[8] Here's a quick example of a use case for the B⁴++:

1. The sensor detects sunlight at a 40% brightness level.

2. The feeding doors open.

3. Birds arrive, eat, and drink.

4. Birds leave.

5. The sensor detects a decrease in sunlight to a 25% brightness level.

6. The feeding doors close.

Given the simplicity of the B4++, that's about all we can expect out of a use case. In fact, steps 3 and 4 aren't technically part of the use case, because they aren't part of the program—but they're good to have so we can get a more complete picture of how the B⁴++ is operating. Use cases are very useful in requirements analysis because they give you an idea, in English, of what the program needs to do in a particular situation, and because they often help you uncover new requirements. Note that in the use case we don't talk about *how* a program does something, we only concentrate on *what* the program has to do to reach the goal. This can also include the inputs, outputs, and errors that occur. And it can include alternative lists of steps for different situations—for example, if the user makes an error, create two alternative use cases, one for how to treat the error and one for when the user doesn't make the error. Most times there will be several use cases for every program you write. We've only got one because this version of the B⁴++ is so simple.

---

[8]Cockburn, 2000.

Decompose the Problem

Now that we've got our use case, we can probably just decompose the problem and identify the objects in the program.

This problem is quite simple. If you look at the use case and pick out the nouns, you see that we can identify several objects. Each object has certain characteristics and contributes to reaching the goal of getting the birds fed. (Yes, *birds* is a noun in the use case, but they are the actors in this little play, so for the purposes of describing the objects we ignore them—they're not part of the program.) The other two nouns of interest are *sensor* and *doors*. These are the critical pieces of the B^4++ because the use case indicates that they're the parts that accomplish the goal of opening and closing the feeding doors at sunrise and sunset. It's logical that they're objects in our design. Here are the objects I came up with for this first version of the B^4++ and a short description:

- `BirdFeeder`: The top-level object. The bird feeder has one or more feeding doors at which the birds will gather, and a sensor to detect sunrise and sunset. The `BirdFeeder` class needs to control the querying of the light sensor and the opening and closing of the feeding doors.

- `Sensor`: There will be a hardware light sensor that detects different light levels. We'll need to ask it about light levels.

- `FeedingDoor`: There will be several feeding doors on the bird feeder. They have to open and close.

That's probably about it for classes at this point. Now, what do they all do? To describe classes and their components, we can use another UML feature: *class diagrams*.

Class Diagrams

A *class diagram* allows you to describe the attributes and the methods of a class. A set of class diagrams will describe all the objects in a program and the relationships between them. We draw arrows of different types between class diagrams to describe the relationships. Class diagrams give you a visual description of the object model you've created for your program. We saw a set of class diagrams for the Fox and Rabbit program we described in Chapter 5.

Class diagrams have three sections:

- *Name*: The name of the class

- *Attributes*: The instance data fields and their types used by the class

- *Methods*: The set of methods used by the class and their visibility.

An example of a class diagram for our `BirdFeeder` class is shown in Figure 8-1.

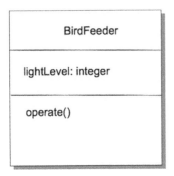

Figure 8-1. *The BirdFeeder class*

The diagram shows that the BirdFeeder class has a single integer attribute, lightLevel, and a single method, operate(). By themselves, class diagrams aren't terribly interesting, but when you put several of them together and show the relationships between them, you can get some interesting information about your program. What else do we need in the way of class diagrams? In our program, the BirdFeeder class uses the FeedingDoor and Sensor classes, but they don't know (or care) about each other. In fact, although BirdFeeder knows about FeedingDoor and Sensor and uses them, they don't know they're being used. Ah, the beauty of object-oriented programming! This relationship can be expressed in the class diagram of all three classes, shown in Figure 8-2.

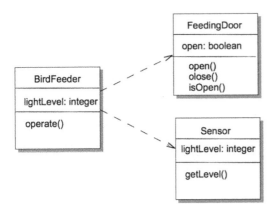

Figure 8-2. *BirdFeeder uses FeedingDoor and Sensor*

In UML, the dotted line with the open arrow at the end indicates that one class (in our case, BirdFeeder) is *associated* with another class (in our case, either FeedingDoor or Sensor) by *using* it.

Code Anyone?

Now that we've got the class diagrams and know the attributes, the methods, and the association between the classes, it's time to flesh out our program with some code.

In the BirdFeeder object, the operate() method needs to check the light levels and open or close the feeding doors depending on the current light level reported by the Sensor object—and does nothing if the current light level is above or below the threshold values.

In the Sensor object, the getLevel() method just reports back the current level from the hardware sensor.

In the FeedingDoor object, the open() method checks to see if the doors are closed. If they are, it opens them and sets a Boolean to indicate that they're open. The close() method does the reverse.

Listing 8-1 shows the code for each of the classes described.

Listing 8-1. Code for B^4++ Bird Feeder

```
/**
 * class BirdFeeder
 *
 * @author John F. Dooley
 * @version 1.0
 */

import java.util.ArrayList;
import java.util.Iterator;

public class BirdFeeder
{
    /* instance variables */
    private static final int ON_THRESHOLD = 40;
    private static final int OFF_THRESHOLD = 25;
    private int lightLevel;
    private Sensor s1;
    private ArrayList<FeedingDoor> doors = null;

    /*
     * Default Constructor for objects of class BirdFeeder
     */
    public BirdFeeder()
    {
        doors = new ArrayList<FeedingDoor>();
        /* initialize lightLevel */
        lightLevel = 0;
        s1 = new Sensor();
        /* by default we have a feeder with just one door */
        doors.add(new FeedingDoor());
    }

    /*
     * The operate() method operates the birdfeeder.
     * It gets the current lightLevel from the Sensor and
     * checks to see if we should open or close the doors
     */
    public void operate()
    {
        lightLevel = s1.getLevel();

        if (lightLevel > ON_THRESHOLD) {
            Iterator door_iter = doors.iterator();
```

```
                while (door_iter.hasNext()) {
                    FeedingDoor a = (FeedingDoor) door_iter.next();
                    a.open();
                    System.out.println("The door has opened.");
                }
            } else if (lightLevel < OFF_THRESHOLD) {
                Iterator door_iter = doors.iterator();
                while (door_iter.hasNext()) {
                    FeedingDoor a = (FeedingDoor) door_iter.next();
                    a.close();
                    System.out.println("The door has closed.");
                }
            }
        }
    }
}

/**
 * class FeedingDoor
 *
 * @author John Dooley
 * @version 1.0
 */
public class FeedingDoor
{
    /* instance variables */
    private boolean doorOpen;

    /*
     * Default constructor for objects of class FeedingDoors
     */
    public FeedingDoor()
    {
        /* initialize instance variables */
        doorOpen = false;
    }

    /*
     * open the feeding doors
     * if they are already open, do nothing
     */
    public void open( )
    {
        /** if the door is closed, open it */
        if (doorOpen == false) {
            doorOpen = true;
        }
    }
    /*
     * close the doors
     * if they are already closed, do nothing
     */
```

```java
    public void close( )
    {
        /* if the door is open, close it */
        if (doorOpen == true) {
            doorOpen = false;
        }
    }
    /*
     * report whether the doors are open or not
     */
    public boolean isOpen()
    {
        return doorOpen;
    }
}

/**
 * class Sensor
 *
 * @author John Dooley
 * @version 1.0
 */
public class Sensor
{
    /* instance variables */
    private int lightLevel;

    /*
     * Default constructor for objects of class Sensor
     */
    public Sensor()
    {
        /** initialize instance variable */
        lightLevel = 0;
    }

    /**
     * getLevel - return a light level
     *
     * @return the value of the light level
     * that is returned by the hardware sensor
     */
    public int getLevel( )
    {
        /* till we get a hardware light sensor, we just fake it */
        lightLevel = (int) (Math.random() * 100);
        return lightLevel;
    }
}
```

Finally, we have a BirdFeederTester class that operates the B⁴++:

```java
/**
 * The class that tests the BirdFeeder, Sensor, and
 * FeedingDoor classes.
 *
 * @version 0.1
 */
public class BirdFeederTester
{
    private BirdFeeder feeder;

    /*
     * Constructor for objects of class BirdFeederTest
     */
    public BirdFeederTester()
    {
        this.feeder = new BirdFeeder();
    }

    public static void main(String [] args)
    {
        BirdFeederTester bfTest = new BirdFeederTester();

        for (int i = 0; i < 10; i++) {
            System.out.println("Testing the bird feeder");
            bfTest.feeder.operate();
            try {
                Thread.currentThread().sleep(2000);
            } catch (InterruptedException e) {
                System.out.println("Sleep interrupted" + e.getMessage());
                System.exit(1);
            }
        }
    }
}
```

When Alice and Bob take delivery of the B⁴++, they're thrilled. The doors automatically open and close, the birds arrive and eat their fill. Birdsong fills the air. What else could they possibly want?

Conclusion

Object-oriented design is a methodology that works for a very wide range of problems. Solutions to many problems in the real world are easily characterized as groups of cooperating objects. This single simple idea promotes simplicity of design, reuse of both designs and code, and the ideas of encapsulation and information hiding that Parnas advocated in his paper on modular decomposition. It's not the right way to solve some problems, including problems like communications protocol implementations, but it opens up a world of new and better solutions for many others. It also closes the "intellectual distance" between the real-world description of a problem and the resulting code.

References

Beck, K., and B. Boehm. "Agility through Discipline: A Debate." *IEEE Computer* 36 (6):44-46 (2003).

Cockburn, A. *Writing Effective Use Cases*. (Boston, MA: Addison-Wesley, 2000.)

Fowler, M. *UML Distilled*. (Boston, MA: Addison-Wesley, 2000.)

Graham, Paul. "Why Arc Isn't Especially Object Oriented," retrieved from `www.paulgraham.com/noop.html` on October 12, 2009.

McLaughlin, Brett D., et. al. *Head First Object-Oriented Analysis & Design*. (O'Reilly Media, Inc. Sebastopol, CA: 2007.)

Wirfs-Brock, R. and A. McKean. *Object Design: Roles Responsibilities, and Collaborations*. (Boston, MA: Addison-Wesley, 2003.)

CHAPTER 9

Object-Oriented Analysis and Design

When doing analysis you are trying to understand the problem. To my mind this is not just listing requirements in use cases. . . . Analysis also involves looking behind the surface requirements to come up with a mental model of what is going on in the problem. . . . Some kind of conceptual model is a necessary part of software development, and even the most uncontrolled hacker does it.

—Martin Fowler[1]

Object-oriented design is, in its simplest form, based on a seemingly elementary idea. Computing systems perform certain actions on certain objects; to obtain flexible and reusable systems, it is better to base the structure of software on the objects than on the actions.

Once you have said this, you have not really provided a definition, but rather posed a set of problems: What precisely is an object? How do you find and describe the objects? How should programs manipulate objects? What are the possible relations between objects? How does one explore the commonalities that may exist between various kinds of objects? How do these ideas relate to classical software engineering concerns such as correct- ness, ease of use, efficiency?

Answers to these issues rely on an impressive array of techniques for efficiently producing reusable, extendible and reliable software: inheritance, both in its linear (single) and multiple forms; dynamic binding and polymorphism; a new view of types and type checking; genericity; information hiding; use of assertions; programming by contract; safe exception handling.

—Bertrand Meyer[2]

[1]Martin, Robert, "Single Responsibility Principle." www.butunclebob.com/ArticleS.UncleBob.PrinciplesOfOod, retrieved on December 10, 2009.
[2]Meyer, Bertrand. *Object-Oriented Software Construction*. (Upper Saddle River , NJ: Prentice Hall, 1988.)

© John F. Dooley 2017
J. F. Dooley, *Software Development, Design and Coding*, https://doi.org/10.1007/978-1-4842-3153-1_9

When defining object-oriented analysis and design, it's best to keep in mind your objectives. In both of these process phases we're producing a *work product* that's closer to the code that is your end goal. In *analysis*, you're refining the feature list you've created and producing a model of what the customer wants. In design you're taking that model and creating the classes that will end up being code.

In analysis you want to end up with a description of what the program is supposed to do, its *essential features*. This end product takes the form of a *conceptual model* of the problem domain and its solution. The model is made up of a number of things, including use cases, user stories, scenarios, preliminary class diagrams, user interface storyboards, and possibly some class interface descriptions.

In *design* you want to end up with a description of how the program will implement the conceptual model and do what the customer wants. This end product takes the form of an *object model* of the solution. This model is made up of groups of related class diagrams—their associations and descriptions of how they interact with each other. This includes the programming interface for each class. From here you should be able to get to the code pretty quickly.

Analysis

What is object-oriented analysis? Well, it depends on whom you talk to. For our purposes, we'll define *object-oriented analysis* as a method of studying the nature of a problem and *determining its essential features and their relations to each other*.[3] Your objective is to end up with a conceptual model of the problem solution that you can then use to create an object model—your design. This model doesn't take into account any implementation details or any constraints on the target system. It looks at the domain that the problem is in and tries to create a set of features, objects and relations that describe a solution in that domain. What makes a feature essential? Typically, a feature is *essential* if it's a feature the customer has said they must have, if it's a non-functional requirement that the program won't run without, or if it's a core program element that other parts of the program depend on.

The conceptual model describes *what* the solution will do and will typically include use cases,[4] user stories,[5] user scenarios, and UML sequence diagrams.[6] It can also include a description of the user interface and a preliminary set of UML class diagrams (but that, of course, is shading over into design).

How do you create this conceptual model? As with all the other methodologies we've talked about, the correct answer is: it depends.

It depends on understanding the problem domain, on understanding the feature list you've already come up with, and on understanding how the customer reacts to each of the program iterations they'll see. As we'll see, change is constant.

The key part of object-oriented analysis is the creation of use cases. With *use cases* you create a detailed walkthrough of a scenario from the user's perspective, and that walkthrough gives you an understanding of what the program is supposed to do from the outside. A program of any size will normally have several use cases associated with it. In fact, a single use case may have alternative paths through the scenario. When using an agile methodology, you'll normally start with *user stories* that the product owner will create and then a set of *scenarios* that flesh out the user stories. The scenarios are then used to generate use cases. More on this later.

Once you get a few use cases created, how do you get to the class diagrams? There are several methods suggested, but we'll just go over one now and save the rest for later. The first method we'll look at is called *textual analysis*. With textual analysis, you take your uses cases and examine the text for clues about classes in your programs. Remember that the object-oriented paradigm is all about objects and the behavior of those objects, so those are the two things to pluck out of your use cases.

---

[3]McLaughlin, Brett D., et. al. *Head First Object-Oriented Analysis & Design*. (Sebastopol, CA: O'Reilly Media, Inc., 2007.)
[4]Cockburn, A. (2000). *Writing Effective Use Cases*. (Boston, MA: Addison-Wesley, 2000.)
[5]Beck, K. *Extreme Programming Explained: Embrace Change*. (Boston, MA: Addison-Wesley, 2000.)
[6]Fowler, M.*UML Distilled*. (Boston, MA: Addison-Wesley, 2000.)

In textual analysis, you pluck potential objects out of the text by picking out the *nouns* in your use case. Because nouns are things and objects are (usually) things, the nouns stand a good chance of being objects in your program. In terms of behavior, you look at the *verbs* in the use case. Verbs provide you with action words that describe changes in state or actions that report state. This usually isn't the end, but it gives you your first cut at method names and parameter lists for the methods.

An Analytical Example

Let's go back to Burt's Bird Buffet and Bath, and the B⁴++. When last we left the B⁴++ it automatically opened the feeding doors at sunrise and closed them at sunset. The B⁴++ was a hit, and Alice and Bob were thrilled with its performance. Once again the B⁴ models were flying off the shelves.

Then one day Burt gets a call from Alice. It seems she has an issue. Although the B⁴++ works just fine, Alice has noticed that she's getting unwanted birds at her bird feeder. Recall that Alice is a songbird fanatic and she's thrilled when cardinals, painted buntings, scarlet tanagers, American goldfinches, and tufted titmice show up at the feeder. But she's not so thrilled when grackles, blue jays, and starlings drive away the songbirds and have their own feast. So Alice wants to be able to close the B⁴++ feeding doors when the bad birds show up and open them again when the songbirds come back. And you're just the guy to do it.

The first obvious question you ask Alice is, "How do you want to open and close the feeding doors?" "Well," she says, "how about a remote control? That way I can stay inside the house and just open and close the doors when the birds arrive." And so the game begins again.

Lets assume that we're an agile team and we'll do our updated design using agile techniques. The first thing we'll need is a new user story. Recall that a user story usually takes the form: "As a <role>, I want to <action>, in order to <benefit>." In this case we might say, "As Alice, the owner, I want to open and close the bird feeder doors with a remote control, in order to keep the predator birds away from the feeder."

From this user story we can generate a scenario that fleshes out what Alice wants to do, which might look like this: "Alice is sitting at her kitchen table having her morning coffee. The B⁴++ doors opened when the sun came out this morning and the feeder has attracted several songbirds. As Alice is watching the songbirds, a couple of blue jays arrive, chase the songbirds off, and begin feasting on the birdseed. Alice reaches for the remote control and presses the button. The bird feeder doors close smoothly and the blue jays fly off. Alice presses the remote control button again and the doors open. After a while the songbirds return and Alice can finish her coffee."

Just like last time, we can take this now fleshed-out problem statement and try to put together a use case. Our previous use case looked like this:

1. The sensor detects sunlight at a 40% brightness level.

2. The feeding doors open.

3. The birds arrive, eat, and drink.

4. The birds leave.

5. The sensor detects a decrease in sunlight to a 25% brightness level.

6. The feeding doors close.

The first thing we need to decide is whether our new problem is an alternate path in this use case, or whether we need an entirely new use case.

Let's try a new use case. Why? Well, using the remote control doesn't really fit into the sensor use case, does it? The remote can be activated at any time and requires a user interaction, neither of which fits with our sensor. So let's see what we can come up with for a remote control use case:

1. Alice hears or sees birds at the bird feeder.

2. Alice determines that they are *not* songbirds.

3. Alice presses the remote control button.

4. The feeding doors close.

5. The birds give up and fly away.

6. Alice presses the remote control button.

7. The feeding doors open again.

Does this cover all the situations? Are there any we've missed? There are two things to think of. First, in step #1 we have "Alice hears or sees birds." The question is should the *or* matter to us? In this case the answer is no, because Alice is the one deciding and she's the actor in this use case. We can't control the actor; we can only respond to something the actor wants to do and make available options for the actor to exercise. In our case, our program will need to wait for the signal from the remote control and then do the right thing. (Not to get ahead of ourselves, but look at our program now as an event-driven system, and the program has to wait, or listen, for an event before it does something).

Secondly, what are the steps in the use case that will help us identify new objects? This is where our textual analysis comes in. In our previous version of this application, we've already got BirdFeeder, Sensor, and FeedingDoor objects. These are identified in the use case easily. What's new now? The only new object here is the remote control. What does the remote control do? How many buttons does it have? What does the program do when a remote control button is pressed?

In our example, the remote control seems relatively simple. Opening and closing the feeding doors is a toggle operation. The doors open if they are closed, and close if they are open. Those are the only options. So the remote really just needs a single button to implement the toggle function.

At the end of the day we've got a new use case and a new class for the B⁴++ program (see Figure 9-1).

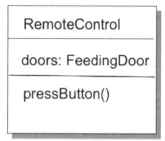

Figure 9-1. *The new RemoteControl class*

And that seems to be all the analysis we need for this version of the program.

This exercise provides us with a couple of guidelines we can use for analysis:

- *Make simple classes that work together by sending and responding to messages*: In our example, the simple classes FeedingDoor and Sensor encapsulate knowledge about the current state of the BirdFeeder and allow us to control the bird feeder with simple messages. This simplicity allows us to easily add a new way of controlling the bird feeder with the RemoteControl class.

- *Classes should have one responsibility*: Not only are the FeedingDoor and Sensor simple and easy to control, but they each only do one thing. That makes them easier to change later and easier to reuse.

Design

Now what about design? Assuming you've got a conceptual model from your analysis in the form of a few use cases and possibly a few class diagrams, your more detailed design should follow from this. In object-oriented design, the next steps are to firm up the class designs, decide on the methods your classes will contain, determine the relationships between the classes, and figure out how each of the methods will do what it's supposed to do.

In our current example, we've decided on four classes: BirdFeeder, FeedingDoor, Sensor, and RemoteControl. The first three classes we've already developed, so the question here is do we need to change any of these classes in order to integrate the RemoteControl class into the program? Figure 9-2 shows what we've got right now.

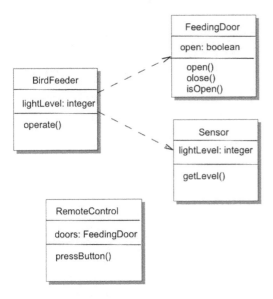

Figure 9-2. *How to integrate the RemoteControl class?*

Thinking about it, it seems that nothing in FeedingDoor or Sensor should have to change. Why?

Well, it's because the BirdFeeder class uses those two classes, and they don't need to use or inherit anything from any other class; they are pretty self-sufficient. If you recall, it's the operate() method in the BirdFeeder class that does all the hard work. It has to check the light level from the Sensor and, if appropriate, send a signal to the doors to open or close. So it seems that maybe the RemoteControl class will work the same way. The question for our design is: does the BirdFeeder class also use the RemoteControl class, or does the RemoteControl class stand alone and just wait for an "event" to happen?

Let's take a look at the code for the operate() method again:

```
public void operate() {
    lightLevel = s1.getLevel();

    if (lightLevel > ON_THRESHOLD) {
        Iterator door_iter = doors.iterator();
        while (door_iter.hasNext()) {
            FeedingDoor a = (FeedingDoor) door_iter.next();
            a.open();
        }
```

```
    } else if (lightLevel < OFF_THRESHOLD) {
        Iterator door_iter = doors.iterator();
        while (door_iter.hasNext()) {
            FeedingDoor a = (FeedingDoor) door_iter.next();
            a.close();
        }
    }
}
```

In this method, we check the light level from the Sensor object, and if it's above a certain level (the sun has risen), then we ask the doors to open. It's the doors themselves that check to see if they are already open or not. Regardless, when the open() method returns, each door is open. The same thing happens with the close() method. Regardless of how they start out, when each invocation of close() returns its door is closed. It seems as if this is just the behavior we want from the RemoteControl object, except that instead of a light threshold, it responds to a button press. So, the pseudo-code for pressButton() will look like this:

```
pressButton()
        while (there are still doors left to process) do
                if (the door is open) then
                        door.close()
                else
                        door.open()
                end-if
        end-while
end-method.
```

And from here you can just write the code.

Change in the Right Direction

A key element of the last two sections is that object-oriented analysis and design are *all about change*. Analysis is about understanding behavior and *anticipation of change*, while design is about implementing the model and *managing change*. In a typical process methodology, analysis and design are iterative. As you begin to create a new program, you uncover new requirements; as the user begins to use your prototypes, they discover new ideas, things that don't work for them, and new features they hadn't mentioned previously. All these things require you to go back and re-think what you already know about the problem and what you have designed. In order to avoid what's known as *analysis paralysis*, you need to manage this neverending flow of new ideas and requirements.

Recognizing Change

There are a number of techniques that can be used to see and deal with change. The first we'll look at is recognizing what might change in your design. Let's look at the B⁴++ again. Right now, our B⁴++ will open and close the bird feeder's doors at sunrise and sunset in response to the light levels returned by the sensor. It will also open and close the feeding doors in response to a button push from the remote control. What might change here?

Well, the hardware might change. If the sensor changes, that might affect the Sensor class or it might cause your boss to re-think how the Sensor class should work. You might also get new hardware. This is just like the remote control addition we made above. And just like the remote control example, new hardware can result in the appearance of new use cases or changes to existing use cases. These changes can consequently ripple down through your class hierarchy.

The requirements might change. Most likely new requirements would crop up. A requirement change can lead to alternate paths through use cases. This implies that behavior will change requirements, which then leads to design changes. Design change happens because requirements change.

By thinking about what things can change in your program and design, you can begin to anticipate change. *Anticipating change* can lead you to be careful about encapsulation, inheritance, dependencies of one class on another, and so on.

Songbirds Forever

While we're talking about change, let's look at B^4++ again. It's several weeks now since Alice and Bob received delivery of their new and improved B^4++ with remote control. Alice loves it. She can watch the birds out her kitchen window, and when the grackles swoop in she just hits the remote control button and the doors shut. The grackles leave disappointed, she hits the button again, and the doors open. The new version works like a charm and does everything they had asked for.

There's just one little thing . . .

Alice has discovered that sometimes she has to run errands, or go to the bathroom, or watch her favorite nature show on the Discovery Channel. When she does this, she can't close the door with the remote, and the grackles can come and feed to their hearts' content, chasing away all the songbirds.

So, Alice would like yet another small, insignificant change to the B^4++, one that's hardly worth mentioning, really. She wants the B^4++ to detect the pesky birds and close the doors automatically. How to do this?

A New Requirement

The new requirement is that "The B^4++ must be able to detect the unwanted birds and close the doors automatically." Is this a complete requirement? It doesn't seem to be because it begs the obvious question: when do the doors open again? It seems we have at least a couple of things to decide:

1. How does the bird feeder detect the birds?

2. How do we distinguish between the unwanted birds and the songbirds?

3. When does the bird feeder open the doors again after they've been closed?

Luckily for us, our sensor supplier, SensorsRUs, has just come out with a programmable audio sensor that will let us identify birdsong. If we integrate that hardware into the B^4++, that takes care of item #1 above. It also turns out that the pesky birds have way different songs from the songbirds we want to attract, so that the audio sensor can be programmed via firmware to distinguish between the different bird species. That takes care of issue #2. What about issue #3—getting the closed doors open again?

It seems as if there are two ways you can get the B^4++ to open the doors again. We can have a timer that keeps the doors shut for a specific amount of time and then opens them again. This has the advantage of simplicity, but it's also a pretty simplistic bit of programming. Simplistic in the sense that the timer program just implements a countdown timer with no information about the *context* in which it operates. It could easily open the door while there are still a bunch of unwanted birds around. Another way we could implement the bird identifier is to have it only open the door when it hears one of our songbirds. If you reason that the songbirds won't be around if the pesky birds are still there, then the only time you'll hear songbirds singing is if there are no pesky birds around. If that's the case, then it's safe to open the feeding doors.

Let's do a use case. Because opening and closing the feeding doors with the song identifier is a lot like using the remote control, let's start with the RemoteControl use case and add to it:

1. Alice hears or sees birds at the bird feeder.

   1.1 The songbird identifier hears birdsong.

2. Alice determines that they are *not* songbirds.

   2.1 The songbird identifier recognizes the song as from an unwanted bird.

3. Alice presses the remote control button.

   3.1 The songbird identifier sends a message to the feeding doors to close.

4. The feeding doors close.

5. The birds give up and fly away.

   5.1 The songbird identifier hears birdsong.

   5.2 The songbird identifier recognizes the song as from a songbird.

6. Alice presses the remote control button.

   6.1 The songbird identifier sends a message to the feeding doors to open.

7. The feeding doors open again.

What we've created here is an *alternate path* in the use case. This use case looks pretty awkward now, because the sub-cases look like they flow from the upper cases when, in fact, one or the other of them should be done. We can rewrite the use case to look like Table 9-1.

Table 9-1. The Song Identifier Use Case and Its Alternate

Main Path	Alternate Path
1. Alice hears or sees birds at the bird feeder.	1.1 The songbird identifier hears birdsong.
2. Alice determines that they are *not* songbirds.	2.1 The songbird identifier recognizes the song as from an unwanted bird.
3. Alice presses the remote control button.	3.1 The songbird identifier sends a message to the feeding doors to close.
4. The feeding doors close.	
5. The birds give up and fly away.	5.1 The songbird identifier hears birdsong.
	5.2 The songbird identifier recognizes the song as from a songbird.
6. Alice presses the remote control button.	6.1 The songbird identifier sends a message to the feeding doors to open.
7. The feeding doors open again.	

These two paths aren't exactly the same. For instance, in the main path, Alice sees the birds give up and fly away before she presses the remote control button. In the alternate path, the bird song identifier must wait until it hears birdsong before it can consider opening the feeding doors again. So, we could easily make these two different use cases. It depends on *you*. Use cases are there to illustrate different scenarios in the use of the program, so you can represent them in any way you want. If you want to break this use case up into two different ones, feel free. Just be consistent. You're still managing change.

Separating Analysis and Design

As mentioned, it's difficult to separate analysis and design. The temptation for every programmer, particularly beginning programmers, is to start writing code *now*. That temptation bleeds over into doing analysis, design, and coding all at once and thinking about all three phases together. This is usually a *bad idea* unless your program is only about 10 lines long. It's nearly always better to abstract out requirements and architectural ideas from your low-level design and coding. Chapters 5 and 6 talked about this separation.

Separating object-oriented analysis and design is a particularly difficult task. In analysis, we're trying to understand the problem and the problem domain from an object-oriented point of view. That means we start thinking about objects and their interactions with each other *very* early in the process. Even our scenarios and use cases are littered with loaded object words. Analysis and design are nearly inseparable—when you're "doing analysis" you can't help but "think design" as well. What should you do when you really want to start thinking about design?

Your design must produce, at minimum, the classes in your system, their public interfaces, and their relationships to other classes, especially base or super classes. If your design methodology produces more than that, ask yourself if all the pieces produced by that methodology have value over the lifetime of the program. If they do not, maintaining them will cost you. Members of development teams tend not to maintain anything that doesn't contribute to their productivity; this is a fact of life that many design methods don't account for.

All software design problems can be simplified by introducing an extra level of conceptual indirection. This one idea is the basis of *abstraction*, the primary feature of object-oriented programming. That's why in UML, what we call *inheritance* in Java is called *generalization*. The idea is to identify common features in two or more classes and abstract those features out into a higher-level, more general class that the lower level classes then inherit from.

When designing, make your classes as atomic as possible; that is, give each class a single, clear purpose. This is the *Single Responsibility Principle* that is discussed more about in the next chapter on design principles.[7] If your classes or your system design grows too complicated, break complex classes into simpler ones. The most obvious indicator of this is sheer size: if a class is big, chances are it's doing too much and should be broken up.

You also need to look for and separate things that change from things that stay the same. That is, search for the elements in a program that you might want to change without forcing a redesign, and then encapsulate those elements in classes.

All these guidelines are key to managing the changes in your design. In the end, you want a clean, understandable design that's easy to maintain.

---

[7]Martin, 2009.

Shaping the Design

Your goal is to invent and arrange objects in a pleasing fashion. Your application will be divided into neighborhoods where clusters of objects work toward a common goal. Your design will be shaped by the number and quality of abstractions and by how well they complement one another. Composition, form, and focus are everything.

—Rebecca Wirfs-Brock and Alan McKean[8]

Identifying objects (or object classes) is a difficult part of object-oriented design. There is no "magic formula" for object identification. It relies on the skill, experience, and domain knowledge of system designers (that would be you). Object identification is an iterative process. You're not likely to get it right the first time.

You begin finding objects by looking for real-world analogues in your requirements. That gets you started, but it's only the first step. Other objects hide in the abstraction layers of your domain. Where to find these hidden objects? You can look to your own knowledge of the application domain. You can look for operations that crop up in your requirements and in your architectural concepts of the system. You can even look to your own past experience designing other systems.

Here are some steps to finding candidate objects in your system:

1. *Write a set of use cases*: These will describe how the application will work for a number of different scenarios. Remember, each use case must have a goal. Alternate paths through a use case may indicate new requirements that require a new use case.

2. *Identify the actors*: Identify the actors in each use case, the operations they need to perform, and the other things they need to use in performing their actions.

3. *Name and describe each candidate object*: Base the identification on tangible things in the application domain (like nouns). Use a behavioral approach and identify objects based on what participates in what behavior (use verbs).

Objects can manifest themselves in a number of ways. They can be

- External entities that produce or consume information

- Things that are part of the information domain (reports, displays, and the like)

- Occurrences or events that occur within the system

- Internal producers (objects that make something)

- Internal consumers (objects that consume what producers make)

- Places (remote systems, databases, and so on)

- Structures (windows, frames)

- People or characteristics of people (person, student, teacher, and so on)

- Things that are owned or used by other objects (like bank accounts or automobile parts).

- Things that are lists of other objects (like parts lists, any kind of collection, and so on)

---

[8]Wirfs-Brock, R. and A. McKean. *Object Design: Roles Responsibilities, and Collaborations*. (Boston, MA, Addison-Wesley, 2003).

4. *Organize the candidate objects into groups*: Each group represents a cluster of objects that work together to solve a common problem in your application. Each object will have several characteristics:

   - *Required information*: The object has information that must be remembered so the system can function.

   - *Needed services*: The object must provide services relating to the system goals.

   - *Common attributes*: The attributes defined for the object must be common to all instances of the object.

   - *Common operations*: The operations defined for the object must be common to all instances of the object.

5. *Make sure the groups you've created represent good abstractions for objects and work in the application*: Good abstractions will help make your application easier to re-work when you inevitably need to change some feature or relationship in the application.

Abstraction

Let's change tack here and talk about a different example. Alice and Bob have just moved to a new city and need to transfer their old Second City Bank and Trust bank accounts to First Galactic Bank. Alice and Bob are typically middle class and have several bank accounts they need to transfer: a checking account, a passbook savings account, and an investment account.

Nobody actually opens a generic "bank account." Instead they open different types of accounts, and each type has different characteristics. You can write checks on a checking account, but you can't write checks on a passbook savings account. You can earn interest on a savings account, but you normally don't earn interest on a checking account; you pay a monthly service fee instead. But all different types of bank accounts have some things in common. All of them use your personal information (name, social security number, address, city, state, ZIP), and they all allow you to deposit money and withdraw money.

So, when putting together a program that handles "bank accounts," you may realize that there will be common attributes and behaviors among several classes. Let's look at some classes for a bank account example.

Because we know that checking accounts, savings accounts, and investment accounts are all different, let's first create three different classes and see what we've got (see Figure 9-3).

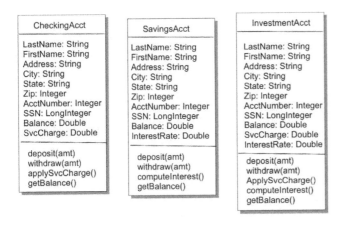

Figure 9-3. Bank accounts with a lot in common

Notice that all three classes have a lot in common. One of the things we always try to do, no matter what design or coding techniques we're using, is to avoid duplication of design and code. This is what abstraction is all about! If we abstract out all the common elements of these three classes, we can create a new (super) class BankAccount that incorporates all of them. The CheckingAcct, SavingsAcct, and InvestmentAcct classes can then inherit from BankAccount.

BankAccount is shown in Figure 9-4.

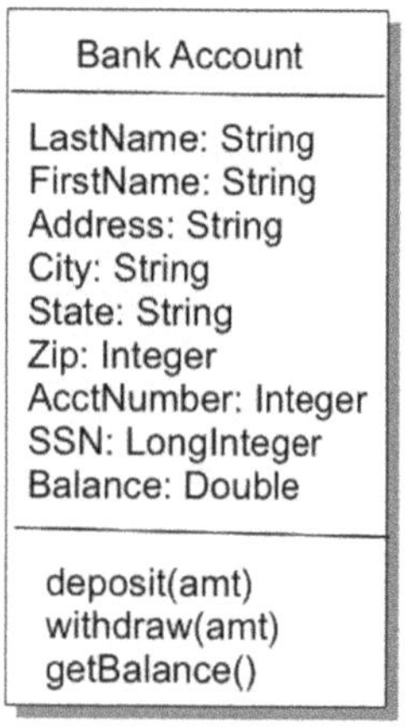

Figure 9-4. *A cleaner BankAccount class*

But wait! Is the BankAccount class one that we would want to instantiate? If you look, you'll see that each of the other classes is much more specific than the BankAccount class is. So, there isn't enough information in the BankAccount class for us to use. This means we'll always be inheriting from it, but never instantiating it. It's a perfect *abstract class*. (Note the little bit of UML in Figure 9-5—class diagrams of abstract classes put the class name in *italics*.)

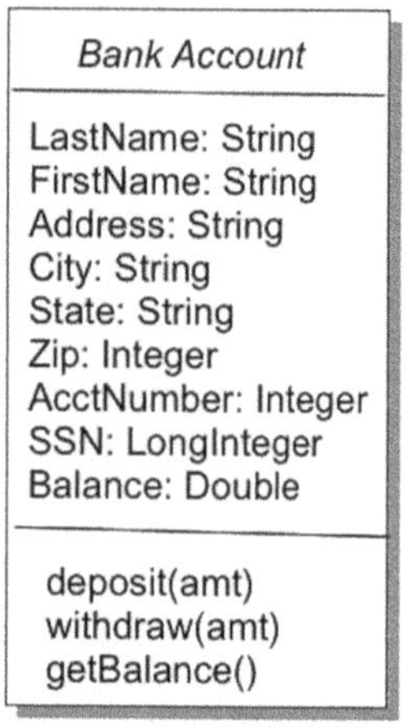

Figure 9-5. *BankAccount as an abstract class*

Abstract classes are templates for actual *concrete classes*. They encapsulate shared behavior and define the protocol for all subclasses. The abstract class defines behavior and sets a common state, and then concrete subclasses inherit and implement that behavior. You can't instantiate an abstract class; a new concrete class must be created that extends the abstract class. As a guideline, whenever you find common behavior in two or more places, you should look to abstract that behavior into a class and then reuse that behavior in the common concrete classes.

Here's what we end up with after abstracting out all the personal data and common behavior into the BankAccount abstract class. Notice one more little bit of UML in Figure 9-6: the new UML arrow types, open arrow ends. These open arrows indicate *inheritance*; so the CheckingAcct class inherits attributes and methods from the BankAccount abstract class. UML calls it *generalization* because the super class generalizes the subclasses. That's why the arrows point up to the super class.

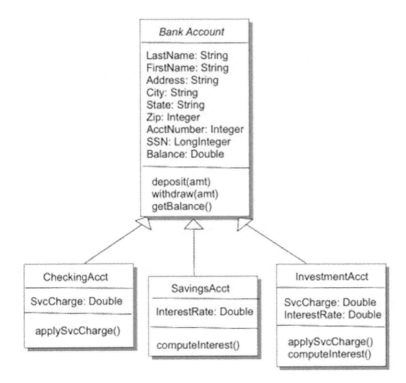

Figure 9-6. *The concrete account classes inherit from BankAccount*

Conclusion

In object-oriented analysis and design, it's best to keep your objectives in mind. In analysis, you're refining the feature list you've created and producing a model of what the customer wants. You want to end up with a description of what the program is supposed to do—its essential features. This creates a conceptual model of the problem domain and its solution. The model is made up of a number of things including user stories, scenarios, use cases, preliminary class diagrams, user interface storyboards, and possibly some class interface descriptions.

In design, you're taking that conceptual model and creating the classes that will end up being code. You want to end up with a description of how the program will implement the conceptual model and do what the customer wants. This is an object model of the solution. This model is made up of groups of related class diagrams, their associations, and descriptions of how they interact with each other. This includes the programming interface for each class. This design is an abstraction of the class details and code you'll create later. From here you should be able to get to code pretty quickly.

References

Beck, K. *Extreme Programming Explained: Embrace Change.* (Boston, MA: Addison-Wesley, 2000.)

Cockburn, A. (2000). *Writing Effective Use Cases.* (Boston, MA: Addison-Wesley, 2000.)

Fowler, M. *UML Distilled.* (Boston, MA: Addison-Wesley, 2000.)

McLaughlin, Brett D., et. al. *Head First Object-Oriented Analysis & Design.* (Sebastopol, CA: O'Reilly Media, Inc., 2007.)

Meyer, Bertrand. *Object-Oriented Software Construction.* (Upper Saddle River , NJ: Prentice Hall, 1988.)

Martin, Robert, "Single Responsibility Principle." `www.butunclebob.com/ArticleS.UncleBob.PrinciplesOfOod`. Retrieved on December 10, 2009.

Wirfs-Brock, R. and A. McKean. *Object Design: Roles Responsibilities, and Collaborations.* (Boston, MA, Addison-Wesley, 2003.)

CHAPTER 10

Object-Oriented Design Principles

Devotion to the facts will always give the pleasures of recognition; adherence to the rules of design, the pleasures of order and certainty.

—Kenneth Clark

How can I qualify my faith in the inviolability of the design principles? Their virtue is demonstrated. They work.

—Edgar Whitney

Now that we've spent some time looking at object-oriented analysis and design, let's recapitulate some of what we've already seen and add some more prose. First, let's talk about some *common design characteristics*.

First, designs have a purpose. They describe how something will work in a context, using the requirements (lists of features, user stories, and use cases) to define the context.

Second, designs must have enough information in them that someone can implement them. You need enough details in the design so that someone can come after you and implement the program correctly.

Next, there are different styles of design, just like there are different types of house architectures. The type of design you want depends on what it is you're being required to build. It depends on the context (see, we're back to context): if you're an architect, you'll design a different kind of house at the seashore than you will in the mountains.

Finally, designs can be expressed at different levels of detail. When building a house, the framing carpenter needs one level of detail, the electrician and plumber another, and the finish carpenter yet another.

There are a number of rules of thumb about object-oriented design that have evolved over the last few decades. These *design principles* act as guidelines for you the designer to abide by so that your design ends up being a good one: easy to implement, easy to maintain, and that does just what your customer wants. We've looked at several of them already in previous chapters, and here I've pulled out nine fundamental design principles of object-oriented design that are likely to be the most useful to you as you become that designer extraordinaire. I'll list them in the next section and then explain them and give examples in the rest of the chapter.

© John F. Dooley 2017

J. F. Dooley, *Software Development, Design and Coding*, https://doi.org/10.1007/978-1-4842-3153-1_10

List of Fundamental Object-Oriented Design Principles

Here are the nine fundamental principles:

1. *Encapsulate* things in your design that are *likely to change*.

2. *Code to an interface* rather than to an implementation.

3. The *Open-Closed Principle* (OCP): Classes should be open for extension and closed for modification.

4. The *Don't Repeat Yourself Principle* (DRY): Avoid duplicate code. Whenever you find common behavior in two or more places, look to abstract that behavior into a class and then reuse that behavior in the common concrete classes. Satisfy one requirement in one place in your code.

5. The *Single Responsibility Principle* (SRP): Every object in your system should have a single responsibility, and all the object's services should be focused on carrying out that responsibility. Another way of saying this is that a cohesive class does one thing well and doesn't try to do anything else. This implies that higher cohesion is better. It also means that each class in your program should have only one reason to change.

6. The *Liskov Substitution Principle* (LSP): Subtypes must be substitutable for their base types. (In other words, inheritance should be well designed and well behaved.)

7. The *Dependency Inversion Principle* (DIP): Don't depend on concrete classes; depend on abstractions.

8. The *Interface Segregation Principle* (ISP): Clients shouldn't have to depend on interfaces they don't use.

9. The *Principle of Least Knowledge* (PLK) (also known as the *Law of Demeter*): Talk only to your immediate friends. This also relates to the idea of *loose coupling*. Objects that interact should be loosely coupled with well-defined interfaces.

As you probably notice, there's some overlap here, and one or more of the design principles may depend on others. That's okay. It's the fundamentals that count. Let's go through these one at a time.

Encapsulate Things in Your Design That Are Likely to Change

This first principle means to protect your classes from unnecessary change by separating the features and methods of a class that remain relatively constant throughout the program from those that will change. By separating the two types of features, we isolate the parts that will change a lot into a separate class (or classes) that we can depend on changing, and we increase our flexibility and ease of change. We also leave the stable parts of our design alone, so that we just need to implement them once and test them once. (Well, we hope.) This protects the stable parts of the design from any unnecessary changes.

Let's create a very simple class called Violinist. Figure 10-1 is a class diagram for the Violinist class.

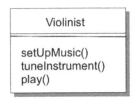

Figure 10-1. *A Violinist*

Notice that the setUpMusic() and tuneInstrument() methods are pretty stable. But what about the play() method? It turns out that there are several different types of playing styles for violins: classical, bluegrass, and Celtic, just to name three. That means the play() method will vary, depending on the playing style. Because we have a behavior that will change depending on the playing style, maybe we should abstract that behavior out and encapsulate it in another class? If we do that, we get something like Figure 10-2.

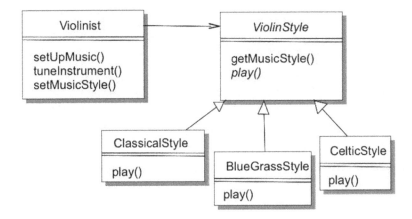

Figure 10-2. *Violinist and playing styles*

Notice that we're using association between the Violinist class and the ViolinStyle abstract class. This allows Violinist to use the concrete classes that inherit the abstract method from the abstract ViolinStyle class. We've abstracted out and encapsulated the play() method—which will vary—in a separate class so that we can isolate any changes we want to make to the playing style from the other stable behaviors in Violinist.

Code to an Interface Rather Than to an Implementation

The normal response to this design principle is: "Huh? What does that mean?" Well, here's the idea. This principle, like many of the principles in this chapter, has to do with inheritance and how you use it in your program. Say you have a program that will model different types of geometric shapes in two dimensions. We'll have a class Point that will represent a single point in 2D, and we'll have an interface named Shape that will abstract out a couple of things that all shapes have in common: areas and perimeters. (Okay, circles and ellipses call it *circumference*—bear with me.) Figure 10-3 shows what we've got.

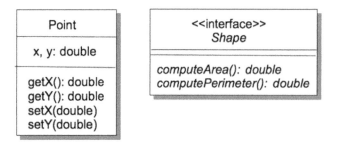

Figure 10-3. *A simple* Point *class and the common* Shape *interface*

If we want to create concrete classes of some different shapes, we'll *implement* the Shape interface. This means the concrete classes must implement each of the abstract methods in the Shape interface. See Figure 10-4.

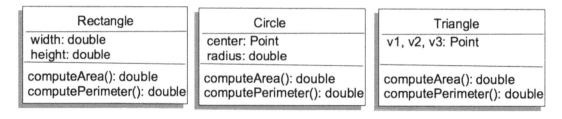

Figure 10-4. Rectangle, Circle, *and* Triangle *all implement* Shape

Now we've got a number of classes that represent different geometric shapes. How do we use them? Say we're writing an application that will manipulate a geometric shape. We can do this in two different ways. First, we can write a separate application for each geometric shape, as shown in Figure 10-5.

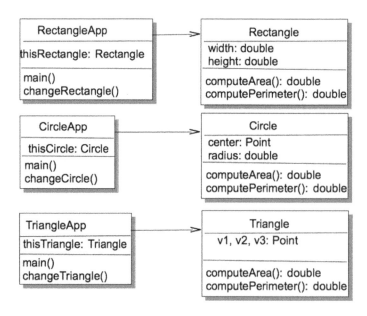

Figure 10-5. *Using the geometric objects*

What's wrong with these apps? Well, we've got three different applications doing the same thing. If we want to add another shape—say, a rhombus—we'd have to write two new classes, the Rhombus class, which implements the Shape interface, and a new RhombusApp class. Yuk! This is inefficient. We've coded to the implementation of the geometric shape rather than coding to the interface itself.

How do we fix this? The thing to realize is that the interface is the top of a class hierarchy of all the classes that implement the interface. As such, it's a class type, and we can use it to help us implement polymorphism in our program. In this case, because we have some number of geometric shapes that implement the Shape interface, we can create an array of Shapes that we can fill up with different types of shapes and then iterate through. In Java, we'll use the List collection type to hold our shapes:

```java
import java.util.*;

/**
 * ShapeTest - test the Shape interface implementations.
 *
 * @author fred
 * @version 1.0
 */
public class ShapeTest {

    public static void main(String [] args) {
        List<Shape> figures = new ArrayList<Shape>();

        figures.add(new Rectangle(10, 20));
        figures.add(new Circle(10));
        Point p1 = new Point(0.0, 0.0);
        Point p2 = new Point(5.0, 1.0);
        Point p3 = new Point(2.0, 8.0);
        figures.add(new Triangle(p1, p2, p3));

        Iterator<Shape> iter = figures.iterator();

        while (iter.hasNext()) {
            Shape nxt =  iter.next();
            System.out.printf("area = %8.4f perimeter = %8.4f\n",
                nxt.computeArea(), nxt.computePerimeter());
        }
    }
}
```

When you code to the interface, your program becomes easier to extend and modify. Your program will work with all the interface's sub-classes seamlessly.

As an aside, the principles just given let you know that you should be constantly reviewing your design. Changing your design will force your code to change because of the need to *refactor*. Your design is iterative. Pride kills good design; don't be afraid to revisit your design decisions.

The Open-Closed Principle

The Open-Closed Principle (OCP) says that classes should be open for extension and closed for modification.[1]

What this means is to find the behavior in a class that doesn't vary and abstract that behavior up into a super/base class. That locks the base code away from modification, but all sub-classes will inherit that behavior. You are encapsulating the behavior that varies in the sub-classes (those classes that extend the base class) and closing the base class from modification. The bottom line here is that in your well-designed code, you add new features not by modifying existing code (it's closed for modification), but by adding new code (it's open for extension).

The BankAccount class example that we did in the previous chapter is a classic example of the Open-Closed Principle at work. In that example, we abstracted all the personal information into the abstract BankAccount class along with any methods to access and modify the data, closed it from modification, and then extended that class into the different types of bank accounts. In this situation, it's very easy to add new types of bank accounts just by extending the BankAccount class again. We avoid duplication of code and we preserve the integrity of the BankAccount properties. See Figure 10-6.

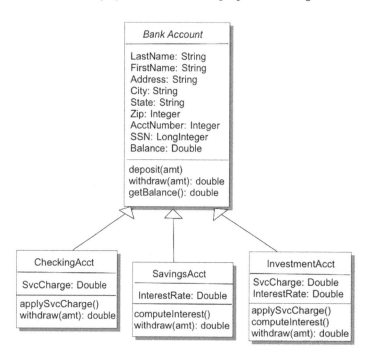

Figure 10-6. *The classic BankAccount example for OCP*

For example, in the BankAccount class, we define the withdraw() method that allows a customer to withdraw funds from an account. But the way in which withdrawals occur can differ in each of the extended account classes. While the withdraw() method is closed for modification in the BankAccount class, it can be overridden in the sub-classes to implement the specific rules for that type of account and thus extend the power of the method. It's closed for modification but open for extension.

---

[1]Larman, C. "Protected Variation: The Importance of Being Closed." *IEEE Software* **18**(3): 89-91 (2001).

The Open-Closed Principle doesn't have to be limited to inheritance either. If you have several private methods in a class, those methods are closed for modification, but if you then create one or more public methods that use the private methods, you've opened up the possibility of extending those private methods by adding functionality in the public methods.

The Don't Repeat Yourself Principle

This principle says to avoid duplicate code by abstracting out things that are common and placing those things in a single location.[2]

Don't repeat yourself (DRY) is the motherhood and apple pie design principle. It's been handed down ever since developers started thinking about better ways to write programs. Go back and look at Chapters 6 and 7 for discussion of this. With DRY, you have each piece of information and each behavior in a single place in the design. Ideally you have one requirement in one place. This means you should create your design so that there is one logical place where a requirement is implemented. Then if you have to change the requirement you have only one place to look to make the change. You also remove duplicate code and replace it with method calls. If you're duplicating code, you're duplicating behavior.

DRY doesn't have to apply just to your code either. It's always a good idea to comb your feature list and requirements for duplications. Rewriting requirements to avoid duplicating features in the code will make your code much easier to maintain.

Consider the final version of the B⁴++ bird feeder discussed in Chapter 9. The last thing we worked on was adding a song identifier to the feeder so that the feeding doors would open and close automatically. But let's look at the two use cases we ended up with (see Table 10-1).

Table 10-1. *The Song Identifier Use Case and Its Alternate*

Main Path	Alternate Path
1. Alice hears or sees birds at the bird feeder.	1.1 The songbird identifier hears birdsong.
2. Alice determines that they are *not* songbirds.	2.1 The songbird identifier recognizes the song as from an unwanted bird.
3. Alice presses the remote control button.	3.1 The songbird identifier sends a message to the feeding doors to close.
4. The feeding doors close.	
5. The birds give up and fly away.	5.1 The songbird identifier hears birdsong.
	5.2 The songbird identifier recognizes the song as from a songbird.
6. Alice presses the remote control button.	6.1 The songbird identifier sends a message to the feeding doors to open.
7. The feeding doors open again.	

Notice that we're opening and closing the feeding doors in two different places—via the remote control and via the song identifier. But if you think about it, regardless of where we request the doors to be open or closed, they always open and close in the same way. So, this is a classic opportunity to abstract out the open and close door behavior and put them in a single place—say, the FeedingDoor class. DRY at work!

---

[2]Hunt, A. and D. Thomas. *The Pragmatic Programmer: From Journeyman to Master*. (Boston, MA: Addison-Wesley, 2000.)

The Single Responsibility Principle

This principle says that a class should have one, and only one, reason to change.[3]

Here's an example of the overlap between these design principles that was mentioned above: SRP, the first principle about encapsulation, and DRY all say similar but slightly different things. *Encapsulation* is about abstracting behavior and putting things in your design that are likely to change in the same place. DRY is about avoiding duplicating code by putting identical behaviors in the same place. SRP is about designing your classes so that each does just one thing, and does it very well.

Every object should have a single responsibility, and all the object's services are targeted towards carrying out that responsibility. *Each class should have only one reason to change.* Put simply, this means beware of having your class try to do too many things.

As an example, let's say we're writing the embedded code for a mobile phone. After months (really) of discussions with the marketing folks, our first cut at a MobilePhone class looks like Figure 10-7.

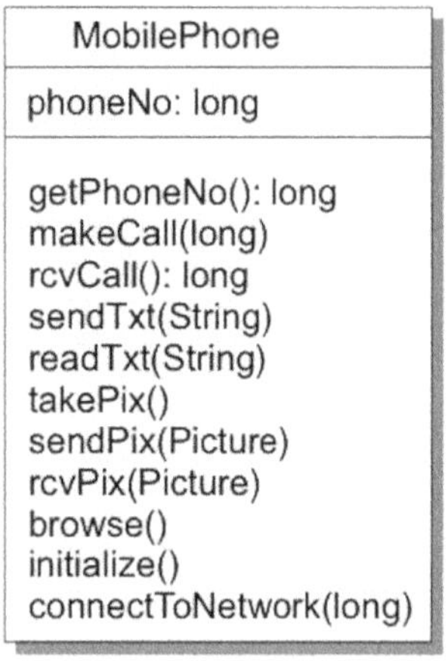

```
┌─────────────────────────────┐
│  MobilePhone                │
├─────────────────────────────┤
│  phoneNo: long              │
├─────────────────────────────┤
│  getPhoneNo(): long         │
│  makeCall(long)             │
│  rcvCall(): long            │
│  sendTxt(String)            │
│  readTxt(String)            │
│  takePix()                  │
│  sendPix(Picture)           │
│  rcvPix(Picture)            │
│  browse()                   │
│  initialize()               │
│  connectToNetwork(long)     │
└─────────────────────────────┘
```

Figure 10-7. A very busy MobilePhone *class*

This class seems to incorporate a lot of what we would want a mobile phone to do, but it violates the SRP in several different ways. This class is not trying to do a single thing—it's trying to do way too many things: make and receive phone calls, create, send, and receive text messages, create, send, and receive pictures, browse the Internet. The class doesn't have a *single responsibility*. It has many.

But we don't want a single class to be impacted by these completely different forces. We don't want to modify the MobilePhone class every time the picture format is changed, or every time we want to add a new picture-editing feature, or every time the browser changes. Rather, we want to separate these functions out into different classes so that they can change independently of each other. So how do we recognize the things that should move out of this class, and how do we recognize the things that should stay? Have a look at Figure 10-8.

---

[3]McLaughlin, Brett D., et. al., *Head First Object-Oriented Analysis & Design*. (Sebastopol, CA: O'Reilly Media, Inc., 2007.)

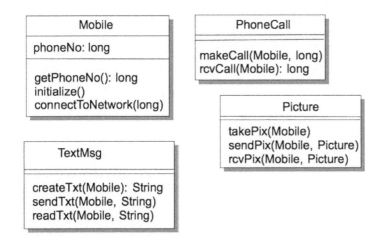

Figure 10-8. *Mobile phone classes each with a single responsibility*

In this example, we ask the question "What does the mobile phone do (to itself)?" as opposed to "What services are offered by the mobile phone?" By asking questions like this, we can start to separate out the responsibilities of the objects in the design. In this case, we can see that the phone itself can get its own phone number, initialize itself, and connect itself to the mobile phone network. The services offered, on the other hand, are really independent of the actual mobile phone, and so can be separated out into PhoneCall, TextMsg, and Picture classes. So we divide up the initial one class into four separate classes, each with a single responsibility. This way we can change any of the four classes without affecting the others. We then add a controller class that runs the whole phone. That way we can add new features as well. We've simplified the design (although we've got more classes), and made it easier to extend and modify. Is that a great principle, or what?

The Liskov Substitution Principle

The Liskov Substitution Principle (LSP), named after Turing Award–winner Dr. Barbara Liskov of MIT, tells us that all sub-classes must be substitutable for their base class.[4] This principle says that inheritance should be well designed and well behaved. In any case, a user should be able to instantiate an object as a sub-class and use all the base class functionality invisibly.

To illustrate the LSP, most books give an example that violates it and say, "Don't do that," which is just what we'll do. One of the best and canonical examples of violating the LSP is the Rectangle/Square example. The example is all over the Internet. Robert Martin gives a great variation on this example in his book *Agile Software Development, Principles, Patterns, and Practices,*[5] and we'll follow his version of the example. Here it is in Java.

---

[4]Wintour, Damien. "The Liskov Substitution Principle." 1988. Downloaded on September 14, 2010 from www.necessaryandsufficient.net/2008/09/design-guidelines-part3-the-liskov-substitution-principle/.
[5]Martin, R. C. *Agile Software Development: Principles, Patterns, and Practices*. (Upper Saddle River, NJ: Prentice Hall, 2003.)

Say you have a class Rectangle that represents the geometric shape of a rectangle:

```
/**
 * class Rectangle
 */
public class Rectangle
{
    private double width;
    private double height;

    /**
     * Constructor for objects of class Rectangle
     */
    public Rectangle(double width, double height) {
        this.width = width;
        this.height = height;
    }

    public void setWidth(double width) {
        this.width = width;
    }

    public void setHeight(double height) {
        this.height = height;
    }

    public double getHeight() {
        return this.height;
    }

    public double getWidth() {
        return this.width;
    }
}
```

And, of course, one of your users wants to have the ability to manipulate squares as well as rectangles. You already know that squares are just a special case of rectangles. In other words, a Square *is a* Rectangle. This problem therefore seems to require using inheritance. So, you create a Square class that inherits from Rectangle:

```
/**
 * class Square
 */
public class Square extends Rectangle
{
    /**
     * Constructor for objects of class Square
     */
    public Square(double side) {
        super(side, side);
    }
```

```
    public void setSide(double side) {
        super.setWidth(side);
        super.setHeight(side);
    }

    public double getSide() {
        return super.getWidth();
    }
}
```

This seems to be okay. Notice that because the width and height of a Square are the same, we couldn't run the risk of changing them individually, so setSide() uses setWidth() and setHeight() to set both for the sides of a Square. No big deal, right?

Well, if we have a function like

```
void myFunc(Rectangle r, double newWidth) {
        r.setWidth(newWidth);
}
```

and we pass myFunc() a Rectangle object, it works just fine, changing the width of the Rectangle. But what if we pass myFunc() a Square object? It turns out that in Java the same thing happens as before, but that's *wrong*. It violates the integrity of the Square object by just changing its width without changing its height as well. So we've violated the LSP here, and the Square can't substitute for a Rectangle without changing the behavior of the Square. The LSP says that the sub-class (Square) should be able to substitute for the super class (Rectangle), but it doesn't in this case.

We can get around this. We can override the Rectangle class' setWidth() and setHeight() methods in Square like this:

```
public void setWidth(double w) {
    super.setWidth(w);
    super.setHeight(w);
}

public void setHeight(double h) {
    super.setWidth(h);
    super.setHeight(h);
}
```

These will both work and we'll get the right answers and preserve the invariants of the Square object, but what's the point in that? If we have to override a bunch of methods we've inherited, then what's the point of using inheritance to begin with? That's what the LSP is all about: getting the *behavior* of derived classes right and thus getting inheritance right. If we think of the base class as being a contract that we adhere to (remember the Open-Closed Principle?), then the LSP is saying that you must adhere to the contract even for derived classes. Oh, by the way, this works in Java because Java public methods are all *virtual methods* and are thus able to be overridden. If we had defined setWidth() and setHeight() in Rectangle with a final keyword or if they had been private, then we couldn't have overridden them. In fact, private versions of those methods would not have been inherited to begin with.

In this example, although a square is mathematically a specialized type of rectangle and one where the invariants related to rectangles still hold, that mathematical definition just doesn't work in Java. In this case, you don't want to have Square be a sub-class of Rectangle; inheritance doesn't work for you in this case because you think about rectangles having two different kinds of sides—length and width—and squares having only one kind of side. So, if a Square class inherits from a Rectangle class, the image of what a Square is versus what a Rectangle is gets in the way of the code. Inheritance is just the wrong thing to use here.

131

How can you tell when you're likely to be violating the Liskov Substitution Principle? Indications that you're violating LSP include the following:

- A sub-class doesn't keep all the external observable behavior of its super class.

- A sub-class modifies, rather than extends, the external observable behavior of its super class.

- A sub-class throws exceptions in an effort to hide certain behavior defined in its super class.

- A sub-class that overrides a virtual method defined in its super class using an empty implementation in order to hide certain behavior defined in its super class.

- Method overriding in derived classes is the biggest cause of LSP violations.[6]

Sometimes inheritance just isn't the right thing to do. Luckily, you've got options. It turns out there are other ways to share the behavior and attributes of other classes. The three most common are *delegation*, *composition*, and *aggregation*.

Delegation is what every manager should do: give away work and let someone else do it. If you want to use the behaviors in another class but you don't want to change that behavior, consider using delegation instead of inheritance. Delegation says to give responsibility for the behavior to another class; this creates an association between the classes. *Association* in this sense means that the classes are related to each other, usually through an attribute or a set of related methods. Delegation has a great side benefit: it shields your objects from any implementation changes in other objects in your program; you're not using inheritance, so encapsulation protects you.[7] Let's show a bit of how delegation works with an example.

When last we left Alice and Bob and their B⁴++, Alice was tired of using the remote to open and close the feeding doors to keep away the non-song birds. So, they'd requested yet another new feature: an automatic song identifier. With the song identifier, the B⁴++ itself would recognize songbird songs and open the doors, and keep them closed for all other birds. We can think of this in a couple of ways.

The BirdFeeder class, because of the Single Responsibility Principle, shouldn't do the identification of bird songs, but it should know what songs are allowed. We'll need a new class, SongIdentifier, that will do the song identification. We'll also need a Song object that contains a birdsong. Figure 10-9 shows what we've got so far.

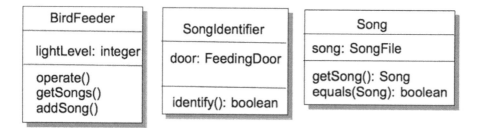

Figure 10-9. *A first cut at the song identifier feature*

---

[6]Wintour, 1998.
[7]Mclaughlin, 2007.

The BirdFeeder knows about birdsong and keeps a list of the allowed songs for the feeder. The SongIdentifier has the single job of identifying a given song. There are two ways that this can happen. The first is that the SongIdentifier class can do the work itself in the identify() method. That would mean that SongIdentifier would need an equals() method in order to do the comparison between two songs (the allowed song from the door, and the song that the new B⁴++ hardware just sent to us). The second way of identifying songs is for the Song class to do it itself, using its own equals() method. Which should we choose?

Well, if we do all the identification in the SongIdentifier class, that means that any time anything changes in a Song, we'll have to change both the Song class *and* the SongIdentifier class. This doesn't sound optimal. But! If we delegate the song comparison work to the Song class, then the SongIdentifier's identify() method could just take a Song as an input parameter and call that method, and we've isolated any Song changes to just the Song class. Figure 10-10 shows the revised class diagrams.

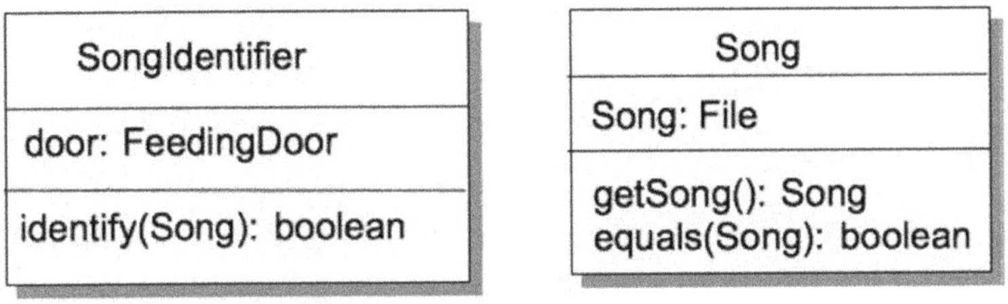

Figure 10-10. Simplifying SongIdentifier and Song

And our corresponding code might look like this:

```java
public class SongIdentifier {
    private BirdFeeder feeder;
    private FeedingDoor door;

    public SongIdentifier(BirdFeeder feeder) {
        this.door = feeder.getDoor();
    }

    public void identify(Song song) {
        List<Song> songs = feeder.getSongs();
        Iterator<Song> song_iter = songs.iterator();

        while (song_iter.hasNext()) {
            Song nxtSong = song_iter.next();
            if (nxtSong.equals(song)) {
                door.open();
                return;
            }
        }
        door.close();
    }
}

public class Song {
    private File song;
```

```
    public Song(File song) {
        this.song = song;
    }

    public File getSong() {
        return this.song;
    }

    public boolean equals(Object newSong) {
        if (newSong instanceof Song) {
            Song newSong2 = (Song) newSong;
            if (this.song.equals(newSong2.song)) {
                return true;
            }
        }
        return false;
    }
}
```

In this implementation, if we change anything with regards to a Song, then the only changes we make will be in the Song class, and SongIdentifier is insulated from those changes. The *behavior* of the Song class doesn't change, although how it *implements* that behavior might. SongIdentifier doesn't care how the behavior is implemented as long as it's always the same behavior. BirdFeeder has delegated the work of handling birdsong to the SongIdentifier class, and SongIdentifier has delegated the work of comparing songs to the Song class, all without using inheritance.

Delegation allows you to give away the responsibility for a behavior to another class and not have to worry about changing the behavior in your class. You can count on the behavior in the delegated class not changing. But sometimes you will want to use an entire set of behaviors simultaneously, and delegation doesn't work for that. Instead, if you want to have your program use that set of behaviors, you need to use composition. We use *composition* to assemble behaviors from other classes.

Say you're putting together a space-based role playing game (RPG) called *Space Rangers*. One of the things you'll model in your game is the spaceships themselves. Spaceships will have lots of different characteristics. For example, there are different types of ships: shuttles, traders, fighters, freighters, capital ships, and so on. Each ship will also have different characteristics, weapons, shields, cargo capacity, number of crew, and so on. But what will all the ships have in common?

Well, if you want to create a generic Ship class, it will be hard to gather all these things together in a single Ship super class so you can create sub-classes for things like Shuttle, Fighter, Freighter, and the like. They're all just too different. This seems to imply that inheritance isn't the way to go here. So back to our question: what do all the ships have in common?

We can say that all the Ships in *Space Rangers* have just two things in common: a ship type and a set of properties that relate to that ship type. This gets us to our first class diagram, shown in Figure 10-11.

```
┌──────────────────────────────┐
│         SpaceShip            │
├──────────────────────────────┤
│ shipType: String             │
│ properties: Map              │
├──────────────────────────────┤
│ getType(): String            │
│ setType(String)              │
│ getProperty(String): Object  │
│ setProperty(String, Object)  │
└──────────────────────────────┘
```

Figure 10-11. *What do all spaceships have in common?*

This allows us to store the spaceship type and a map of the various properties for an instance of a ship. It means we can then develop the properties independently from the ships, and then different ships can share similar properties. For example, all ships can have weapons, but they can have different ones with different characteristics. This leads us to develop a weapons interface that we can then use to implement particular classes. We get to use these weapons in our SpaceShip by using composition. Remember that composition allows us to use an entire family of behaviors that we can be guaranteed won't change. See Figure 10-12.

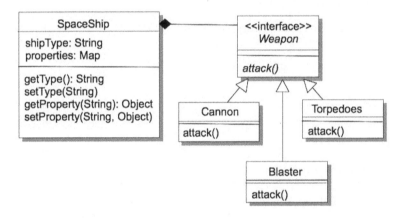

Figure 10-12. *Using composition to allow the SpaceShip to use Weapons*

Remember that the open triangle in the UML diagram means inheritance (or in the case of an interface, it means *implements*). The closed diamond in UML means composition. So, in this design we can add several weapons to our properties map, and each weapon can have different characteristics, but all of them exhibit the same behavior.

Note that in composition the component objects (Weapons) become part of a larger object (SpaceShip), and when the larger object goes away (you get blown up), so do the components. The object that's composed of other behaviors owns those behaviors. When that object is destroyed, so are all its behaviors. The behaviors in a composition don't exist outside of the composition itself. When your SpaceShip is blown up, so are all your Weapons.

Of course, sometimes you want to put together a set of objects and behaviors in such a way that when one of them is removed, the others continue in existence. That's what aggregation is all about. If the behaviors need to persist, then you must aggregate. *Aggregation* is when one class is used as a part of another class, but still exists outside of that other class. If the object does make sense existing on its own, then use aggregation—otherwise use composition. For example, a library is an example of aggregation. Each book makes sense on its own, but the aggregation of them all is a library. The key is to show an instance where it makes sense to use a component outside a composition, implying that it should have a separate existence.

In *Space Rangers,* we can have Pilot objects in addition to SpaceShip objects. A Pilot can also carry weapons. Different ones, of course—Pilots probably don't carry Cannon objects with them. Say a Pilot is carrying around a HandBlaster, so in object-oriented speak he's using the behaviors of the HandBlaster. If a mad SpaceCow accidentally crushes the Pilot, is the weapon destroyed along with the Pilot? Probably not, hence the need for a mechanism where the HandBlaster can be used by a Pilot but has an existence outside of the Pilot class. Ta-da! Aggregation!

We've seen three different mechanisms that allow objects to use the behaviors of other objects, none of which requires inheritance. As it's said in Object-Oriented Analysis and Design, "If you favor delegation, composition, and aggregation over inheritance, your software will usually be more flexible and easier to maintain, extend, and reuse.[8] "

The Dependency Inversion Principle

Robert C. Martin introduced the Dependency Inversion Principle (DIP) in his C++ Report and later in his classic book *Agile Software Development.*[9] In his book, Martin defined the DIP as follows:

1. High-level modules should not depend on low-level modules. Both should depend on abstraction.

2. Abstractions should not depend on details. Details should depend on abstractions.

The simple version of this is: *don't depend on concrete classes, depend on abstractions.* Martin's contention is that object-oriented design is the inverse of traditional structured design. In structured design, as we saw in Chapter 7, one either works from the top down, pushing details and design decisions as low in the hierarchy of software layers as possible, or one works from the bottom up, designing low-level details first and later putting together a set of low-level functions into a single higher-level abstraction. In both cases, the higher-level software depends on decisions made at the lower levels, including interface and behavioral decisions.

Martin contends that for object-oriented design, this is backward. The Dependency Inversion Principle implies that higher-level (more abstract) design levels should create an interface that lower (more concrete) levels should code to. This will mean that as long as the lower level—concrete—classes *code to the interface* of the upper level abstraction, the upper level classes are safe. As Martin puts it, "The modules that contain the high-level business rules should take precedence over, and be independent of, the modules that contain the implementation details. High-level modules simply should not depend on low-level modules in any way."

Here's a simple example. Traditionally, in structured design we write many programs with this general format:

1. Get input data from somewhere.

2. Process the data.

3. Write the data to somewhere else.

[8]McLaughlin, 2007.
[9]Martin, 2003.

In this example, the Processor uses the Collector to get data. It then packages the data and uses the Writer to write the data to, say, a database. If we draw this out, we get something that looks like Figure 10-13.

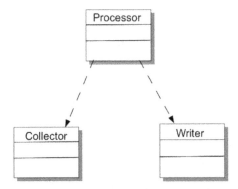

Figure 10-13. *A traditional input-process-output model*

One problem with this implementation is that the Processor must create and use the Writer whose interface and parameter types it must know in order to write correctly. This means that the Processor must be written to a concrete implementation of a Writer and so must be rewritten if we want to change what kind of Writer we want. Say the first implementation writes to a File; if we then want to write to a printer or a database, we need to change Processor every time. That's not very reusable. The Dependency Inversion Principle says that the Processor should be coded to an interface (we abstract Writer), and then the interface is implemented in separate concrete classes for each type of Writer destination. The resulting design looks like Figure 10-14.

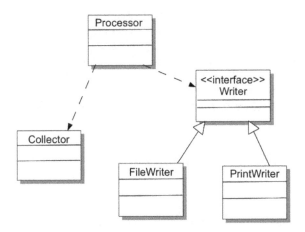

Figure 10-14. *Using an interface to allow different writer implementations*

In this way, different writers can be added, and as long as they adhere to the interface, Processor never needs to change. Note that the DIP is closely related to Principle #2: Code to an Interface.

The Interface Segregation Principle

This principle tells us that clients shouldn't have to depend on interfaces they don't use. In particular, they shouldn't have to depend on *methods* they don't use.[10]

We've talked a lot about interfaces in this chapter. Coding to interfaces, using interfaces to abstract out common details, and so on. We use interfaces to make our code more flexible and maintainable. So overall, interfaces are a great thing, right? Well, there are a few things you must beware of.

One of the greatest temptations with respect to interfaces is to make them bigger. If an interface is good, then a bigger interface must be better, right? After all, you can then use the interface in many more objects and *the user just has to not implement certain methods that they don't need*. However, by doing that you are ruining the *cohesion* of your interface. By "generalizing" an interface too much, you're moving away from that single lightning bolt of a set of methods that are all closely related to each other to a jumble of methods that say hello to each other in passing. Remember: *cohesion is good*. Your applications should be cohesive, and the classes and interfaces they depend on should also be cohesive.

You make your interfaces less cohesive and begin to violate the Interface Segregation Principle when you start adding new methods to your interface because one of the sub-classes that implements the interface needs it—*and others do not*. So what's the answer here? How do we keep our interfaces cohesive and still make them useful for a range of objects?

The answer is to make more interfaces. The Interface Segregation Principle implies that instead of adding new methods that are only appropriate to one or a few implementation classes, you *make a new interface*. You divide your bloated interface into two or more smaller, *more cohesive* interfaces. That way, new classes can just implement the interfaces they need and not implement ones that they don't.

The Principle of Least Knowledge

Also known as the Law of Demeter, the Principle of Least Knowledge (PLK) says to talk only to your immediate friends.[11]

The complement to strong cohesion in an application is *loose coupling*. That's what the Principle of Least Knowledge is all about. It says that classes should collaborate *indirectly* with as few other classes as possible.[12]

Here's an example. You've got a computer system in your car—we all do these days. Say you're writing an application that graphs temperature data in the car. There are a number of sensors that provide temperature data and that are part of a family of sensors in the car's engine. Your program should select a sensor and gather and plot its temperature data. (This example is derived from one found in Hunt).[13] Part of your program might look like this:

```
public void plotTemperature(Sensor theSensor) {
        double temp = theSensor.getSensorData().getOilData().getTemp();
        ...
}
```

This will likely work—once. But now you've coupled your temperature-plotting method to the Sensor, SensorData, and OilSensor classes. Which means that a change to *any one of them* could affect your plotTemperature() method and cause you to have to refactor your code. Not good.

---

[10]Martin, 2003.
[11]Martin, 2003.
[12]Lieberherr, K., I. Holland, et al. *Object-Oriented Programming: An Objective Sense of Style*. OOPSLA '88, Association for Computing Machinery, 1988.
[13]Hunt, 2000.

This is what the PLK urges you to avoid. Instead of linking your method to a hierarchy and having to traverse the hierarchy to get the service you're looking for, just ask for the data directly:

```
public void plotTemperature(double theData) {
     ...
}
...
plotTemperature(aSensor.getTemp());
```

Yup, we had to add a method to the Sensor class to get the temperature for us, but that's a small price to pay for cleaning up the mess (and the possible errors) earlier. Now your class is just collaborating directly with *one* class and letting that class take care of the others. Of course, your Sensor class will do the same thing with SensorData, and so on.

This leads us to a corollary to the PLK: *keep dependencies to a minimum*. This is the crux of loose coupling. By interacting with only a few other classes, you make your class more flexible and less likely to contain errors.

Class Design Guidelines

Finally, I'd like to present a list of 23 class design guidelines. These guidelines are somewhat more specific than the general design guidelines described earlier, but they're handy to have around.

These 23 class design guidelines are taken from Davis[14] and McConnell[15]:

1. Present a *consistent level of abstraction* in the class interface.
2. Be sure you understand what abstraction the class is implementing.
3. Move unrelated information to a different class (ISP).
4. Beware of erosion of the class's interface when you're making changes (ISP).
5. Don't add public members that are inconsistent with the interface abstraction.
6. Minimize accessibility of classes and members (OCP).
7. Don't expose member data in public.
8. Avoid putting private implementation details into the class's interface.
9. Avoid putting methods into the public interface.
10. Watch for coupling that's too tight (PLK).
11. Try to implement "has a" relations through containment within a class (SRP).
12. Implement "is a" relations through inheritance (LSP).
13. Only inherit if the derived class is a more specific version of the base class.
14. Be sure to inherit only what you want to inherit (LSP).
15. Move common interfaces, data, and operations as high in the inheritance hierarchy as possible (DRY).

[14]Davis, A. M. *201 Principles of Software Development*. (New York, NY: McGraw-Hill, Inc., 1995.)
[15]McConnell, Steve, *Code Complete,* 2nd Edition. (Redmond, WA: Microsoft Press, 2004.)

139

16.   Be suspicious of classes of which there is only one instance.

17.   Be suspicious of base classes that only have a single derived class.

18.   Avoid deep inheritance trees (LSP).

19.   Keep the number of methods in a class as small as possible.

20.   Minimize indirect method calls to other classes (PLK).

21.   Initialize all member data in all constructors, if possible.

22.   Eliminate data-only classes.

23.   Eliminate operation-only classes.

Conclusion

This chapter examined a number of rules of thumb about object-oriented design that have evolved over the last few decades. These design principles act as guidelines for you, the designer, to abide by so that your design ends up being a good one, easy to implement, easy to maintain, and that does just what your customer wants. Importantly, these design principles give guidance when you're feeling your way from features to design. They talk about ways to examine and implement the important object-oriented principles of inheritance, encapsulation, polymorphism, and abstraction. They also reinforce basic design principles like cohesion and coupling.

References

Davis, A. M. *201 Principles of Software Development*. (New York, NY: McGraw-Hill, Inc., 1995.)

Hunt, A. and D. Thomas. *The Pragmatic Programmer: From Journeyman to Master*. (Boston, MA: Addison-Wesley, 2000.)

Larman, C. "Protected Variation: The Importance of Being Closed." *IEEE Software* 18(3): 89-91 (2001).

Lieberherr, K., I. Holland, et al. *Object-Oriented Programming: An Objective Sense of Style*. OOPSLA '88, Association for Computing Machinery, 1988.

Martin, R. C. *Agile Software Development: Principles, Patterns, and Practices*. (Upper Saddle River, NJ: Prentice Hall, 2003.)

McConnell, Steve, *Code Complete,* 2nd Edition. (Redmond, WA: Microsoft Press, 2004.)

McLaughlin, Brett D., et. al., *Head First Object-Oriented Analysis & Design*. (Sebastopol, CA: O'Reilly Media, Inc., 2007.)

Wintour, Damien. "The Liskov Substitution Principle." 1988. Downloaded on September 14, 2010 from `www.necessaryandsufficient.net/2008/09/design-guidelines-part3-the-liskov-substitution-principle/`.

CHAPTER 11

Design Patterns

Each pattern describes a problem which occurs over and over again in our environment, and then describes the core of the solution to that problem, in such a way that you can use this solution a million times over, without ever doing it the same way twice.

—Christopher Alexander[1]

Do you reinvent the wheel each time you write code? Do you have to relearn how to iterate through an array every time you write a program? Do you have to reinvent how to fix a dangling else in every if-statement you write? Do you need to relearn insertion sort or binary search every time you want to use them? Of course not!

Over the time you've spent writing programs, you've learned a *set of idioms* that you employ whenever you're writing code. For example, if you need to iterate through all the elements of an array in Java, you're likely to do the following:

```
for (int i = 0; i < myArray.length; i++) {
        System.out.printf(" %d ", myArray[i]);
}
```

or

```
for (int nextElement: myArray) {
        System.out.printf(" %d ", nextElement);
}
```

And the code just flows out of your fingertips as you type. These *code patterns* are sets of rules and templates for code that you accumulate as you gain more experience writing programs.

---

[1]Alexander, C., S. Ishikawa, et al. *A Pattern Language: Towns, Buildings, Construction*. (Oxford, UK: Oxford University Press, 1977.)

© John F. Dooley 2017
J. F. Dooley, *Software Development, Design and Coding*, https://doi.org/10.1007/978-1-4842-3153-1_11

Design patterns are the same thing—but for your design. If you take the time to learn a core group of design patterns, it will make your code more uniform and readable and improve its overall quality over time. The famous architect Christopher Alexander, in his book *A Pattern Language*, defined patterns for design in architecture. The same ideas carry over into software design. If you go back and read the Alexander quote at the top of this chapter, you'll see the following three key elements in Alexander's definition of design pattern:

- *Recurring*: The problem that evokes the design pattern must be a common one.

- *Core solution*: The pattern provides a template for the solution; it tries to extract out the essence of the solution.

- *Reuse*: The pattern must be easily reusable when the same problem appears in different domains.

In fact, you've already seen at least one design pattern so far in this book: the Model-View-Controller pattern (MVC) discussed in Chapter 5 is one of the earliest published examples of a software design pattern[2]. The MVC design pattern is used with programs that use graphical user interfaces. It divides the program into three parts: the *Model* that contains the processing rules for the program, the *View* that presents the data and the interface to the user, and the *Controller* that mediates communication between the *Model* and the *View*. In a typical object-oriented implementation, each of these abstractions becomes a separate object.

The *Gang of Four* (Gamma, Helm, Johnson, and Vlissides), in their seminal book on design patterns, *Design Patterns: Elements of Reusable Object-Oriented Software*,[3] define a design pattern as something that "names, abstracts, and identifies the key aspects of a common design structure that makes it useful for creating a reusable object-oriented design." In other words, a design pattern is a *named abstraction* from a *concrete example* that represents a *recurring solution* to a *particular, but common, problem*—recurring, core solution, reuse.

But why do we need design patterns in the first place? Why can't we just get along with the object-oriented design principles we studied in Chapter 10 and with our old favorites abstraction, inheritance, polymorphism, and encapsulation?

Well, it turns out that design is hard, that's why. Design for reuse is even harder. Design is also much more of an art than a science or an engineering discipline. Experienced software designers rarely start from first principles; they look for similarities in the current problem to problems they've solved in the past. And they bring to the design table the set of design idioms they've learned over time. Design patterns provide a *shared vocabulary* that makes this expert knowledge available to everyone.

Design Patterns and the Gang of Four

In their book, the Gang of Four describe design patterns as having four essential features:

- *The Pattern Name*: ". . . a handle we can use to describe a design problem, its solution, and consequences in a word or two. Naming a pattern immediately increases our design vocabulary."

- *The Problem*: Describes when to use the pattern. "It explains the problem and its context."

---

[2]Krasner, G. E. and S. T. Pope. "A cookbook for using the Model-View-Controller user interface paradigm in Smalltalk-80." *Journal of Object-Oriented Programming* **1**(3): 26-49 (1988).
[3]Gamma, E., Helm, R., Johnson, R., Vlissides. *Design Patterns: Elements of Reusable Object-Oriented Software*. (Boston, MA: Addison-Wesley, 1995.)

- *The Solution*: "... describes the elements that make up the design, their relationships, responsibilities, and collaborations ... the pattern provides an abstract description of a design problem and how a general arrangement of elements solves it."

- *The Consequences*: The results and tradeoffs of applying the pattern to a problem. These include time and space tradeoffs, but also flexibility, extensibility, and portability, among others.[4]

Design patterns are classified using two criteria: scope and purpose. *Scope* deals with the relationships between classes and objects. Static relationships between classes are fixed at compile time, whereas, dynamic relationships apply to objects and these relationships can change at run-time. *Purpose*, of course, deals with what the pattern does with respect to classes and objects. Patterns can deal with object creation, composition of classes or objects, or the ways in which objects interact and distribute responsibilities in the program.

The Gang of Four describe 23 different design patterns in their book, dividing them into three different classes of patterns: *creational*, *structural*, and *behavioral*.

- *Creational design patterns*: Dealing with when and how objects are created, these patterns typically create objects for you, relieving you of the need to instantiate those objects directly.

- *Structural design patterns*: These describe how objects are composed into larger groups.

- *Behavioral design patterns*: These generally talk about how responsibilities are distributed in the design and how communication happens between objects.

The list is not meant to be complete, and over the years since the publication of the Gang of Four's *Design Patterns* book, many more patterns have been added to this original list by developers everywhere. A recent Google search for the phrase "design patterns" yielded more than 10.6 million hits, so lots of object-oriented developers have jumped on the design patterns bandwagon.

The Classic Design Patterns

The 23 (classic) design patterns described by the Gang of Four are as follows (in the remainder of this chapter we'll go over the design patterns that are in italics):

- Creational Patterns
  - Abstract Factory
  - Builder
  - *Factory Method*
  - Prototype
  - *Singleton*

---

[4]Gamma et. al, 1995.

- Structural Patterns
  - *Adapter*
  - Bridge
  - Composite
  - Decorator
  - *Façade*
  - Flyweight
  - Proxy
- Behavioral Patterns
  - Chain of Responsibility
  - Command
  - Interpreter
  - *Iterator*
  - Mediator
  - Memento
  - *Observer*
  - State
  - *Strategy*
  - Template Method
  - Visitor

Patterns We Can Use

The patterns in this section are a representative sample of the classic design patterns, and are those that you'll find the most useful right away.

Creational Patterns

Creational patterns all have to do with creating objects. If we think about class definitions as templates for producing objects, then these patterns are all about how to create those templates. The two patterns we'll look at next, Singleton and Factory Method, show us two different ways of thinking about creating objects.

The Singleton Pattern

Singleton[5] is almost certainly the easiest of the design patterns to understand and to code. The idea is simple: you are writing a program and you have a need for one—*and only one*—instance of a class. And you need to enforce that "and only one" requirement. Examples of programs that would use a Singleton pattern are things like print spoolers, window managers, device drivers, and the like.

What are the implications of the "one, and only one" requirement? Well, first, it means your program can only say new Singleton() once, right? But what's to stop other objects in your program (or objects in the program that you didn't write) from issuing another new Singleton()? The answer is—nothing! As long as your class can be instantiated once, other objects should be able to instantiate it again and again.

What we need to do is to create a class that can be instantiated, once and only once, and which *doesn't use* new to do the instantiation.

You heard me right: we need a class that can be instantiated without using new. Go ahead, think about it.

Here's what we'll do. The method that gets called when an object is instantiated is the constructor. In Java you can say new Singleton() because the Singleton() constructor is *public*—it's visible from outside the class definition. If we want to keep the constructor so we can make instances of Singleton objects, but we don't want anyone to be able to use new to do that, we must make the constructor *private*. "But wait!" you cry. "If the constructor is private then we can't instantiate the object at all!" There is a way around this problem. If the constructor is private, then it can only be accessed from inside the class definition, so it's entirely possible to instantiate the object from within the class definition itself!

But this then recurses to the problem of how do we get to the constructor from *outside* the class definition? Well, in Java is there a way to access a method inside a class without having to have an instantiation of the class? (Think the Math class.)

Aha! Class methods! If you create a *public* method that is *static* (a class method), then that method is visible outside the class definition without having the object actually instantiated. So, if you create a class with a private constructor and then use a static method to create an instance of the class, you can control how many instances of the class you create. Here's the code:

```java
public class Singleton {
        // this is the reference to the instance that will hang around
        private static Singleton uniqueInstance;

        // the private constructor - can't be accessed from outside
        private Singleton() {
                // do stuff here to initialize the instance
        }

        // here's the static method we'll use to create the instance
        public static Singleton getInstance() {
                if (uniqueInstance == null) {
                        uniqueInstance = new Singleton();
                }
                // if uniqueInstance is not null, then it already exists
                return uniqueInstance;
        }

        // Other methods - after all Singleton is a real class
}
```

---

[5]Gamma et. al, 1995.

And in order to use the Singleton class, we'd do something like this:

```
public class SingletonTest {

        public static void main(String [] args) {
                Singleton mySingle;
                mySingle = Singleton.getInstance();
                // and we do other stuff here
        }
}
```

When we instantiate the Singleton instance by calling the getInstance() method, it will test to see if we've done this before. If not, it creates the instance using the private constructor in the Singleton class. If the instance already exists (the uniqueInstance variable is not null), then we just return the reference to the object.

This version of the Singleton pattern isn't without its problems; for one thing, it can fail if you're writing a multi-threaded Java program. The solution just mentioned isn't "thread safe." It's possible that, in between the test for the existing of a Singleton instance and the actual creation of an instance, your program could be swapped out while another thread executes. When it swaps back in, it could erroneously create another instance of the Singleton. There are relatively easy solutions to this.

The simplest way to make your Singleton pattern thread-safe is to make the getInstance() method a *synchronized* method. That way it will execute to completion and not be swapped out. Here's a version of the getInstance() method that is thread-safe:

```
public synchronized static Singleton getInstance() {
        if (uniqueInstance == null) {
                uniqueInstance = new Singleton();
        }
        return uniqueInstance;
}
```

Notice that the only difference is the inclusion of the synchronized keyword in the method signature. I'll give an example of how to use the Singleton pattern later in this chapter.

The Factory Method Pattern

Say you've got a small company that's expanding across multiple cities in several states. Whenever you sell an item, you need to compute the sales tax for the locale your store is in. Every state and city has a different sales tax rate, and so you'll need to keep track of the locations and only use the correct rate in any particular location. As you add new stores in new locations you don't want to have to continue to change lots of your code in order to compute the sales tax in the new locations. And, of course, you have a program to model your operations and compute the sales tax on each sale. The question is, how do you write the program in such a way that you don't have to change it every day or change a lot of it every time you open a new store? That's where the Factory Method design pattern comes in.

The *Factory Method* pattern[6] creates objects for you. The Factory Method pattern says that you just define an interface or abstract class for creating an object but let the sub-classes themselves decide which class to instantiate. In other words, sub-classes are responsible for creating the instance of the class. You use the Factory Method pattern when you need to create several types of objects that are usually related to each other—they usually have the same abstract parent class so they are in the same class hierarchy—but that are different.

---

[6]Gamma, et. al, 1995.

In the Factory method, you create an object without exposing the creation logic to the client and refer to the newly created object using a common interface. The Factory Method pattern allows the sub-classes to choose the type of objects to create, and they do that at run-time.

Factory Method promotes loose coupling by eliminating the need to bind application-specific classes into the client code. That means the client code interacts solely with the resultant interface or abstract class, so that it will work with any classes that implement that interface or that extend that abstract class.

When do you use the Factory pattern?

1. When you don't know ahead of time what class object you will need

2. When all the potential classes are in the same sub-class hierarchy

3. To centralize class selection code

4. When you don't want the user to have to know every sub-class

5. To encapsulate object creation

You ask the factory to create an object of type X and it creates one; you ask it to create an object of type Y and it creates one. This forces the creation of concrete classes to be relegated to sub-classes of an interface that knows how to create concrete classes and keeps your other classes closed for modification. All without changing X or Y or the store. In our example, we can create sales tax calculation objects, using a SalesTaxFactory class to generate the objects that will compute sales tax for different locations. The Factory method pattern allows you to define an interface for creating a family of objects, and it allows sub-classes to decide which members of the family to instantiate. It defers instantiation down into the sub-classes.

In our example, we'll have several classes:

- SalesTax: An interface that defines our sales tax objects

- BostonTax: A concrete class that inherits from Tax

- ChicagoTax: A concrete class that inherits from Tax

- StLouisTax: A concrete class that inherits from Tax

- SalesTaxFactory: Our concrete implementation that makes different Tax objects

- SalesTaxDriver: A driver class that lets us sell items and compute sales tax

The Factory Method pattern depends on defining an interface for the objects we need and then allowing sub-classes that implement that interface to actually implement the objects. We can either use a Java interface or an abstract class to define our SalesTax interface. We'll use an abstract class. Our SalesTax abstract class will look like the following:

```java
abstract class SalesTax {
    protected double rate;
    abstract void getRate();

    public void calculateTax(double amount) {
        System.out.printf("$%6.2f\n", amount * (1.0 +rate));
    }

}
```

And our SalesTax sub-classes end up as concrete classes that override one or more of the methods from the SalesTax abstract class:

```
public class BostonTax extends SalesTax {
    public void getRate() {
        rate = 0.0875;
    }
}

public class ChicagoTax extends SalesTax {
        public void getRate() {
            rate = 0.075;
        }
}

public class StLouisTax extends SalesTax {
    public void getRate() {
        rate = 0.05;
    }
}
```

Finally, our concrete SalesTaxFactory, which will actually make a concrete SalesTax object object looks like this:

```
public class SalesTaxFactory {
    /**
     * use the makeTaxObject() method to get object of type SalesTax
     */
    public SalesTax makeTaxObject(String location) {

        if(location == null) {
            return null;
        } else if(location.equalsIgnoreCase("boston")) {
            return new BostonTax();
        } else if(location.equalsIgnoreCase("chicago")) {
            return new ChicagoTax();
        } else if(location.equalsIgnoreCase("stlouis"))  {
            return new StLouisTax();
        }

        return null;
    }
}
```

In order to test our factory, we create a *driver*. This is the client code that uses the Factory to create the correct types of objects:

```
/**
 * Test the Factory Method pattern.
 * We use the SalesTaxFactory to get the object of concrete classes
 */
```

```
import java.io.*;
import java.util.Scanner;

public class SalesTaxDriver {

    public static void main(String args[])throws IOException {
        Scanner stdin = new Scanner(System.in);

        SalesTaxFactory salesTaxFactory = new SalesTaxFactory();
        //get an object of type SalesTax and call its getTax()method.

        System.out.print("Enter the location (boston/chicago/stlouis): ");
        String location= stdin.nextLine();

        System.out.print("Enter the dollar amount: ");
        double amount = stdin.nextDouble();

        SalesTax cityTax = salesTaxFactory.makeTaxObject(location);

        System.out.printf("Bill amount for %s of  $%6.2f is: ", location, amount);
        cityTax.getRate();
        cityTax.calculateTax(amount);
    }
}
```

Figure 11-1 shows what the entire program looks like in UML.

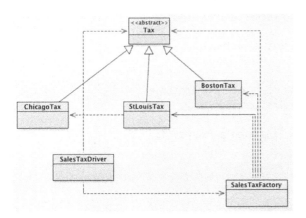

Figure 11-1. *SalesTaxFactory example*

What should we notice about this Factory method pattern example? The following tells us some things about how the Factory method pattern works in this case:

- The factory method makeTaxobject() encapsulates the creation of the SalesTax object. Our driver just tells the factory which location to use.

- The SalesTax interface provides the interface for the sub-classes to create the actual objects.

- The SalesTaxFactory concrete class actually creates the objects by implementing the makeTaxObject() method.

- This leaves the *SalesTax* classes alone and makes it easier for the SalesTaxDriver to create new objects.

- Notice also that the SalesTaxDriver class only deals with SalesTax objects. It doesn't have to know anything about particular sales tax rates. The concrete SalesTax objects implement the methods from the SalesTax abstract class, and the SalesTaxDriver just uses them regardless of which type of SalesTax object you've created.

- It also means that you can change the implementation of a particular type of SalesTax object without changing either the interface or the SalesTaxDriver.

There's another variation of the Factory Method pattern. If you think about it, in our example we only ever need a single factory. If that's the case, we could use the Singleton pattern to generate the factory and then just use it. This would change our SalesTaxFactory and SalesTaxDriver classes. They would end up looking like this:

```java
public class SingletonTaxFactory {
    /**
     * We'll just create one SalesTaxFactory using the Singleton pattern
     * To do that we need to make the constructor private and create a
     * variable to hold the reference to the SalesTaxFactory object.
     */
    // this is the instance that will hang around
    private static SingletonTaxFactory uniqueInstance;

    // the private constructor - can't be accessed from outside
    private SingletonTaxFactory() {
        // do stuff here to initialize the instance
    }

    // here's the static method we'll use to create the instance
    public static SingletonTaxFactory getInstance() {
        if (uniqueInstance == null) {
            uniqueInstance = new SingletonTaxFactory();
        }
        return uniqueInstance;
    }
    /**
     * use getTax method to get object of type Tax
     */
    public SalesTax getTax(String location) {
        if(location == null) {
            return null;
        }
        if(location.equalsIgnoreCase("boston")) {
            return new BostonTax();
        }   else if(location.equalsIgnoreCase("chicago")) {
            return new ChicagoTax();
```

```
    }    else if(location.equalsIgnoreCase("stlouis"))  {
         return new StLouisTax();
    }
    return null;
  }
}
```

And the client code then becomes:

```
import java.io.*;
import java.util.Scanner;

  public class SingletonTaxDriver {

    public static void main(String args[])throws IOException {
       Scanner stdin = new Scanner(System.in);

       /* get the single SalesTaxFactory that we need */
       SingletonTaxFactory salesTaxFactory =
                              SingletonTaxFactory.getInstance();

       System.out.print("Enter the location (boston/chicago/stlouis): ");
       String location= stdin.nextLine();

       System.out.print("Enter the dollar amount: ");
       double amount = stdin.nextDouble();

       SalesTax cityTax = salesTaxFactory.getTax(location);

       System.out.printf("Bill amount for %s of  $%6.2f is: ", location, amount);
       cityTax.getRate();
       cityTax.calculateTax(amount);
    }
  }
```

Structural Patterns

Structural patterns help you put objects together so you can use them more easily. They're all about grouping objects together and providing ways for objects to coordinate to get work done. Remember, composition, aggregation, delegation, and inheritance are all about structure and coordination. The first Structural pattern we'll look at here—the Adapter—is all about getting classes to work together.

The Adapter Pattern

Here's the problem. You've got a client program Foo that wants to access another class or library or package, Bar. The problem is, Foo is expecting a particular interface, and that interface is different from the public interface that Bar presents to the world. What are you to do?

Well, you could rewrite Foo to change the interface it expects to conform to the interface that Bar is presenting. But if Foo is large, or if it's being used by other classes, that may not be a viable possibility. Or you could rewrite Bar so it presents the interface that Foo is expecting. But maybe Bar is a commercial package and you don't have the source code?

That's where the Adapter design pattern comes in[7]. You use the Adapter pattern to create an intermediate class that wraps the Bar interface inside a set of methods that presents the interface that Foo is looking for. Here's the idea: the Adapter can interface with Foo on one side and with Bar on the other. So the interface to Bar doesn't have to change, and Foo users gets the interface it expects. Everyone is happy! By the way, the Adapter design pattern is also called the *Wrapper* pattern because it wraps an interface[8]. Figure 11-2 illustrates.

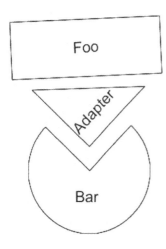

Figure 11-2. *The Adapter lets Foo use Bar*

There are two ways to implement adapters: *class adapters,* where the adapter will inherit from the target class, and *object adapters* that use delegation to create the adapter. Note the difference: a c*lass adapter* will sub-class an existing class and implement a target interface. An *object adapter* will sub-class a target class and delegate to an existing class. Figure 11-3 shows the UML for a generic class adapter.

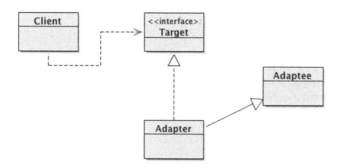

Figure 11-3. *A class adapter example*

---

[7]Gamma et. al, 1995.
[8]Gamma et. al, 1995.

Note that the Adapter class inherits from the Adaptee class and implements the same Target interface that the Client class uses. Here's the code for this example:

```
public class Client {

    public static void main(String [] args) {
        Target myTarget = new Adapter();

        System.out.println(myTarget.sampleMethod(12));
    }
}

public interface Target {
    int sampleMethod(int y);
}

public class Adapter extends Adaptee implements Target {
    public int sampleMethod(int y) {
        return myMethod(y);
    }
}

public class Adaptee {

    public Adaptee() {

    }

    public int myMethod(int y) {
        return y * y;
    }
}
```

The object adapter, on the other hand, still implements the Target interface but uses composition with the Adaptee class in order to accomplish the wrapping. It looks like this:

```
public class Adapter implements Target {
    Adaptee myAdaptee = new Adaptee();

    public int sampleMethod(int y) {
        return myAdaptee.myMethod(y);
    }
}
```

In both cases, the Client doesn't have to change! That's the beauty of Adapter. You can change which Adaptee you're using by changing the Adapter and not the Client.

The Façade Pattern

For a second example, we try to simplify interfaces. Say you have a set of classes that constitute a subsystem. They could be individual classes that make up a more complex system or part of a large class library. Let's also say that each of those classes in the subsystem has a different interface. Finally, let's say that you want to write a client program that uses some or all of those classes to get some work done. This would normally mean that to write the client program, you'd need to learn all the interfaces of all the classes in the subsystem in order to communicate with the subsystem and get your work done. Pictorially, this will look like Figure 11-4.

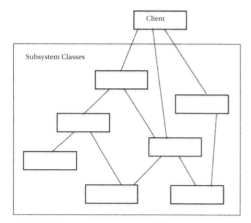

Figure 11-4. *A client using several interfaces*

Clearly, this will make your client program complicated and very hard to maintain. This problem is what the Façade design pattern is here to fix. The idea behind Façade is to provide a single, simple, unified interface that makes it easier for your client to interact with the subsystem classes. When you use a Façade, you learn a single interface and use it to interact with all the subsystem classes. Pictorially, this looks like Figure 11-5.

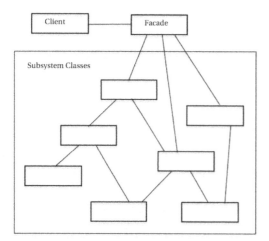

Figure 11-5. *A client using a Façade interface*

In addition to providing you with a single interface to use, the Façade pattern also hides any interface changes or additions from the client. It's a classic example of the Principle of Least Knowledge from Chapter 10.

Note that the Façade pattern may look a lot like the Adapter pattern from earlier. But don't be fooled. What the Adapter pattern does is wrap a target interface and allow a client to use the interface it expects. The Façade simplifies one or more interfaces and presents that simplified interface for the client to use.

Here's an example for the Façade design pattern. Say you're creating an online store and you're putting together a simple program to compute the total amount a customer would have to pay for an item they want to order. In this program, you would need to look up the item, compute the payment, compute the sales tax, compute the delivery charge, and then total all that up and send it to the user. That leaves you with classes for SalesTax, Delivery, Payment, and Inventory. If we want to simplify the interface using Façade, we can create a new class, Order, that will hide the several interfaces and produce a simpler interface for a client program to use. In UML, this would look like Figure 11-6.

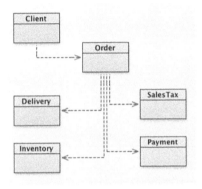

Figure 11-6. *Façade example*

And the code for this simple example would look like the following:

```
/**
 * Facade Design Pattern Example
 */

/** Check the Inventory for the item */
public class Inventory {
    public String checkInventory(String itemID) {
        /* code in here to check the database */
        return "Inventory checked";
    }
}

/** compute the payment for an item */
public class Payment {
    public String computePayment(String itemID, String currency) {
        return "Payment computed successfully";
    }
}
```

```java
/** compute the sales tax for an item */
public class SalesTax {
    public String computeTax(String itemID, double rate) {
        return "Tax computed";
    }
}

/** compute the delivery charge for an item */
public class Delivery {
    public String computeDelivery(String itemID, String location) {
        return "Delivery amount computed";
    }
}

/**
 * Here's the Facade
 */
public class Order {
    private Payment pymt = new Payment();
    private Inventory inventory = new Inventory();
    private SalesTax salestax = new SalesTax();
    private Delivery deliver = new Delivery();

    /**
     *  This is the new interface for buying an item
     *  it incorporates all the different steps into a single
     *  method call
     */
    public void placeOrder(String itemID, String currency, String location, double rate) {
        String step1 = inventory.checkInventory(itemID);
        String step2 = pymt.computePayment(itemID, currency);
        String step3 = salestax.computeTax(itemID, rate);
        String step4 = deliver.computeDelivery(itemID, location);

        System.out.printf("%s\n", step1);
        System.out.printf("%s\n", step2);
        System.out.printf("%s\n", step3);
        System.out.printf("%s\n", step4);
    }

  /** add more methods here for performing other actions */
}

/**
 * Here's the client code.
 * Note how the Facade makes ordering something simple
 * by using it's interface
 */
```

```
public class Client {
      public static void main(String args[]){
        Order order = new Order();

        order.placeOrder("OR123456", "USD", "Chicago", 0.075);
        System.out.println("Order processing completed");
      }
}
```

Behavioral Patterns

Where creational patterns are all about how to create new objects, and structural patterns are all about getting objects to communicate and cooperate, behavioral patterns are all about getting objects to do things. They examine how responsibilities are distributed in the design and how communication happens between objects. The three patterns we'll look at here all describe how to assign behavioral responsibilities to classes. The Iterator pattern is about how to traverse a collection of objects. The Observer pattern tells us how to manage push and pull state changes. The Strategy pattern lets us select different behaviors behind a single interface.

The Iterator Pattern

If you've programmed in Java, you've seen iterators. I'll get to that, but let's start at the beginning. If you have a *collection of elements*, you can organize them in many different ways. They can be arrays, linked lists, queues, hash tables, sets, and so on. Each of these collections will have its own unique set of operations, but there's usually one operation that you might want to perform on all of them: *traverse the entire collection from beginning to end, one element at a time.* Oh, and you want to traverse the elements in such a way that *you don't need to know the internal structure of the collection.* And you may want to be able to traverse the collection backwards, and you may want to have several traversals going on at the same time.

That's what the Iterator pattern is for[9]. It creates an object that allows you to traverse a collection, one element at a time.

Because of the requirement that you don't need to know about the internal structure of the collection, an Iterator object doesn't care about sorting order; it just returns each object as it's stored in the collection, one at a time from first to last. The simplest iterator needs just two methods:

- hasNext( ): Returns a true if there is an element to be retrieved—that is, if we've not reached the end of the collection yet—and false if there are no elements left.

- getNextElement( ): Returns the next element in the collection.

In the Iterator pattern, we have an Iterator interface that's implemented to make a concrete Iterator object that's used by a concrete Collections object. A client class then creates the Collection object and gets the Iterator from there. Figure 11-7 shows the UML version of this from Gamma et. al.

---

[9]Gamma et. al, 1995.

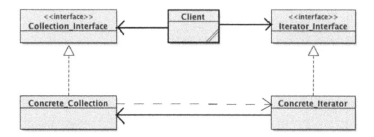

Figure 11-7. *An example of using the Iterator pattern*

You can see that the client class uses the `Collection` and the `Iterator` interfaces, and the `Concrete_Iterator` is part of and uses the `Concrete_Collection`. Note that the `Collection_Interface` will contain an abstract method to create an iterator for the `Collection`. This method is implemented in the `Concrete_Collection` class, and when the client calls the method, a `Concrete_Iterator` is created and passed to the client to use.

Starting in version 1.2, Java contained the Java Collections Framework (JCF) that included a number of new classes and interfaces to allow you to create collections of objects, including an `Iterator` interface. All these new types contained iterators. Java even included (just for collections of type `List`) an expanded Iterator called a `ListIterator`. With the `ListIterator`, you can go backwards through the list.

Here's an example of typical Iterator code in Java using both the `Iterator` and the `ListIterator` implementations:

```
/**
 * Iterate through elements Java ArrayList using an Iterator
 * We then use ListIterator to go backwards through the same
 * ArrayList
 */

import java.util.ArrayList;
import java.util.Iterator;
import java.util.ListIterator;

public class ArrayListIterator {
    public static void main(String[] args) {
        //create an ArrayList object
        ArrayList<Integer> arrayList = new ArrayList<Integer>();
        //Add elements to ArrayList
        arrayList.add(1);
        arrayList.add(3);
        arrayList.add(5);
        arrayList.add(7);
        arrayList.add(11);
        arrayList.add(13);
        arrayList.add(17);

        //get an Iterator object for ArrayList
        Iterator iter = arrayList.iterator();
```

```
        System.out.println("Iterating through ArrayList elements");
        while(iter.hasNext()) {
            System.out.println(iter.next());
        }

        ListIterator list_iter = arrayList.listIterator(arrayList.size());

        System.out.println("Iterating through ArrayList backwards");
        while(list_iter.hasPrevious()) {
            System.out.println(list_iter.previous());
        }
    }
}
```

Note that when we create the ListIterator object, we pass it the number of elements in the ArrayList. This is to set the cursor that the ListIterator object uses to point to just past the last element in the ArrayList so it can then look backwards using the hasPrevious() method. In both the Iterator and ListIterator implementations in Java, the *cursor* always points between two elements so that the hasNext() and hasPrevious() method calls make sense; for example, when you say iter.hasNext(), you're asking the iterator if there is a next element in the collection. Figure 11-8 is the abstraction of what the cursors look like.

Figure 11-8. *Cursors in the Iterator abstraction*

Finally, some iterators will allow you to insert and delete elements in the collection while the iterator is running. These are called *robust iterators*. The Java ListIterator interface (not the *Iterator*) allows both insertion (via the add() method) and deletion (via the remove() method) in an iterator with restrictions. The add() method only adds to the position immediately before the one that would be the next element retrieved by a next() or immediately after the next element that would be returned by a previous() method call. The remove() method can only be called between successive next() or previous() method calls; it can't be called twice in a row, and never immediately after an add() method call.

The Observer Pattern

I love NPR's *Talk of the Nation: Science Friday* radio show (http://sciencefriday.com). But I hardly get to listen to it when it's broadcast because it's on from 2:00–4:00 PM EST on Fridays and, because I work for a living, I can't listen to it then. But I subscribe to the podcast and so every Saturday morning I get a new podcast of *SciFri* so I can listen to it on my iPod while I mow the lawn. If I ever get tired of *SciFri*, I can just unsubscribe, and I won't get any new podcasts. That, ladies and gentlemen, is the Observer pattern.

According to the Gang of Four, the Observer Pattern ". . . defines a one-to-many dependency between objects so that when one object changes state, all of its dependents are notified and updated automatically[10]." So in my *SciFri* example, NPR is the "publisher" of the *SciFri* podcast, and all of us who "subscribe"

[10]Gamma et. al, 1995.

(or register) to the podcast are the observers. We wait for the *SciFri* state to change (a new podcast gets created) and then the publisher updates us automatically. How the updates happen differentiate between two different types of Observer—push and pull. In a *push Observer*, the Publisher (also known as the *Subject* in object-oriented speak) changes state and then *pushes* the new state out to all the Observers. In a *pull Observer*, the Subject changes state, but doesn't provide a full update until the Observers ask for it—they *pull* the update from the Subject. In a variation of the *pull* model, the Subject may provide a minimal update to all the Observers notifying them that the state has changed, but the Observers still need to ask for the details of the new state.

With the Observer pattern, we need a Subject interface so that the Subject and the Observer and the Client all can tell what the state interface they're using is. We also need an Observer interface that just tells us how to update an Observer. Our publisher will then implement the Subject interface and the different "listeners" will implement the Observer interface. Figure 11-9 is a UML diagram of this.

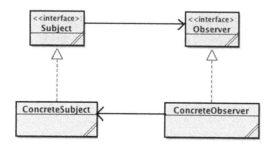

Figure 11-9. *The canonical Observer Pattern*

The client class is missing, but it will use both the ConcreteSubject and ConcreteObserver classes. Here's a simple implementation of a push model version of all of these. Remember, it's a *push model* because the ConcreteSubject object is notifying all the Observers whether they request it or not.

First, we create the Subject interface that tells us how to register, remove, and notify the Observers:

```
public interface Subject {
    public void addObserver(Observer obs);
    public void removeObserver(Observer obs);
    public void notifyAllObservers();
}
```

Next, we write the implementation of the Subject interface. This class is the real publisher, so it also needs the attributes that form the state of the Subject. In this simple version we use an ArrayList to hold all the Observers:

```
import java.util.ArrayList;

public class ConcreteSubject implements Subject {
    private ArrayList<Observer> observerList;
        // these two variables are our state
    private int subj_id;
    private String msg;
```

```
    public ConcreteSubject() {
        observerList = new ArrayList<Observer>();
        this.subj_id = 0;
        this.msg = "Hello";
    }

    public void addObserver(Observer obs) {
        observerList.add(obs);
    }

    public void removeObserver(Observer obs) {
        observerList.remove(obs);
    }

    public void notifyAllObservers() {
        for (Observer obs: observerList) {
            obs.update(this.subj_id, this.msg);
            }
    }

    public void setState(int foo, String bar) {
        this.subj_id = subj_id;
        this.msg = msg;
        notifyAllObservers();
    }
}
```

Next, the Observer interface tells us how to update our Observers:

```
public interface Observer {
    public void update(int obs_id, String msg);
}
```

And then we write the implementation of the Observer interface:

```
public class ConcreteObserver implements Observer {
    private int obs_id;
    private String msg;
    Subject subj;

    /**
     * Constructor for objects of class ConcreteObserver
     */
    public ConcreteObserver(Subject subj) {
        this.subj = subj;
        subj.addObserver(this);
    }

    public void update(int obs_id, String msg) {
        this.obs_id = obs_id;
        this.msg = msg;
        show();
    }
```

```
    private void show() {
        System.out.printf("Id = %d Msg = %s\n", this.obs_id, this.msg);
    }
}
```

And finally, the driver program that creates the publisher and each of the observers and puts them all together.

```
public class ObserverDriver {
    public static void main(String [] args) {
        ConcreteSubject subj = new ConcreteSubject();

        ConcreteObserver obj = new ConcreteObserver(subj);

        subj.setState(12, "Monday");
        subj.setState(17, "Tuesday");
    }
}
```

And the output of executing the driver (which all comes from the show() method in the ConcreteObserver object will look like this:

```
Id = 12 Msg = Monday
Id = 17 Msg = Tuesday
```

In many ways, the Observer design pattern works like the Java events interface. In Java you create a class that registers as a "listener" (our Observer) for a particular event type. You also create a method that is the actual observer and which will respond when the event occurs. When an event of that type occurs, the Java events object (our Subject) notifies your observer by making a call to the method you wrote, passing the data from the event to the observer method—Java events use the *push model* of the Observer pattern.

For example, if you create a Button object in a Java program, you use the addActionListener() method of the Button object to register to observe ActionEvents. When an ActionEvent occurs, all the ActionListeners are notified by having a method named actionPerformed() called. This means that your Button object must implement the actionPerformed() method to handle the event.

The Strategy Pattern

Sometimes you have an application where you have several ways of doing a single operation or you have several different behaviors, each with a different interface. One of the ways to implement something like this is using a switch statement, like so:

```
switch (selectBehavior) {
        case Behavior1:
                Algorithm1.act(foo);
                break;
        case Behavior2:
                Algorithm2.act(foo, bar);
                break;
```

```
    case Behavior3:
            Algorithm3.act(1, 2, 3);
            break;
}
```

The problem with this type of construct it that if you add another behavior, you need to change this code and potentially all the other code that has to select different behaviors. This is not good.

The Strategy design pattern gets you around this. It says that if you have several behaviors (algorithms) you need to select from dynamically, you should make sure they all adhere to the same interface—a Strategy interface—and then that they're selected dynamically via a driver, called the Context, that is told which to call by the client software. The Strategy pattern embodies two of our fundamental object-oriented design principles: *encapsulate the idea that varies* and *code to an interface, not an implementation*. This is illustrated in Figure 11-10.

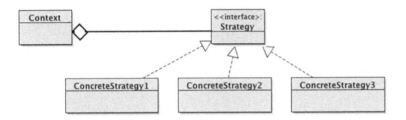

Figure 11-10. *A typical Strategy pattern layout*

Here are some examples of when you might use the Strategy pattern:

- Capture video using different compression algorithms
- Compute taxes for different types of entities (people, corporations, nonprofits)
- Plot data in different formats (line graphs, pie charts, bar graphs)
- Compress audio files using different formats

In each of these examples you can think of having the application program telling a driver—the Context—which of the strategies to use and then asking the Context to perform the operation.

As an example, let's say you're a newly minted CPA and you're trying to write your own software to compute your customers' tax bills. (Why a CPA would write their own tax program, I have no idea—work with me on this.) Initially, you've divided your customers into individuals who only file personal income taxes, corporations that file corporate income taxes, and nonprofit organizations that file hardly any taxes at all. Now, all these groups have to compute taxes, so the behavior of a class to compute taxes should be the same for all, but they'll compute taxes in different ways. What we need is a Strategy setup that will use the same interface—to encapsulate what varies in our application, and to code the concrete classes to an interface—and allow our client class to select which type of tax customer to use. Figure 11-11 is a diagram of what our program will look like.

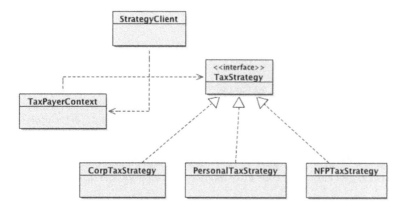

Figure 11-11. *Using the Strategy pattern to select a tax behavior*

We create a TaxStrategy interface that all the concrete TaxStrategy classes will implement:

```
public interface TaxStrategy {
  public double computeTax(double income);
}
```

Because the only thing that varies here is how the tax is computed, our TaxStrategy interface just includes the computeTax() method:

Then we create each of the concrete TaxStrategy classes, each of which implements the tax computation for that particular type of customer:

```
public class PersonalTaxStrategy implements TaxStrategy {
    private final double RATE = 0.25;

    public double computeTax(double income) {
        if (income <= 25000.0) {
            return income * (0.75 * RATE);
        } else {
            return income * RATE;
        }
    }
}

public class CorpTaxStrategy implements TaxStrategy {
    private final double RATE = 0.45;

    public double computeTax(double income) {
        return income * RATE ;
    }
}

public class NFPTaxStrategy implements TaxStrategy {
    private final double RATE = 0.0;
```

```java
    public double computeTax(double income) {
        return income * RATE;
    }
}
```

Next, we create the Context class that does the heavy lifting of creating strategy objects requested by the client program and executing the correct ones:

```java
public class TaxPayerContext {
    private TaxStrategy strategy;
    private double income;

    /** constructor for Context */
    public TaxPayerContext(TaxStrategy strategy, double income) {
        this.strategy = strategy;
        this.income = income;
    }
    public double getIncome() {
        return income;
    }
    public void setIncome(double income) {
        this.income = income;
    }
    public TaxStrategy getStrategy() {
        return strategy;
    }
    public void setStrategy(TaxStrategy strategy) {
        this.strategy = strategy;
    }
    public double computeTax() {
        return strategy.computeTax(income);
    }
}
```

Note that here we write a separate version of the computeTax() method (we're not overriding the method because we're not extending any of the concrete classes—the Strategy pattern uses composition, not inheritance). This version calls the computeTax() method of the strategy that the client has selected.

Finally, we implement the client that controls who gets instantiated and when:

```java
public class StrategyClient {
        public static void main(String [] args) {
                double income;
                TaxPayerContext tp;

                income = 35000.00;
                tp = new TaxPayerContext(new PersonalTaxStrategy(), income);
                System.out.println("Tax is " + tp.computeTax());

                tp.setStrategy(new CorpTaxStrategy());
                System.out.println("Tax is " + tp.computeTax());
        }
}
```

165

The `client` class selects which algorithm to use and then gets the `context` object to execute it. This way we've encapsulated the tax computation in separate classes. We can easily add new customer types just by adding new concrete `TaxStrategy` classes and making the change in the `client` to use that new concrete type. Piece of cake!

Conclusion

Design patterns are reusable, commonly occurring core solutions to design problems. They're not a finished design. Rather a design pattern is a template you can use to solve similar problems in many different domains. Design patterns offer you proven strategies for solving common proglems and so they can help speed up your design process. And because these patterns describe *proven solutions*, they can help reduce defects in your design as well.

Be careful, though. Like all design techniques, design patterns are heuristics, so there will be cases where they just don't fit. Trying to squeeze a pattern into a problem where it just doesn't belong is asking for trouble.

The goal of design patterns is to define a common vocabulary for design. They may not get us all the way there, but design patterns, plus the design principles described in Chapter 10, get us a long way down that road.

References

Alexander, C., S. Ishikawa, et al. *A Pattern Language: Towns, Buildings, Construction.* (Oxford, UK: Oxford University Press, 1977.)

Freeman, E. and E. Freeman *Head First Design Patterns.* (Sebastopol, CA: O'Reilly Media, Inc., 2004.)

Gamma, E., Helm, R., Johnson, R., Vlissides. *Design Patterns: Elements of Reusable Object-Oriented Software.* (Boston, MA: Addison-Wesley, 1995.)

Krasner, G. E. and S. T. Pope. "A cookbook for using the Model-View-Controller user interface paradigm in Smalltalk-80." *Journal of Object-Oriented Programming* 1(3): 26-49 (1988).

Lieberherr, K., I. Holland, et al. *Object-Oriented Programming: An Objective Sense of Style.* OOPSLA '88, Association for Computing Machinery, 1988.

Martin, R. C. *Agile Software Development: Principles, Patterns, and Practices.* (Upper Saddle River, NJ: Prentice Hall, 2003.)

CHAPTER 12

Parallel Programming

Concurrency is a property of the algorithm. Parallelism is a property of the machine.

—Douglas Eadline

For about 40 years, Moore's law has said that the number of transistors on an integrated circuit would double about every 18 months to 2 years while the size of the circuit would stay about the same or get smaller and the price of that integrated circuit would stay about the same or get cheaper. This means that we'd have more powerful processors for about the same amount of money on a regular basis. This prediction worked really well until the beginning of the 2000s, when some things changed. There are a couple of reasons for this. Moore's law implies that to get twice as many transistors on a similarly sized chip, the size of the transistors would shrink and the distance between the transistors would also shrink. Clearly, quantum physics being what it is, this couldn't continue indefinitely, and by the early 2000s we were beginning to see some problems with making the transistors a lot smaller. The other problem is heat. If you pack twice as many transistors on a chip and expect to run the chip at the same or a higher clock speed, you'll need more electricity going through the circuit. More electricity means more heat. This is known as the *power wall*.

So, by about 2001 it was becoming clear that primarily because of heat considerations, the current generation of microprocessors couldn't be pushed much past about 3 or 4 billion cycles per second (3–4 GHz), and if we wanted to go faster we needed a different idea. Enter the multi-core microprocessor. The basic idea with that is to put two or more CPUs on a single, slightly larger integrated circuit, run them on the same—slower—clock and have the processors share some cache memory (typically at L3) and use a shared main memory. This allows the processors to use less electricity, generating less heat and being able to run two or more programs simultaneously to make up for the slower clock speed. All the major chip manufacturers got on board with this idea. IBM was first, introducing the POWER4 PowerPC dual-core processor in late 2001, followed by AMD with its Athlon dual-core processor in 2005 and then Intel with its Core Duo in 2006. Since then, nearly all new processors and processor architectures have been multi-core, and programmers and language developers have been working hard to create new software that would take advantage of the new parallel machines.

In this chapter we'll first take a brief look at how parallel computers are organized. Then we'll describe some of the issues that make writing programs that can take advantage of a parallel computer architecture very difficult. Next, we'll talk about how to write parallel programs and how to take a serial program and convert it into a parallel program. Finally, we'll look at writing parallel programs using different computer languages and libraries.

© John F. Dooley 2017
J. F. Dooley, *Software Development, Design and Coding*, https://doi.org/10.1007/978-1-4842-3153-1_12

Concurrency vs. Parallelism

Traditionally, software has been written for *serial* or *sequential* computation. A problem solution is broken into a discrete series of instructions that are executed sequentially one after another on a single processor. These (single-core) computers only allow one instruction to execute at any moment in time. A classic example might be a loop to sum all the elements of a list. In this example, we iterate over all the elements in the list and add each of them to the sum one at a time:

```
int sum = 0;
for (int i = 0; i < n; i++) {
    sum += list[i];
}
print(sum);
```

This will normally be executed serially with these results:

```
sum = 0
sum = sum + list[0]
sum = sum + list[1]
sum = sum + list[2]
...
```

This is clearly an $O(n)$ operation requiring n additions and taking about $T(n)$ time proportional to n. We can improve on this by recognizing that we can add pairs of numbers together in any order and then add partial sums to get the total. The code might change to look like this:

```
sum = 0;
for (int i = 0; i < n-1; i+=2) {
    sum += (list[i] + list[i+1]);
}
print(sum);
```

Note that because of commutativity of addition, the order in which we execute the two additions inside the loop doesn't matter. Although this version goes through the loop half the number of times, it will still require the same overall number of additions and the same amount of time. So, with just one processor we don't really gain anything. But this loop serves as the genesis of an idea. If we had n/2 processors instead of just 1, we could do many of the computations *simultaneously*, using the same number of operations, $O(n)$, but reducing the time, $T(n)$, required from proportional to n to proportional to log n (by assuming a binary tree hierarchy of processors)—a substantial drop in time, particularly as n gets large.

This brings us to the difference between concurrency and parallelism:

- *Concurrency*: The recognition that we can divide up a computation (an algorithm) into separate pieces where the *order of execution* of the pieces doesn't matter. Concurrency is a function of the algorithm you use to solve a problem. This also means that even if you create a concurrent program, if you run it on a single processor it will still run serially.

- *Parallelism*: The mechanism used to execute a program on a particular machine or machine architecture in order to improve the performance of the program. Parallelism allows a concurrent program to execute on many different processors and thus potentially improve the overall performance of the program.

The left side of Figure 12-1 illustrates the idea of executing a concurrent program broken up into two threads of execution and running on a single processor, whereas the right side illustrates the idea of using two processors to execute a program that's divided up into two threads of execution.

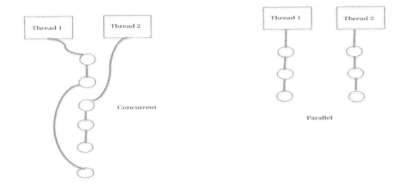

Figure 12-1. *Concurrency vs. parallelism*

As an example, here's a slightly different version of a way to tell the difference between concurrency and parallelism that appeared in Stack Overflow[1]:

Assume that your local chess club organizes a demonstration tournament where 10 local players, all with approximately the same skill level, will be pitted against a chess Grandmaster. So the club organizers have to arrange 10 chess games and want to make them time efficient so everyone can go out and celebrate. There are several ways to organize the match:

- *Serial*: The boards are all lined up in a room and the chess master sits down at the first table to play. The game is played to completion and the chess master then moves to the next table to play the next game. If each game lasts 10 minutes, that's a total of 100 minutes. If it takes the chess master about 6 seconds to move from one table to the next, then that's about another minute (well, it's 54 seconds, but we'll fudge it a bit) for a total of 101 minutes. Not bad.

- *Concurrent*: The boards and players are all lined up the same way, but for this version the chess master plays differently. The chess master sits down at the first table to play, makes the first move in 6 seconds and then immediately moves to the next player to make the next first move. Once again, it takes 6 seconds to move between tables. This continues until after one minute (6 * 10 seconds) the chess master is back at the first table for the second move. If we assume that each game will take the same 10 minutes that the serial games took, then we need to know how many rounds the chess master will have to make. If each of the local players takes about 50 seconds for their move, then we have each move taking 50 + 6 = 56 seconds. Each game takes 10 minutes or 600 seconds, so we have 600 seconds / 56 seconds per move = about 11 rounds to complete all 10 games. This will give us a total of 11 * 56 + 11 * 60 = 616 + 660 seconds = 1,276 seconds = 21.27 minutes to complete the match. Much better.

[1]https://stackoverflow.com/questions/1050222/concurrency-vs-parallelism-what-is-the-difference Retrieved July 24, 2017. If you don't know Stack Overflow, you should go there right now.

- *Parallel*: Lets say the chess club wants to add a bit more competition to the event and hires a second chess master. With two chess masters, the club organizers can have each master play just 5 games. If they use the serial method from above, then each chess master will sit down, play a complete game and then move to the next table. But this time since two games are being played simultaneously, the tournament is finished in half the time, 101 / 2 = 50.5 minutes. Better, but not as good as the concurrent approach.

- *Concurrent* and *Parallel*. In this case we have two chess masters, and each of them plays all 5 games at the same time. Each chess master sits down, makes a move in 6 seconds, gets up and moves to the next table also in 6 seconds. If the games still take 10 minutes each, and if each player still takes 50 seconds for each move, then we still end up with 11 rounds, but the total time to move between games only takes 30 seconds now (because there are only 5 games going on for each chess master). That gives us 11 * 56 + 11 * 30 = 616 + 330 = 946 seconds = 15.77 minutes for the entire match. This appears to be the minimum value that we get from the four different ways of playing the match, and it seems that creating a concurrent program and running it on a parallel machine is clearly better than the other possibilities.

Remember, concurrency is a property of the algorithm, whereas parallelism is a property of the machine[2].

Parallel Computers

Computer scientists have recognized that parallelism can be used to improve performance and to scale large problems for 50 years. In this section we'll look at some different forms of parallel machines that allow us to improve the performance of concurrent programs.

Flynn's Taxonomy

In 1966 Michael Flynn proposed a taxonomy for different types of computer architectures. This taxonomy persists to today, with a couple of extensions I'll mention.

The taxonomy originally contained four model architectures:

- *SISD—single instruction stream, single data stream*: This is the classic von Neumann computer architecture for uniprocessor computers. A single program runs on the machine at a time, handling a single stream of data.

- *MISD—multiple instruction stream, single data stream*: This architecture assumes that a number of different programs will all execute on the same data stream, producing possibly different results. The programs all run in lockstep. Machines that use this architecture are very rare. One possible application might be a machine that tries to break a cryptogram using several different algorithms all running on different processing units.

---

[2]A great talk on the differences between concurrency and parallelism by Rob Pike is at https://vimeo.com/49718712.

- *SIMD—single instruction stream, multiple data stream*: This is one of the most common architectures. In it a single program is run on different processors, each using a different data stream. These data streams can be a partitioned set of data where each subset must have the same computation run on it. For example, weather models can use this architecture to predict hurricane paths. One characteristic of the SIMD model is that all the machines in the system are running the same program in lockstep. Because all the machines are running the same program at the same time, SIMD machines aren't suitable to improve the performance of concurrent programs.

- *MIMD—multiple instruction stream, multiple data stream*: The most general architecture where multiple programs run simultaneously on different machines, each using a different data stream. These programs are not required to run in lockstep, so they can execute concurrent programs and improve their performance. In the early 21st century, this is the most common model for supercomputers. Your multi-core laptop or desktop system is also an MIMD machine.

There are two other variations on these models that have evolved in the last decade or so:

- *SIMT—single instruction stream, multi-threading*: This execution model uses SIMD as its base, but allows each instruction stream to execute multiple threads at a time. This model was proposed in the mid-2000s and is generally used in multi-core graphics processors. It's very useful for applications where there is a lot of redundancy in the data stream.

- *SPMD—single program, multiple data stream*: This is a common parallel programming execution model today. It allows each processor to execute a program independently, and so not in step with other processors, all on different (possibly partitioned) data streams. Because the programs run independently, they can take advantage of concurrent sections of the program in order to improve performance. Despite its name, SPMD is a sub-category of the MIMD model above.

Parallel Programming

A *thread*, also called a *thread of execution*, is a unit of parallelism. A thread is a piece of code that contains everything it needs to execute a sequence of instructions, a private list of instructions, a call or system stack, a program counter, and a small amount of thread-specific data (usually on its call stack). A thread shares access to memory with other threads. This allows multiple threads to cooperate and communicate via shared variables.

A *process* is a thread that also has its own private address space. Instead of using shared memory, processes communicate with each other using messages, so they share an interface for sending and receiving messages. A process is dynamic, whereas programs are static. A process is a program in execution. Processes have more state associated with them than do threads. This means it costs more to create and destroy processes. It also means that processes are intended to stay around longer.

Latency is the amount of time it takes to complete a given unit of work, whether that's a process, a thread, or a smaller unit of the program. Latency can be a problem in program execution. If one part of a program or process takes much longer to execute than others, then nothing else can get done while we are waiting on that one part. A way around this has been used in operating systems since the early 1970s: *context switching*. Say you're executing a program and the program attempts to open a disk file. Disk operations are orders of magnitude slower than other memory operations, and having to wait on the disk operation to complete will slow down your program considerably and also prevent any other program from executing. In cases like this, the operating system swaps out your program and allows other programs to execute until the disk operation completes. (The system must be able to let the disk to perform operations independently for this to work.) It can then switch your program back into memory to continue executing. This context switching doesn't make the latency any shorter, but it hides the latency from the rest of the system and allows other programs to make progress towards completion. This improves the overall performance of the machine, if not the individual programs. This technique is like the *Concurrent* technique in the earlier chess example.

Throughput is the amount of work that can be computed in a unit of time. Our objective is to use parallelism to increase throughput. As an example, if you have a pipelined processor, this exhibits a form of parallelism. The pipeline may be made up of different stages—for example, (1) fetch instruction, (2) decode instruction, (3) fetch data, (4) execute instruction, and (5) write data. In this example, we can have five different instructions all being "executed" simultaneously as each of them is in a different stage at any given time. This architecture improves the throughput of the machine by allowing it to retire more instructions per unit time than a processor that only has a single instruction active at a time.

Speedup is the execution time of the sequential version of a program divided by the execution time of a parallel version of the same program. *Speedup = Ts / Tp*. (See also *Amdahl's law*, discussed shortly.) Related to speedup, *efficiency* is a measure that shows how efficiently each processor is being used. *Efficiency = Speedup / P*, where P is the number of processors in the parallel machine.

The two main goals of parallel programming are *scalability* and *improved performance* to a large number of processors. In the next, sections we'll look at these two goals briefly. For a more detailed look, see Lin & Snyder[3].

Scalability

Scalability is a simple idea: as the amount of data grows, we want our program to be able to use more processors to accommodate the growth in data size and do it efficiently. This doesn't seem hard. As the amount of data increases, we merely spawn more copies of our program and set them loose to act on the data. But there are a number of issues with scalability that make this not such an easy problem. These include the memory model of the system. Are we using a shared memory or a distributed memory? Does each processor have its own copy of the data? Are we running in lockstep or independently and does this matter for this program? What is the topology of the network system that connects the processors and how does that affect communication latency (the time it takes to pass data from one processing element to another when it needs it)? Well-written parallel programs must explore and compensate for all these issues.

Performance

One would think that *improving performance* by using more processors would also be easy. One would be wrong. Ideally, if a program takes time T to execute to completion on a single processor, we would like it to take T / P time on a machine with P processors. It turns out this is hardly ever the case for a number of reasons. First, you must be able to divide your program into P different concurrent sections in order to achieve optimal performance improvement. If you can't do this, you won't be able to take advantage of all P processors. Next, it turns out that creating a concurrent program adds *overhead* to your program that is not there in the serial version. This overhead comes in the form of creating the control sections that the program will use to fork off the concurrent pieces of your program and the communications overhead needed to move data and results back and forth between processors. Then we know that even highly parallelizable programs will have sections that are inherently serial. So, not all of the program can be divided up. Finally, even for well-designed parallel programs, scaling your program for larger values of P creates overhead that may drown out any advantage you gain from having more processors. In short, you may end up with too many processors.

---

[3]Lin, Calvin, and Lawrence Snyder. *Principles of Parallel Programming*. Hardcover. Boston, MA: Addison-Wesley (2009).

Obstacles to Performance Improvement

There are a number of potential roadblocks to improving scalability and performance in your parallel programs. Here are a few:

- *Overhead*: In converting a serial program into a parallel one, you may need to add code to *manage* the parallel bits. All this code is considered overhead and will impact your performance. There is also overhead in creating and destroying your threads of execution; this code is usually in a library or in the operating system and is invisible to you, but nonetheless will slow down your parallel program. *Communication* between threads and other processes is another source of overhead. If you have one thread that must wait on another thread for an event or a computation to complete, that's called *synchronization* overhead.

- *Non-parallelizable code*: As mentioned earlier, in your serial program there is bound to be code that can't be parallelized. For example, loop overhead, input/output, and network communications are all examples of code that normally can't be parallelized. This will prove an impediment to your efforts to create concurrent sections of your program and will limit the benefits you can get from parallelizing the program. The fact of non-parallelizable code leads us to the next obstacle.

- *Amdahl's law*: In 1967 Gene Amdahl wrote a paper that tried to express the relationship between performance and the serial portion of a parallel program. This expression is now known as Amdahl's law. If the fraction of time for the parallel part of your program to execute on a single processor is P, and the fraction of time for the inherently serial fraction of your program is 1 – P, then Amdahl's law says that the speedup you'll get from using N processors is as follows:

  ```
  S(N) = 1 / ((1-P) + P/N)
  ```

  Note that $S(1) = 1$. It's also true that as N goes to infinity, $S(N) = 1 / (1 - P)$. This gives us a limit on the amount of parallelism we can expect for individual programs. It means there's likely an upper bound on the number of processors we'll be able to use to improve the performance of any given program. There are arguments about this conclusion.

- *Idle time*: The next roadblock to optimum parallel performance is idle time. Ideally, we'd like all the available processors to be working all the time, but this may not be the case. There may be instances like load imbalances (your concurrent program puts more work on certain parts than others) and delays waiting for memory operations that will cause some processors to have to wait on others. This will hurt your performance gains.

- *Contention*: Finally, in any computer system, the processors are only one resource that your program will use. There are also various I/O devices, the connectivity network, and so on. If one of these resources is scarce, or if your program is overly dependent on a single resource, then there may be contention for that resource among your parallel code parts. This will cause some of them to have to wait, slowing down your overall performance.

How to Write a Parallel Program

In order to write a parallel program, we'll often start with a serial version of the program, or with serial algorithms that implement the solution to a problem we'd like to parallelize. To convert a serial solution into a parallel one, we need to identify the portions of the solution that are inherently serial and those that may be parallelized. We also need a series of abstractions that we can use to think about parallel problems. Finally, we need a set of language features to allow us to talk about the parallel program.

Parallel Programming Models

We can divide parallel computations into several different types:

- Data parallel

- Task parallel

- Shared memory

- Threaded

- Message passing (a.k.a. distributed memory)

- Single program multiple data (SPMD)

In a problem that exhibits *data parallel computations* we can apply parallelism by performing the same set of computations to different parts of the data all in parallel and hence on different processors. Because we're running the same code on all the processors, but on different data, this type of computation is *scalable*. We can maintain efficiency by just adding more processors as the size of the data increases. The most popular current programming language that works with the data parallel model is Chapel[4].

On the other hand, if can divide up a program into a set of tasks, each of which does something different but all of which contributes to the solution of the whole problem, then we have a *task parallel computation*. Because there are a finite number of tasks in any given problem solution, and because there are bound to be some number of dependencies in the computation (some tasks need to execute before others), task parallel types of computations are usually not scalable beyond the number of tasks.

In the *shared memory* model, all the tasks, whether serial or parallel, share the same address space. They read and write to this shared address space asynchronously. This typically requires the use of locks or semaphores to control access to the memory and prevent contention and deadlocks. This is one of the simplest models and is an example of the PRAM (parallel random access machine) model, which implements a shared memory abstract machine.

In the *threads* model, a single process starts up and acquires a set of resources. It then spawns some number of threads that will execute in parallel. All the threads have some local data (usually on their call stack) but all of them also share the memory and resources of the parent process. This means that the threads model is a form of shared memory model. POSIX Threads, Java Threads, OpenMP, and CUDA threads are all examples of this model.

The *message passing* (distributed memory) model has all the processes on different processors with their own set of memory resources. The processes communicate not by sharing memory but by passing messages over the interconnection network. These messages usually take the form of library subroutine calls. The messages can include control and data messages. All the processes must be programmed to cooperate with the other processes. Messages are usually sent synchronously (for example, for every send() function call there must be a receive() function call). The standard for this model is the *Message Passing Interface* (MPI) standard created by the MPI Forum[5].

---

[4]See http://chapel.cray.com/
[5]See https://computing.llnl.gov/tutorials/mpi/

The *single program multiple data* (SPMD) model is a meta-model that can be built on top of any of the models mentioned earlier. In this model, all the tasks spawned are identical and execute simultaneously, but on different slices of the data stream. Because they act on different parts of the data, each task may, in fact, execute different instructions as they move forward.

Designing Parallel Programs

The first issue with designing a parallel program is to decide who is going to do it. Originally it was up to the developer to identify all the parallel parts of a problem solution or an existing serial program, design the program using one of the models just mentioned, and then write the program by hand. This process is difficult and prone to many errors. But over the last few decades, a number of tools have been developed to at least partially automate the parallelization of programs. Mostly these tools are built into modern compilers.

Modern compilers can parallelize serial programs in two different ways: (1) a fully automatic option where the compiler does all the work, and (2) a programmer directed option where the programmer identifies areas of possible parallelization using compiler directives, pragmas, or command line options. Fully automatic compilers are good at recognizing low-level parallelization opportunities, for example in loops, but they typically don't do large-scale parallelization well. Programmer-directed parallelization is more effective because the programmer is explicitly suggesting areas of the program ripe for parallelizing. This means that modern developers will typically use a combination of manual examination and writing and automatic tools to create parallel programs.

We'll spend the next few sections examining this hybrid approach to parallel programming.

Parallel Design Techniques

Here we'll talk about several techniques to use when you begin to think about a parallel program. This is not a complete tutorial on parallel design. There are many online courses and books devoted just to that. Here's a short list of things to consider as you design a parallel program:

- First of all, you must *understand the problem and the solution in terms of concurrency*. Given an algorithm to solve a problem, you must understand how to create a concurrent solution. If you've already got a serial program that solves your problem, you must understand it before you start thinking of concurrency.

- Once you understand the problem, you should consider whether it can be parallelized at all. It won't do you any good to try to parallelize a problem that isn't amenable to parallelization to begin with (these are known as *inherently sequential* problems).

- The biggest thing to look for when you're thinking about parallelism is *data dependency*. If you have a problem or a solution where the partial solutions always depend on previous partial solutions, this severely limits your ability to find concurrency and hence to parallelize the algorithm. Computing the Fibonacci sequence (0, 1, 1, 2, 3, 5, 8, 13, 21, 34, . . .) is an example of a problem whose solution benefits very little from parallelization. The standard definition of the sequence is that $F(n) = F(n-1) + F(n-2)$ and so at every step, the next partial solution in the sequence is dependent on the values of the two previous partial solutions, which *must* be computed first. This offers us little opportunity in the way of parallelization.

- If you're looking at a serial program, one thing to do is to find the program's *hotspots*—those portions of the code where the program spends most of its time. If you can find hotspots in the serial program, and if they can be parallelized, then this is one way to quickly improve the program's performance. Loops and recursive calls are prime places to look for hotspots.

- In addition to hotspots, you should identify parts of the program that will act as *choke points* or *bottlenecks*. Areas where the existing program is considerably slower than other parts. The classic example here is any part of the program doing input or output, particularly disk I/O. These parts can't normally be parallelized, but you can improve them by taking advantage of things like large, fast, shared memory (for example, so instead of reading a single block at a time, you read several blocks at once into main or cache memory where they can be accessed much faster).

- *Task decomposition* is another technique that's useful as you're looking at ways to parallelize a program. Just as we looked for opportunities to decompose larger problems into smaller ones in the section on structured decomposition in Chapter 5, you can look for opportunities to break a large amount of work into several smaller tasks that could be executed independently. For example, a climate modeling is often made up of several smaller independent models—an atmospheric model, an ocean model, a hydrology model, and a land surface model. Each of these smaller pieces of a large problem can be separated out for independent computation, with a fifth piece that brings the partial results together.

- When designing a parallel program you should always think about *communication* between the different, independent parts of the program. If you have an embarrassingly parallel program (the next chapter talks more about this), then there will be very little communication between processing units, so communication is not much of an issue. For example, if I have a graphics application that's inverting all the color elements in each pixel, the program is making changes to individual pixels that are independent of the pixels surrounding it. On the other hand, in a hurricane model, computations of things like wind speed and direction and barometric pressure in one small geographic area will affect the same computations in adjacent areas so communication overhead and synchronization must be taken into account.

- The *memory model* used in the target parallel computer is also an issue that must be considered when writing a parallel program. A shared memory model typically makes reading and writing to and from memory easier, but also brings in problems with contention for reads and writes. A distributed memory model typically requires that the program synchronize the memories from time to time, which can hinder performance.

- Finally, as you design your parallel program you should always consider *synchronization* and *coordination*. In some applications the order in which tasks or threads execute must be coordinated to ensure that any data dependencies are met. This can take the form of language or library features that, for example, allow the developer to stop execution of a thread until all the other threads catch up. Or the developer may also write code to require synchronizing execution to force memory writes to take place in the correct order.

Programming Languages and APIs (with examples)

The next few sections look at two modern programming languages (and libraries and APIs) with parallel programming features: Java and OpenMP. I won't attempt to cover all the features in each language, leaving that to the references at the end of the chapter. We'll just try to get a feel for how parallel programming is approached in each language.

Parallel Language Features

Nearly all parallel programming languages (and APIs and libraries) include certain features that facilitate the process of turning your serial algorithm or program into a scalable parallel program. Just to get us started, here's a partial list of parallel language features:

- *Threads*: Most parallel languages include the concept of a *thread of execution*. They typically provide a set of language features to allow the developer to create and destroy threads, to manage them, to cause them to wait, and to join back up to the main program thread. These languages may also allow the threads to share data.

- *Synchronization*: All parallel languages include features that allow the developer to synchronize the work of different processors and combine answers from partial solutions. This is particularly important in fine-grained programs running on shared memory machines (like multi-core processors). A common type of synchronization technique is the barrier. A *barrier* is a piece of code that will force all threads to stop execution until all other threads have reached the same point in their computation. For example, in OpenMP the parallel for loop construction creates a barrier that doesn't let any thread proceed past the loop until all threads have completed executing the loop. A second common synchronization technique is *mutual exclusion*.

- *Mutual exclusion and locking*. Many times in concurrent programming two or more threads of execution must share resources. When this happens, care must be taken to avoid *race conditions*—for example, if one thread changes a shared variable value while another thread is attempting to either read or write that same value. Mutual exclusion solves this problem by requiring that each thread include a *critical section* of code where the thread has sole control of the resource and no other thread can access the resource—the other thread is forbidden from being it its critical section at the same time. This exclusion is usually accomplished by using a separate variable (called a *mutex*) that a thread will set to acquire control of the resource and to lock out all other threads until the resource is released. The original idea for mutual exclusion comes from Dijkstra[6]. All parallel programming languages contain features to implement mutual exclusion. As an example of how a mutex works, consider the following class in an object-oriented language:

```
class Mutex {
        public void lock() { // definition in here }
        public void unlock() { // definition in here }
        private boolean locked;
}
```

---

[6]Dijkstra, Edsger W. 1965. "Solution of a Problem in Concurrent Programming Control." *Commun. ACM* 8 (9): 569. doi: https://doi.org/10.1145/365559.365617.

This would be used in a program as in

```
Mutex m = new Mutex(); // create a single instance of the Mutex class
...
m.lock();
// critical section
...
m.unlock();
```

while a thread is inside its critical section. Any other threads that call the lock() method will have to wait until the first thread unlocks the mutex. In this way, changes to shared variables are kept inside the critical section and remain synchronized.

- *Access to shared memory*: Most parallel programming languages assume that the developer is using some variation on the shared memory model and so contain features that allow threads to access shared memory variables and to control access to them (see mutual exclusion earlier).

- *Reduction*: When your program spawns a number of threads that are each going to compute part of a solution to a problem, you have to have a way to gather the partial solutions together and *reduce* them into a single solution for the entire problem. Many parallel languages provide a feature that lets you tell the program how to do the reduction. We'll see how this works below when we talk about OpenMP.

Java Threads

Java has several libraries that are used for creating parallel programs. The most basic library available is the Thread class in the java.lang package. The Thread class provides the basic functionality to create and manage threads of execution. You can also make new Threads by creating a class that implements the Runnable interface, or by using the utilities provided in the java.util.concurrent package. When a Java program executes, there's always at least one thread of execution running, the main thread. Here's probably the simplest example of creating and using a new Thread in Java:

```
/**
 * just about the simplest example of starting and running a Java Thread
 * This new thread will just print "MyThread is running" and exit.
 */
public class MakeAThread {

    /** make an inner class that will be the new thread */
    public static class MyThread extends Thread {
        /** the Thread must have a run method */
        @Override
        public void run(){
            System.out.println("MyThread is running");
        }
    }
```

```
    public static void main(String [] args) {
        MyThread myThread = new MyThread();

        /** always start a new thread using the start() method */
        myThread.start();
    }
}
```

In this program we create an inner class that is a sub-class of the Thread class and whose instances do the work of the new Thread. In our main() method we create the new Thread and start it. We don't really have a Thread until the start() method is called, at which point we now have two threads executing. The start() method automatically called the new thread's run() method and when it exits, the Thread object also exits. We can also create new threads of execution by implementing the Runnable interface and then creating new Thread objects. Here's the same example, but this time using the Runnable interface:

```
/**
 * a second way to
 * make a simple example of starting and running a Java Thread
 */

public class MakeARunnableThread {

    /** make an inner class that will be the new thread */
    public static class MyRunnable implements Runnable {
        /** the Runnable must have a run method */
        @Override
        public void run(){
            System.out.println("MyRunnableThread is running");
        }
    }

    public static void main(String [] args) {
        /* we create a new thread and pass it the Runnable object to execute */
        Thread myThread = new Thread(new MyRunnable());

        /** always start a new thread using the start() method */
        myThread.start();
    }
}
```

Note that in this example, we still have to create a new Thread instance, but we can pass the Thread constructor an instance of the new Runnable object. Everything else is the same as above.

When you use Java Threads, each new thread is given a *priority*, and the Java Virtual Machine (JVM) contains a thread scheduler that's charged with ordering the thread executions. The scheduler will vary executions based on how many processors are available and the priority of each thread. There are several ways that you as the developer can control the scheduling of your threads.

The first is to use the Thread.sleep() method to force a thread to go to sleep. The thread will be blocked, and another thread will be selected to execute. When the sleeping thread wakes up it will be put in a queue to execute. Another way you can change the scheduling of a thread is by changing its priority. All threads are created with an integer value that is the priority of the thread. The values range from 1 through 10, with higher numbers having higher priority. The Thread methods getPriority() and setPriority() allow the developer to manipulate a thread's priority and hence when it's scheduled to run.

The Threads interface in Java gives the developer very low-level control over the creation and management of threads. This actually makes programming threads in Java more difficult than it might be otherwise. If a developer writes a program that creates several threads, then the scheduling of these threads and the management of shared variables add significantly to the overhead of the program. It also can lead to possible run-time errors in the form of *race conditions* and *lost updates*.

In a race condition, two or more threads are sharing a variable and they all want to read and write the variable. The order in which each thread executes and the fact that a thread can be forced to suspend execution either by a sleep() or by the operating system because it has exhausted its current quantum of allowed time can cause the shared variable to have the wrong value when the next thread reads it. Here's an example.

Say that Fred and Gladys both share a bank account. Let's also say that the algorithm for withdrawing money from the bank account is as follows:

1.   You check the account balance to make sure there's enough money in the account.

2.   You withdraw the money you want from the account.

Note that although each of these two operations is atomic (can't be interrupted once started), the algorithm could be interrupted between steps 1 and 2. And now let's throw in another step and allow Fred or Gladys to take a nap at some time while they are thinking about withdrawing money. This can lead to the following situation:

1.   Fred wants to withdraw $100 from the bank account.

2.   He checks the account balance, and it's $150.

3.   Fred takes a nap.

4.   Gladys checks the account balance and it's $150.

5.   Gladys withdraws $100.

6.   Fred wakes up and tries to withdraw $100.

7.   Oops. The account is now overdrawn.

That's a race condition. Here's a program that can illustrate this problem:

```
/*
 * example of a race condition
 * with Java Threads
 *  Here we are going to create two threads and have
 *  each of them withdraw $10 from the account
 *  10 times in a row.
 */
public class FredAndGladys implements Runnable  {
    private BankAccount account = new BankAccount();

    /** The run() method does the actual work of the thread */
    public void run()  {
        for (int x = 0; x < 10; x++) {
            makeWithdrawal(10);
            if (account.getBalance() < 0) {
                System.out.println("Overdrawn!");
            }
        }
    }
}
```

```java
    /**
     *  The method that makes each withdrawal.
     *  It checks to see if the balance is OK
     *  goes to sleep for 500msec and then
     *  attempts to withdraw the money.
     */
    private void makeWithdrawal(int amount)  {
        /** so we know which thread this is */
        String name = Thread.currentThread().getName();
        if (account.getBalance() >= amount)
        {
            System.out.println(name + " is about to withdraw " + amount);
            try {
                System.out.println(name + " is going to sleep");
                Thread.sleep(500);
            } catch (InterruptedException ex) {
                ex.printStackTrace();
            }

            System.out.println(name + " woke up");
            account.withdraw(amount);
            System.out.printf("%s completes the withdrawal\n", name);
            System.out.printf("New balance is $%d\n", account.getBalance());
        } else {
            System.out.println("Sorry, not enough for "
                        + Thread.currentThread().getName());
        }
    }
}

/**
 *  inner class to represent a simple bank account
 */
class BankAccount {
    private int balance = 100;

    public int getBalance () {
        return balance;
    }

    public void withdraw(int amount) {
        balance = balance - amount;
    }
}

/**
 * the driver to run the experiment
 */
class FGMain
{
    public static void main(String[] args) {
        FredAndGladys theJob = new FredAndGladys();
```

```
        Thread one = new Thread(theJob);
        Thread two = new Thread(theJob);

        one.setName("Fred");
        two.setName("Gladys");

        one.start();
        two.start();
    }
}
```

When we compile and execute this program, the first part of what we get is shown next. All things being equal, Fred and Gladys can alternate making withdrawals, but there's a race condition. (Note that the balance is first reported as $80 and then as $90 because both threads are holding copies of the balance variable in their caches before they write it back to memory. Gladys writes first (after Fred has withdrawn) and we see an $80. Then Fred writes and we see a $90. Gladys then gets in before Fred again and the amount is correct:

```
Gladys is about to withdraw 10
Gladys is going to sleep
Fred is about to withdraw 10
Fred is going to sleep
Fred woke up
Fred completes the withdrawal
Gladys woke up
Gladys completes the withdrawal
New balance is $80
Gladys is about to withdraw 10
Gladys is going to sleep
New balance is $90
Fred is about to withdraw 10
Fred is going to sleep
Fred woke up
Fred completes the withdrawal
New balance is $70
Fred is about to withdraw 10
Fred is going to sleep
Gladys woke up
Gladys completes the withdrawal
New balance is $60
```

This all happens because it's the JVM (or the operating system) that controls when threads get to use the CPU again. Luckily, Java has a way to fix this. There's a keyword, synchronized, that you can use in a method signature and that creates a critical section so that only one thread at a time is allowed to execute in that method. Any other thread that attempts to enter the synchronized method is blocked. If we synchronize the makeWithdrawal(int amount) method, then when we run it we get the following:

```
Fred is about to withdraw 10
Fred is going to sleep
Fred woke up
Fred completes the withdrawal
```

```
New balance is $90
Gladys is about to withdraw 10
Gladys is going to sleep
Gladys woke up
Gladys completes the withdrawal
New balance is $80
Fred is about to withdraw 10
Fred is going to sleep
Fred woke up
Fred completes the withdrawal
New balance is $70
Fred is about to withdraw 10
Fred is going to sleep
Fred woke up
Fred completes the withdrawal
New balance is $60
```

Which now has everyone in sync[7].

Another way to try avoiding race conditions (available since Java 5) is to use the volatile keyword on the variable balance in the BankAccount class. If this is done, then no cache copies of balance are kept, and the values are correctly updated most of the time. Because the variable is always stored in main memory (and not in the cache) and is always written back to main memory, then multiple threads could be writing to a shared volatile variable and still have the correct value stored in main memory. But if a thread needs to first read the value of a shared volatile variable and then update that value with a new one, using a volatile variable is no longer good enough to guarantee that the variable's value remains synchronized. Because there's a gap in time between reading the current value of the variable from main memory and then writing the new value, there's still a race condition where Fred and Gladys might both read the current value of balance and generate (the same) new value and write it. The volatile variable is now out of sync. There's no way to fix this other than being careful about when and how a shared volatile variable is used in your program.

One should also be careful about the use of the synchronized keyword, because it adds more overhead and thus impacts performance. And although synchronized methods provide mutual exclusion and thread-safe code, they don't protect against deadlock. *Deadlock* occurs when two processes or threads are contending for the same resources, the resources can be locked, and the processes refuse to give them up. As an example, the following sequence of events leads to deadlock:

- Thread a enters synchronized method foo (and gets the key, locking out any other thread).

- Thread a goes to sleep.

- Thread b enters synchronized method bar (and gets the key, locking out any other thread).

- Thread b tries to enter foo, can't get the key, and waits.

- Thread a wakes up, tries to enter bar, can't get the key and waits.

- *Neither can proceed until they acquire the other key.*

---

[7]https://docs.oracle.com/javase/tutorial/essential/concurrency/syncmeth.html

This is known (from Dijkstra) as a *deadly embrace*. How to fix a deadlock? Well, you shouldn't depend on Java to do it because Java can't detect a deadlock. The best methods involve mitigation; work carefully to make sure that this situation doesn't happen.

For more on concurrency and parallel programming in Java, see the online Java Tutorials[8].

OpenMP[9]

OpenMP stands for *Open Multi-Processing*. It's a very popular open source application programming interface (API) that enables simple creation of parallel programs. There are OpenMP implementations for practically all hardware architectures and bindings for C, C++, and Fortran. OpenMP assumes a shared memory model where threads share variables, so there are race condition possibilities like in Java already discussed. It's not really a programming language. Rather it consists of compiler directives (#pragma's in C & C++), library routines (which gives you an API), and environment variables.

OpenMP uses a *fork-join parallelism* model. In this model there is one *master thread*. This thread is charged with dynamically creating N parallel threads (called a *team of threads*) for a parallel region of the code. The number of threads created depends on OpenMP's assessment of how much parallelism is needed to execute the parallel region. When all those threads finish, program execution goes back to one master thread again until another parallel region is encountered. Figure 12-2 illustrates what fork-join parallelism looks like.

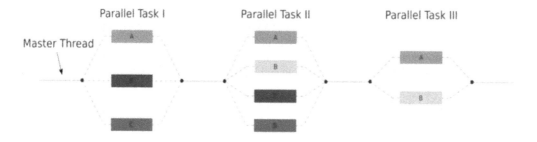

Figure 12-2. *Fork-join parallelism*

The programmer indicates to the compiler where the parallel regions should be using the compiler directive #pragma omp parallel. This directive creates an SPMD (*single program multiple data*) program where each thread executes the same code. The threads are created dynamically as needed. The maximum number of threads can be controlled with the OMP_NUM_THREADS environment variable or with the omp_set_num_threads(N) OpenMP library function.

The programmer can figure out which thread they currently are using omp_get_thread_num() library function, which returns the current thread number. OpenMP will add parallelism dynamically until the demands of the program are met (or until it reaches the maximum number of threads allowed).

---

[8]https://docs.oracle.com/javase/tutorial/essential/concurrency/index.html
[9]The name OpenMP is the property of the OpenMP Architecture Review Board. See www.openmp.org.

The master thread will create threads with the OpenMP `parallel` compiler directive. This directive tells the compiler that the next code statement block is to be considered a *parallel region* to be executed by each processor. For example, #pragma omp parallel num_threads(8) will instruct OpenMP to create up to seven threads of the parallel region that immediately follows the #pragma. Seven threads are created instead of eight because the master thread is also used in the parallel computation. In C or C++, this might look like the following:

```
long list[1000];
#pragma omp parallel num_threads(8)
{
        int threadID = omp_get_thread_num();
        foo(list, threadID);
}
```

Note that because OpenMP uses a shared memory model, we need to guarantee *synchronization* and that the program can also still encounter race conditions. Recall that two common techniques for enforcing synchronization are *barriers* and *mutual exclusion*. OpenMP has a compiler directive to set a barrier, #pragma omp barrier. It can also create critical sections (and thus enforce mutual exclusion) by using another directive, #pragma omp critical. Only one thread at a time can enter a critical section. OpenMP also allows a very fine-grained form of synchronization by allowing the programmer to create an *atomic* operation. Using the #pragma omp atomic compiler directive, the programmer can apply mutual exclusion to a single statement that must update a memory location. Allowable operations in an atomic region include: x op= expression, x++, ++x, x--, and --x.

If the #pragma omp parallel compiler directive creates an SPMD program and forces the program to execute the code in the parallel region, how do we get a loop to divide up the work into the threads (known as *worksharing*) so that we can execute the entire program faster? OpenMP assures this will happen with another directive, #pragma omp for. This directive has the effect of splitting up the work in the loop among all the threads in the team.

To illustrate how you would use all these OpenMP directives and library functions, let's take a look at a fairly common example in parallel computing. If you took calculus in school, you remember that one way to look at the integral is as the area under a curve. In numerical analysis, there's a technique called the *trapezoid rule* that allows you to approximate the definite integral of a function by measuring and summing up a number of trapezoids (or rectangles) under the curve drawn by your function. It turns out that the function f(x) = 1.0 / (1.0 + x²) using values of x from 0.0 to 1.0 is an approximation to π / 4. So we can write a program that uses the trapezoid rule to compute π / 4 and then just multiply to get a value for π. Figure 12-3 shows what the function looks like.

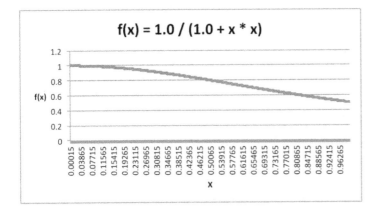

Figure 12-3. Function to compute π / 4

And here's a serial version of this program in C:

```c
/*
 *  Serial program to estimate the area under a curve f(x)
 *  It really computes pi/4 and approximates the trapezoidal rule
 *  using rectangles instead of trapezoids.
 */
#include <stdio.h>
#include <stdlib.h>

/*
 * Here's the function we'll be computing
 */
double f(double x) {
    return 1.0 / (1.0 + x * x);
}

int main (int argc, char **argv) {
    int steps = 1000000000;      /* number of rectangles - 1 billion */
    double width = 0.0;          /* width of each rectangle */
    double x, pi4, sum = 0.0;

    /* get the width of each rectangle */
    width = 1.0 / (double) steps;

    /* loop to compute the area under f(x) */
    for (int i = 0; i <= steps; i++) {
        x = i * width;
        sum = sum + f(x);
    }
    pi4 = width * sum;
    printf("Sum is %8.4f and Area: pi/4 is %8.6f\n", sum, pi4);
    printf("Approximation to pi is %8.6f\n", pi4 * 4.0);
    return 0;
}
```

Compiling and executing this program on an 8-core Intel Linux computer running the Fedora operating system and using the GNU C compiler produces the following results:

```
Sum is 785398164.1474 and Area: pi/4 is 0.785398
Approximation to pi is 3.141593
real 16.19
user 16.11
sys 0.00
```

The real processor time for the execution of 1 billion loop iterations is 16.19 seconds on a lightly loaded machine. Of course, this version of the program is running serially on only a single core. To speed it up, we want to use OpenMP to try to parallelize the loop. Here's a version of the program using OpenMP:

```c
/*
 *  Parallel program to estimate the area under a curve f(x)
 *  it really computes pi/4 and approximates the trapezoidal rule
 *  using rectangles instead of trapezoids.
 *  Uses OpenMP with the gcc 7.1.0 compiler.
 */
#include <stdio.h>
#include <stdlib.h>
#include <omp.h>

/*
 * Here's the function we'll be computing
 */
double f(double x) {
    return 1.0 / (1.0 + x * x);
}

int main (int argc, char **argv) {
    int steps = 1000000000;    /* number of rectangles - 1 billion */
    double width = 0.0;        /* width of each rectangle */
    double x, pi4, sum = 0.0;

    /* get the width of each rectangle */
    width = 1.0 / (double) steps;

    /*
     * here we define the parallel region to be the for loop
     * We declare x to be private and tell OpenMP
     * to reduce the partial sums as each thread finishes.
     */
    #pragma omp parallel for private(x) reduction(+:sum)
    /* loop to compute the area under f(x) */
    for (int i = 0; i <= steps; i++) {
        x = i * width;
        sum = sum + f(x);
    }
    pi4 = width * sum;
    printf("Sum is %8.4f and Area: pi/4 is %8.6f\n", sum, pi4);
    printf("Approximation to pi is %8.6f\n", pi4 * 4.0);
    return 0;
}
```

When this version of the program is compiled and run on the same system and using the same compiler (but including the OpenMP library), we get the following results:

```
Sum is 785398164.1475 and Area: pi/4 is 0.785398
Approximation to pi is 3.141593
real 2.24
user 17.06
sys 0.00
```

Note that the sum variable in the compute_p4 program is accumulated in the for loop. How does this work if we do *worksharing* and separate the work in the loop into multiple threads? This idea, that inside a loop we accumulate partial values each time through the loop, is called a *reduction*. What we do in this case is use another OpenMP compiler directive, reduction(<operator> : <list of variables>). This operator causes several things to happen: (1) a local copy of each variable is made and initialized, (2) updates in the thread only happen to the local copy, and (3) at the end of the loop execution the local copies are reduced into a single value and combined (both using the designated operator) into the original global variable. Operators that can be used for reduction include +, -, *, max, min, &, |, ^, &&, and ||.

In this version, the running time is down to 2.24 seconds—a speedup of 7.2 on a lightly loaded system. This indicates that OpenMP was using all eight cores to do the work, and with the for and reduction compiler directives, the compiler was dividing up the work in the for loop efficiently, and the answers ended up the same, but in a much shorter time.

Just as in Java, there's much more to the details of OpenMP that we haven't gone into here. This was just a taste of the very cool and interesting things you can do with parallel programming. If you really want to do parallel programming, you're strongly encouraged to go to the references at the end of this chapter and learn more.

The Last Word on Parallel Programming

Coding is the heart of software development. Code is what you produce. Performance is the key to good code and to programming the solutions to large and interesting problems. With Moore's law beginning to fade and the power wall a reality, parallel programming is what everyone will be doing in the future.

And finally:

> *"The way the processor industry is going is to add more and more cores, but nobody knows how to program those things. I mean, two, yeah; four, not really; eight, forget it."*

—Steve Jobs, Apple

References

Anonymous. (2007). *Example of fork-join parallelism*. Retrieved from By Wikipedia user A1 w:en:File:Fork_ join.svg, CC BY 3.0, `https://commons.wikimedia.org/w/index.php?curid=32004077`.

Barney, B. (2017a). *Introduction to Parallel Programming* [government]. Retrieved July 31, 2017, from `https://computing.llnl.gov/tutorials/parallel_comp/#top`.

Barney, B. (2017b, June). *OpenMP* [government]. Retrieved July 31, 2017, from `https://computing.llnl. gov/tutorials/openMP/`.

Cherneyshev, A. (2008, December 2). *Writing Parallel Programs: a Multi-Language Tutorial Introduction* [industrial]. Retrieved July 31, 2017, from `https://software.intel.com/en-us/articles/writing-parallel-programs-a-multi-language-tutorial-introduction`.

Dijkstra, E. W. (1965). "Solution of a problem in concurrent programming control." *Commun. ACM, 8*(9), 569. `https://doi.org/10.1145/365559.365617`.

Downey, A. B. (2016). *The Little Book of Semaphores* (2nd edition). Needham, MA: Green Tea Press. Retrieved from `http://greenteapress.com/semaphores/LittleBookOfSemaphores.pdf`.

Eadline, D. (2009, July 7). *Concurrent and Parallel are not the Same* [Online magazine]. Retrieved July 27, 2017, from `http://www.linux-mag.com/id/7411/`.

Flynn, M. (1972). "Some Computer Organizations and Their Effectiveness." *IEEE Transactions on Computers, C-21*(9), 948-960. `https://doi.org/10.1109/TC.1972.5009071`.

Hoare, C. A. R. (1978). Communicating Sequential Processes. *CACM, 21*(8), 666-677.

Lin, C., & Snyder, L. *Principles of Parallel Programming* (Hardcover). Boston, MA: Addison-Wesley (2009).

Mattson, T. G., Sanders, B. A., & Massingill, B. L.. *Patterns for Parallel Programming* (hardcover). Boston, MA: Addison-Wesley (2005).

Parri, J., Shapiro, D., Bolic, M., & Groza, V. (2011). "Returning control to the programmer: SIMD intrinsics for virtual machines." *CACM, 54*(4), 38-43. `https://doi.org/10.1145/1924421.1924437`.

Vishkin, U. (2011). "Using simple abstraction to reinvent computing for parallelism." *CACM, 54*(1), 75-85. `https://doi.org/10.1145/1866739.1866757`.

CHAPTER 13

Parallel Design Patterns

> *Software typically outlives hardware, so over the course of a program's life it may be used on a tremendous range of target platforms. The goal is to obtain a design that works well on the original target platform, but at the same time is flexible enough to adapt to different classes of hardware.*

—Tim Mattson, et. al.

Design patterns (refer to Chapter 11) were introduced in the 1990s in order to "describe simple and elegant solutions to specific problems in object-oriented software design. Design patterns capture solutions that have developed and evolved over time. Hence, they aren't the designs people tend to generate initially. They reflect untold redesign and recoding as developers have struggled for greater reuse and flexibility in their software. Design patterns capture these solutions in a succinct and easily applied form.[1]"

A *design pattern* is a representation of a common programming problem along with a tested, efficient solution for that problem. Although design patterns are normally presented in an object-oriented programming framework, the idea is completely general and can be applied to different programming models, including parallel ones.

Parallel Patterns Overview

Parallel design patterns have the same objectives as the classical sequential design patterns, namely to describe solutions to recurrent problems, but now in the context of parallel software design rather than object-oriented software design.

This chapter provides an overview of parallel patterns, the abstractions, and how to think about converting serial programs into parallel programs. We'll also go through several sample parallel design patterns, including those for solving the problem of efficient implementation of recursive, divide and conquer computations, of staged computations, and of computations split in a number of independent tasks. As in Chapter 11, I won't examine all the parallel design patterns. Instead, I'll take a representative sample, mostly from Mattson, et. al.[2]

---

[1]Gamma, E., Helm, R., Johnson, R., & Vlissides, J. *Design Patterns: Elements of Reusable Object-Oriented Software* (Vol. Hardcover). Boston: Addison-Wesley (1995).
[2]Mattson, T. G., Sanders, B. A., & Massingill, B. L. *Patterns for Parallel Programming*. Boston, MA: Addison-Wesley (2005).

© John F. Dooley 2017

J. F. Dooley, *Software Development, Design and Coding*, https://doi.org/10.1007/978-1-4842-3153-1_13

In the next several sections we'll develop a vocabulary of parallel patterns so that we can illustrate several different patterns later. To begin the language definition, Mattson, et. al. in their seminal book use four different design elements, called *design spaces*, to describe each of the parallel patterns.

Parallel Design Pattern Design Spaces

One of the most interesting aspects related to parallel design patterns is the partitioning of the design of a parallel application into four separate but related *design spaces* that roughly coincide with the steps in creating a parallel program:

- *Finding concurrency*: This design space is "concerned with structuring the problem to expose exploitable concurrency[3]." The programmer will take a problem or an existing serial program and search out the areas of possible concurrency that can be utilized.

- *Algorithm structure*: In this design space, the programmer attempts to find and structure the algorithms that can take advantage of the exposed concurrency.

- *Supporting structures*: Where the programmer begins to map the algorithms to data structures and to more detailed program structures like loops and recursion.

- *Implementation mechanisms*: Finally, the design is mapped into particular parallel programming frameworks.

  Figure 13-1 shows the hierarchy of the design spaces, the general areas in which the patterns are organized, and lists the parallel meta-patterns associated with each space.

---

[3]Mattson, p. 24.

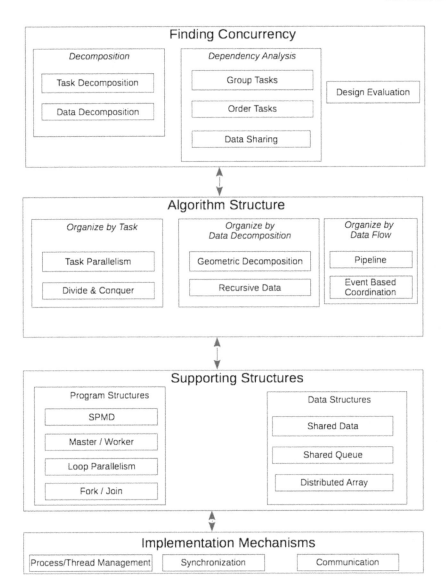

Figure 13-1. *The parallel design spaces and related meta-patterns*

Finding Concurrency

The meta-patterns in the *finding concurrency* design space are used to start designing a parallel application. The developer enters this design space after having considered the top-level elements of the problem to be solved. Our objective is to tease out the parts of the algorithm or program that are inherently sequential and those that contain elements of concurrency. This typically has the developer looking at the parts of the program or algorithm that are the most computationally intensive because these are the areas where are most likely to find concurrency. Finding concurrency is divided up into three dimensions.

The first two dimensions, the *Decomposition* and *Dependency Analysis* dimensions, are related to the ways in which the developer will implement the parallel application.

In particular, the *Decomposition* meta-patterns are used to decompose the problem into pieces that can execute concurrently, whereas the *Dependency Analysis* meta-patterns help group the tasks to be executed and analyze the dependencies among these tasks.

The *Decomposition* dimension includes just two meta-patterns that are used to find and divide the problem into parts that can execute concurrently:

- *Task Decomposition*: This pattern views a complex algorithm as a set of instructions that can be grouped into a set of tasks that can be executed concurrently.

- *Data Decomposition*: This pattern takes the data used by the program and attempts to divide it into chunks that can be used by each of the tasks.

The *Dependency Analysis* dimension includes three different meta-patterns whose job it is to group the tasks found above and to analyze the dependencies between them:

- *Group Tasks*: This pattern aims at modeling the more convenient grouping of tasks such that the management of dependencies is simplified,

- *Order Tasks*: This pattern aims at figuring out how tasks (or groups of tasks) may be ordered to satisfy the application constraints related to task execution.

- *Data Sharing*: This pattern aims to model the accesses to a shared data structure.

The main forces influencing the design of these meta-patterns are flexibility, efficiency, and simplicity. Flexibility is needed to adapt the program design to different implementation requirements. Efficiency is usually related to scalability; how does the solution scale with the size of the target parallel computer? Finally, simplicity is required for understandability and maintenance.

The third dimension, *Design Evaluation*, isn't really a pattern in the sense that we've used the word so far. Rather, it's used to "guide the algorithm designer through an analysis of what has been done so far before moving to the patterns in the *algorithm structure* design space[4]." Design evaluation is really a process that encourages the developer to evaluate the design iteratively in order to arrive at the best design possible. In this process, the developer asks a number of questions that force them to think about the current version of the design. For example, how suitable is the design for the target platform? How many processing elements (PEs) are available and how many of them and how often will they be used? How are the data structures shared among the PEs? How regular are the tasks and their data dependencies? Are the tasks grouped in the most efficient and scalable way?

The overall output resulting from the analysis of the *finding concurrency* design space is a decomposition of the problem into different design elements, namely: 1) a task decomposition identifying the tasks that can be executed concurrently, 2) a data decomposition that identifies the data local to each of the tasks, 3) a way of grouping tasks and ordering the tasks groups such that temporal and data dependencies are satisfied, and 4) an analysis of the dependencies among the tasks.

Algorithm Structure

The output from the *finding concurrency* design space is used in the *algorithm structure* design space to refine the design of our concurrent tasks and to create a parallel program structure closer to an actual parallel program suitable to be run on a parallel target architecture.

---

[4]Mattson, p. 26.

There are three major ways of organizing a parallel algorithm:

- *Task decomposition*: The tasks themselves drive your design. That is, consider the tasks that can be computed in parallel, which tasks in your set are concurrent, and then how they're enumerated, linearly or recursively. For linear decompositions, use the Task Parallelism pattern, and for the recursive decompositions, use Divide & Conquer. The *organize by tasks* meta-pattern group includes these two meta-patterns:

  - *Task Parallelism*: This pattern that governs the efficient execution of collections of tasks. The common factor here is that "the problem can be decomposed into a collection of tasks that execute concurrently[5]." These tasks can be independent or there may be some dependencies between them. In many cases, the tasks are also associated with a loop program structure. The proposed solution to implement the pattern works out three different points: how tasks are defined, the dependencies among tasks, and the scheduling of the tasks for concurrent execution, including assigning tasks to different processors or threads.

  - *Divide & Conquer*: This pattern implements the well-known *divide and conquer* recursive solution schema: a problem is divided up into a number of smaller, identical sub-problems, which are then solved, and the solutions are combined into a single final solution for the original problem.

- *Data decomposition*: Here, the data is driving the design. Consider the decomposition of data into (possibly disjoint) subsets to be used by each task. Again, this decomposition can be either linear or recursive. If the data can be distributed into discrete data sets and the entire problem can be solved by operating on each data set independently, then choose the Geometric Decomposition meta-pattern. If the data is organized recursively (say, as a binary tree), choose the Recursive Data meta-pattern. The *organize by data* decomposition pattern group includes two meta-patterns:

  - *Geometric Decomposition*: This pattern represents all those computations where the algorithm is recognized as a series of computations on some core data structure and where that data structure is inherently *linear* in nature, such as an array, table, or matrix. With these types of data structures, the data can be broken up into contiguous subsets and acted on independently by the program. That means the tasks operating on this data can execute concurrently. See the *Distributed Array* meta-pattern for an example of how the *Geometric Distribution* pattern would organize its data.

  - *Recursive Data*: This pattern works with those parallel computations created to work with some recursively defined data structure, where the data appears to be acted upon sequentially. These tasks generally use links to move from one data element to another, as in a linked list, binary tree, or graph, but the computations involve things like following a path in the tree or partitioning the graph. Solving these problems usually involves restructuring the computations over the linked data structure that exposes more concurrency.

---

[5]Mattson, p. 65.

- *Organize by flow of data*: You would consider using the *flow of data* when the organizing principle of the algorithm is how the flow of data imposes an ordering on the tasks that make up the algorithm. If the flow of data is one-way and consistent, then the Pipeline meta-pattern is the choice. If the flow of data is dynamic or unpredictable, then you want the Event-Based Coordination meta-pattern. The organize by flow of data pattern group hosts two meta-patterns:

  - *Pipeline*: This pattern is for where the flow of data is traversing a linear chain of stages, each representing a function computed on the input data coming from the previous stage whose result is delivered to the next stage. Note that the data flow is assumed to be one-way in this pattern. This should look and sound just like the idea of a multi-stage CPU architecture, or a pipe-and-filter execution sequence in the Unix shell.

  - *Event-Based Coordination*: This pattern is for where a number of semi-independent concurrent activities interact in an irregular way, and interactions are determined by the flow of data between the concurrent activities. The flow of data implies a set of ordering dependencies between the tasks. Note that here, the data flow isn't assumed to be one-way, nor is the flow assumed to be linear. There are many examples of problems that fit this pattern, including many discrete event-simulation problems. Hence many of the solutions that use this pattern use events as basic building blocks. There is usually at least one task that generates events, and then some number of them process the events. (Think of a multi-stall car wash where cars arrive at random and are assigned to a stall, or a bank with either a single queue or multiple queues and several tellers to serve customers as they reach the front of the queue).

Note that in the *organize by flow of data* design space, the three ways of organizing the parallel algorithm are alternatives, whereas in the *finding concurrency* design space the developer will normally go through all the groups of patterns. Here the programmer is required to choose one of the three alternatives and exploit one of the parallel design patterns in the group.

Supporting Structures

After having explored different possibilities to find concurrency and express parallel algorithms in the *finding concurrency* and *algorithm structure* design spaces, implementation is taken into account with two more design spaces. The first one is called the *supporting structures* design space, which starts investigating those structures/patterns suitable to support the implementation of the algorithms planned when exploring the *algorithm structure* design space. Two groups of meta-patterns are included in this design space. The first group is related to how to structure the program in order to maximize parallelism—the *program structures* meta-pattern group—and the second is related to commonly used shared data structures: the *data structures* meta-pattern group.

The *program structures* group includes four meta-patterns:

- *Single Program, Multiple Data (SPMD)*: In this meta-pattern, all the processing elements (PEs) run the same program in parallel, but each PE has its own subset of the data. Unlike in an SIMD architecture, the PEs aren't required to stay in lockstep, and so different parallel tasks may follow different paths through the code. Because each of the PEs runs its own copy of the program, an important feature of the SPMD is that the extra overhead associated with starting and stopping the loops is implemented at the beginning and end of the program rather than inside the loop itself. Each data set will typically be split so that a loop in the program runs just a fraction of the total number of iterations. Also, the PEs only communicate infrequently with their neighbors, increasing efficiency.

- *Master/Worker*: In this meta-pattern, a single Master task sets up a number of concurrent Worker threads or processes and a single bag of tasks. Each Worker will take a task out of the bag and execute it in parallel; as they finish, Workers will continue to take tasks out of the bag and execute them until the bag is empty or some other ending condition has occurred. The bag of tasks is typically implemented as a shared queue. The *Master/Worker* pattern is particularly useful for *Embarrassingly Parallel* programs (discussed a little later), where a large number of worker tasks have no dependencies.

- *Loop Parallelism*: This meta-pattern solves the problem of how to execute an algorithm with one or more compute-intensive loops. The pattern describes how to create a parallel program where the distinct iterations of the loop are executed in parallel. The program to compute the value of π using OpenMP in Chapter 12 is an example of the *Loop Parallelism* pattern at work.

- *Fork/Join*: This meta-pattern (see the example in Chapter 12) is an example of the concurrent execution of different portions of the overall computation that proceed unrelated up to the (possibly coordinated) collective termination. Typically, a single thread or process will fork off some number of sub-processes that will all execute in parallel. The originating process will typically wait until the child processes all join before resuming its own execution. Each time the original thread forks off sub-processes, there may be a different number of them. This meta-pattern, like many of the patterns we've seen so far, assumes a shared memory model where all the tasks are sharing values and results that are available to the Master at the end. The Fork/Join pattern is the standard programming model in OpenMP.

These meta-patterns are well known in the parallel computing community. The SPMD pattern is the computational model used by MPI and is one of the most popular patterns used to structure parallel computations, along with the Master/Worker. Loop Parallelism has been exploited in vector architectures and it is currently one of the main sources of parallelism in both OpenMP and GPUs. Last but not least, the Fork/Join pattern perfectly models the pthread_create/pthread_join model of POSIX threads[6] and is also used as the basis for OpenMP.

The *data structures* group includes three meta-patterns:

- *Shared Data*: This meta-pattern implements those features related to the management of data shared among a number of different concurrent activities. Shared data is managed in a number of different parallel applications. The correct and efficient management of the shared data is usually the most time- and effort-consuming activity in the whole parallel program development/design process. This pattern requires simplicity of execution, careful abstraction of how the data is to be manipulated, and awareness that explicitly managing the shared data will incur some parallel overhead—and it must guarantee the correctness of any computation, regardless of the order of the tasks (reading and writing, in particular) that will occur during the computation[7]. It needs to consider locking, memory synchronization, and task scheduling. An example of the use of this meta-pattern is managing shared data in the Task Parallelism meta-pattern, where tasks are first duplicated and then partial answers reduced.

---

[6]Barney, B. (2017, March). "POSIX Threads Programming" [government]. Retrieved August 7, 2017, from `https://computing.llnl.gov/tutorials/pthreads/`.
[7]Mattson, p. 174.

- *Shared Queue*: This meta-pattern creates queue data types implemented in such a way that the queues may be accessed concurrently. Shared queues are used to support the interaction of concurrent activities in different contexts, from threads to processes and concurrent activities running on CPU co-processors. A good example of where this meta-pattern would be used is in the Master/Worker meta-pattern to create the concurrent queue that dispenses tasks for the Worker processes.

- *Distributed Array*: This meta-pattern models all the aspects of the parallel program related to the management of arrays partitioned and distributed among different concurrent activities. Distributed arrays are often used to implement data structures that are logically shared among concurrent activities but may be somehow partitioned in such a way that a single one of the concurrent activities owns and manages a single portion of the distributed array. "The challenge is to organize the arrays so that the elements needed by each UE are nearby at the right time in the computation. In other words, the arrays must be distributed about the computer so that the array distribution matches the flow of the computation[8]." This meta-pattern is particularly useful for programs using the Geometric Decomposition meta-pattern in order to help with the algorithm construction, and to organize the program structure when using the SPMD meta-pattern.

Mattson, et. al. classify the different meta-patterns in this design with respect to their suitability to support the implementation of the different patterns in the algorithm structure design space. As an example, Task Parallelism is well supported by the four meta-patterns in the program structures group, whereas the Recursive Data pattern is only (partially) supported by the SPMD and Master/Worker patterns.

Implementation Mechanisms

The second (and lowest-level) design space related to implementation of parallel applications is called the *implementation mechanisms* design space, which includes the meta-patterns representing the base mechanisms needed to support the parallel computing abstractions typical of parallel programming:

- Concurrent activities

- Synchronization

- Communication

In fact, this design space hosts only three distinct meta-patterns corresponding to the abstractions mentioned:

- *UE Management*: This meta-pattern is related to the management of the *units of execution* (processes, threads). The UE Management meta-pattern deals with all the aspects related to the concurrent activities in a parallel application, including their creation, destruction, and management. Although in Mattson only threads and processes are taken into account, the UE Management meta-pattern may be adapted to handle the concurrent activities placed on CPU co-processors such as the GPU kernels.

---

[8]Mattson, p. 199.

- *Synchronization*: This meta-pattern handles all those aspects related to ordering of events/computations in the UE used to execute the parallel application. The Synchronization meta-pattern deals with all aspects related to synchronization of concurrent activities and memory and therefore covers aspects such as lock/fence mechanisms, higher-level mutual exclusion constructs (for example, monitors), and collective synchronizations (such as barriers).

- *Communication*: This meta-pattern manages all the aspects related to the communications happening between the different UEs implementing the parallel application. The Communication meta-pattern deals with the aspects related to data exchange among concurrent activities and therefore covers aspects related to different kinds of point-to-point message passing (for example, send and receive, synchronous and asynchronous) and multi-point or collective communications (for example, broadcast, scatter, gather, reduce) where multiple UEs are involved in a single communication event.

A List of Parallel Patterns

This section examines in more detail a few of the meta-patterns mentioned earlier. I'll also include some other common parallel patterns and match these patterns with the meta-patterns already discussed.

Embarrassingly Parallel

Not really a pattern, this is rather a class of problems. There are some problems where the division of the work into independent tasks is so obvious and simple that the problem is known as *Embarrassingly Parallel* or *Pleasingly Parallel*.

Examples include the trapezoid rule program to compute π in Chapter 12, where we could compute the areas of any number of trapezoids in parallel, or any program that uses a loop to accumulate values using multiplication or addition, password-cracking programs, rendering of computer graphics images, computing the points for the Mandelbrot set, facial-recognition systems, and many computer simulations such as climate models.

Other examples of Embarrassingly Parallel problems can depend on the type and size of the input data. For example, if you have several million (say M) TIFF files that you want to convert to GIF files, you can just distribute M/P TIFF files (where P is the number of processing elements) to each PE and do the conversions there (see the upcoming Map pattern). Or if you have an entire catalog of text documents and you want to compute word frequencies across the entire catalog, you can again divide the documents across all the processing elements you have, do the counts on each subset, and then combine all the subsets (see the MapReduce pattern, discussed shortly). It turns out that there are many types of Pleasingly Parallel problems where you have a large number of independently distributed computations across a large set of data that fit this split-compute-combine pattern. We'll look at these in upcoming sections.

Master/Worker

In this pattern, a single Master task will set up a number of concurrent Worker threads or processes and a single bag of tasks. Each Worker will take a task out of the bag and execute it in parallel; as they finish, Workers will continue to take tasks out of the bag and execute them until the bag is empty or some other ending condition has occurred. The bag of tasks is typically implemented as a shared queue. The Master/Worker pattern is particularly useful for Embarrassingly Parallel programs (see Figure 13-2), where a large number of worker tasks have no dependencies.

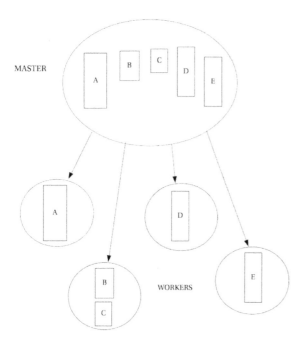

Figure 13-2. *Master/Worker pattern implementing an Embarrassingly Parallel problem*

Map and Reduce

The Map pattern is likely the simplest pattern you'll run into. Like Master/Worker, the Map and Reduce patterns are very well suited for Embarrassingly Parallel problems. Map applies part of the program—call it a function—to every element of the data in parallel. The functions must have no side-effects and must be identical and independent. Because of this independence, Map can take advantage of as many units of execution as are available.

Used with the Map pattern, the Reduce pattern combines all the elements of the collection of partial solutions pairwise and creates a summary value as the final solution. Though commutativity is not required for the combination of the partial solutions, most applications of Reduce assume commutativity and associativity. Figure 13-3 shows an example of how combining Map and Reduce works.

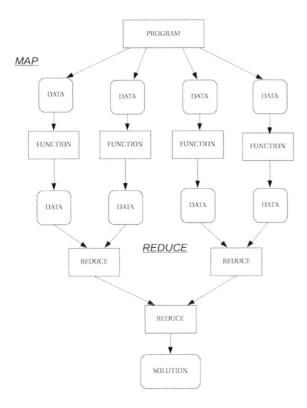

Figure 13-3. *Illustration of an implementation of Map, followed by Reduce*

In OpenMP, the `#pragma omp parallel for` compiler directive will initiate a Map operation for a for-loop that is in an Embarrassingly Parallel program. Adding a `reduction(+: <var-list>)` to the compiler directive will add the Reduce component. For the trapezoid rule program in Chapter 12, the main for loop looked like this:

```
#pragma omp parallel for private(x) reduction(+:sum)
    /* loop to compute the area under f(x) */
    for (int i = 0; i <= steps; i++) {
        x = i * width;
        sum = sum + f(x);
    }
```

Of course, the Map and Reduce patterns can be used separately and often are.

MapReduce

This variation of using the Map and Reduce patterns combines the two to accomplish a common task. The MapReduce pattern, first published in 2004[9], is intended solve problems where the main goal is to input, process, and generate large data sets and where the implementation is scalable across many processors. The implementation of MapReduce performs three essential functions:

- *Mapping*: The program divides up a large data set (or a large set of files) into N discrete and independent subsets, each of which will be processed on a single processor. The output is typically a map data structure of some kind containing lists of not necessarily unique (key, value) pairs.

- *Shuffle*: The program extracts similar (key, value) pairs and assigns them to a new processor where the reduce operation will happen.

- *Reduce*: The elements in an input data set are combined into a single result that's output. The list of the results from each processor constitutes the generated output data set.

As an example of a use of MapReduce to solve a large problem, say we have a large catalog of text documents. Our objective is to create a single list of (word, frequency) pairs that tells us all the unique words in all the documents and how many times each of those words occurs. A solution to this type of problem would be useful in problems in cryptography or in the statistical analysis of texts, say for author-attribution studies. Figure 13-4 shows what the system might look.

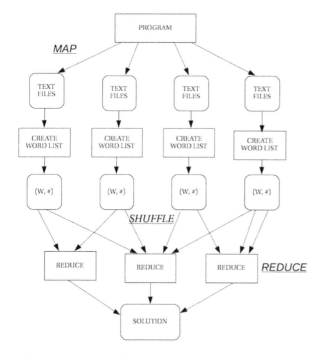

Figure 13-4. *A use of MapReduce to find word frequencies across a large set of text files*

---

[9]Dean, J., & Ghemawat, S. "MapReduce: Simplified Data Processing on Large Clusters." In *Proceedings of the 6th Conference on Symposium on Operating Systems Design & Implementation*. Berkeley, CA, USA: USENIX Association. pp. 137–149 (2004).

In this solution, we start with a catalog of text files. We divide the files up into subsets and assign each subset to an instance of the program on a processor. The program then creates a list of words and their frequencies for each of the words in all the documents in its subset. The shuffle operation then takes each unique word in each of the words lists and assigns it to a reduce process. For example, all the ("cat", value) pairs from all the word lists end up as inputs to the same reduce process. Each reduce process then accumulates all the values of all the unique words to create the final solution.

Pseudo-code for the map and reduce portions of this program might look like[10] the following:

```
map(DocumentID docID_key, String input_value) {
    /* docID_key is the name of the document */
    /* input_value is the contents of the document */
    Create a Map called myMap;
    for each word in input_value do {
        if (myMap.contains(word)) then
            myMap.put(word, myMap.get(word) + 1);
        else
            myMap.put(word, 1);
    }
    return myMap;
}
```

The shuffle operation goes here. The input to the shuffle is the set of all the myMap map output files that contain (word, frequency) pairs for all the words in the text file subsets. The output of the shuffle function is an intermediate key (the word) and the list of all the word frequency counts for that word in all the files in the catalog. Each of these goes to a reduce function and this operation continues until all the myMap output files are exhausted. The shuffle operation can take a long time (longer than the map or reduce) because it will end up doing a lot of I/O between processing elements as it moves data from the map output files to the reduce inputs:

```
reduce(String intermediate_key, Iterator value_list) {
    /* intermediate_key is a word from the documents */
    /* value_list is the list of counts of that word */
    int result = 0;
    for each value in value_list do {
        result += value;
    }
    return result;
}
```

At the end we have a final output map that contains entries for each unique word and its total frequency in all the files in the catalog. So we see that the MapReduce pattern is a useful set of operations that allow a parallel program to implement a solution to the split-compute-combine problem.

MapReduce is so common, and the solution so popular, that a standard framework called Hadoop has been created with MapReduce as its fundamental basis of operation. Hadoop is now part of the Apache project. "Apache Hadoop is a framework for running applications on large cluster built of commodity hardware. The Hadoop framework transparently provides applications both reliability and data motion. Hadoop implements a computational paradigm named MapReduce where the application is divided into many small fragments of work, each of which may be executed or re-executed on any node in the cluster. In addition, it provides a

---

[10]Dean and Gehmawat, p. 138.

distributed file system, the Hadoop Distributed Files System (HDFS), which stores data on the compute nodes, providing very high aggregate bandwidth across the cluster. Both MapReduce and the Hadoop Distributed File System are designed so that node failures are automatically handled by the framework[11]."

Divide & Conquer

Among the many problems with recursive solutions, a large number of them are amenable to a divide and conquer strategy. In this strategy, the data is typically large and contiguous, and the problem has the characteristic that smaller versions of the problem are solved independently as the larger versions of the problem and the larger solution depends on the smaller solutions. Thus, the original large problem can be broken down into smaller sub-problems (along with a discretized subset of the data), and each sub-problem can be solved independently in turn, and the partial solutions combined back into a solution for the larger problem. This characteristic of these problems makes them easily amenable to parallelization. Figure 13-5 shows how Divide & Conquer works.

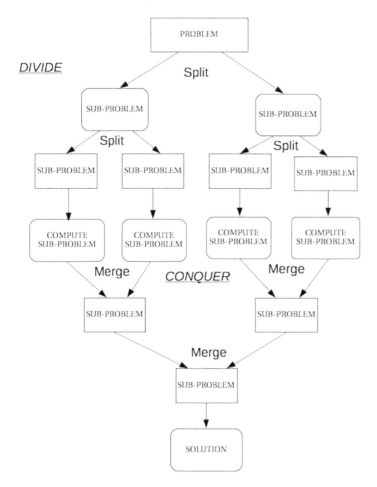

Figure 13-5. *An illustration of the Divide & Conquer strategy*

---

[11]https://wiki.apache.org/hadoop/FrontPage

Note in Figure 13-5 that in a program that uses the Divide & Conquer strategy, the amount of concurrency will vary over the course of the execution of the program. At the beginning and end of the program, there is little in the way of concurrency, but as the program divides the data into more levels, the amount of concurrency grows, at some point reaching a maximum, after which as the merging operations occur, the amount of concurrency shrinks. Also, at some level in the recursion the amount of work involved in coming up with a solution is less than the parallel overhead, and the program should drop out into a sequential algorithm or a base case. There is also the possibility that the division of data won't be regular (a good example here is where the pivot element in Quicksort doesn't divide the current list in half), which also may require more work.

The Divide & Conquer strategy is useful for an entire class of recursive problems, including all the (On log n) sorting algorithms, the Fast Fourier Transform, and problems in linear algebra. This general strategy is typically implemented using either a Fork/Join pattern—where a master thread or instance will spawn some number of child threads and then wait for their completion and combine the partial answers into a final answer—or a Master/Worker pattern. We'll examine the Fork/Join parallel pattern next.

Fork/Join

In some problems, the number of parallel threads will vary as the program executes, making it more difficult to use simple control structures to invoke the parallelism. One way around this is to fork off a different number of threads at different times during the program execution and then wait for them to finish before proceeding. Typically, a single thread or process will fork off some number of sub-processes that will all execute in parallel. The originating process will typically wait until the child processes all join before resuming its own execution. Each time the original thread forks off sub-processes, there may be a different number of them. This pattern also has the possibility of having *nested parallel execution regions* that can complicate the performance of the program.

Pseudo-code for this strategy is simple enough and retains the recursive nature of sequential Divide & Conquer algorithms:

```
ResultType solve(Problem problem) {
    if (problem.size is small enough)
        return solveSequentially(problem);
    else {
        ResultType left, right;
        Divide problem into K subproblems;
        Fork the K subproblems;
        join; // wait for all the subproblems to finish
        return combine(left, right);
    }
}
```

This also illustrates a problem with this type of pattern. The combine() function looks to be inherently serial and will be executed every time solve() is executed. This might slow down the parallel implementation of the problem. We'll next examine a version of the mergesort algorithm. Pseudo-code for the parallel version looks like this:

```
mergesort(list, start, end) {
    if (start < end) then
        mid = floor(start + (end - start)) / 2
        fork mergesort(list, start, mid)
        mergesort(list, mid+1, end)
        join
        merge(list, start, mid, end)
```

We implement this program in C using the OpenMP parallel package. In this C version, in the main() function, we first tell OpenMP to allow nested parallel regions. This is necessary because of the recursion in mergesort. Then, in the mergesort() function we create a parallel region around the two recursive calls to mergesort(). We tell OpenMP to limit the number of threads created in this region to two, so that each recursive call will get exactly one thread. This will create the proper number of threads of execution:

```
/*
 * parallel version of mergesort in C using openMP
 */
#include <stdio.h>
#include <stdlib.h>
#include <omp.h>

/* Here's the merge; it's sequential and the normal one you'd write */
void merge(int* array, int start, int end) {
    int middle = (start + end) / 2;
    int temp_index = 0;

    /* create a temporary array */
    int* temp = malloc(sizeof(int) * (end - start + 1));

    /* merge in sorted data from the 2 halves */
    int left = start;
    int right = middle + 1;

    /* while both halves have data */
    while((left <= middle) && (right <= end)) {
        /* if the left half value is less than right */
        if (array[left] < array[right]) {
            /* take from left */
            temp[temp_index] = array[left];
            temp_index++;
            left++;
        }
        else {
            /* take from right */
            temp[temp_index] = array[right];
            temp_index++;
            right++;
        }
    }

    /* add the remaining elements from the left half */
    while(left <= middle) {
        temp[temp_index] = array[left];
        temp_index++;
        left++;
    }
```

```
    /* add the remaining elements from the right half */
    while(right <= end) {
        temp[temp_index] = array[right];
        temp_index++;
        right++;
    }

    /* move from temp array to the original array */
    int i;
    for(i = start; i <= end; i++) {
        array[i] = temp[i - start];
    }

    /* free the temporary array */
    free(temp);
}

/* the parallel version of mergesort */
void mergeSort(int* array, int start, int end) {
    if(start < end) {
        int middle = (start + end) / 2;

/* sort both halves in parallel;
 * we limit the number of threads to 2
 */
        #pragma omp parallel sections num_threads(2)
        {
            /* require that only one thread execute this task */
            #pragma omp section
            {
                mergeSort(array, start, middle);
            }
            #pragma omp section
            {
                mergeSort(array, middle + 1, end);
            }
        }

        /* merge the two halves */
        merge(array, start, end);
    }
}

int main(int argc, char **argv ) {
    int i;

        if (argc < 2) {
                printf("Usage: %s <arraySize>\n", argv[0]);
                exit(1);
        }
```

```
      int SIZE = atoi(argv[1]);
   int* nums = malloc(sizeof(int) * SIZE);

   /* enable recursive parallel blocks */
   omp_set_nested(1);

   /* put in random numbers */
   for(i = 0; i < SIZE; i++) {
       nums[i] = rand( ) % 1000;
   }

   /* sort them */
   mergeSort(nums, 0, SIZE - 1);

   return 0;
}
```

Notice that we use the OpenMP sections directive in this program. This directive guarantees that each section inside the parallel pragma will be executed once by a thread from the team. Different sections are allowed to be executed by different threads. There is also an implicit barrier at the end of the parallel block so that the merge() function won't be called until the two mergesort() threads are completed. So, with the Fork/Join pattern, we can separate the partitioned array, do the independent mergesort()s, and then merge when each pair is complete. With this setup, each call to mergesort(), except for the last ones, will divide the current sub-list in half and then create two new threads of execution that will execute until complete; when both finish, the merge() function will execute, and then the thread will end. The array being sorted will be shared among all the threads. The number of threads active will increase until we get to a maximum (after $\log_2 n$ steps), at which time the threads will begin to end and the joins will happen. There is overhead incurred every time a new thread is created and destroyed.

The sequential version of this program executes everything in a single thread but uses the system stack to keep track of the recursive calls to mergesort(). Every time mergesort() is called, a new activation record is created on the system stack, and when each mergesort() call ends, that activation record is removed. In this way, the system stack grows and shrinks during the course of the execution. Again, the array is shared by all the active instances of the mergesort() function. The temporary array created in the merge() function is local to that function and disappears when merge() exits. The major overhead in the sequential version is creation and destruction of the activation records on the system stack.

Although this parallel version works and we're able to take advantage of the multiple cores in our test system, it turns out Amdahl's law will be our undoing here. The merge() function as written is inherently sequential and thus slows down the entire program so that our potential speedup is very small. The parallel version of the mergesort program ends up being slower than the sequential version on a two-core, shared memory system running Linux. With larger sizes of the array, we also have to be careful of how many threads we will create simultaneously (that's why we limited the number of threads in the parallel pragma); most operating systems create limits on the number of simultaneously active threads or processes that a single user can create.

How might we fix this problem with the parallel version? There are two changes that might be made. First, in the mergesort() function, the test for the base case - if (start < end) can be changed to be a threshold test instead. We can keep track of either the number of recursive calls or the length of the current sub-list and if it drops below a certain threshold we stop recursing and switch to a different sorting algorithm—say, insertion sort, which approaches linear time complexity for small arrays. This fix doesn't change the sequential nature of the merge() function, though. We can make the program faster by creating a parallel merge function. The merge function is already a O(n) algorithm, so we don't want to make it any slower. It's also not an obvious candidate for parallelization. The goal should be a parallel algorithm that is

O(n) or faster (possibly by reducing the coefficient size in the complexity estimate?). A Divide & Conquer algorithm might be what we are looking for. The development of this algorithm is somewhat beyond the scope of this book, but there's a nice parallel merge algorithm in the 3rd edition of the famous CLRS *Introduction to Algorithms* book, which I commend to the interested reader[12].

A Last Word on Parallel Design Patterns

As you should have noticed by now, parallel design patterns can be very similar. That's because they typically follow the process of creating a parallel algorithm/program from a corresponding serial algorithm/program. The process is to (1) identify concurrency, (2) split the program into the concurrent pieces, (3) split the data if the updated algorithm calls for it, (4) execute the concurrent pieces in parallel, and (5) put all the answers back together to make a final answer. That said, parallel design patterns provide a useful set of abstractions for thinking about parallel programming.

References

Barney, B. (2017a). *Introduction to Parallel Programming* [government]. Retrieved July 31, 2017, from https://computing.llnl.gov/tutorials/parallel_comp/#top.

Barney, B. (2017b, March). POSIX Threads Programming [government]. Retrieved August 7, 2017, from https://computing.llnl.gov/tutorials/pthreads/.

Barney, B. (2017c, June). *OpenMP* [government]. Retrieved July 31, 2017, from https://computing.llnl.gov/tutorials/openMP/.

Cormen, T. H., Leiserson, C. E., Rivest, R. L., & Stein, C. *Introduction to Algorithms, 3rd Edition* (hardcover). Cambridge, MA: The MIT Press (2009).

Dean, J., & Ghemawat, S. "MapReduce: Simplified Data Processing on Large Clusters." In *Proceedings of the 6th Conference on Symposium on Operating Systems Design & Implementation*. Berkeley, CA, USA: USENIX Association. pp. 137–149 (2004).

Gamma, E., Helm, R., Johnson, R., & Vlissides, J. *Design Patterns: Elements of Reusable Object-Oriented Software* (Hardcover). Boston: Addison-Wesley (1995).

Lin, C., & Snyder, L. *Principles of Parallel Programming* (Hardcover). Boston, MA: Addison-Wesley (2009).

Mattson, T. G., Sanders, B. A., & Massingill, B. L. *Patterns for Parallel Programming* (hardcover). Boston, MA: Addison-Wesley (2005).

McCool, M., Robison, A. D., & Reinders, J. *Structured Parallel Programming: Patterns for Efficient Computation* (paperback). Waltham, MA: Morgan Kaufmann Publishers (2012).

---

[12]Cormen, T. H., Leiserson, C. E., Rivest, R. L., & Stein, C. *Introduction to Algorithms, 3rd Edition* (hardcover). Cambridge, MA: The MIT Press. pp. 797–804 (2009).

CHAPTER 14

Code Construction

Mostly, when you see programmers, they aren't doing anything. One of the attractive things about programmers is that you cannot tell whether or not they are working simply by looking at them. Very often they're sitting there seemingly drinking coffee and gossiping, or just staring into space. What the programmer is trying to do is get a handle on all the individual and unrelated ideas that are scampering around in his head.

—Charles M. Strauss

Great software, likewise, requires a fanatical devotion to beauty. If you look inside good software, you find that parts no one is ever supposed to see are beautiful too. I'm not claiming I write great software, but I know that when it comes to code I behave in a way that would make me eligible for prescription drugs if I approached everyday life the same way. It drives me crazy to see code that's badly indented, or that uses ugly variable names.

—Paul Graham, "Hackers and Painters," 2003

We're finally getting to the real heart of software development: writing the code. The assumption here is that you already *do* know how to write code in at least one programming language; this chapter presents examples in a few languages, each chosen for the appropriate point being made. The purpose of this chapter is to provide some tips for writing *better* code. Because we can all write better code.

For plan-driven process developers (see Chapter 2), coding is the tail that wags the development-process dog. Once you finish detailed requirements, architecture, and detailed design, the code should just flow out of the final design, right? Not. In 20 years of industry software development experience, I never saw this happen. Coding is hard; translating even a good, detailed design into code takes a lot of thought, experience, and knowledge, even for small programs. Depending on the programming language you're using and the target system, programming can be a very time-consuming and difficult task. On the other hand, for very large projects that employ dozens or even hundreds of developers, having a very detailed design is critical to success; so don't write off the plan-driven process just yet.

For the agile development process folks, coding is it. The agile manifesto (http://agilemanifesto.org) says it at the very beginning: "Working software over comprehensive documentation." Agile developers favor creating code early and often; they believe in delivering software to their customers frequently, and using feedback from the customers to make the code better. They welcome changes in requirements and see them as an opportunity to refactor the code and make the product more usable for their customer and easier to maintain. This doesn't mean that coding gets any easier when using an agile process; it means that your focus is different. Rather than focus on requirements and design and getting them nailed down as early as possible, in agile processes you focus on delivering working code to your customer as quickly and as often as possible. You change the code often, and the entire team owns all the code and so has permission to change anything if it's appropriate.

© John F. Dooley 2017
J. F. Dooley, *Software Development, Design and Coding*, https://doi.org/10.1007/978-1-4842-3153-1_14

Your code has two audiences:

- The machine that's the target of the compiled version of the code, what will actually get executed

- The people, including you, who will *read* it in order to understand it and modify it

To those ends, your code needs to fulfill the requirements, implement the design, and be readable and easy to understand. We'll be focusing on the readability and understandability parts of these ends first, and then look at some issues related to performance and process. This chapter won't give you all the hints, tips, and techniques for writing great code; there are entire books for that, some of which are in the references at the end of this chapter. Good luck!

Before we continue, I'd be remiss if I didn't suggest the two best books on coding around. The first is Steve McConnell's *Code Complete 2: A Practical Handbook of Software Construction*, a massive, 960-page tome that takes you through what makes good code[1]. McConnell discusses everything from variable names, to function organization, to code layout, to defensive programming, to controlling loops. It's in McConnell's book where the "software construction" metaphor comes from. The metaphor suggests that building a software application is similar to constructing a building. Small buildings (Fido's dog house, for example) are easier to build, require less planning, and are easier to change (refactor) if something goes wrong. Larger buildings (your house) require more detail, more planning, and more coordination largely because it's more than a one-person job. Really big buildings (skyscrapers) require many detailed levels of both design and planning, close coordination, and many processes to handle change and errors. Although the building construction model isn't perfect—it doesn't handle incremental development well, and McConnell also talks about an accretion model where one layer of software is added to an existing layer much like a pearl is created in an oyster—the metaphor gives you a clear view of the idea that software gets much more complicated and difficult to build the larger it gets.

The second classic book is Hunt and Thomas's *The Pragmatic Programmer*[2]. The book is organized as 46 short sections containing 70 tips that provide a clear vision of how you should act as a programmer. It provides practical advice on a range of topics from source code control, to testing, to assertions, to the DRY principle, some of which we'll cover later in this chapter. Hunt and Thomas themselves do the best job of describing what the book and what pragmatic programming is all about:

> *Programming is a craft. At its simplest, it comes down to getting a computer to do what you want it to do (or what your user wants it to do). As a programmer, you are part listener, part advisor, part interpreter, and part dictator. You try to capture elusive requirements and find a way of expressing them so that a mere machine can do them justice. You try to document your work so that others can understand it, and you try to engineer your work so that others can build on it. What's more, you try to do all this against the relentless ticking of the project clock. You work small miracles every day. It's a difficult job[3].*

---

[1]McConnell, S. *Code Complete 2: A Practical Handbook of Software Construction*. (Redmond, WA, Microsoft Press, 2004.)

[2]Hunt, A. and D. Thomas. *The Pragmatic Programmer: From Journeyman to Master*. (Boston, MA: Addison-Wesley, 2000.)

[3]Hunt, 2000.

A Coding Example

In *Code Complete 2*, Steve McConnell gives an example of bad code that's worth examining so we can begin to see what the issues of readability, usability, and understandability are about. I've converted it from C++ to Java, but the example is basically McConnell's[4]. Here's the code; we'll look at what's wrong with it:

```java
void HandleStuff(CORP_DATA inputRec, int crntQtr, EMP_DATA empRec, Double estimRevenue,
    double ytdRevenue, int screenx, int screeny, Color newColor, Color prevColor, StatusType
    status, int expenseType) {
int i;
for ( i = 0; i < 100; i++ )
        {
        inputRec.revenue[i] = 0;
        inputRec.expense[i] = corpExpense[crntQtr][i];
        }
UpdateCorpDatabase( empRec );
estimRevenue = ytdRevenue * 4.0 / (double) crntQtr;
newColor = prevColor;
status = SUCCESS;
if ( expenseType == 1 ) {
        for ( i = 0; i < 12; i++ )
                profit[i] = revenue[i] - expense.type1[i];
        }
else if ( expenseType == 2 ) {
                profit[i] = revenue[i] - expense.type2[i];
        }
else if ( expenseType == 3 )
                profit[i] = revenue[i] - expense.type3[i];
                }
```

So what's wrong with this code? Well, what isn't? Let's make a list:

- Because this is Java, it should have a *visibility modifier*. No, it's not required, but you should always put one in. You're not writing for the compiler here, you're writing for the human. Visibility modifiers make things explicit for the human reader.

- The method name is terrible. HandleStuff doesn't tell you anything about what the method does.

- Oh, and the method does too many things. It seems to compute something called profit based on an expenseType. But it also seems to change a color and indicate a success. Methods should be small. They should do just one thing.

- Where are the comments? There's no indication of what the parameters are or what the method is supposed to do. All methods should tell you at least that.

- The layout is just awful. And it's not consistent. The indentation is wrong. Sometimes the curly braces are part of the statement, and sometimes they're separators. And are you sure that that last right curly brace really ends the method?

- The method doesn't protect itself from bad data. If the crntQtr variable is zero, then the division in line 8 will return a divide-by-zero exception.

---

[4]McConnell, 2004. p. 162.

213

- The method uses magic numbers including 100, 4.0, 12, 2, and 3. Where do they come from? What do they mean? Magic numbers are bad.

- The method has way too many input parameters. If we knew what the method was supposed to do, maybe we could change this.

- There are also at least two input parameters—screenx and screeny—that aren't used at all. This is an indication of poor design; this method's interface may be used for more than one purpose and so is "fat," meaning it has to accommodate all the possible uses.

- The variables corpExpense and profit are not declared inside the method, so they're either instance variables or class variables. This can be dangerous. Because instance and class variables are visible inside every method in the class, we can also change their values inside any method, generating a side-effect. Side-effects are bad.

- Finally, the method doesn't consistently adhere to the Java naming conventions.

This example is terrible code for a bunch of different reasons. In the rest of the chapter, we'll take a look at the general coding rules that are violated here and give suggestions for how to make your code correct, readable, and maintainable.

Functions and Methods and Size

First things first. Your classes, functions, and methods should all *do just one thing*. This is the fundamental idea behind encapsulation. Having your methods do just one thing isolates errors and makes them easier to find. It encourages reuse because small, single-feature methods are easier to use in different classes. Single-feature (and single-layer of abstraction) classes are also easier to reuse.

The phrase *single feature* implies small. Your methods/functions should be small. And I mean small—20 lines of executable code is a good upper bound for a function. Under no circumstances should you write 300-line functions. I know; I've done it. It's not pretty. Back in Chapter 7 we talked about *stepwise refinement* and *modular decomposition*. Taking an initial function definition and refactoring it so that it does just a single, small thing will decompose your function into two or more smaller, easier-to-understand and easier-to-maintain functions. Oh, and as we'll see in Chapter 16, smaller functions are easier to test because they require fewer unit tests (they have fewer paths to get through the code). As the book said, *Small Is Beautiful*.

Formatting, Layout, and Style

Formatting, layout, and style are all related to how your code looks on the page. It turns out that, as we've already seen, how your code looks on the page is also related to its correctness. McConnell's Fundamental Theorem of Formatting says, "good visual layout shows the logical structure of a program[5]." Good visual layout not only makes the program more readable, it helps reduce the number of errors because it shows how the program is structured. The converse is also true; a good logical structure is easier to read. So, the objectives of good layout and formatting should be as follows:

- To accurately represent the logical structure of your program

- To be consistent so there are few exceptions to whatever style of layout you've chosen

---

[5]McConnell, 2004, p. 732.

- To improve readability for humans

- To be open to modifications. (You do know you're code is going to be modified, right?)

General Layout Issues and Techniques[6]

Most layout issues have to do with laying out blocks of code; there are different types of block layout, some of which are built into languages, some you get to choose on your own. The three most prevalent kinds of block layouts are built-in block boundaries, begin-end block boundaries, and emulating built-in blocks.

Some languages have *built-in block boundaries* for every control structure in the language. In this case you have no choice—because the block boundary element is a language feature, you must use it. Languages that have built-in block boundaries include Ada, PL/1, Lisp and Scheme, and Visual Basic. As an example, an if-then statement in Visual Basic looks like this:

```
if income > 25000 then
        statement1
        statement2
else
        statement3
        ...
end if
```

You can't write a control structure in Visual Basic without using the ending block element, so blocks are easier to find and distinguish.

But most languages don't have built-in block boundary lexical elements. Most languages use a begin-end block boundary requirement. With this requirement, a block is a sequence of zero or more statements (where a statement has a particular definition) that are delimited by *begin* and *end* lexical elements. The most typical begin and end elements are the keywords begin and end, or left and right curly braces { and }. For example:

Pascal:

```
if income > 25000 then
    begin
        statement1;
        statement2
    end
else
        statement3;
```

C/C++/Java:

```
if (income > 25000)
{
        statement1;
        statement2;
} else
        statement3;
```

---

[6]There are a number of tools available that will help with coding and testing issues. Some links to popular tools are https://www.owasp.org/index.php/Source_Code_Analysis_Tools, https://en.wikipedia.org/wiki/List_of_tools_for_static_code_analysis, https://www.jetbrains.com/resharper/, and http://www.softwaretest-inghelp.com/tools/top-40-static-code-analysis-tools/

Note in both examples that a single statement is considered a block and doesn't require the block delimiter elements. Note also in Pascal the semicolon is the statement *separator* symbol, so is required between statements, but because else and end are not the end of a statement, you don't use a semi-colon right before else or end (confused? most people are); in C, C++, and Java, the semicolon is the statement *terminator* symbol, and must be at the end of every statement. This is easier to remember and write; you just pretty much put a semicolon everywhere except after curly braces. Simplicity is good.

Finally, when we format a block, we can try to emulate the built-in block boundary in languages that don't have it by requiring that every block use the block delimiter lexical elements.

C/C++/Java:

```
if (income > 25000) {
        statement1;
        statement2;
} else {
        statement3;
}
```

In this example, we want to pretend that the left and right curly braces are part of the control structure syntax, and so we use them to delimit the block, no matter how large it is. To emphasize that the block delimiter is part of the control structure, we put it on the same line as the beginning of the control statement. We can then line up the closing block boundary element with the beginning of the control structure. This isn't a perfect emulation of the built-in block element language feature, but it comes pretty close and has the advantage that you're less likely to run into problems with erroneous indentation, like the following:

C/C++/Java:

```
if (income > 25000)
        statement1;
        statement2;
        statement3;
```

In this example, the erroneous indentation for statement2 and statement3 can lead the reader to believe that they are part of the if statement. The compiler is under no such illusions.

Overall, using an emulating block-boundaries style works very well, is readable, and clearly illustrates the logical structure of your program. It's also a great idea to put block boundaries around every block, including just single statement blocks. That lets you eliminate the possibility of the erroneous indentation error from earlier. So if you say

```
if (income > 25000) {
        statement1;
}
```

it's then clear that in

```
if (income > 25000) {
        statement1;
}
        statement2;
        statement3;
```

`statement2` and `statement3` are not part of the block, regardless of their indentation. It also means that you can now safely add extra statements to the block without worrying about whether they're in the block or not:

```
if (income > 25000) {
        statement1;
        statement2;
        statement3;
        statement4;
        statement5;
}
```

White Space

White space is your friend. You wouldn't write a book without any spaces between words, or line breaks between paragraphs, or chapter divisions, would you? Then why would you write code with no white space? White space allows you to logically separate parts of the program and to line up block separators and other lexical elements. It also lets your eyes rest between parts of the program. Resting your eyes is a good thing. The following are some suggestions on the use of white space:

- Use blank lines to separate groups (just like paragraphs).

- Within a block, align all the statements to the same tab stop (the default tab width is normally four spaces).

- Use indentation to show the logical structure of each control structure and block.

- Use spaces around operators.

- In fact, use spaces around array references and function/method arguments as well.

- Do not use double indentation with begin-end block boundaries.

Block and Statement Style Guidelines

As mentioned previously, the "emulating block boundaries" style works well for most block-structured languages:

- *Use more parentheses than you think you'll need*: I especially use parentheses around all my arithmetic expressions—mostly just to make sure I haven't screwed up the precedence rules.

  ```
  fx = ((a + b) * (c + d)) / e;
  ```

- *Format single statement blocks consistently*: Use the emulating block-boundaries technique:

  ```
  if (average > MIN_AVG) {
      avg = MIN_AVG;
  }
  ```

- *For complicated conditional expressions, put separate conditions on separate lines*:

```
if (('0' <= inChar && inChar <= '9') ||
    ('a' <= inChar && inChar <= 'z') ||
    ('A' <= inChar && inChar <= 'Z')) {
    mytext.addString(inChar);
    mytext.length++;
}
```

- *Wrap individual statements at column 70 or so*: This is a holdover from the days of 80-column punch cards, but it's also a great way to make your code more readable. Having very long lines of code forces your readers to scroll horizontally, or it makes them forget what the heck was at the beginning of the line!

- *Don't use* goto, *no matter what Don Knuth says*[7]: Some languages, such as Java, don't even have goto statements. Most don't need them (assembly languages excepted). Take the spirit of Knuth's paper and only use gotos where they make real sense and make your program more readable and understandable.

- *Use only one statement per line*: (Don't write code as if you were entering the annual International Obfuscated C Code Contest! See www.ioccc.org.) The following is legal, but just doesn't look good, and it's easy to just slide right over that statement in the middle:

```
g.setColor(Color.blue); g.fillOval(100, 100, 200, 200);
mytext.addString(inChar);mytext.length++;System.out.println();
```

This looks much, much better:

```
g.setColor(Color.blue);
g.fillOval(100, 100, 200, 200);

mytext.addString(inChar);
mytext.length++;
System.out.println();
```

Declaration Style Guidelines

Just like in writing executable code, your variable declarations need to be neat and readable.

- *Use only one declaration per line*: Well, I go both ways on this one. Although I think that

```
int max,min,top,left,right,average,bottom,mode;
```

---

[7]Knuth, D. "Structured Programming with goto Statements." *ACM Computing Surveys* 6(4): 261-301 (1974).

is a bit crowded; I'd rewrite this as

```
int max, min;
int top, bottom;
int left, right;
int average, mode;
```

That's not one per line, but the variables that are related are grouped together. That makes more sense to me.

- *Declare variables close to where they're used*: Most procedural and object-oriented programming languages have a *declaration before use* rule, requiring that you declare a variable before you can use it in any expression. In the olden days, say in Pascal, you had to declare variables at the top of your program (or subprogram), and you couldn't declare variables inside blocks. This had the disadvantage that you might declare a variable pages and pages before you'd actually use it. (But see the section later in this chapter where I talk about how long your functions should be.) Python is one exception to the declaration before use rule. Because Python is usually interpreted (instead of being compiled), the interpreter will guess at the variable type the first time it's seen.

  These days you can normally declare variables in any block in your program. The scope of that variable is the block in which it is declared and all the blocks inside that block.

  This tip says that it's a good idea to declare those variables in the closest block in which they are used. That way you can see the declaration and the use the variables *right there*.

- *Order declarations sensibly*: Group your declarations by types and usage (see the previous example).

- *Use white space to separate your declarations*: Once again, white space is your friend. The key idea in these last couple of tips is to make your declarations visible and to keep them near the code where they'll be used.

- *Don't nest header files—ever!* (This is for you C and C++ programmers.) Header files are designed so that you only need to define constants, declare global variables, and declare function prototypes once, and you can then reuse the header file in some (possibly large) number of source code files. Nesting header files hides some of those declarations inside the nested headers. This is bad—because visibility is good. It allows you to erroneously include a header file more than once, which can lead to redefinitions of variables and macros and errors.

  The only header files you might nest in your own header files are system headers like stdio.h or stdlib.h, and I'm not even sure I like that.

- *Don't put source code in your header files—ever!* (Again, this is for you C and C++ programmers.) Headers are for declarations, not for source code. Libraries are for source code. Putting a function in a header file means that the function will be re-defined everywhere you include the header. This can easily lead to multiple definitions—which the compiler may not catch until the link phase. The only source that should be in your headers are macro definitions in #define pre-processor statements, and even those should be used carefully.

Commenting Style Guidelines

Just like white space, comments are your friend. Every programming book in existence tells you to put comments in your code—and none of them (including this one) tells you just where to put comments or what a good comment should look like. That's because how to write good, informative comments falls in the "it depends" category of advice. A good, informative comment depends on the *context* in which you're writing it, so general advice is pretty useless. The only good advice about writing comments is: just do it. Oh, and because you'll change your code—do it again. That's the second hardest thing about comments—keeping them up to date.

Here's my advice:

- *Write comments when you first write your program*: This gives you an idea of *where* they should be. Then, when you finish your unit testing of a particular function, write a final set of comments for that function by updating the ones that are already there. That way, you'll come pretty close to having an up-to-date set of comments in the released code.

- *Indent a comment with its corresponding statement*: This is important for readability because then the comment and the code line up:

```
/* make sure we have the right number of arguments */
if (argc < 2) {
        fprintf(stderr, "Usage: %s <filename>\n", argv[0]);
        exit(1);
}
```

- *Set off block comments with blank lines*: Well, I go both ways on this one. If you line up the start and end of the block comments on lines by themselves, then you don't need the blank lines. But if you stick the end of comment marker at the end of a line, you should use a blank line to set it apart from the source code. So if you do this

```
/*
 * make sure we have the right number of arguments
 * from the command line
 */
if (argc < 2) {
fprintf(stderr, "Usage: %s <filename>\n", argv[0]);
                                exit(1);
}
```

you don't need the blank line; but if you do this

```
/* make sure we have the right number of arguments
from the command line */

if (argc < 2) {
                fprintf(stderr, "Usage: %s <filename>\n", argv[0]);
exit(1);
}
```

then you do (but I wouldn't recommend this style of comment in the first place).

- *Don't let comments wrap—use block comments instead*: This usually occurs if you tack a comment onto the end of a line of source code:

```
if (argc < 2) { // make sure we have the right number of arguments from the
command line
```

Don't do that. Make this a block comment above the `if` statement instead (see the previous bullet point). It's just way easier to read.

- *All functions/methods should have a header block comment*: The purpose of this bit of advice is so your reader knows what the method is supposed to do. The necessity of this is mitigated if you use good identifier names for the method name and the input parameters. Still, you should tell the user what the method is going to do and what the return values are, if any. See the next tip for the version of this advice for Java programmers. In C++ we can say:

```
#include <string>
/*
 * getSubString() - get a substring from the input string.
 *  The substring starts at index start
 *  and goes up to but doesn't include index stop.
 *  returns the resulting substring.
 */
string getSubString(string str, int start, int stop) { }
```

- *In Java use JavaDoc comments for all your methods*: JavaDoc is built into the Java environment and all Java SDKs come with the program to generate JavaDoc web pages, so why not use it? JavaDoc can provide a nice overview of what your class is up to at very little cost. Just make sure and keep those comments up to date:

```
/**
 * getSubString() - get a substring from the input string.
 *      The substring starts at index start
 *      and goes up to but doesn't include index stop.
 * @param str the input string
 * @param start the integer starting index
 * @param stop the integer stopping index
 * @return the resulting substring.
 */
public String getSubString(String str, int start, int stop) { }
```

- *Use fewer, but better comments*: This is one of those useless motherhood and apple pie pieces of advice that everyone feels obliged to put in any discussion of comments. Okay, so you don't need to comment every line of code. Everyone knows that a comment like

```
index = index + 1;      // add one to index
```

is not an informative comment. So don't do it. Enough said.

- *"Self-documenting code" is an ideal*: Self-documenting code is the Holy Grail of lazy programmers who don't want to take the time to explain their code to readers. Self-documenting code is the Platonic ideal of coding that assumes that everyone who reads your code can also read your mind. If you have an algorithm that's at all complicated, or input that's at all obscure, you need to explain it. Don't depend on the reader to understand every subtlety of your code. Explain it. Just do it. All that said, some programming languages and tool sets allow you to embed documenting tags in comments in your code. JavaDocs is the canonical example here.

Identifier Naming Conventions

As Rob Pike puts it so well in his terrific white paper on programming style, "Length is not a virtue in a name; clarity of expression *is*[8]." As Goldilocks would put it, you need identifier names that are not too long, not too short, but just right. Just like comments, this means different things to different people. Common sense and readability should rule:

- *All identifiers should be descriptive*: Remember that someday you may be back to look at your code again. Or, if you're working for a living, somebody else will be looking at your code. Descriptive identifiers make it much, much easier to read your code and figure out what you were trying to do at 3:00 AM. A variable called `interestRate` is much easier to understand than `ir`. Sure, `ir` is shorter and faster to type, but believe me, you'll forget what it stood for about 10 minutes after you ship that program. Reasonably descriptive identifiers can save you a lot of time and effort.

- `OverlyLongVariableNamesAreHardToRead` *(and type)*: On the other hand, don't make your identifiers too long. For one thing they're hard to read, for another they don't really add anything to the context of your program, they use up too much space on the page, and finally, they're just plain ugly.

  `Andtheyareevenharderwhenyoudontincludeworddivisions`: Despite what Rob Pike says[9], using *camel case* (those embedded capital letters that begin new words in your identifiers) can make your code easier to read. Especially if the identifier isn't overly long. At least to me, `maxPhysAddr` is easier to read than `maxphysaddr`.

- *Single-letter variable names are cryptic, but sometimes useful*: Using single-letter variable names for things like mortgage payments, window names, or graphics objects is not a good example of readability. `M`, `w`, and `g` don't mean anything even in the context of your code. `mortPmnt`, `gfxWindow`, and `gfxObj` have more meaning. The big exception here is variables intended as index values—loop control variables and array index variables. Here, `i`, `j`, `k`, `l`, `m`, etc. are easily understandable, although I wouldn't argue with you about using `index` or `indx` instead.

```
for (int i = 0; i < myArray.length; i++) {
    myArray[i] = 0;
}
```

---

[8]Pike, Rob. 1980. *Notes on Programming in C*, retrieved from http://www.literateprogramming.com/pikestyle.pdf on 29 September 2010. 1999.
[9]Pike. 1980. p. 2.

looks much better and is just as understandable as

```
for (int arrayIndex = 0; arrayIndex < myArray.length; arrayIndex++) {
    myArray[arrayIndex] = 0;
}
```

- *Adhere to the programming language naming conventions when they exist*: Sometime, somewhere you'll run into a document called Style Guide or something like that. Nearly every software development organization of any size has one. Sometimes you're allowed to violate the guidelines, and sometimes during a code review you'll get dinged for not following the guidelines and have to change your code.

  If you work in a group with more than one developer, style guidelines are a good idea. They give all your code a common look and feel and make it easier for one developer to make changes to code written by somebody else.

  A common set of guidelines in a Style Guide is about naming conventions. Naming conventions tell you what your identifier names should look like for each of the different kind of identifiers. Java has a common set of naming conventions:

  - *For classes and interfaces*: The identifier names should be nouns, using both upper- and lowercase alphanumerics and with the first character of the name capitalized:

    ```
    public class Automobile {}
    public interface Shape {}
    ```

  - *For methods*: The identifier names should be verbs, using both upper- and lowercase alphanumerics and with the first character of the name in lowercase:

    ```
    private double computeAverage(int [] list)
    ```

  - *For variables*: The identifier names should use both upper- and lowercase alphanumerics, with the first character of the name in lowercase. Variable names should not start with $ or _ (underscore).

    ```
    double average;
    String firstSentence;
    ```

  - *For all identifiers (except constants)*: Camel case should be used, so that internal words are capitalized:

    ```
    long myLongArray;
    ```

  - *For constants*: All letters should be uppercase, and words should be separated by underscores:

    ```
    static final int MAX_WIDTH = 80;
    ```

Refactoring

An important part of code construction is keeping the design in mind as you code, and especially keeping the design as simple as possible. Design simplicity is particularly important when you're fixing a bug or adding something new to existing code. In these cases, you should think about whether the code you're working on is as simple as it can be or whether it's getting old, crusty, and complicated. If so, then think about changing the code to bring back that simplicity of design. This is known as refactoring.

Martin Fowler defines *refactoring* as "a change made to the internal structure of the software to make it easier to understand and cheaper to modify without changing its observable behavior[10]. " Refactoring is key to all agile methodologies, which strongly encourage it every time you change code.

There are a number of times, reasons, and techniques for refactoring code. In *Code Complete 2*, Steve McConnell gives a number of them. Martin Fowler gives a longer list at his website[11].

When to Refactor

Lets look at a number of reasons for refactoring code:

- *You have duplicate code*: If you have duplicate code, remember the DRY principle. Create a new method that encapsulates the code and then call it.

- *A function or method is too long*: A function or method should only ever do one thing. That means it should be short. Typically, a method should not be more than one screen height long; that's somewhere between 24 and 50 lines long.

- *A class has poor (not tight enough) cohesion*: If you have a class that's doing more than one thing (than a single responsibility), you should break it up into two or more classes.

- *A class interface doesn't project a consistent level of abstraction*: Over time as you've made changes to a class, its interface may become complicated and difficult to understand. This is the time to simplify the interface by moving methods to other classes or combining methods.

- *A formal parameter list has too many input parameters*: Too many input parameters means that the method is just being used to transfer data to another method or it's doing too many things. In either case, the parameter list should be simplified.

- *Changes to code require parallel changes to multiple classes or modules*: If you end up with a situation where a change in the code in one class requires changes in one or more other classes as well, then you need to think about rearranging data and/or methods to simplify the structure.

- *Related pieces of data that are used together are in different places*: Just like the preceding item, if you find that data across methods or classes need to be used together (such as two or more pieces of data are always used to compute a third, but the input data is in two different places), then they should be moved together to the same class.

- *A method uses more features of some other class than of its own class*: If you find you have a method that's calling several methods from a different class, maybe it should be moved to the other class.

---

[10]Fowler, Martin, and Kent Beck. *Refactoring: Improving the Design of Existing Code*. (Boston, MA: Addison-Wesley, 1999.)
[11]https://refactoring.com/catalog/index.html

- *A chain of method calls is used to pass data via parameters*: If you find yourself with input parameters to a method that aren't used but are just passed on to other methods, you should take a look at your flow of control to see if changes need to be made.

- *A middleman object doesn't do anything itself*: If you find you have a class whose main work is just to call methods in another object, then maybe you can eliminate the middleman and call the methods directly.

- *Instance variables are public*: One of the fundamental ideas behind object-oriented programming is *information hiding*. The advice here is that all instance variables in an object should be private.

- *A subclass uses only a few of its super class's inherited methods*: If you've created an inheritance hierarchy, and a subclass only uses a few of the inherited methods, you may want to re-think this relationship. As McConnell puts it: "Typically this indicates that that subclass has been created because a parent class happened to contain the routines it needed, not because the subclass is logically a descendent of the super- class. Consider achieving better encapsulation by switching the subclass's relationship to its superclass from an is-a relationship to a has-a relationship; convert the superclass to member data of the former subclass, and expose only the routines in the former subclass that are really needed."

- *Comments are used to document difficult or complicated code*: Although you should always have comments in your code, you should always take a look at them when you refactor code. As the saying goes, "Don't document bad code—rewrite it[12] ".

- *The code uses global variables*: It's very simple. Don't use global variables (or at least use them very carefully). If you find global variables in code you're refactoring, consider them carefully and see if you can eliminate them by passing data to methods via parameters.

- *A method uses setup or takedown code with another method call*: This is another example of carefully considering your class's interface. Say you're going to add an item to an inventory of CarParts, and your code looks like this:

```
AddInventory transaction = new AddInventory();
transaction.setPartID(partID);
transaction.setPartName(partName);
transaction.setPartCost(partCost);
transaction.setDate(transactionDate);
```

And then you do the actual add:

```
processAdd(transaction);
```

You might consider whether the method call that requires this type of setup is using the right level of abstraction. In order to eliminate the setup code and make the code simpler, you might change the formal parameter list for the processAdd() method to something like this:

```
processAdd(partID, partName, partCost, transactionDate);
```

---

[12]Kernighan, Brian W., and P. J. Plauger. *The Elements of Programming Style, 2nd Edition*. (New York, NY: McGraw Hill, Inc., 1978).

Types of Refactoring

You can make many types of changes to improve your code. The following list isn't complete, but it's a good start:

- *Replace a magic number with a named constant*: Magic numbers are bad for a couple of reasons. First, if you have to use a magic number more than once, that means if you need to change it, you have to change it everywhere you've used it. Second, if someone comes along after you, they may not know what the number means. Named constants allow you to change the value of the number in only one place, and they give a hint as to what the number means.

- *Rename a variable with a name that's more informative*: There are occasions when using short or cryptic variable names is okay. For example, using i, j, or k as loop control variables is always clear. But using other short variable names like a, b, c, inv, and so on is just confusing. Replace those with names that mean something to the reader.

- *Replace variables with expressions*: In some cases, where you have a complex expression, you break it up into several parts and create an intermediate variable for each part, with the final variable just the combination of the intermediate values. This rule says to examine those and check to see if you can replace some of the intermediate variables with the expressions themselves.

- *Replace expressions with methods*: In this case, you have an expression that might be duplicated in two or more parts of the code. If so, replace that expression with a single method and just call the method. Think DRY.

- *Convert a variable that's used for different things into several variables each used for one thing*: Here someone has been lazy and is reusing a variable name for two or more different purposes. Replace all the duplicates with new variables to make the code more understandable.

- *Create a local variable instead of overusing an input parameter*: This is the same as the preceding rule, but someone is reusing an input parameter name in a method. Just create a local variable instead and use it. It's just one more entry on the system stack.

- *Create a class instead of using a data primitive*: If you create a variable using a data primitive type (say using double to create a variable called money) and if that variable may need extra behaviors, then replace the primitive type with a class declaration.

- *Convert a set of named constants (type codes) into a class or an enumeration*: Earlier I said that using magic numbers was bad and you should use named constants instead. But if you have a set of named constants that are related to each other, you should consider putting them in a separate class or in an enumeration type instead. It will make your code more maintainable and more readable.

- *Decompose a Boolean expression into variables*: If you have a complex Boolean expression, you might consider separating the clauses into intermediate variables and then combining the results at the end.

- *Move a complex Boolean expression into a method that returns a Boolean*: If your Boolean expression is complex and likely to be repeated elsewhere in the program, put it into a method that evaluates the expression and returns a Boolean result.

- *Use break or return instead of a Boolean loop control variable*: Many times you'll see a while loop that looks something like this:

```
boolean done = false;
while (!done) {
        // do stuff here
        if (some-expression)
                done = true;
}
```

This creates a bit of unnecessary work, and the suggestion here is to replace the done = true; with a return or a break statement.

- *Return from a method as soon as you know the answer*: This also means don't use a Boolean or other variable to tell yourself you've found the return value from a method. As soon as you know the answer, just return it.

- *Move the code from simple routines to where it is used*: If you have a method that contains code that's only used in one place, just put the code inline where it's used instead of having it in a method.

- *Separate queries from calculations*: Normally a query operation will just return a value. If you have a method that does both calculation and returns a value for a query (say something like getAverage() or getTotal()) consider separating it into two methods—one to do the calculation and one to do the query. This allows you to adhere to the "methods should just do one thing" principle.

- *Combine methods that are similar*: You may have two different methods that differ only by a constant used in a calculation. Consider consolidating those methods and making the constant an input parameter instead.

- *Move specialized code into its own class or subclass*: If you have code that's only used by a subset of the instances of a super class, move that code into its own class or sub-class.

- *Move similar code from classes into a super class*: On the other hand, if you have code in several classes that is similar, then create a new super class and move the code up into it.

- *Divide a class with multiple responsibilities into two*: Adhering to the single responsibility principle, if you have a class that does multiple things, separate it into two or more classes that each just do one thing.

- *Delete a class*: If you have a class that ends up not doing much (for example, it only has a single method, or it only contains data members), then move that work into another class.

- *Encapsulate public instance variables*: If you have an instance variable declared as public, convert it to private and create a getter method to access it. Now you're obeying the information hiding principle.

- *Only use* get() *and* set() *methods when necessary*: Only use get() methods for instance variables that need to be used outside the object, and only use set() methods when you really need to change the value of an instance variable. For example, if you have an instance variable for a part number, you probably don't need a set() method because part numbers don't usually change. By default, all instance variables should be private.

- *Hide public methods*: Only expose methods if they need to be in the class's interface. Just like with instance variables, all methods should be private unless there's a good reason to make them public.

- *Combine similar super and sub-classes*: If you have a super and sub-class pair that are nearly identical, consider consolidating them into a single class.

Defensive Programming

By *defensive programming* I mean that your code should protect itself from bad data. The bad data can come from user input via the command line, a graphical text box or form, or a file. Bad data can also come from other routines in your program via input parameters, as in the first example given earlier.

How do you protect your program from bad data? Validate! As tedious as it sounds, you should always check the validity of data that you receive from outside your routine. This means you should check the following:

- Check the number and type of command line arguments.

- Check file operations:

    - Did the file open?

    - Did the read operation return anything?

    - Did the write operation write anything?

    - Did we reach EOF yet?

- Check all values in function/method parameter lists.

    - Are they all the correct type and size?

- Always initialize variables and don't depend on the system to do the initialization for you.

What else should you check for? Here's a short list:

- Null pointers (references in Java)

- Zeros in denominators

- Wrong type

- Out of range values

As an example, here's a C program that takes in a list of house prices from a file and computes the average house price from the list. The file is provided to the program from the command line:

```
/*
 * program to compute the average selling price of a set of homes.
 * Input comes from a file that is passed via the command line.
 * Output is the Total and Average sale prices for
 * all the homes and the number of prices in the file.
 *
 * jfdooley
 */
#include <stdlib.h>
#include <stdio.h>
```

```c
int main(int argc, char **argv)
{
        FILE *fp;
        double totalPrice, avgPrice;
        double price;
        int numPrices;

        /* check that the user entered the correct number of args */
        if (argc < 2) {
                fprintf(stderr,"Usage: %s <filename>\n", argv[0]);
                exit(1);
        }

        /* try to open the input file */
        fp = fopen(argv[1], "r");
        if (fp == NULL) {
                fprintf(stderr, "File Not Found: %s\n", argv[1]);
                exit(1);
        }
        totalPrice = 0.0;
        numPrices = 0;

        /* read the file, total the prices and count the number of houses */
        while (!feof(fp)) {
                fscanf(fp, "%10lf\n", &price);
                totalPrice += price;
                numPrices++;
        }

        avgPrice = totalPrice / numPrices;
        printf("Number of houses is %d\n", numPrices);
        printf("Total Price of all houses is $%10.2f\n", totalPrice);
        printf("Average Price per house is $%10.2f\n", avgPrice);

        return 0;
}
```

Assertions Are Helpful

Defensive programming means that using assertions is a great idea if your language supports them. Java, C99, C11, and C++ all support assertions. Assertions will test an expression that you give them, and if the expression is false, it will throw an error and normally abort the program. You should use error handling code for errors you think might happen—erroneous user input, for example—and use assertions for errors that should *never* happen—off-by-one errors in loops, for example. Assertions are great for testing your program, but because you should remove them before giving programs to customers (you don't want the program to abort on the user, right?), they aren't good to use to validate input data in a production program.

Exceptions

The preceding section talked about using assertions to handle truly bad errors, ones that should never occur in production code. But what about handling "normal" errors? Part of defensive programming is to handle errors in such a way that no damage is done to any data in the program or the files it uses, and so that the program stays running for as long as possible (making your program *robust*).

Let's look at exceptions first. You should take advantage of built-in exception handling in whatever programming language you're using. The exception-handling mechanism will give you information about what bad thing has just happened. It's then up to you to decide what to do. Normally, in an exception-handling mechanism, you have two choices: handle the exception yourself or pass it along to whoever called you and let them handle it. What you do and how you do it depends on the language you're using and the capabilities it gives you. We'll talk about exception handling in Java later.

Error Handling

As with validation, you're most likely to encounter errors in input data, whether it's command line input, file handling, or input from a graphical user interface form. Here we're talking about errors that occur at run-time (compile time and testing errors are covered in Chapter 15, on debugging and testing). Other types of errors can be data that your program computes incorrectly, errors in other programs that interact with your program—the operating system, for instance—race conditions, and interaction errors where your program is communicating with another and your program is at fault.

The main purpose of error handling is to have your program survive and run correctly for as long as possible. When it gets to a point where your program can't continue, it needs to report what's wrong as best as it can and then exit gracefully. Exiting is the last resort for error handling. So what should you do? Well, once again, "it depends." What you should do depends on what your program's context is when the error occurs and what its purpose is. You won't handle an error in a video game the same way you handle one in a cardiac pacemaker. In every case, your first goal should be *try to recover*.

Trying to recover from an error will have different meanings in different programs. *Recovery* means that your program needs to try to ignore the bad data, fix it, or substitute something else that's valid for the bad data. See McConnell[13] for a further discussion of error handling. Here are a few examples of how to recover from errors:

- You might just *ignore the bad data and keep going*, using the next valid piece of data. Say your program is a piece of embedded software in a digital pressure gauge. You sample the sensor that returns the pressure 60 times a second. If the sensor fails to deliver a pressure reading once, should you shut down the gauge? Probably not; a reasonable thing to do is just skip that reading and set up to read the next piece of data when it arrives. Now, if the pressure sensor skips several readings in a row, then something might be wrong with the sensor and you should do something different (like yell for help).

- You might *substitute the last valid piece of data* for a missing or wrong piece. Taking the digital pressure gauge again, if the sensor misses a reading, because each time interval is only a 1/60 of a second, it's likely that the missing reading is very close to the previous reading. In that case, you can substitute the last valid piece of data for the missing value.

---

[13]McConnell, 2004.

- There may be instances where you don't have any previously recorded valid data. Your application uses an asynchronous event handler, so you don't have any history of data, but your program knows that the data should be in a particular range. Say you've prompted the user for a salary amount, and the value you get back is a negative number. Clearly, no one gets paid a salary of negative dollars, so the value is wrong. One way (probably not the best) to handle this error is to *substitute the closest valid value in the range*—in this case, a zero. Although not ideal, at least your program can continue running with a valid data value in that field.

- In C programs, nearly all system calls and most of the standard library functions return a value. You should test these values! Most functions will return values that indicate success (a non-negative integer) or failure (a negative integer, usually –1). Some functions return a value that indicates how successful they were. For example, the printf() family of functions returns the number of characters printed, and the scanf() family returns the number of input elements read. Most C functions also set a global variable named errno that contains an integer value that is the number of the error that occurred. The list of error numbers is in a header file called errno.h. A zero on the errno variable indicates success. Any other positive integer value is the number of the error that occurred. Because the system tells you two things—(1) an error occurred, and (2) what it thinks is the cause of the error—you can do lots of different things to handle it, including just *reporting the error* and bailing out. For example, we try to open a file that doesn't exist:

```
#include <stdio.h>
#include <stdlib.h>
#include <errno.h>

int main(int argc, char **argv)
{
    FILE *fd;
    char *fname = "NotAFile.txt";

    if ((fd = fopen(fname, "r")) == NULL) {
        perror("File not opened");
        exit(1);
    }
    printf("File exists\n");
    return 0;
}
```

The program will return the error message

```
File not opened: No such file or directory
```

if the file really doesn't exist. The function perror() reads the errno variable and, using the string provided plus a standard string corresponding to the error number, writes an error message to the console's standard error output. This program could also prompt the user for a different filename or could substitute a default filename. Either of these would allow the program to continue rather than exit on the error.

There are other techniques to use in error handling and recovery. These examples should give you a flavor of what you can do within your program. The important idea to remember here is to attempt recovery if possible, but most of all, *don't fail silently!*

Exceptions in Java

Some programming languages have built-in error reporting systems that will tell you when an error occurs and leave it up to you to handle it one way or another. These errors that would normally cause your program to die a horrible death are called *exceptions*. The code that encounters the error throws the exception. Once something is *thrown*, like a baseball, for example, it's usually a good idea if someone *catches* it. It's the same with exceptions. There are two sides to exceptions that you need to be aware of when you're writing code:

- When you have a piece of code that can encounter an error, you *throw* an exception. Systems like Java will throw some exceptions for you. These exceptions are listed in the Exception class in the Java API documentation (see http://download.oracle. com/javase/8/docs/api). You can also write your own code to throw exceptions. I'll show you an example later in the chapter.

- Once an exception is thrown, somebody has to *catch* it. If you don't do anything in your program, this *uncaught exception* will percolate through to the Java Virtual Machine (JVM) and be caught there. The JVM will kill your program and provide you with a stack backtrace that should lead you back to the place that originally threw the exception and show you how you got there. On the other hand, you can also write code to encapsulate the calls that might generate exceptions and catch them yourself using Java's try...catch mechanism. Java requires that some exceptions must be caught. We'll see an example later.

Java has three different types of exceptions: checked exceptions, errors, and unchecked exceptions. *Checked exceptions* are those that you should catch and handle yourself using an exception handler; they're exceptions that you should anticipate and handle as you design and write your code. For example, if your code asks a user for a filename, you should anticipate that they will type it wrong and be prepared to catch the resulting FileNotFoundException. Checked exceptions must be caught.

Errors, on the other hand, are exceptions that are usually related to things happening outside your program. Errors are things you can't do anything about except fail gracefully. You might try to catch the error exception and provide some output for the user, but you will still usually have to exit.

The third type of exception is the *run-time exception*. Run-time exceptions all result from problems within your program that occur as it runs and almost always indicate errors in your code. For example, a NullPointerException nearly always indicates a bug in your code and shows up as a run-time exception. Errors and run-time exceptions are collectively called *unchecked exceptions* (that would be because you usually don't try to catch them, so they're unchecked). The following program deliberately causes a run-time exception:

```java
public class TestNull {
  public static void main(String[] args) {
      String str = null;
      int len = str.length();
  }
}
```

This program will compile just fine, but when you run it you'll get this as output:

```
Exception in thread "main" java.lang.NullPointerException
        at TestNull.main(TestNull.java:4)
```

This is a classic run-time exception. There's no need to catch this exception because the only thing we can do is exit. If we do catch it, the program might look like this

```
public class TestNullCatch {
        public static void main(String[] args) {
                String str = null;

                try {
                        int len = str.length();
                } catch (NullPointerException e) {
                        System.out.println("Error. Found a pointer: " + e.getMessage());
                        System.exit(1);
                }
        }
}
```

which gives us the output

```
Error. Found a pointer: null
```

Note that the getMessage() method will return a String containing whatever error message Java deems appropriate—if there is one. Otherwise it returns a null. This is somewhat less helpful than the default stack trace shown.

Let's rewrite the short C program in Java and illustrate how to catch a *checked exception*:

```
import java.io.*;
import java.util.*;

public class FileTest {
        public static void main(String [] args) {
                File fd = new File("NotAFile.txt");
                System.out.println("File exists " + fd.exists());

                try {
                        FileReader fr = new FileReader(fd);
                } catch (FileNotFoundException e) {
                        System.out.println(e.getMessage());
                }
        }
}
```

The output we get when we execute FileTest is as follows:

```
File exists false
NotAFile.txt (No such file or directory)
```

By the way, if we don't use the `try-catch` block in the preceding program, then it won't compile. We get the following compiler error message:

```
FileTestWrong.java:11: unreported exception java.io.FileNotFoundException; must be caught
or declared to be thrown
                FileReader fr = new FileReader(fd);
```

```
                                      ^
```

```
1 error
```

Remember, in Java checked exceptions *must* be caught. This type of error doesn't show up for unchecked exceptions. This is far from everything you should know about exceptions and exception handling in Java; start digging through the Java tutorials and the Java API!

The Last Word on Coding

Coding is the heart of software development. Code is what you produce. But coding is hard—translating even a good, detailed design into code takes a lot of thought, experience, and knowledge, even for small programs. Depending on the programming language you're using and the target system, programming can be a very time-consuming and difficult task. That's why taking the time to make your code readable and have the code layout match the logical structure of your design is essential to writing code that works and is understandable by humans. Adhering to coding standards and conventions, keeping to a consistent style, and including good, accurate comments will help you immensely during debugging and testing. And it will help you six months from now when you come back and try to figure out what the heck you were thinking.

And finally:

> *I am rarely happier than when spending an entire day programming my computer to perform automatically a task that it would otherwise take me a good ten seconds to do by hand.*

—Douglas Adams, "Last Chance to See"

References

Fowler, Martin, and Kent Beck. *Refactoring: Improving the Design of Existing Code*. (Boston, MA: Addison-Wesley, 1999.)

Hunt, A. and D. Thomas. *The Pragmatic Programmer: From Journeyman to Master*. (Boston, MA: Addison-Wesley, 2000.)

Kernighan, Brian W., and P. J. Plauger. *The Elements of Programming Style, 2nd Edition*. (New York, NY: McGraw Hill, Inc., 1978.)

Knuth, D. "Structured Programming with goto Statements." *ACM Computing Surveys* 6(4): 261-301 (1974).

Krasner, G. E. and S. T. Pope. "A cookbook for using the Model-View-Controller user interface paradigm in Smalltalk-80." *Journal of Object-Oriented Programming* 1(3): 26-49 (1988).

Lieberherr, K., I. Holland, et al. *Object-Oriented Programming: An Objective Sense of Style*. OOPSLA '88, Association for Computing Machinery, 1988.

Martin, R. C. *Agile Software Development: Principles, Patterns, and Practices*. (Upper Saddle River, NJ: Prentice Hall, 2003.)

McConnell, S. *Code Complete 2: A Practical Handbook of Software Construction*. (Redmond, WA, Microsoft Press, 2004.)

Pike, Rob, *Notes on Programming in C*, retrieved from http://www.literateprogramming.com/pikestyle.pdf on 29 September 2010 (1999).

CHAPTER 15

Debugging

As soon as we started programming, we found to our surprise that it wasn't as easy to get programs right as we had thought. Debugging had to be discovered. I can remember the exact instant when I realized that a large part of my life from then on was going to be spent in finding mistakes in my own programs.

—Maurice Wilkes, 1949

It is a painful thing to look at your own trouble and know that you yourself and no one else has made it.

—Sophocles

Congratulations! You've finished writing your code, so now it's time to get it working. I know. You're thinking, "I can write perfect code; I'm careful. I won't have any errors in my program." Get over it. Every programmer thinks this at one point or another. There's just no such thing as a perfect program. Humans are imperfect, so we all make mistakes when we write code. After writing code for over 40 years, I've gotten to the point where most of the time my programs that are less than about 50 lines long don't have any *obvious* errors in them, and lots of times they even compile the first time. I think that's a pretty good result. You should shoot for that.

Getting your program to work is a process with three parts, the order of which is the subject of some debate:

- *Debugging* is the process of finding the *root cause* of an error and fixing it. This doesn't mean treating the symptoms of an error by coding around it to make it go away; it means to find the real reason for the error and fixing that piece of code so the error is removed. Debugging is normally done once you finish writing the code and before you do a code review or unit testing (but see coverage of test-driven development later in this chapter).

- *Reviewing* (or inspecting) is the process of reading the code as it sits on the page and *looking for errors*. The errors can include mistakes in how you've implemented the design, other kinds of logic errors, wrong comments, and so on. Reviewing code is an inherently *static* process because the program isn't running on a computer—you're reading it off a screen or a piece of paper. So, although reviewing is very good for finding static errors, it can't find dynamic or interaction errors in your code. That's what *testing* is for. I'll talk more about reviews and inspections in Chapter 17.

J. F. Dooley, *Software Development, Design and Coding*, https://doi.org/10.1007/978-1-4842-3153-1_15

- *Testing* is the process of *finding errors* in the code, as opposed to fixing them, which is what *debugging* is all about. Testing occurs, at minimum, at the following three different levels:

  - *Unit testing*: Where you test small pieces of your code, notably at the function or method level.

  - *Integration testing*: Where you put together several modules or classes that relate to each other and test them together.

  - *System testing*: Where you test the entire program from the user's perspective; this is also called *black-box testing*, because the tester doesn't know how the code was implemented—all they know is what the requirements are, so they're testing to see whether the code as written implements all the requirements correctly.

This chapter focuses on debugging.

What Is an Error, Anyway?

We define three types of errors in code:

- Syntactic errors
- Semantic errors
- Logic errors

Syntactic errors are errors you make with respect to the syntax of the programming language you're using. Spelling a keyword wrong, failing to declare a variable before you use it, forgetting to put that closing curly brace in a block, forgetting the return type of a function, and forgetting that semicolon at the end of a statement are all typical examples of syntactic errors. Syntactic errors are by far the easiest to find because the compiler finds nearly all of them for you. Compilers are very rigid taskmasters when it comes to enforcing lexical and grammar rules of a language, so if you get through the compilation process with no errors *and no warnings*, then it's very likely your program has no syntax errors left. Notice the "and no warnings" in the preceding sentence. You should *always* compile your code with the strictest syntax checking turned on, and you should *always* eliminate all errors and warnings before you move on to reviews or testing. If you're sure you've not done anything wrong syntactically, then that's just one less thing to worry about while you're finding all the other errors. And the good news is that modern integrated development environments (IDEs) like Eclipse, NetBeans, XCode, or Visual Studio do this for you automatically once you've set up the compiler options. So, after you set the warning and syntax checking levels, every time you make a change, the IDE will automatically re-compile your file and let you know about any syntactic errors!

Semantic errors, on the other hand, occur when you fail to create a proper sentence in the programming language. You do this because you have some basic misunderstanding about the grammar rules of the language. Not putting curly braces around a block, accidentally putting a semicolon after the condition in an `if` or `while` statement in C/C++ or Java, forgetting to use a `break;` statement at the end of a `case` statement inside a `switch`—all these are classic examples of semantic errors. Semantic errors are harder to find because they're normally syntactically correct pieces of code, so the compiler passes your program and it compiles correctly into an object file. It's only when you try to execute your program that semantic errors surface. The good news is that they're usually so egregious that they show up pretty much immediately. The bad news is they can be very subtle. For example, in this code segment

```
while (j < MAX_LEN);
{
        // do stuff here
        j++;
}
```

the semicolon at the end of the while statement's conditional expression is usually very hard to see; your eyes will just slide right over it, but its effect is to either put the program into an infinite loop, because the conditional test passes and the loop control variable j is never being incremented, or to never execute the loop because the test fails the first time, but then erroneously execute the block because it's no longer semantically connected to the while statement.

The third type of error, logic errors, are by far the most difficult to find and eradicate. A *logic error* is one that occurs because you've made a mistake in translating the design into code. These errors include things like computing a result incorrectly, off-by-one errors in loops (which can also be a semantic error if your off-by-one error is because you didn't understand array indexing, for example), misunderstanding a network protocol, returning a value of the wrong type from a method, and so on. With a logic error, either your program seems to execute normally but you get the wrong answers, or it dies a sudden and horrible death because you've walked off the end of an array, tried to dereference a null pointer, or attempted to go off and execute code in the middle of a data area. It's not pretty.

Unit testing involves finding the errors in your program, and *debugging* involves finding the root cause and fixing those errors. Debugging is about finding out why an error occurs in your program. You can look at errors as opportunities to learn more about the program, and about how you work and approach problem solving. Because after all, debugging is a problem-solving activity, just as developing a program is problem solving. Look at debugging as an opportunity to learn about yourself and improve your skill set.

What Not To Do

Just like in any endeavor, particularly problem-solving endeavors, there's a wrong way and a right way to approach the task. This section discusses a few things you shouldn't do as you approach a debugging problem[1].

- *Don't guess about where the error might be*: This implies that (1) you don't know anything about the program you're trying to debug, and (2) you're not going about the job of finding the root cause of the error systematically. Stop, take a deep breath, and start again.

- *Don't fix the symptom—fix the problem*: Lots of times you can "fix" a problem by forcing the error to go away by adding code. This is particularly true if the error involves an outlier in a range of values. The temptation here is to "special case" the outlier by adding code to handle just that case. Don't do it! You haven't fixed the underlying problem here; you've just painted over it. There's almost always some other special case out there waiting to break free and squash your program. Study the program, figure out what it's doing at that spot, and fix the problem.

---

[1]McConnell, S. *Code Complete 2: A Practical Handbook of Software Construction*. (Redmond, WA: Microsoft Press, 2004.)

- *Avoid denial*: It's always tempting to say "the compiler must be wrong" or "the system must be broken" or "Ralph's module is obviously sending me bad data" or "that's impossible" or some such excuse. Those are all almost certainly incorrect. If you just "changed one thing," and the program breaks, then guess who probably just injected an error into the program and where it is? (Or at the very least, who uncovered one?) Review the quote from Sophocles at the beginning of this chapter: "*. . . you yourself and no one else has made it*." You will make mistakes. We all do. The best attitude to display is "By golly, this program can't beat me, I'm going to fix this thing!" One of the best discussions of careful coding and how hard it is to write correct programs is the discussion of how to write binary search in Column 5 of Jon Bentley's *Programming Pearls*.[2] You should read it.

An Approach to Debugging

Here's an approach to debugging that will get the job done. Remember, you're solving a problem here, and the best way to do that is to have a systematic way of sneaking up on the problem and whacking it on the head. The other thing to remember about debugging is that, as in a murder mystery, you're working backwards from the conclusion.[3] The bad thing has already happened—your program failed. Now you need to examine the evidence and work back toward a solution. Here's the approach, in the order in which you should work:

1. Reproduce the problem reliably.

2. Find the source of the error.

3. Fix the error (just that one).

4. Test the fix (now you've got a regression test for later).

5. Optionally look for other errors in the vicinity of the one you just fixed.

Reproduce the Problem Reliably

This is the key first step. If your error only shows up periodically, it will be much, much harder to find. The classic example of how hard this can be is the "but it works fine on my computer" problem. This is the one sentence you never want to hear. This is why people in tech support retire early. Reproducing the problem—in different ways, if possible—will allow you to see what's happening and will give you a clear indication of where the problem is occurring. Luckily for you, most errors are easy to find. Either you get the wrong answer and you can look for where the `print` statement is located and work backwards from there, or your program dies a horrible death and the system generates a backtrace for you. The Java Virtual Machine does this automatically for you. With other languages, you may need to use a debugger to get the backtrace.

Remember, errors are not random events. If you think the problem is random, then it's usually one of the following:

- *Initialization problem*: This can be that you're depending on a side-effect of the variable definition to initialize the variable, and it's not acting as you expect.

- *Timing error*: Something is happening sooner or later than you expect.

---

[2]Bentley, J. *Programming Pearls, 2nd Edition.* (Reading, MA: Addison-Wesley, 2000.)
[3]Kernighan, B. W. and R. Pike. *The Practice of Programming.* (Boston, MA, Addison-Wesley, 1999.)

- *Dangling pointer problem*: You returned a pointer from a local variable, and the memory in which that local variable was stored has been given back to the system.

- *Buffer overflow or walking off the end of an array*: You have a loop that iterates through a collection and you're walking off the end and stomping on either a piece of code, or another variable, or the system stack.

- *Concurrency issue (a race condition)*: In a multi-threaded application or in an application that uses shared memory, you've not synchronized your code, and a variable you need to use is getting overwritten by someone else before you can get to it.

Reproducing the problem isn't enough, though. You should reproduce it using the simplest test case that will cause the error to occur. It's a matter of eliminating all the other possibilities so you can focus on the single one (well, maybe one or two) that probably causes the error. One way to do this is to try to reproduce the problem using half the data you had the first time. Pick one half or the other. If the error still occurs, try it again. If the error doesn't happen, try the other half of the data. If there's still no error, then try with three-quarters of the data. You get the idea. You'll know when you've found the simplest case because with anything smaller the behavior of the program will change—either the error will disappear, or you'll get a slightly different error.

Find the Source of the Error

Once you can reproduce the problem from the outside, you can now find where the error is occurring. Once again, we need to do this systematically. For most errors this is easy. There are a number of techniques you can use:

- *Read the code*: What a concept! The first thing you should do once you've run your test case is examine the output, make a guess where the error might be (look at the last thing that got printed and find that print statement in the program), and then sit back, grab a cup of coffee, and just read the code. Understanding what the code is trying to do in the area where the error occurs is key to figuring out what the fix should be. It's also key to finding the source of the error in the first place. Nine times out of ten, if you just sit back and read the code for five minutes or so you'll find just where the error is. Don't just grab the keyboard and start hacking away. Read the code.

- *Gather data*: Since you've now got a test case that will reproduce the error, gather data from running the test case. The data can include what kinds of input data cause the error, what do you have to do to get it to appear—the exact steps you need to execute, how long it takes to appear, and what exactly happens. Once you have this data, you can form a hypothesis on where the error is in the code. For most types of errors, you'll have some output that is correct, and then either the program crashes or you get bad output. That will help isolate the error.

- *Insert print statements*: The simplest thing to do once you figure out what output is incorrect is to start putting print statements at that point and at other interesting points in the code. Interesting points can be the entrance and exit to functions, "Entering sort routine," "Exiting partition routine," and so on. When using an integrated development environment (IDE), there are built-in debugging features, including setting breakpoints, watchpoints, the ability to step through code, and so on that make inserting print statements less useful. I'll come back to some of these in a minute.

- You can also put print statements at the top and bottom of loops, at the beginning of the then and else blocks of if-statements, in the default case of a switch statement, and so on. Unless something very spooky is going on, you should be able to isolate where the error is occurring pretty quickly using this method. Once again, work your way backwards from the point where you think the error makes itself known. Remember that many times where an error *exhibits* its behavior may be many lines of code after where the error actually *occurs*.

    In some languages you can encase your print statements inside debugging blocks that you can turn on and off on the command line when you compile. In C/C++ you can insert

    ```
    #ifdef DEBUG
        printf("Debug statement in sort routine\n");
    #endif
    ```

    blocks in various places, and then when you compile the program you can either put a #define DEBUG in a header file or you can compile using gcc -DDEBUG foo.c and the printf function call will be included in your program. Leaving out the #define or the -DDEBUG will remove the printf function call from the executable program (but not your source). Beware, though, that this technique makes your program harder to read because of all the DEBUG blocks scattered around the code. You should remove DEBUG blocks before your program releases. Unfortunately, Java doesn't have this facility because it doesn't have a pre-processor. But all is not lost. You can get the same effect as the #ifdef DEBUG by using a named Boolean constant. Here's an example of code:

    ```
    public class IfDef {
        final static boolean DEBUG = true;

        public static void main(String [] args) {
          System.out.printf("Hello, World \n");

          if (DEBUG) {
              System.out.printf("max(5, 8) is %d\n", Math.max(5, 8));
              System.out.printf("If this prints, the code was included\n");
          }
        }
    }
    ```

    In this example we set the Boolean constant DEBUG to true when we want to turn the DEBUG blocks on, and we'll then turn it to false when we want to turn them off. This isn't perfect because you have to re-compile every time you want to turn debugging on and off, but you have to do that with the earlier C/C++ example as well.

- *Use logging*: Many IDEs and scripting languages (such as JavaScript) have built-in logging routines that you can turn on and use in place of putting in your own print statements. Typically you can identify which variables to log and where to log the values. The logging routines will usually create a log file that you can then examine when the program finishes running. If you're doing interactive debugging, you may be able to examine the log file as you go.

- *Look for patterns*: The next thing to try is to see if there's a pattern to the code or the error that you've seen before. As you gain more programming experience and get a better understanding of how you program and what kind of mistakes you make, this will be easier.

The extra semicolon at the end of the earlier `while` loop is one example of a mistake that can be a pattern. Here's another:

```
for (int j = 0; j <= myArray.length; j++) {
    // some code here
}
```

You will step off the end of the array because you're testing for `<=` rather than `<`. This is the classic off-by-one error.

A classic in C/C++ is using one = where you meant to use two == in a conditional expression. Say you're checking an array of characters for a particular character in a C/C++ program, like this:

```
for (int j = 0; j < length; j++) {
    if (c = myArray[j]) {
        pos = j;
        break;
    }
}
```

The single equals sign will cause the `if` statement to stop early every time; `pos` will always be zero. By the way, Java doesn't let you get away with this. It gives you an error that says the type of the assignment expression is not a Boolean:

```
TstEql.java:10: incompatible types
found   : char
required: boolean
    if (c = myArray[j]) {
          ^
1 error
```

That's because in Java, as in C and C++, an assignment operator returns a result, and every result has a type. In this case, the result type is `char` but the `if`-statement is expecting a Boolean expression there. The Java compiler checks for this because it's more strongly typed than C and C++; their compilers don't do the check.

- Forgetting a break statement in a switch is another. Writing this

```
switch(selectOne) {
    case 'p':  operation = "print";
               break;
    case 'd':  operation = "display";
    default:   operation = "blank";
               break;
}
```

  will reset operation to blank because there is no break statement after the
  second case.

- *Use a debugger*: Pretty much all the IDEs you'll run into, whether open source or
  proprietary, have built-in debuggers. This includes Eclipse, XCode, Visual Studio,
  BlueJ, and many others. These debuggers will allow you to set breakpoints, watch
  variables, step into and out of functions, single-step instructions, change code on the
  fly, examine registers and other memory locations, and so on so that you can learn
  as much as possible about what's going on in your code. If a quick and dirty look
  through the code and a sprinkling of print statements doesn't get you any closer to
  finding the error, then use the debugger. See the next section for more on these.

- *Explain the code to someone*: How many times have you started explaining a problem
  to one of your peers and two minutes later, all of a sudden, you solve it? When you
  start explaining the problem to someone else, you're really explaining it to yourself
  as well. That's when the inspiration can hit. Give it a try.

- *Other problems*: I've only scratched the surface of the possible errors you can make
  and ways to find them in your code. Because there are nearly an infinite number
  of programs you can write in any given programming language, there are nearly an
  infinite number of ways to insert errors into them. Memory leaks, typing mistakes,
  side-effects from global variables, failure to close files, not putting a default case in
  a switch statement, accidentally overriding a method definition, bad return types,
  hiding a global or instance variable with a local variable—there are thousands of
  them.

Don't be discouraged. Most errors you'll make really are simple. Most of them you'll catch during code
reviews and unit tests. The ones that escape into system test or (heaven forbid) released code are the really
interesting and subtle ones. Debugging is a great problem-solving exercise. Revel in it.

Debugging Tools

So far, the only debugging tools we've talked about using are compilers to remove syntax errors and
warnings, print statements you can insert in your code to give you data on what is happening where, and
inline debugging statements that you can compile in or out. There are other tools you can use that will help
you find the source of an error. The first among these are debuggers.

Debuggers are special programs that execute instrumented code and allow you to peek inside the
code as it's running to see what's going on. Debuggers allow you to stop your running code (breakpoints),
examine variable values as the code executes (watchpoints), execute a single instruction at a time, step into
and out of functions, and even make changes to the code and the data while the program is running.

Gdb

Debuggers are the easiest way to get a backtrace for C and C++ programs. For C and C++ developers, the gdb command line debugger that comes with nearly all Unix and Linux systems is usually the debugger of choice. For Java, gdb is also integrated in some interactive development environments like Eclipse (www.eclipse.org) and also comes with a graphical user interface in the DDD debugger (www.gnu.org/software/ddd/). The NetBeans IDE (www.netbeans.org) comes with its own graphical debugger. The Java debuggers in Eclipse and NetBeans allow you to set breakpoints at individual lines of code, watch variables values change via watchpoints, and step through the code one line or one method at a time.

gdb does all those things and more, but you should use it, and any other debugger, cautiously. By their nature, debuggers have tunnel vision when it comes to looking at code. They're great at showing you all the code for the current function, but they don't give you a feel for the organization of the program as a whole. They also don't give you a feel for complicated data structures, and it's hard to debug multi-threaded and multi-process programs using a debugger. Multi-threaded programs are particularly hard for a number of reasons, one of which is that while executing, timing is crucial for the different threads, and running a multi-threaded program in a debugger changes the timing.

Eclipse

The Eclipse IDE has a built-in debugger that gives you many tools all in one. We'll focus on the Java debugger that's built into Eclipse. The easiest way to get a debugging session started is to first to change to the Java perspective in Eclipse, open your project, open the files you're interested in so they appear in the Editor pane, and then go to the upper right of the screen and open the Debug perspective. Several new panes will open, and your screen will look something like Figure 15-1.

Figure 15-1. *The Debug perspective in Eclipse*

   With this new perspective, you'll see several panes, including Debug, Variables, Breakpoints, Outline, Mulitcore Visualizer, Console, and the Editor pane. The first thing you should do is to set Breakpoints. You can do that in the Editor pane just by double-clicking the line number of a source code file where you want execution to stop. You can now run your program by clicking the bug icon in the upper left of the window. Your program will execute and then stop at the first breakpoint. You can then start to look around and examine the current state of your program. The debugger also allows you to set watchpoints on variables, single-step through instructions, skip over method calls (the method executes, the debugger just doesn't go into the method), change the current value of a variable, and change the code in your program on the fly. The Eclipse website has extensive documentation on the Eclipse debugger[4].

XCode

Apple's XCode IDE allows you to create applications for Mac OS, iOS, and WatchOS devices. XCode lets you program in several different programming languages, including C, C++, Swift, and Objective-C. Just like Eclipse, XCode has a built-in debugger that allows you to set breakpoints, watch variables, step through code, and make changes on the fly[5].

   XCode's debugger can be set to automatically start when you build and execute your program; just insert a breakpoint. You can insert breakpoints by double-clicking the line number to the left of the source line of code where you want to stop execution. Once you've stopped at a breakpoint, XCode also allows you to watch variables and then step through the code execution one line at a time. Figure 15-2 gives you a view of what a stopped program looks like in XCode. Note the left pane of the window that provides options and information about the currently running program. The blue flag in the Editing pane indicates the breakpoint where the program is currently stopped (just before it prints "Hello World").

---

[4]http://help.eclipse.org/neon/index.jsp?topic=%2Forg.eclipse.jdt.doc.user%2Ftasks%2Ftask-running_and_debugging.htm&cp=1_3_6

[5]https://developer.apple.com/library/content/documentation/DeveloperTools/Conceptual/debugging_with_xcode/chapters/debugging_tools.html#//apple_ref/doc/uid/TP40015022-CH8-SW4

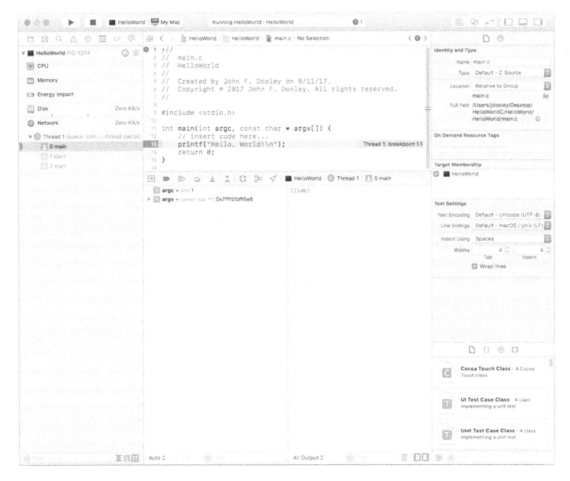

Figure 15-2. *A program stopped in the XCode debugger*

Fix the Error (Just That One)!

Once you've found where the error is, you need to come up with a fix for it. Most of the time the fix is obvious and simple because the error is simple. That's the good news. But sometimes even though you can find the error, the fix isn't obvious, or the fix will entail rewriting a large section of code. In cases like that, be careful! Take the time necessary to understand the code and then rewrite the code and fix the error correctly. The biggest problem in debugging is haste.

When you're fixing errors remember two things:

- Fix the actual error, don't fix the symptom.

- Only fix one error at a time.

This second item is particularly important. We've all been in situations where you're fixing an error and you find another one in the same piece of code. The temptation is to fix them both right then and there. Resist! Fix the error you came to fix. Test it and make sure the fix is correct. Integrate the new code back into the source code base. *Then* go back to step 1 and fix the second error. You might ask, "Why do all this extra work when I can just make the fix right now?"

Well, here's the situation. By the time you get to this step in the debugging process, you already have a test for the first error, you've educated yourself about the code where the error occurs, and you're ready to make that one fix. Why should you confuse the issue by fixing two things now? Besides, you don't have a test for the second error. So how do you test that fix? Trust me, it's a little more work, but doing the fixes one at a time will save you lots of headaches down the road.

Test the Fix

Well, this sounds obvious, doesn't it? But you'd be surprised how many fixes don't get tested. Or if they're tested, it's a simple test with generic sample data and no attempt to see if your fix broke anything else.

First of all, rerun the original test that uncovered the error—not just the minimal test that you came up with in step 1, but the first test that caused the error to appear. If that test now fails (in the sense that the error doesn't occur any more), that's a good sign that you've at least fixed the proximate cause of the error. Then run every other test in your regression suite (see Chapter 16 for more discussion on regression tests) so you can make sure you've not re-broken something that was already fixed. Finally, integrate your code into the source code base, check out the new version, and test the entire thing. If all that still works, then you're in good shape. Now go have a beer.

Look for More Errors

If there was one error in a particular function or method, there might be another, right? One of the truisms of programming is that 80% of the errors occur in 20% of the code, so it's likely there's another error close to where you've just fixed one[6]. This rule is also known as the **Pareto Principle**[7]. So, while you're here, you might as well take a look at the code in the general vicinity of the error you just fixed and see if anything like it happens again. This is another example of looking for patterns. Patterns are there because developers make the same mistakes over and over again (we're human, after all). Grab another cup of coffee and a doughnut and read some more code. It won't hurt to take a look at the whole module or class and see if there are other errors or opportunities for change. In the agile world, this is called *refactoring*. This means rewriting the code to make it simpler. Making your code simpler will make it clearer, easier to read, and it will make finding that next error easier. So have some coffee and read some code.

Source Code Control

I've mentioned a source code base and integrating changes into that base. That is a sneaky way of starting a brief discussion of *source code control*, also known as *software version control*.

Whenever you work on a project, whether you're the only developer or are part of a team, you should keep backups of the work you're doing. That's what a version control system (VCS) does for you, but with a twist. A VCS will not only keep a backup of all the files you create during a project, it will keep track of all the changes you've made to them, so that in addition to saying, "Give me the latest version of PhoneContact.java," you can say, "I want the version of PhoneContact.java from last Thursday."

A VCS keeps a *repository* of all the files you've created and added to it for your project. The repository can be a flat file or a more sophisticated database, usually organized hierarchically as a file system tree structure. A client program allows you access the repository and retrieve different versions of one or more of the files stored there. Normally, if you just ask the VCS for a particular file or files, you get the latest version. Whatever version of the file you extract from the repository is called the *working copy* in VCS-speak. Extracting the file is called a *checkout*.

---

[6]https://www.utest.com/articles/principles-of-testing-the-8020-rule
[7]https://en.wikipedia.org/wiki/Pareto_principle

If you're working on a project all alone, then the working copy you check out from the VCS repository is the only one out there, and any changes you make will be reflected in the repository when you check the file back in (yes, that's a *check-in*). The cool part of this is that if you make a change and it's wrong, you can just check out a previous version that doesn't have the change in it. The other interesting part of a VCS is when there's more than one developer working on a project. When you're working on a development team, it's quite likely that somebody else on the team may check out the same file that you did. This brings up the problem of file sharing. The problem here is if both of you make changes to the file and then both want to check the file back into the repository, who gets to go first and whose changes end up in the repository? Ideally, both, right?

The Collision Problem

Well, maybe not. Say Alice and Bob both check out PhoneContact.java from the repository and each of them makes changes to it. Bob checks his version of PhoneContact.java back into the repository and goes to lunch. A few minutes later Alice checks in her version of PhoneContact.java. Two problems occur: (1) if Alice hasn't made any changes in the same lines of code that Bob did, her version is still newer than Bob's and it hides Bob's version in the repository. Bob's changes are still there, but they're now in an older version than Alice's. (2) Worse, if Alice did make changes to some of the same code that Bob did, then her changes actually overwrite Bob's, and PhoneContact.java is a very different file. Bummer. We don't want either of these situations to occur. How do we avoid this problem?

Version-control systems use the following two different strategies to avoid this collision problem:

- lock-modify-unlock
- copy-modify-merge

Using Lock-Modify-Unlock

The first strategy is *lock-modify-unlock*. In this strategy, Bob checks out PhoneContact.java and locks it for edit. This means that Bob now has the only working copy of PhoneContact.java that can be changed. If Alice tries to check out PhoneContact.java, she gets a message that she can only check out a read-only version and so can't check it back in until Bob gives up his lock. Bob makes his changes, checks PhoneContact.java back in, and then releases the lock. Alice can now check out and lock an editable version of PhoneContact.java (which now includes Bob's changes) and make her own changes and check the file back in, giving up her lock. The lock-modify-unlock strategy has the effect of serializing changes in the repository.

This *serialization of changes* is the biggest problem with lock-modify-unlock. While Bob has the file checked out for editing, Alice can't make her changes. She just sits around twiddling her thumbs until Bob is done. Alice's boss doesn't like this thumb-twiddling stuff. However, there is an alternative.

Using Copy-Modify-Merge

The second strategy is *copy-modify-merge*. In this strategy, Alice and Bob are both free to check out editable copies of PhoneContact.java. Let's say that Alice makes her changes first and checks her new version of the file back into the repository and goes out for cocktails. When Bob is finished making his changes, he tries to check his new version of PhoneContact.java into the repository only to have the VCS tell him his version of the file is "out of date"—Bob can't check in. What happened here? Well, the VCS stamps each file that's checked out with a timestamp and a version number. It also keeps track of what's checked out and who checked it out and when. It checks those values when you try to check in.

When Bob tried to check in, his VCS realized that the version of the code he was trying to check in was older than the current version (the new one that Alice had checked in earlier), so it let him know that. So what is Bob to do? That's where the third part of copy-modify-merge comes in. Bob needs to tell the VCS to merge his changes with the current version of PhoneContact.java and then check in the updated version. This all works just fine if Alice and Bob have changed different parts of the file. If their changes don't conflict, then the VCS can just do the merge automatically and check in the new file. A problem occurs if Alice and Bob have made changes to the same lines of code in the file, known as a *merge conflict*. In that case, Bob must do a manual merge of the two files. In a manual merge, the VCS will normally put both versions of the file on the screen, side-by-side, highlighting the conflicting lines of code, and then Bob can decide which version he wants, or he can make changes that resolve any inconsistencies. Bob is in control. Bob has to do this because the VCS isn't smart enough to choose between the conflicting changes. Usually, a VCS will provide some help in doing the merge, but ultimately the merge decision must be Bob's. Copy-modify-merge can occasionally make for extra work for whomever checks-in second, but it allows both developers to work on the same file simultaneously and doesn't lose any changes.

There's still one problem (well, okay, more than one, but we'll just talk about this one) with copy-modify-merge. If your repository allows you to store binary files, you can't merge them. Say you have two versions of the same .jpg file. How do you decide which of the bits is correct? In this case, the VCS will require you to use lock-modify-unlock.

So, to summarize, a typical working cycle for any version-control system will look like the following. Before anything else starts, the developer must create a *local repository* for the project. This can happen automatically using a client program, or the developer can manually create a directory that will house the repository. Some systems allow the developer to do an initial checkout and will create the repository for them. Then:

1. The developer *checks out* the code they want from the project.

2. The developer edits, compiles, debugs, and tests the code.

3. When ready to upload their changes to the main repository, the developer will *commit* the changes; this will automatically check in the changed files.

4. Usually the system will attempt to do an *automatic merge* of the changes. If there is a *merge conflict*, the developer will be notified and will be prompted to do a manual merge.

5. Once all merge conflicts are resolved, the changed files are in the main repository and ready to be checked out again by other developers.

Source Code Control Systems

The following sections discuss various source code control systems.

Subversion

Copy-modify-merge is the strategy used by most version-control systems these days, including the popular open source distributed version-control system Subversion (http://subversion.apache.org)[8]. *Subversion (SVN)* was first developed in 2000 and is a rewrite and update of an older VCS called the Concurrent Versions System (CVS). CVS itself is a front end to a version-control system developed in 1982 called the

---

[8]Collins-Sussman, B., Fitzpatrick, B. W., and Pilato, C. M. *Version Control with Subversion*. (Sebastapol, CA: O'Reilly Press, 2010.) Retrieved from http://svnbook.red-bean.com/ on 15 October 2010.

Revision Control System (RCS). Subversion is much more fully featured and sophisticated than either CVS or RCS. Although it's primarily used in software development projects, it can be used as a version-control system for any type of file in any type of project. Subversion comes in both command line versions and in GUI versions, like RapidSVN, TortoiseSVN, and SmartSVN. There are also plug-ins for various IDEs, like subclipse for the Eclipse IDE.

Subversion is an example of a *centralized version-control* system (also known as client-server) where there is a centralized database of all the source code and users access the database via a local client. This centralized database can be on the local machine, on a remote *svnserve* server machine, or on a remote Apache server. The user can set things up so the local svn client knows where the version-control database is located. Checked out—*working copies*—of files are stored locally in a tree hierarchy repository. Working copies are the developer's own private copy of the file. Subversion defaults to the copy-modify-merge version-control model, but can also be configured to use the lock-modify-unlock model on individual files. For more information and a link to the online copy of the aptly named *Subversion Book*, go to `http://subversion.apache.org`.

Git and GitHub

Git (`http://git-scm.com`), a candidate for most popular open source *distributed version-control system*, uses a model in which each developer has a local repository of the source files that includes the entire development history of the project. Developers working on a project have their own local repository of the files in the project. When a developer makes a change to a file, the changes are synced to the other local repositories via the use of `git` commands. Git uses a model called an *incomplete merge* along with a number of plug-in merge tools to coordinate merges across repositories. Git can also connect with and sync remote repositories on different computers across a network (including the Internet). Note that two developers' local repositories may be out of sync at any given time, but the totality of all the developer's repositories is what constitutes the project's source code. This is what makes Git a *distributed* version-control system. It's up to the developers to keep their repositories in sync (but see GitHub and Bitbucket below). Git's main virtue is speed. It may be the fastest distributed VCS around. Linus Torvalds, who also famously developed the Linux kernel, originally developed Git.

Git is typically run via the command line and when installed just comes with command line tools. Like other version-control systems, Git uses the idea of a *master branch* of the code that a developer can *pull* from in order to get copies of the code to work on. Developers can also make separate branches of the master so that their work doesn't interfere with other developers until they merge. Git makes it trivially easy to create repositories (just create a directory and type `% git init`) and the typical sequence of actions is also simple. Typical Git workflow looks like this:

- *Branch* a master so you can work on it or check out an existing master branch.

- *Edit* the files you want to make changes to.

- Do *compiling, debugging,* and *testing.*

- *Add* the files to the *staging* area (an abstract area Git uses to indicate which files are candidates for committing back into the source code repository).

- *Commit* the files from the staging area back into the repository.

- *Push* to a remote branch in order to update it. The remote branch can be on the same computer or across a network.

- *Pull* from a remote version of the repository to sync with other developer changes.

- *Merge* the changes you just pulled into your repository.

An extension of Git called GitHub is a web-based version of Git that allows the creation and maintenance of remote repositories accessible across the Internet. GitHub provides all the regular services of Git but also features access control, bug tracking, a web-hosting service, wikis, and project-management services. GitHub has more than 20 million users and hosts more than 50 million repositories. See `https://github.com/`.

You can find all the Git commands and tutorials at `https://git-scm.com/doc`.[9] Needless to say, there are also graphical interfaces to Git. The two most popular are the GitHub desktop application, which you can find at `https://desktop.github.com`, and the gitKraken application at `www.gitkraken.com`, which can attach to GitHub and Mercurial (discussed next).

Mercurial

Mercurial is another popular, free, distributed version-control system. Like Git, it's primarily a command line tool. It uses practically the same repository and workflow models as Git, including the ideas of pulling and pushing branches, commits, and merges. Instead of staging, Mercurial has the idea of a *changeset*—that is, the set of all the files that have been modified since the last commit. It also allows you to view changes between different versions of files, look at the current status of the repository since the last commit, and view a summary of the work that's gone on in the repository. Mercurial is available free online at `www.mercurial-scm.org`, and a free online book and tutorial are available at `https://book.mercurial-scm.org`. In addition to gitKraken, there's another popular graphical interface for Mercurial called TortoiseHg available at `https://tortoisehg.bitbucket.io`.

One Last Thought on Coding and Debugging: Pair Programming

Pair programming is a technique to improve software quality and programmer performance (it was discussed in Chapter 2). It's been around for many years but only recently has been formalized[10]. In pair programming, two people share one computer and one keyboard. One person "drives," controlling the keyboard and writing the code, and the other "navigates," watching for errors in the code and suggesting changes and test cases. Periodically the driver and the navigator switch places. Pairs can work together for long periods of time on a project, or pairs can change with each programming task. Pair programming is particularly popular in agile development environments; in the eXtreme Programming (EP) process, all developers are required to pair program, and no code that has not been written by two people is allowed to be integrated into the project. Several studies[11] have shown that pair programming decreases the number of errors in code and improves the productivity of programmers. So, this is your final debugging technique—pair program!

---

[9]See Chacon, S., & Straub, B. (2014). *Pro Git: Everything You Need to Know About Git, 2nd. Ed.* (paperback). New York, NY: Apress. Also free online at `https://git-scm.com/book/en/v2`.

[10]Williams, L., & Kessler, R. "All I Really Need to Know about Pair Programming I Learned in Kindergarten." *CACM*, *43*(5), 108–114 (2000).

[11]Cockburn, A. and L. Williams. "The Costs and Benefits of Pair Programming." *Extreme Programming Examined*. (Boston, MA: Addison-Wesley Longman, 2001). Page 592.

Conclusion

Just like writing good, efficient code, debugging is a skill that all programmers need to acquire. Being a careful coder will mean you have less debugging to do, but there will always be debugging. Programmers are all human, and we'll always make mistakes. Having a basket of debugging skills will help you find the root causes of errors in your code faster and will help you from injecting more errors. The combination of reviews (Chapter 17), debugging, and unit testing—as we'll see in Chapter 16—is the knock-out punch that a developer uses to release defect-free code.

References

Bentley, J. *Programming Pearls,* 2nd Edition. (Reading, MA, Addison-Wesley, 2000.)

Chacon, S., & Straub, B. *Pro Git: Everything You Need to Know About Git,* 2nd. Edition (paperback). New York, NY: Apress (2014). Also free online at `https://git-scm.com/book/en/v2`.

Chelf, B. "Avoiding the most common software development goofs." Retrieved from `http://www.drdobbs.com/architecture-and-design/avoiding-the-most-common-software-develo/193001588` on September 6, 2017.

Cockburn, A. and L. Williams. "The Costs and Benefits of Pair Programming." *Extreme Programming Examined.* (Boston, MA: Addison-Wesley Longman, 2001.) Page 592.

Collins-Sussman, B., Fitzpatrick, B. W., and Pilato, C. M. *Version Control with Subversion.* (Sebastapol, CA: O'Reilly Press, 2010.) Retrieved from `http://svnbook.red-bean.com` on 15 October 2010.

Kernighan, B. W. and R. Pike. *The Practice of Programming.* (Boston, MA: Addison-Wesley, 1999.)

McConnell, S. *Code Complete 2: A Practical Handbook of Software Construction.* (Redmond, WA: Microsoft Press, 2004.)

Williams, L., & Kessler, R. "All I Really Need to Know about Pair Programming I Learned in Kindergarten." *CACM*, 2000, *43*(5), 108–114.

CHAPTER 16

Unit Testing

> *More than the act of testing, the act of designing tests is one of the best bug preventers known. The thinking that must be done to create a useful test can discover and eliminate bugs before they are coded—indeed, test-design thinking can discover and eliminate bugs at every stage in the creation of software, from conception to specification, to design, coding and the rest.*
>
> —Boris Beizer

> *You can see a lot by just looking.*
>
> —Yogi Berra

As was emphasized in the last chapter, nobody's perfect, including software developers. Chapter 15 talked about different things to look for when you *know* there are errors in your code. Now we're going to talk about how to *find* those errors. Of the three types of errors in your code, the compiler will find the syntax errors and the occasional semantic error. In some language environments, the run-time system will find others (to your users' chagrin). The rest of the errors are found in two different ways: testing and code reviews and inspections. In this chapter, we'll discuss testing, when to do it, what it is, how to do it, what your tests should cover, and the limitations of testing. Chapter 17 will talk about code reviews and inspections.

There are three levels of testing in a typical software development project: unit testing, integration testing, and system testing. *Unit testing* is typically done by you, the developer. With unit testing, you're testing individual methods and classes, but you're generally not testing larger configurations of the program. You're also not usually testing interfaces or library interactions—except those that your method might actually be using. Because you're doing unit testing, you know how all the methods are written, what the data is supposed to look like, what the method signatures are, and what the return values and types should be. This is known as *white-box testing*. It should really be called *transparent-box testing*, because the assumption is you can see all the details of the code being tested.

Integration testing is normally done by a separate testing organization. This is the testing of a collection of classes or modules that interact with each other; its purpose is to test interfaces between modules or classes and the interactions between the modules. Testers write their tests with knowledge of the interfaces but not with information about *how* each module has been implemented. From that perspective the testers are users of the interfaces. Because of this, integration testing is sometimes called *gray-box testing*. Integration testing is done after unit-tested code is integrated into the source code base. A partial or complete version of the product is built and tested, to find any errors in how the new module interacts with the existing code. This type of testing is also done when errors in a module are fixed and the module is reintegrated into the code base. As a developer you'll do some integration testing yourself because you'll usually be working in a separate code branch and will integrate your new or updated code into that branch and then test the entire application to make sure you've not broken anything.

© John F. Dooley 2017
J. F. Dooley, *Software Development, Design and Coding*, https://doi.org/10.1007/978-1-4842-3153-1_16

System testing is normally done by a separate testing organization. This is the testing of the entire product (the system). System testing is done on both internal baselines of the software product and on the final baseline that's proposed for release to customers. System testing is like integration testing on steroids. All the recent changes by all developers are used to build a version of the product, which is then tested as a whole. The separate testing organization uses the requirements and writes their own tests without knowing anything about how the program is designed or written. This is known as *black-box testing* because the program is opaque to the tester except for the inputs it takes and the outputs it produces. The job of the testers at this level is to make sure the program implements all the requirements. Black-box testing can also include stress testing, usability testing, and acceptance testing. End users may be involved in this type of testing.

The Problem with Testing

So, if we can use testing to find errors in our programs, why don't we find all of them? After all, we wrote the program, or at least the fix or new feature we just added, so we must understand what we just wrote. We also wrote the tests. Why do so many errors escape into the next phase of testing or even into users' hands?

Well, there are two reasons we don't find all the errors in our code. First, we're not perfect. This seems to be a theme here. But we're not. If we made mistakes when we wrote the code, why should we assume we wouldn't make some mistakes when we read it or try to test and fix it? This happens for even small programs, but it's particularly true for larger programs. If you have a 50,000-line program, that's a lot to read and understand, and you're bound to miss something. Also, static reading of programs won't help you find those dynamic interactions between modules and interfaces. So, we need to test more intelligently and combine both static (code reading) and dynamic (testing) techniques to find and fix errors in programs.

The second reason errors escape from one testing phase to another and ultimately to the user of that software is that software, more than any other product that humans manufacture, is very complex. Even small programs have many pathways through the code and many different types of data errors that can occur. This large number of pathways through a program is called a *combinatorial explosion*. Every time you add an if-statement to your program, you double the number of possible paths through the program. Think about it; you have one path through the code if the conditional expression in the if-statement is true, and a different path if the conditional expression is false. Every time you add a new input value, you increase complexity and increase the number of possible errors. This means that, for large programs, you can't possibly test every possible path through the program with every possible input value. There are an exponential number of code path/data value combinations to test every one.

So what to do? If brute force won't work, then you need a better plan. That plan is to identify those use cases that are the most probable and test those. You need to identify the likely input data values and the boundary conditions for data, figure out what the likely code paths will be, and test those. That, it turns out, will get you most of the errors. Steve McConnell says in *Code Complete* that a combination of good testing and code reviews can uncover more than 95% of errors in a good-sized program[1]. That's what we need to shoot for.

That Testing Mindset

There's actually another problem with testing—you. Well, actually, you, the developer. You see, developers and testers have two different, one might say *adversarial*, roles to play in code construction. Developers are there to produce a design that reflects the requirements and write the code that implements the design. Your job as a developer is to *get code to work*.

---

[1]McConnell, S. *Code Complete 2: A Practical Handbook of Software Construction*. (Redmond, WA: Microsoft Press, 2004.)

A tester's job, on the other hand, is to take those same requirements and your code and *get the code to break*. Testers are supposed to do unspeakable, horrible, wrenching things to your code in an effort to get the errors in it to expose themselves to the light of day. Their job is to break stuff. You, the developer, then get to fix it. This is why being a tester can be a very cool job.

You can see where this might be an adversarial relationship. You can also see where developers might make pretty bad testers. If your job is to make the code work, you're not focused on breaking it, so your test cases may not be the nasty, mean test cases that someone whose job it is to break your code may come up with. In short, because they're trying to build something beautiful, *developers make lousy testers*. Developers tend to write tests using typical, clean data. They tend to have an overly optimistic view of how much of their code a test will exercise. They tend to write tests assuming that the code will work; after all, it's their code, right?

This is why most software development organizations have a *separate testing team* for integration and system testing. The testers write their own test code, create their own frameworks, do the testing of all new baselines and the final release code, and report all the errors back to the developers—who then must fix them. The one thing testers normally *do not* do is unit testing. Unit testing is the developer's responsibility, so you're not completely off the hook here. You *do* need to think about testing, learn how to write tests, how to run them, and how to analyze the results. You need to learn to be mean to your code. And you still need to fix the errors.

When to Test?

Before we get around to discussing just how to do unit testing and what things to test, let's talk about *when* to test. Current thinking falls into two areas: the more traditional approach is to write your code, get it to compile so you've eliminated the syntax errors, and then write your tests and do your unit testing *after* you feel the code for a function or a module is finished. This has the advantage that you've understood the requirements and written the code and while you were writing the code you had the opportunity to think about test cases. Then you can write clear test cases. In this strategy, testing and debugging go hand in hand and occur pretty much simultaneously. It allows you to find an error, fix it, and then rerun the failed test right away.

An approach that flows out of the agile methodologies, especially out of eXtreme Programming (XP), is called *test-driven development* (TDD). With TDD, you write your unit tests *before* you write any code. Clearly if you write your unit tests first, they will all fail—at most, you'll have the stub of a method to call in your test. But that's a good thing because in TDD your goal when you write code is to *get all the tests to pass*. So writing the tests up front gives you a benchmark for success. If you've written a bunch of tests, you then write just enough code to make all the unit tests pass, and then you know you're done! This has the advantage of helping you keep your code lean, which implies simpler and easier to debug. You can write some new code and test it; if it fails, write some more code, and if it passes, stop. It also gives you, right up front, a set of tests you can run whenever you make a change to your code. If the tests all still pass, then you haven't broken anything by making the changes. It also allows you to find an error, fix it, and then rerun the failed test right away.

Which way is better? The answer is another of those "it depends" things. Generally, writing your tests first gets you in the testing mind-set earlier and gives you definite goals for implementing the code. On the other hand, until you do it a lot of it and it becomes second nature, writing tests first can be hard because you have to visualize what you're testing. It forces you to come to terms with the requirements and the module or class design early as well. That means that design/coding/testing all pretty much happen at once. This can make the whole code construction process more difficult. Because you're doing design/coding/testing all at the same time, it will also take longer to create that first functional program. But once you have that first piece of functionality working, your development time can speed up. TDD works well for small- to medium-sized projects (as do agile techniques in general), but it may be more difficult for very large programs. TDD also works quite well when you're pair programming. In pair programming, the driver is writing the code while the navigator is watching for errors and thinking about testing. With TDD, the driver is writing a *test* while the navigator is thinking of more tests to write and thinking ahead to the code. This process tends to make writing the tests easier and then flows naturally into writing the code.

Give testing a shot both before and after and then you can decide which is best.

Testing in an Agile Development Environment

It seems like a good time to separate out testing in an agile development environment because although many of the ideas and methods are the same no matter what development process you are using, agile processes have a different viewpoint on testing.

Most agile methodologies strongly encourage (and XP requires) the use of *test-driven development*, so that unit tests are written before the production code is written. On an agile team, this makes a lot of sense because of another agile technique: *continuous integration*. In most agile methodologies, every time a developer finishes developing a task or a feature, they're supposed to integrate their new code into the code base and test it using an automated test suite. This can happen many times a day on a team of 10–20 developers.

One of the rules of *continuous integration* is that if you write a new piece of code that passes the unit tests and if you integrate it and it breaks the product—*you have to fix it right away.* No bug reports, no passing the problem off to a separate bug-fixing and integration team. The developer who wrote the code is supposed to fix the problem immediately. This, combined with the fact that most new features or tasks implemented in an agile project are small (remember, tasks are supposed to be eight hours of effort or less, total) makes integration testing an extension of unit testing.

Another aspect of agile projects that plays into good testing is *pair programming*. Pair programming is required in XP and recommended in all other agile methodologies. To refresh your memory, in pair programming two developers work on the same task at the same time. They share a single computer with one of them (sometimes called the *driver*) at the keyboard and writing code, and the other (called the *navigator*) sits next to the driver and watches, thinks, and comments. The navigator is thinking about design issues and about testing. About every half hour or so, the driver and navigator switch places. The effective part of this is the "two heads are better than one" idea. Two developers think and write tests for the task they're implementing. They take turns writing code and refining their tests and the code. They test often— say, every time they have a new function written. They integrate often and all their new tests are added to the automated test suite for the project. It's a win, win, win.

Finally, in an agile project *the customer, who is part of the team, does system testing.* And in many cases, the customer is on site and so the acceptance tests written by the customer can be executed as soon as an integration takes place. This is another very powerful piece of how agile works.

So, in agile projects, the entire suite of tests—unit tests, integration tests, and system tests—are all part of the normal agile process.

What to Test?

Now that we've talked about different phases of testing and when you should do your unit testing, it's time to discuss just *what* to test. What you're testing falls into two general categories:

- *Code coverage* has the goal of executing every line of code in your program at least once with representative data so you can be sure that all the code functions correctly. Sounds easy? Well, remember that combinatorial explosion problem for that 50,000-line program.

- *Data coverage* has the goal of testing representative samples of good and bad data, both input data and data generated by your program, with the objective of making sure the program handles data and particularly data errors correctly.

Of course, there's overlap between code coverage and data coverage; sometimes in order to get a particular part of your program to execute, you have to feed it bad data, for example. We'll separate these as best we can and come together when we talk about writing actual tests.

Code Coverage: Test Every Statement

Your objective in code coverage is to test every statement in your program. In order to do that, you need to keep several things in mind about your code. Your program is made up of a number of different types of code, each of which you need to test.

First, there's straight-line code. *Straight-line code* illuminates a single path through your function or method. Normally this will require one test per different data type (I talk more about data coverage shortly).

Next there's branch coverage. With *branch coverage*, you want to test everywhere your program can change directions. That means you need to look at control structures here. Take a look at every if and switch statement and every complex conditional expression—those that contain AND and OR operators in them. For every if-statement, you'll need two tests—one for when the conditional expression is true and one for when it's false. For every switch statement in your method, you'll need a separate test for each case clause in the switch, including the default clause (all your switch statements have a default clause, right?). The logical AND (&&) and OR (||) operators add complexity to your conditional expressions, so you'll need extra test cases for those.

Ideally, you'll need four test cases for each (F-F, F-T, T-F, T-T), but if the language you're using uses shortcut evaluation for logical operators, as do C/C++ and Java, then you can reduce the number of test cases. For the OR operator you'll still need two cases if the first sub-expression is false, but you can just use a single test case if the first sub-expression evaluates to true (the entire expression will always be true). For the AND operator, you'll only need a single test if the first sub-expression evaluates to false (the result will always be false), but you need both tests if the first sub-expression evaluates to true.

Then there is *loop coverage*, which is similar to branch coverage. The difference here is that in for, while, or do-while loops, you have the best likelihood of introducing an off-by-one error and you need to test for that explicitly. You'll also need a test for a *normal* run through the loop, but you'll need to test for a couple of other things too. First will be the possibility for the pre-test loops that you never enter the loop body—the loop conditional expression fails the very first time. Then you'll need to test for an *infinite loop*—the conditional expression never becomes false. This is most likely because you don't change the loop control variable in the loop body, or you do change it, but the conditional expression is wrong from the get-go. For loops that read files, you normally need to test for the *end-of-file* marker (EOF). This is another place where errors could occur either because of a premature EOF or because (in the case of using standard input) EOF is never indicated.

Finally, there are *return values*. In many languages, standard library functions and operating system call all return values. For example, in C, the fprintf and fscanf families of functions return the number of characters printed to an output stream and the number of input elements assigned from an input stream, respectively. But hardly anyone ever checks these return values[2]. You should!

Note that Java is a bit different than C or C++. In Java many of the similarly offending routines will have return values declared void rather than int as in C or C++. So, the problem occurs much less frequently in Java than in other languages. It's not completely gone, though. While the System.out.print() and System.out.println() methods in Java are both declared to return void, the System.out.printf() method returns a PrintStream object that is almost universally ignored. In addition, it's perfectly legal in Java to call a Scanner's next() or nextInt() methods or any of the methods that read data and not save the return value in a variable. Be careful out there.

---

[2]Kernighan, B. W. and R. Pike. *The Practice of Programming*. (Boston, MA: Addison-Wesley, 1999.)

Data Coverage: Bad Data Is Your Friend?

Remember Chapter 14 talked about *defensive programming*, and that the key to defending your program was watching out for bad data—detecting and handling it so that your program can recover from bad data or at least fail gracefully. Well, this is where we see if your defenses are worthy. Data coverage should examine two types of data: good data and bad data. Good data is the typical data your method is supposed to handle. These tests will test data that is the correct type and within the correct ranges. They are just to see if your program is working normally. This doesn't mean you're completely off the hook here. There are still a few cases to test. Here's the short list:

- *Test boundary conditions*: This means to test data near the edges of the range of your valid data. For example, if your program is computing average grades for a course, then the range of values is between 0 and 100 inclusive. So you should test grades at, for example, 0, 1, 99, and 100. Those are all valid grades. But you should also test at –1, and 101. Both of these are invalid values, but are close to the range. In addition, if you're assigning letter grades, you need to check at the upper and lower boundaries of each letter grade value. So if an F is any grade below a 60, you need to check 59, 60, and 61. If you're going to have an off-by-one error, that's where to check.

- *Test typical data values*: These are valid data fields that you might normally expect to get. For the grading example just mentioned, you might check 35, 50, 67, 75, 88, 93, and so on. If these don't work, you've got other problems.

- *Test pre- and post-conditions*. Whenever you enter a control structure—a loop or a selection statement—or make a function call, you're making certain assumptions about data values and the state of your computations. These are *pre-conditions*. And when you exit that control structure, you're making assumptions about what those values are now. These are *post-conditions*. You should write tests that make sure that your assumptions are correct by testing the pre- and post-conditions. In languages that have *assertions* (including C, C++, and Java), this is a great place to use them.

Testing valid data and boundary conditions is one thing, but you also need to test bad data:

- *Illegal data values*: You should test data that's blatantly illegal to make sure your data validation code is working. I already mentioned testing illegal data near the boundaries of your data ranges. You should also test some that are blatantly out of the range.

- *No data*: This is where you test the case where you're expecting data and you get nothing, such as where you've prompted a user for input, and instead of typing a value and hitting the Return key they just hit Return. Or you can't open an input file. Or the file you've just opened is empty. Or you're expecting three files on the command line and you get none. You've got to test all these cases.

- *Too little or too much data*: You have to test the cases where you ask for three pieces of data and only get two. Also the cases where you ask for three and you get ten.

- *Uninitialized variables*: Most language systems these days will provide default initialization values for any variable you declare. But you should still test to make sure these variables are initialized correctly. (Really, you shouldn't depend on the system to initialize your data anyway; you should always initialize it yourself.)

Characteristics of Tests

Robert Martin, in his book *Clean Code*, describes a set of characteristics that all unit tests should have using the acronym FIRST[3]:

Fast: Tests should be fast. If your tests take a long time to run, you're liable to run them less frequently. So make your tests small, simple, and fast.

Independent: Tests should not depend on each other. In particular, one test shouldn't set up data or create objects that another test depends on. For example, the JUnit testing framework for Java has separate setup and teardown methods that make the tests independent. We'll examine JUnit in more detail later on.

Repeatable: You should be able to run your tests any time you want, in any order you want, including after you've added more code to the module.

Self-validating: The tests should either just pass or fail; in other words, their output should just be Boolean. You shouldn't have to read pages and pages of a log file to see if the test passed or not.

Timely: This means you should write the tests when you need them, so that they're available when you want to run them. For agile methodologies that use TDD, this means write the unit tests first, just before you write the code that they will test.

Finally, it's important that just like your functions, your tests should only test one thing; there should be a single concept for each test. This is very important for your debugging work because if each test only tests a single concept in your code, a test failure will point you like a laser at the place in your code where your error is likely to be.

How to Write a Test

Before we go any further, let's look at how to write a unit test. We'll do this by hand now to get the feel for writing tests and we'll examine how a testing framework helps us when we talk about JUnit in the next section. We'll imagine that we're writing a part of an application and go from there. We'll do this in the form of a user story, as it might be done in an eXtreme Programming (XP) environment[4].

In XP, the developers and the customer get together to talk about what the customer wants. This is called exploration. During *exploration* the customer writes a series of *stories* that describe features that they want in the program. These stories are taken by the developers and broken up into *implementation tasks* and estimated. These tasks should be small—no more than eight hours of effort. Pairs of programmers take individual tasks and implement them using TDD. We'll present a story, break it up into a few tasks, and implement some tests for the tasks just to give you an idea of the unit-testing process.

---

[3]Martin, R. C. *Clean Code: A Handbook of Agile Software Craftsmanship*. (Upper Saddle River, NJ: Prentice-Hall, 2009.)
[4]Newkirk, J. and R. C. Martin. *Extreme Programming in Practice*. (Boston, MA: Addison-Wesley, 2001.)

The Story

We want to take as input a flat file of phone contacts and we want to sort the file alphabetically and produce an output table that can be printed.

Really, that's all. Stories in agile projects are typically very short—the suggestion is that they be written on 3 × 5 index cards.

So, we can break this story up into a set of tasks. By the way, this will look suspiciously like a design exercise; it is.

The Tasks

- We need a class that represents a phone contact.

- We need to create a phone contact.

- We need to read a data file and create a list of phone contacts. (This may look like two things, but it's really just one thing—converting a file into a list of phone contacts.)

- We need to sort the phone contacts alphabetically by last name.

- We need to create the printable sorted list.

The Tests

First of all, we'll collapse the first two preceding tasks into a single test. It makes sense once we've created a phone contact class to make sure we can correctly instantiate an object—in effect, we're testing the class's constructors. So let's create a test.

In our first test we'll create an instance of our phone contact object and print out the instance variables to prove it was created correctly. We have to do a little design work first. We have to figure out what the phone contact class will be called and what instance variables it will have.

A reasonable name for the class is PhoneContact, and as long as it's all right with our customer, the instance variables will be firstName, lastName, phoneNumber, and emailAddr. Oh, and they can all be String variables. It's a simple contact list. For this class, we can have two constructors: a default constructor that just initializes the contacts to null and a constructor that takes all four values as input arguments and assigns them. That's probably all we need at the moment. Here's what the test may look like:

```
public class TestPhoneContact
{
    /**
     * Default constructor for test class TestPhoneContact
     */
    public TestPhoneContact() {
    }

    public void testPhoneContactCreation() {
        String fname = "Fred";
        String lname = "Flintstone";
        String phone = "800-555-1212";
        String email = "fred@knox.edu";
```

```
        PhoneContact t1 = new PhoneContact();
        System.out.printf("Phone Contact reference is %H\n", t1);    // reference var address

        PhoneContact t2 = new PhoneContact(fname, lname, phone, email);
        System.out.printf("Phone Contact:\n Name = %s\n Phone = %s\n Email = %s\n",
                          t2.getName(), t2.getPhoneNum(),
                          t2.getEmailAddr());
    }
}
```

Now this test will fail to begin with because we've not created the PhoneContact class yet. That's okay. Let's do that now. The PhoneContact class will be simple—just the instance variables, the two constructors, and getter and setter methods for the variables. A few minutes later we have the following:

```
public class PhoneContact {
    /**
     * instance variables
     */
    private String lastName;
    private String firstName;
    private String phoneNumber;
    private String emailAddr;

    /**
     * Constructors for objects of class PhoneContact
     */
    public PhoneContact() {
        lastName = "";
        firstName = "";
        phoneNumber = "";
        emailAddr = "";
    }

    public PhoneContact(String firstName, String lastName,
                        String phoneNumber, String emailAddr) {
        this.lastName = lastName;
        this.firstName = firstName;
        this.phoneNumber = phoneNumber;
        this.emailAddr = emailAddr;
    }

    /**
     * Getter and Setter methods for each of the instance variables
     */
    public String getName() {
        return this.lastName + ", " + this.firstName;
    }

    public String getLastName() {
        return this.lastName;
    }
```

261

```
    public String getFirstName() {
        return this.firstName;
    }

    public String getPhoneNum() {
        return this.phoneNumber;
    }

    public String getEmailAddr() {
        return this.emailAddr;
    }

    public void setLastName(String lastName) {
        this.lastName = lastName;
    }

    public void setFirstName(String firstName) {
        this.firstName = firstName;
    }

    public void setPhoneNum(String phoneNumber) {
        this.phoneNumber = phoneNumber;
    }

    public void setEmailAddr(String emailAddr) {
        this.emailAddr = emailAddr;
    }
}
```

The last thing we need is a driver for the test we've just created. This will complete the *scaffolding* for this test environment:

```
public class TestDriver
{
    public static void main(String [] args)
    {
        TestPhoneContact t1 = new TestPhoneContact();

        t1.testPhoneContactCreation();
    }
}
```

Now, when we compile and execute the TestDriver, the output console will display something like this:

```
Phone Contact reference is 3D7DC1CB
Phone Contact:
 Name = Flintstone, Fred
 Phone = 800-555-1212
 Email = fred@knox.edu
```

The next task is to read a data file and create a phone contact list. Here, before we figure out the test or the code, we need to decide on some data structures.

Because the story says "flat file of phone contacts," we can just assume we're dealing with a text file where each line contains phone contact information. Say the format mirrors the PhoneContact class and is "first_name last_name phone_number email_addr," one entry per line.

Next we need a list of phone contacts that we can sort later and print out. Because we want to keep the list alphabetically by last name, we can use a TreeMap Java Collections type to store all the phone contacts. Then we don't even need to sort the list because the TreeMap class keeps the list sorted for us. It also looks like we'll need another class to bring the PhoneContact objects and the list operations together. So what's the test look like?

Well, in the interest of keeping our tests small and adhering to the "a test does just one thing" maxim, it seems like we could use two tests after all, one to confirm that the file is there and can be opened, and one to confirm that we can create the PhoneContact list data structure. For the file opening test, it looks like we'll need a new class that represents the phone contact list. We can just stub that class out for now, creating a simple constructor and a stub of the one method that we'll need to test. That way we can write the test (which will fail because we don't have a real method yet). The file opening test looks like this:

```java
public void testFileOpen() {
    String fileName = "phoneList.txt";

    PhoneContactList pc = new PhoneContactList();
    boolean fileOK = pc.fileOpen(fileName);

    if (fileOK == false) {
        System.out.println("Open Failed");
        System.exit(1);
    }
}
```

We add that to the testing class we created before. In the TestDriver class from before, we just add the line

```java
t1.testFileOpen();
```

to the main() method. Once this test fails, you can then implement the new class and fill in the stubs we created before. The new PhoneContactList class then looks like this:

```java
import java.util.*;
import java.io.*;

public class PhoneContactList
{
    private TreeMap<String, PhoneContact> phoneList;
    private Scanner phoneFile;

    /**
     * Constructors for objects of class PhoneContactList
     */
    public PhoneContactList() {
    }
```

```
    public PhoneContactList(PhoneContact pc)
    {
        phoneList = new TreeMap<String, PhoneContact>();
        phoneList.put(pc.getLastName(), pc);
    }

    public boolean fileOpen(String name)
    {
        try {
            phoneFile = new Scanner(new File(name));
            return true;
        } catch (FileNotFoundException e) {
            System.out.println(e.getMessage());
            return false;
        }
    }
}
```

This is how your test-design-develop process will work. Try creating the rest of the tests I listed earlier and finish implementing the PhoneContactList class code. Good luck.

JUnit: A Testing Framework

In the previous section, we created our own test scaffolding and hooked our tests into it. Many development environments have the ability to do this for you. One of the most popular for Java is the JUnit testing framework that was created by Eric Gamma and Kent Beck (see http://junit.org/junit4/).

JUnit is a framework for developing unit tests for Java classes. It provides a base class called TestCase that you extend to create a series of tests for the class you're creating. JUnit contains a number of other classes, including an assertion library used for evaluating the results of individual tests and several applications that run the tests you create. A very good FAQ for JUnit is at http://junit.sourceforge.net/doc/faq/faq.htm#overview_1.

To write a test in JUnit, you must import the framework classes and then extend the TestCase base class. A very simple test would look like this:

```
import junit.framework.TestCase;
import junit.framework.Assert.*;

public class SimpleTest extends TestCase {

    public SimpleTest(String name) {
        super(name);
    }

    public void testSimpleTest() {
        LifeUniverse lu = new LifeUniverse();
        int answer = lu.ultimateQuestion();
        assertEquals(42, answer);
    }
}
```

Note that the single-argument constructor is required. The assertEquals() method is one of the assertion library (junit.framework.Assert) methods which, of course, tests to see if the expected answer (the first parameter) is equal to the actual answer (the second parameter). There are many other assert*() methods. The complete list is at http://junit.sourceforge.net/javadoc/.

Because JUnit is packaged in a Java jar file, you either need to add the location of the jar file to your Java CLASSPATH environment variable or add it to the line when you compile the test case from the command line. For example, to compile our simple test case, we would use this:

```
% javac -classpath $JUNIT_HOME/junit.jar SimpleTest.java
```

$JUNIT_HOME is the directory where you installed the junit.jar file.

Executing a test from the command line is just as easy as compiling. There are two ways to do it. The first is to use one of the JUnit pre-packaged runner classes, which takes as its argument the name of the test class:

```
java -cp .:./junit.jar junit.textui.TestRunner SimpleTest
```

That results in

```
.
Time: 0.001

OK (1 test)
```

where there is a dot for every test that is run, the time the entire test suite required, and the results of the tests.

You can also execute the JUnitCore class directly, also passing the name of the test class as an argument to the class:

```
java -cp .:./junit.jar org.junit.runner.JUnitCore SimpleTest
```

That results in the following:

```
JUnit version 4.8.2
.
Time: 0.004

OK (1 test)
```

JUnit is included in many standard integrated development environments (IDEs). BlueJ, NetBeans, and Eclipse all have JUnit plug-ins, making the creation and running of unit test cases nearly effortless.

For example, with our earlier example and using BlueJ, we can create a new unit test class and use it to test our PhoneContact and PhoneContactList classes, as shown in Figure 16-1.

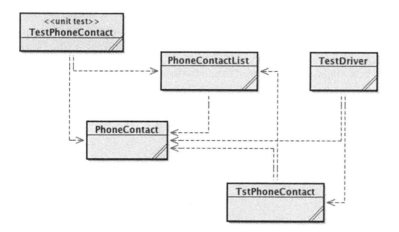

Figure 16-1. *The PhoneContact test UML diagrams*

Our test class, TestPhoneContact now looks like this:

```
public class TestPhoneContact extends junit.framework.TestCase {
    /**
     * Default constructor for test class TestPhoneContact
     */
    public TestPhoneContact(String name) {
        super(name);
    }

    /**
     * Sets up the test fixture.
     * Called before every test case method.
     */
    protected void setUp() {
    }

    /**
     * Tears down the test fixture.
     * Called after every test case method.
     */
    protected void tearDown() {
    }

    public void testPhoneContactCreation() {
        String fname = "Fred";
        String lname = "Flintstone";
        String phone = "800-555-1212";
        String email = "fred@knox.edu";
```

```
        PhoneContact pc = new PhoneContact(fname, lname, phone, email);
        assertEquals(lname, pc.getLastName());
        assertEquals(fname, pc.getFirstName());
        assertEquals(phone, pc.getPhoneNum());
        assertEquals(email, pc.getEmailAddr());
    }

    public void testFileOpen() {
        String fileName = "phoneList.txt";

        PhoneContactList pc = new PhoneContactList();
        boolean fileOK = pc.fileOpen(fileName);
        assertTrue(fileOK);

        if (fileOK == false) {
            System.out.println("Open Failed, File Not Found");
            System.exit(1);
        }
    }
}
```

To run this set of tests in BlueJ, we select Test All from the drop-down menu shown in Figure 16-2.

Figure 16-2. *The JUnit Menu: select Test All to run the tests*

Because we don't have a phoneList.txt file created yet, we get the output shown in Figure 16-3.

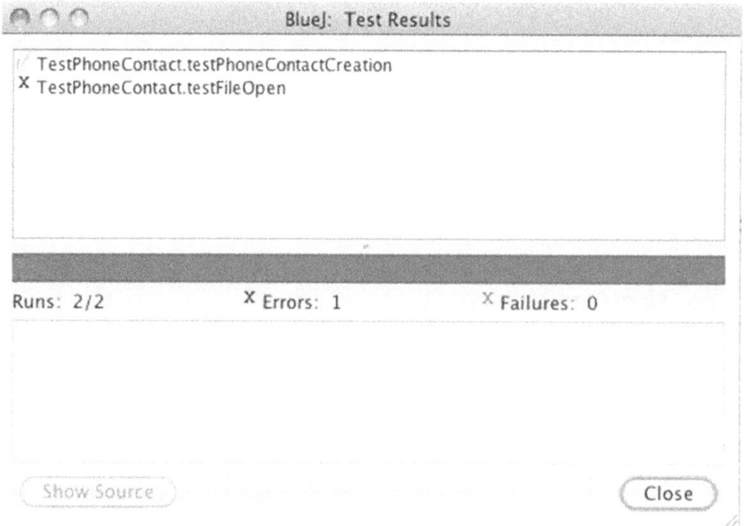

Figure 16-3. *JUnit Testing output*

Here, we note that the `testFileOpen()` test has failed.

Every time we make any changes to our program, we can add another test to the `TestPhoneContact` class and rerun all the tests with a single menu selection. The testing framework makes it much easier to create individual tests and whole suites of tests that can be run every time you make a change to the program. This lets us know every time we make a change whether we've broken something or not. Very cool.

Testing Is Good

At the end of the day, unit testing is a critical part of your development process. Done carefully and correctly, it can help you remove the vast majority of your errors even before you integrate your code into the larger program. TDD, where you write tests first and then write the code that makes the tests succeed, is an effective way to catch errors in both low-level design and coding and allows you to easily and quickly create a regression test suite that you can use for every integration and every baseline of your program.

Conclusion

From your point of view as the developer, unit testing is the most important class of testing your program will undergo. It's the most fundamental type of testing, making sure your code meets the requirements of the design at the lowest level. Despite the fact that developers are more concerned with making sure their program works than with breaking it, developing a good unit-testing mindset is critical to your development as a mature, effective programmer. Testing frameworks make this job much easier than in the past, and so learning how your local testing framework operates and learning to write good tests are skills you should work hard at. Better that you should find your own bugs than the customer.

References

Kernighan, B. W. and R. Pike. *The Practice of Programming.* (Boston, MA: Addison-Wesley, 1999.)

Martin, R. C. *Clean Code: A Handbook of Agile Software Craftsmanship.* (Upper Saddle River, NJ: Prentice-Hall, 2009.)

McConnell, S. *Code Complete 2: A Practical Handbook of Software Construction.* (Redmond, WA: Microsoft Press, 2004.)

Newkirk, J. and R. C. Martin. *Extreme Programming in Practice.* (Boston, MA, Addison-Wesley, 2001.)

CHAPTER 17

Code Reviews and Inspections

Our objective with Inspections is to reduce the Cost of Quality by finding and removing defects earlier and at a lower cost. While some testing will always be necessary, we can reduce the costs of test by reducing the volume of defects propagated to test.

—Ron Radice (2002)

When you catch bugs early, you also get fewer compound bugs. Compound bugs are two separate bugs that interact: you trip going downstairs, and when you reach for the handrail it comes off in your hand.

—Paul Graham (2001)

Here's a shocker: your main quality objective in software development is to get a working program to your user that meets all their requirements and has no defects. That's right: your code should be perfect. It meets all the user's requirements and it has no errors in it when you deliver it. Impossible? Can't be done? Well, *software quality assurance* is all about trying to get as close to perfection as you can—albeit within time and budget.

Software quality is usually discussed from two different perspectives: the user's and the developer's. From the user's perspective, quality has a number of characteristics—things that your program must do in order to be accepted by the user—among which are the following[1]:

- *Correctness*: The software has to work, period.

- *Usability*: It has to be easy to learn and easy to use.

- *Reliability*: It has to stay up and be available when you need it.

- *Security*: The software has to prevent unauthorized access and protect your data.

- *Adaptability*: It should be easy to add new features.

From the developer's perspective, things are a bit different. The developer wants to see the following:

- *Maintainability*: It has to be easy to make changes to the software.

- *Portability*: It has to be easy to move the software to a different platform.

- *Readability*: Many developers won't admit this, but you do need to be able to read the code.

---

[1]McConnell, S. *Code Complete 2: A Practical Handbook of Software Construction*. (Redmond, WA: Microsoft Press, 2004.)

© John F. Dooley 2017

J. F. Dooley, *Software Development, Design and Coding*, https://doi.org/10.1007/978-1-4842-3153-1_17

- *Understandability*: The code needs to be designed in such a way that a new developer can understand how it all hangs together.

- *Testability*: Well, at least the testers think your code should be easy to test. Code that's created in a modular fashion, with short functions that do only one thing, is much easier to understand and test than code that is all just one big `main()` function.

Software Quality Assurance (SQA) has three legs to it:

- *Testing*: Finding the errors that surface while your program is executing, also known as *dynamic analysis*.

- *Debugging*: Getting all the obvious errors out of your code—the ones that are found by testing it.

- *Reviews*: Finding the errors that are inherently in your code as it sits there, also known as *static analysis*.

Many developers—and managers—think that you can test your way to quality. You can't. As we saw in the last chapter, tests are limited. You often can't explore every code path, you can't test every possible data combination, and often your tests themselves are flawed. Tests can only get you so far. As Edsger Dijkstra famously said, ". . . program testing can be a very effective way to show the presence of bugs, but it is hopelessly inadequate for showing their absence[2]."

Reviewing your code—reading it and looking for errors on the page—provides another mechanism for making sure you've implemented the user's requirements and the resulting design correctly. In fact, most development organizations that use a plan-driven methodology will not only review code, they'll also review the requirements document, architecture, design specification, test plan, the tests themselves, and user documentation—in short, all the *work products* produced by the software development organization. Organizations that use an agile development methodology don't necessarily have all the documents just mentioned, but they do have requirements, user stories, user documentation, and especially code to review. This chapter focuses on reviewing your code.

Walkthroughs, Reviews, and Inspections

Testing alone is not a particularly effective way of finding errors in your code. In many cases, the combination of unit testing, integration testing, and system testing will only find about 50% or so of the errors in your program[3]. But if you add some type of code review (reading the code to find errors) to your testing regimen you can bring that percentage up to 93–99% of all the errors in your code. Now *that's* an objective to shoot for.

Three types of reviews are typically done: walkthroughs, code reviews, and inspections. These three work their way up from very informal techniques to very formal methodologies. The reviews are typically done either right after you've got a clean compile of your code and before you unit test, or right after you finish your unit testing. It's better to do the reviews right after unit testing. Then you've got your changes made, you've got a clean compile, and you've done the first round of testing. That's a great time to have someone else take a look at your code.

---

[2]Dijkstra, E. "The Humble Programmer." *CACM* **15**(10): 859–866 (1972).
[3]McConnell, 2004.

Walkthroughs

Walkthroughs, also known as *desk checks* or *code reads*, are the least formal type of a review. Walkthroughs are normally used to confirm small changes to code, say a line or two, that you've just made to fix an error. If you've just added a new method to a class, or you've changed more than about 25 or 30 lines of code, don't do a walkthrough. Do a code review instead (discussed next).

Walkthroughs involve two or at most three people: the author of the code and the reviewer. The author's job in a walkthrough is to explain to the reviewer what the change is supposed to do and to point out where the change was made. The reviewer's job is to understand the change and then read the code. Once the reviewer reads the code, they make one of two judgments: either they agree that the change is correct, or they don't. If not, the author has to go back, fix the code again, and then do another walkthrough. If the reviewer thinks the change is correct, then the author can integrate the changed code back into the code base for integration testing.

If you're using an agile methodology and you're pair programming, a code walkthrough will happen naturally as you are implementing a task. The driver is writing the code, and the navigator is looking over their shoulder, checking for errors and thinking ahead. In this case, it's acceptable to use a walkthrough for a larger piece of code, but for a complete task—or better yet, for each user story that's implemented—you should do a code review or an inspection. I talk more about reviews and agile methodologies in subsequent sections.

Code Reviews

Code reviews are somewhat more formal than a walkthrough. Code reviews are what most software developers do. You should always do a code review if you've changed a substantial amount of code, or if you've added more than just a few lines of new code to an existing program. As mentioned, agile programmers may do code reviews when they finish a user story. Code reviews are real meetings.

There are usually between three and five attendees at a code review. The people who attend a code review should each bring a different perspective to the meeting.

- The *moderator* of the code review is usually the *author*. It's the moderator's job to call the meeting, send out the work to be reviewed well before the meeting time, and to run the code review meeting. The moderator may also take notes at the meeting.

- There should be one or more *developers* at the meeting—someone who's working on the same project as the author. This person will bring detailed knowledge of the project to the meeting and assume that perspective.

- There should be a *tester* at the code review. This person brings the testing perspective and not only reads the code being reviewed, but thinks about ways in which the code should be tested.

- Finally, there should be an experienced developer present who's not on the same project as the author. This person is the *disinterested third party* who represents the quality perspective. Their job at the code review is to understand the code and get the author to explain the changes clearly. This person provides a more strategic vision about the code and how it fits into the project.

Oh, and no managers are allowed at code reviews. The presence of a manager changes the dynamics of the meeting and makes the code review less effective. People who might be willing to honestly critique a piece of code among peers will clam up in the presence of a manager; that doesn't help find errors. No managers, please.

The objective of a code review is to find errors in the code. It's *not* to fix them. Code reviews are informal enough that some discussion of fixes may occur, but that should be kept to a minimum. Before the code review meeting, all the participants should go over the materials sent out by the moderator and prepare a list of errors they find. This step is critical to making the review meeting efficient and successful. Do your homework!

This list should be given to the moderator at the beginning of the meeting. The author (who may also be the moderator) goes through the code changes, explaining them and how they either fix the error they were intended to fix or add the new feature that was required. If an error or a discussion leads the review meeting off into code that wasn't in the scope of the original review—*stop*! Be very careful about moving off into territory that hasn't been pre-read. You should treat any code not in the scope of the review as a black box. Schedule another meeting instead. Remember, the focus of the code review is on a single piece of code and finding errors in that piece of code. Don't be distracted.

A computer and projector are essential at the code review so that everyone can see what's going on all the time. A second computer should be used so that someone (usually the author) can take notes about errors found in the code. A code review should not last more than about two hours or review more than about 200–500 lines of code because everyone's productivity will begin to suffer after that amount of time or reading.

After the code review, the notes are distributed to all the participants and the author is charged with fixing all the errors that were found during the review. If you run out of time, schedule another review. Although metrics aren't required for code reviews, the moderator should at least keep track of how many errors were found, how many lines of code were reviewed, and if appropriate, the severity of each of the errors. These metrics are very useful to gauge productivity and should be used in planning the next project.

Code Inspections

Code inspections are the most formal type of review meeting. The sole purpose of an inspection is to find defects in a work product. Inspections can be used to review planning documents, requirements, designs, or code—in short, any work product that a development team produces. Code inspections have specific rules regarding how many lines of code to review at once, how long the review meeting must be, and how much preparation each member of the review team should do, among other things. Inspections are typically used by larger organizations because they take more training, time, and effort than walkthroughs or code reviews. They're also used for mission- and safety-critical software where defects can cause harm to users. Michael Fagan invented the most widely known inspection methodology in 1976. Fagan's process was the first formal software inspection process proposed and, as such, has been very influential. Most organizations that use inspections use a variation of the original Fagan software code inspection process[4]. Code inspections have several very important criteria, including the following:

- Inspections use checklists of common error types to focus the inspectors.

- The focus of the inspection meeting is solely on finding errors; no solutions are permitted.

- Reviewers are required to prepare beforehand; the inspection meeting will be canceled if everyone isn't ready.

- Each participant in the inspection has a distinct role.

- All participants have had inspection training.

---

[4]Fagan, M. "Design and Code Inspections to Reduce Errors in Program Development." *IBM Systems Journal* 15(3): 182–211 (1976).

- The moderator is not the author and has had special training in addition to the regular inspection training.

- The author is always required to follow up on errors reported in the meeting with the moderator.

- Metrics data is always collected at an inspection meeting.

Inspection Roles

The following are the roles used in code inspections:

- *Moderator*: The moderator gets all the materials from the author, decides who the other participants in the inspection should be, and is responsible for sending out all the inspection materials and scheduling and coordinating the meeting. Moderators must be technically competent; they need to understand the inspection materials and keep the meeting on track. The moderator schedules the inspection meeting and sends out the checklist of common errors for the reviewers to peruse. They also follow up with the author on any errors found in the inspection, so they must understand the errors and the corrections. Moderators attend an additional inspection-training course to help them prepare for their role.

- *Author*: The author distributes the inspection materials to the moderator. If an Overview meeting is required, the author chairs it and explains the overall design to the reviewers. Overview meetings are discouraged in code inspections, because they can "taint the evidence" by injecting the author's opinions about the code and the design before the inspection meeting. Sometimes, though, if many of the reviewers are unfamiliar with the project, an Overview meeting is necessary. The author is also responsible for all rework that's created as a result of the inspection meeting. During the inspection, the author answers questions about the code from the reviewers, but does nothing else.

- *Reader*: The reader's role is to read the code. Actually, the reader is supposed to paraphrase the code, not read it. Paraphrasing implies that the reader has a good understanding of the project, its design, and the code in question. The reader doesn't explain the code, only paraphrases it. The author should answer any questions about the code. That said, if the author has to explain too much of the code, that's usually considered a defect to be fixed; the code should be refactored to make it simpler.

- *Reviewers*: The reviewers do the heavy lifting in the inspection. A reviewer can be anyone with an interest in the code who is not the author. Normally, reviewers are other developers from the same project. As in code reviews, it's usually a good idea to have a senior person who's not on the project also be a reviewer. There are usually between two and four reviewers in an inspection meeting. Reviewers must do their pre-reading of the inspection materials and are expected to come to the meeting with a list of errors that they have found. This list is given to the recorder.

- *Recorder*: Every inspection meeting has a recorder. The recorder is one of the reviewers and is the one who takes notes at the inspection meeting. The recorder merges the defect lists of the reviewers and classifies and records errors found during the meeting. They then prepare the inspection report and distribute it to the meeting participants. If the project is using a defect management system, then it's up to the recorder to enter defect reports for all major defects from the meeting into the system.

- *Managers*: As with code reviews, managers aren't invited to code inspections.

Inspection Phases and Procedures

Fagan inspections have seven phases that must be followed for each inspection[5]:

1. Planning
2. The Overview meeting
3. Preparation
4. The Inspection meeting
5. The Inspection report
6. Rework
7. Follow up

Planning

In the Planning phase, the moderator organizes and schedules the meeting and picks the participants. The moderator and the author get together to discuss the scope of the inspection materials—for code inspections, typically 200–500 uncommented lines of code will be reviewed. The author then distributes the code to be inspected to the participants.

The Overview Meeting

An Overview meeting is necessary if several of the participants are unfamiliar with the project or its design and they need to come up to speed before they can effectively read the code. If an Overview meeting is necessary, the author will call it and run the meeting. The meeting itself is mostly a presentation by the author of the project architecture and design. As mentioned, Overview meetings are discouraged, because they have a tendency to taint the evidence. Like the Inspection meeting itself, Overview meetings should last no longer than two hours.

Preparation

In the Preparation phase, each reviewer reads the work to be inspected. Preparation should take no more than two or three hours. The amount of work to be inspected should be between 200–500 uncommented lines of code or 30-80 pages of text. A number of studies have shown that reviewers can typically review about 125-200 lines of code per hour. In Fagan inspections, the Preparation phase is required. The Inspection meeting can be canceled if the reviewers haven't done their preparation. The amount of time each reviewer spent in preparation is one of the metrics gathered at the Inspection meeting.

The Inspection Meeting

The moderator is in charge of the Inspection meeting. Their job during the meeting is to keep the meeting on track and focused. The Inspection meeting should last no more than two hours. If there is any material that has not been inspected at the end of that time, a new meeting is scheduled. At the beginning of the meeting, the reviewers turn in their list of previously discovered errors to the recorder.

---

[5]Fagan, M. "Advances in Software Inspections." *IEEE Trans on Software Engineering* 12(7): 744–751 (1986).

During the meeting the reader paraphrases the code, and the reviewers follow along. The author is there to clarify any details and answer any questions about the code—and otherwise does nothing. The recorder writes down all the defects reported, their severity, and their classification. Solutions to problems are strongly discouraged. Participants are encouraged to have a different meeting to discuss solutions.

We should look for a minute at defect types and severity as reported in a Fagan inspection. Fagan specifies only two types of defects: minor and major. *Minor* defects are typically typographic errors, errors in documentation, small user interface errors, and other miscellany that don't cause the software to fail. All other errors are *major* defects. This is a bit extreme. Two levels are usually not sufficient for most development organizations. Most organizations will have at least a five-level defect structure:

1. *Fatal*: Yes, your program dies; can you say core dump?

2. *Severe*: A major piece of functionality fails, and there is no workaround for the user. Say, in a first-person shooter game the software doesn't allow you to re-load your main weapon and doesn't let you switch weapons in the middle of a fight. That's bad.

3. *Serious*: The error is severe, but there's a workaround for the user. The software doesn't let you re-load your main weapon, but if you switch weapons and then switch back you can re-load.

4. *Trivial*: A small error—incorrect documentation or something like a minor user interface problem. For example, a text box is 10 pixels too far from its prompt in a form.

5. *Feature request*: A brand new feature for the program is desired. This isn't an error; it's a request from the user (or marketing) for new functionality in the software. In a game, this could be new weapons, new character types, new maps or surroundings, and so on. This is version 2.

In most organizations, software is not allowed to ship to a user with known severity 1 and 2 errors still in it. But severity 3 errors really make users unhappy, so realistically, no known severity 1 through 3 errors are allowed to ship. Ideally, of course, no errors ship, right?

In a Fagan inspection meeting, it's usually up to the recorder to correctly classify the severity of the major defects found in the code. This classification can be changed later. In the Fagan inspection process, all severity 1 through 3 defects must be fixed.

Inspection Report

Within a day of the meeting, the recorder distributes the Inspection report to all participants. The central part of the report is the defects that were found in the code at the meeting.

The report also includes metrics data, including the following:

- Number of defects found

- Number of each type of defect by severity and type

- Time spent in preparation; total time in person-hours and time per participant

- Time spent in the meeting; clock time and total person-hours

- Number of uncommented lines of code or pages reviewed

Rework and Follow-up

The author fixes all the severity 1 through 3 defects found during the meeting. If enough defects were found, or if enough refactoring or code changes had to occur, then another Inspection is scheduled. How much is enough? Amounts vary. McConnell says 5% of the code[6], but this author has typically used 10% of the code inspected. So, if you inspected 200 lines of code and had to change 20 or more of them in the rework, then you should have another Inspection meeting. If it's less than 10%, the author and the moderator can do a walkthrough. Regardless of how much code is changed, the moderator must check all the changes as part of the follow-up. As part of the rework, another metric should be reported—the amount of time required by the author to fix each of the defects reported. This metric plus the number of defects found during the project are critical to doing accurate planning and scheduling for the *next* project. This metric is easier to keep track of if developers use a defect tracking system.

Reviews in Agile Projects

Lets face it: the preceding sections on walkthroughs, code reviews, and inspections don't seem to apply to agile projects at all. They seem like heavyweight processes that might be used in very large projects, but surely not in XP or Scrum or Lean Development, right? The last thing we need during a Scrum sprint is a meeting every time we finish a task and want to integrate the code. Well, it turns out that doing reviews in agile projects is a pretty good idea and seems to work well.

Lets remember what the Agile Manifesto says agile developers value:

- Individuals and interactions over processes and tools

- Working software over comprehensive documentation

- Customer collaboration over contract negotiation

- Responding to change over following a plan

Over the last 40 years or so, quite a bit of research has shown that code reviews produce software with fewer defects, which aligns nicely with the agile emphasis on working software. What could be more interactive than software developers collaborating on the code and making real-time improvements? Code reviews also fully support agile tenets by promoting the development of working software, collaboration, and interaction among teams, continuous attention to technical excellence, and the ability to respond to change—all while maintaining a high level of quality. The only question is: "How do you do code reviews in an agile project?"

First of all, let's change the name. Instead of talking about walkthroughs or code reviews, let's talk about *peer code reviews* instead. This emphasizes the fact that in our agile project *peers* do the reviewing of code. Remember that a typical agile team has members with a wide variety of skills. There are developers, designers, testers, writers, architects, and, of course, the customer. Also remember that one of the hallmarks of an agile team is that they are *self-organizing*. In this case what we want is for anyone on the team to be able to be in a peer code review. This spreads the knowledge of the code around, just as pair programming does, and it gives everyone on the team more skills and knowledge; remember that *collective code ownership* is a trait of agile methodologies.

Secondly, why do you need a meeting? You'll hold the *peer code review* after the code has been written (or fixed) and after all the unit tests have been run. Whoever is to participate in the peer code review will need to read the code before the code review. In addition, if your project is using pair programming, there have already been two sets of eyes on the code and the design and the requirements already. What are

---

[6]McConnell, 2004.

the chances that in a code review meeting you'll uncover more major defects that would require fixing? It turns out that the probability of finding more major defects is pretty low. According to a research study by Lawrence Votta[7], code inspection meetings add only about 4% more defects to the list than those already brought to the meeting by the participants. In other words, the meetings may not add much.

Also remember the ultimate purpose of a peer code review: producing working software. In all agile processes, anything that detracts from the goal of producing working software is to be shunned, and meetings take time away from producing working software.

So, where is the case for having a peer code review? Well the case is the research that says that code reviews *do* find new defects in code, and if we can do a peer code review without slowing down the flow of a sprint that would be a good thing. Also remember that one of the reasons for agile processes (described in Kent Beck's *Extreme Programming Explained* book[8]) is that the earlier you find defects, the cheaper they are to fix.

A last idea here is that the team should allocate part of everyone's time to doing peer code reviews when they're doing the task estimations at the beginning of an iteration or a sprint. Making peer code reviews a part of the culture and the work effort will make it easier to convince developers to fit it into their day.

How to Do an Agile Peer Code Review

There are several ways that you can do a peer code review without having a long, drawn-out meeting and without requiring lots of heavyweight documentation and reporting. Here are a few suggestions:

- *Pair programming + 1*: If your project is already doing pair programming, then you're halfway to a peer code review already. The suggestion here is to just add one more person at the end and go over the code with that person one more time before you integrate it. That's all. You can give the new person a heads-up and have them read the code beforehand, or you can just drag them over to your computer and do it immediately.

- *Over the shoulder*: This is like the walkthrough we visited at the beginning of this chapter and is pretty much what you do in the pair programming + 1 activity. We put it here for those who aren't using pair programming. Once again, the suggestion here is to just add one more person at the end and go over the code with that person one more time before you integrate it. That's all. You can give the new person a heads-up and have them read the code beforehand, or you can just drag them over to your computer and do it immediately.

- *E-mail review*: In this case, you email one or more of your colleagues a link to the code and ask them to read it and provide comments. Assuming that your team has built code review time into all your task estimations, this should be something that everyone on the team is on board with.

Summary of Review Methodologies

Table 17-1 summarizes the characteristics of the three review methodologies we've examined. Each has its place, and you should know how each of them works. The important thing to remember is that reviews and testing go hand in hand and both should be used to get your high-quality code out the door.

---

[7]Votta, Lawrence. "Does every inspection need a meeting?" *SIGSOFT Softw. Eng. Notes*, vol. 18, no. 5, pp. 107–114 (1993).

[8]Beck, Kent. *Extreme Programming Explained: Embrace Change*, Paperback. (Boston, MA: Addison-Wesley, 2000.)

Table 17-1. *Comparison of Review Methodologies*

Properties	Walkthrough	Code Review	Code Inspection
Formal moderator training	No	No	Yes
Distinct participant roles	No	Yes	Yes
Who drives the meeting	Author	Author/moderator	Moderator
Common error checklists	No	Maybe	Yes
Focused review effort	No	Yes	Yes
Formal follow-up	No	Maybe	Yes
Detailed defect feedback	Incidental	Yes	Yes
Metric data collected and used	No	Maybe	Yes
Process improvements	No	No	Yes

Defect Tracking Systems

Most software development organizations and many open source development projects will use an automated defect tracking system to keep track of defects found in their software and to record requests for new features in the program. Popular free and open source defect tracking systems include Bugzilla (`www.bugzilla.org`), YouTrack (`www.jetbrains.com/youtrack/`), Jira (`www.atlassian.com/software/jira`), Mantis (`www.mantisbt.org`), and Trac (`https://trac.edgewall.org`).

Defect tracking systems keep track of a large amount of information about each defect found and entered. A typical defect tracking system will keep track of at least the following:

- The number of the defect (assigned by the tracking system itself)

- The current state of the defect in the system (Open, Assigned, Resolved, Integrated, Closed)

- The fix that was made to correct the error

- The files that were changed to make the fix

- What baseline the fix was integrated into

- What tests were written and where they're stored (ideally, the tests are stored along with the fix)

- The result of the code review or inspection

Defect tracking systems assume that at any given time, a defect report is in some state that reflects where it is in the process of being fixed. A typical defect tracking system can have upwards of ten states for each defect report.

Figure 17-1 shows the states of a typical defect tracking system and the flow of a defect report through the system. In brief, all defects start out as New. They are then assigned to a developer for Analysis. The developer decides whether the reported defect is

- A duplicate of one already in the system.

- Not a defect and so should be rejected.

- A real defect that should be worked on by someone.

- A real defect whose resolution can be postponed to a later date.

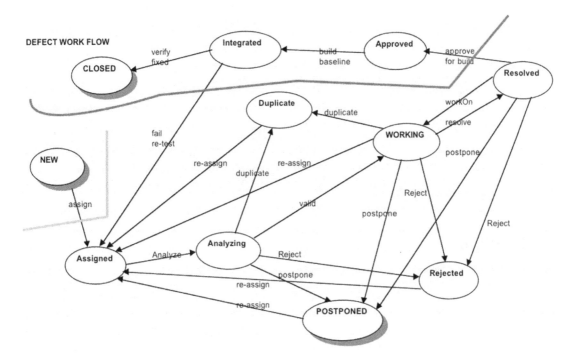

Figure 17-1. *Defect tracking system workflow*

Defects that are worked on are eventually fixed and move to the Resolved state. The fix must then be subjected to a code review. If the code review is successful, the defect fix is then Approved. From Approved, the fix is scheduled for integration into the next baseline of the product, and if the integration tests of that baseline are successful, the defect is Closed.

Defect Tracking in Agile Projects

Once again we're at a place where we realize that a lot of what we've said so far about defect tracking is pretty heavyweight, and so we ask, "How does this apply to agile projects?" Well, first of all, we can ask ourselves which defects we want to track and when do those defects occur?

When defects occur can be divided up into before and after an iteration, and before and after the product release. *Which* defects occur can be those that affect the customer and that they care about, and those that the customer doesn't care about. Let's break these all up.

Defects that are found before the end of an iteration or a sprint are ones we can easily fix. These will normally be found either via unit test failures, during peer code reviews, or by the customer when they're testing an intermediate product build. These defects are typically fixed immediately, or if they uncover some other problem, like in the requirements, they can be made into new tasks that are added to the product or sprint backlog.

Defects that are found after the end of an iteration or sprint, but before the final product release, should probably be made into new tasks that must be added to the backlog for the next iteration. These defects can also lead to refactoring or new tasks that reflect changing requirements.

Defects that are found after product release are all errors that customers find and report. Here the decision of whether to fix them depends on whether the customer cares about the error or not. If the customer does care, then the error should be tagged and tracked, added to the product backlog, and fixed in a subsequent release of the product. If the customer doesn't care, then just ignore it.

This leads us to the problem of who fixes defects found in the product code.

If the error is found during development (during an iteration or a sprint and before product release), then the development team, in consultation with the customer, should decide whether the error should be fixed. If yes, then the development team should fix it by making it a task and adding it to the backlog for the next iteration or sprint. If no, then everyone just moves on.

If the defect is found after the product release, then it's likely that the development team has moved on to another project and may even have dispersed into several projects. This calls for the creation of a separate support team whose job it is to evaluate and fix errors in released code. Ideally, people on this support team will rotate in and out from the company's development teams so that some institutional memory of the project is present on the support team.

Conclusion

A second or third set of eyes on your code is always a good thing. Code that's reviewed by others is improved and brings you closer to the Platonic ideal of defect-free software. Walkthroughs, code reviews, and formal code inspections each have their place in the array of tools used to improve code quality. The more of these tools you have in your toolbox, the better programmer you are. The combination of reviews, debugging, and unit testing will find the vast majority of defects in your code[9] (say, up to 95% of defects) and is the best thing that a developer can do to help release great code.

References

Ackerman, A., et al. "Software Inspections: An Effective Verification Process." *IEEE Software* 6(3): 31–36 (1989).

K. Beck, *Extreme Programming Explained: Embrace Change*, Paperback. (Boston, MA: Addison-Wesley, 2000.)

Dijkstra, E. "The Humble Programmer." *CACM* 15(10): 859–866 (1972).

Doolan, P. "Experience with Fagan's Inspection Method." *Software—Practice & experience* 22(2): 173–182 (1992).

Dunsmore, A., M. Roper, et al. "Practical Code Inspection Techniques for Object-Oriented Systems: An Experimental Comparison." *IEEE Software* 20(4): 21–29 (2003).

Fagan, M. "Design and Code Inspections to Reduce Errors in Program Development." *IBM Systems Journal* 15(3): 182–211 (1976).

Fagan, M. "Advances in Software Inspections." *IEEE Trans on Software Engineering* 12(7): 744–751. 1986.

Martin, R. C. *Agile Software Development: Principles, Patterns, and Practices*. (Upper Saddle River, NJ: Prentice Hall, 2003.)

McConnell, S. *Code Complete 2: A Practical Handbook of Software Construction*. (Redmond, WA: Microsoft Press, 2004.)

Votta, Lawrence, "Does every inspection need a meeting?" *SIGSOFT Softw. Eng. Notes*, vol. 18, no. 5, pp. 107–114 (1993).

---

[9]McConnell, 2004.

▓ ▓ ▓

CHAPTER 18

Ethics and Professional Practice

Ethics is knowing the difference between what you have a right to do and what is right to do.

—Potter Stewart

I'll wrap up our exploration of software development by spending some time talking about ethics and professional practice—that is, how should you act as a computing professional in situations that pose an ethical dilemma? We'll talk about what *ethics* means and how it applies to the software industry, what ethical theories exist that will give us some tools, what an ethical argument or discussion is, and how to evaluate ethical situations. Finally, we'll go through three case studies to give you an idea of how these evaluation techniques will work.

Introduction to Ethics

Simply put *ethics* is the study of how to decide if something is *right or wrong*. Another way of putting this is that it is the study of humans figuring out *how best to live*. For now, we're going to assume that everyone knows what *right* and *wrong* means, but as we'll see in some of the examples, even this can be dicey at times. As for *computer ethics*, we'll say it means those ethical issues that a computer professional (in our case, software developers) will face in the course of their job. It includes your relationships with your colleagues, your managers, and your customers. Computer ethics also includes figuring out how to deal with situations where you must make critical decisions that can affect you, your company, and the users of your products. For example, what if you're asked to ship software that you think has a critical safety bug in it—or any serious bug? What if your company is making illegal copies of software? What if your company is making it easy for others to illegally use or copy the intellectual property of others? What do you do if you think you have a conflict of interest regarding a project you're working on? What do you do if you're offered a job developing software that you find morally objectionable? What if you discover that your company is keeping track of everyone's web searches or keystrokes?

Many decisions that are made in your professional life will have an ethical component. For example, the amount of data that a company collects from web site visitors has one. Whether customers are made aware of the data collection also has an ethical component. A decision to release software that allows users to convert files that use digital rights management (DRM) protection into unprotected files has an ethical component. A company's treatment of its employees also has an ethical component.

The ethical situations you encounter in your professional life aren't something that is categorically or substantially different from those that you encounter outside of your profession. You still need to examine these situations using general ethical principles and theories. That's what we'll start with.

© John F. Dooley 2017
J. F. Dooley, *Software Development, Design and Coding*, https://doi.org/10.1007/978-1-4842-3153-1_18

Ethical Theory

Ethics is the study of what it means to *do the right thing* and how to do the right thing in different situations. Ethics is a huge branch of philosophy, and we won't be able to cover more than a small part of it here. We'll focus on just a couple of different theories and the tools those theories give us to figure out how to do the right thing.

First of all, "ethical theory is based on the assumption that people are rational and make free choices[1]." That assumption isn't always true, obviously, but we'll assume it is and that for the most part people are responsible for their own decisions and actions.

Ethical rules are rules that we follow when we deal with other people and in actions or decisions that affect other people. Most ethical theories have the same goal: "to enhance human dignity, peace, happiness, and well-being.[2]" We'll also assume that the ethical rules from an ethical theory apply to everyone and in all situations. These rules should help to clarify our decision making and help lead us to an ethical decision in a particular situation. This is not as hard as it may sound at first. According to Sara Baase:

> *Behaving ethically, in a personal or professional sphere, is usually not a burden. Most of the time we are honest, we keep our promises, we do not steal, we do our jobs. This should not be surprising. If ethical rules are good ones, they work for people, that is, they make our lives better. Behaving ethically is often practical. Honesty makes interactions among people work more smoothly and reliably, for example. We might lose friends if we often lie or break promises. Also, social institutions encourage us to do right: We might be arrested if caught stealing. We might lose our jobs if we do them carelessly. In a professional context, doing good ethically often corresponds closely with doing a good job in the sense of professional quality and competence. Doing good ethically often corresponds closely with good business in the sense that ethically developed products are more likely to please customers. Sometimes, however, it is difficult to do the right thing. . . . Courage in a professional setting could mean admitting to a customer that your program is faulty, declining a job for which you are not qualified, or speaking out when you see someone else doing something wrong[3].*

We'll now explore some different ethical theories from two different schools, the deontological school and the consequentialist school.

Deontological Theories

The word *deontology* is derived from *deont*, the Greek present participle stem of *dei*, meaning "it is right." Deontologists believe that people's actions ought to be guided by moral laws and that these laws are universal (and in some cases, absolute). Deontologists emphasize duty and absolutist rules without respecting the consequences of the application of those rules. Deontological arguments focus on the *intent* of an act and how that act is or is not defensible as an application of a moral law. They usually do not concern themselves with the consequences of an act.

---

[1]Baase, Sara. *A Gift of Fire, 2nd Ed.* Upper Saddle River, NJ: Prentice-Hall, p. 403 (2003).
[2]Baase, p. 404 (2003).
[3]Baase, p. 404 (2003).

This school of ethical theory comes out of the work of Immanuel Kant (1724–1804). Kant believed that all moral laws were based on rational thought and behavior. Kant stresses fidelity to principles and duty. His arguments focus on duty divorced from any concerns about happiness or pleasure. Kant's philosophy is not grounded in knowledge of human nature, but in a common idea of duty that applies to all rational beings. One should do the right thing in the right spirit.[4]

Kant contributed many ideas to deontological theory. Here are three of the most important fundamental ideas:

1. *There are ethical constants and rules that must apply universally*: This is known as the *categorical imperative* or the *principle of universality*. In the simplest terms, the categorical imperative is a test of whether an action is right or wrong. If you propose a moral law or rule, can your conception of that law when acted upon apply universally? "Can the action in question pass the test of universalization? If not, the action is immoral and one has a duty to avoid it. The categorical imperative is a moral compass that gives us a convenient and tenable way of knowing when we are acting morally[5]."

2. *You should always act so as to treat yourself and others as ends in themselves and not means to an end*: That is, it's wrong to use a person. Rather, every interaction with another person should respect them as a rational human being. "The principle of humanity as an end in itself serves as a limiting condition of every person's freedom of action. We cannot exploit other human beings and treat them exclusively as a means to our ends or purposes[6]." One can look at this as a re-statement of the traditional saying "Do unto others as you would have them do unto you."

3. *Logic or reason determine the rules of ethical behavior*: Actions are intrinsically good if they follow from logic or reason. Rationality is the standard for what is good.

Deontologists believe that it's the act that's important in evaluating a moral decision and that the consequences of the act don't enter into determining whether the act is morally good or not. Kant takes an extreme position on the absolutism of moral rules. For example, take the moral rule *It is always wrong to lie*. If a murderer is looking for his intended victim (whom you just hid in your basement) and asks where they are, according to the *It is always wrong to lie* moral rule it's ethically wrong for you to lie to protect the intended victim. In the real world, most people would agree that this is a circumstance where the ethical rule should be broken because of the consequences if you don't[7]. We'll come back to this problem with Kant a little later.

As another example of a deontological argument and its problems, let's assume that most of us have been involved in experiences where we've been torn between what we want to do and what we ought to do. Kant says that what we want to do is of no importance. We should always focus on what we ought to do—in other words, we must do our duty. People who act in a dutiful way feel compelled to act that way out of belief and respect for some moral law. The moral value of an action depends on the underlying moral law[8].

---

[4]Spinello, Richard A. *Case Studies in Information and Computer Ethics*. (Upper Saddle River, NJ: Prentice-Hall, 1997).
[5]Spinello, p. 33.
[6]Spinello, p. 34.
[7]Baase, p. 405.
[8]Quinn, Michael J. *Ethics for the Information Age*. (Boston: Addison-Wesley, p. 63 (2005.)

In order to determine whether a moral rule is correct or good, we try to apply the principle of universality. Let's work through an example of the application of the principle of universality: Keeping promises.

Say we're in a difficult situation. In order to get out of that situation, we must make a promise that we later intend to break. The moral rule here would be *I am allowed to make promises with the intention of breaking them later*. Following the categorical imperative, we attempt to universalize this rule, so the universal version of the rule is: *It is morally correct for everyone in a difficult situation to make a promise they later break*. If this is true, then promises become worthless because everyone would know they'd be broken later. So there would be no such thing as a promise anymore. Hence, the moral rule that applies to me becomes useless when we try to universalize it. We have a logical contradiction: *a promise is a promise except when it's not a promise*. So this is how, when you're analyzing an ethical dilemma, you apply the principle of universality. In this case, we discover that the rule we started with can't be extended universally, and so it can't be a moral rule.

Where are we with respect to deontological ethics? Well, we have a set of assumptions (or axioms) and a means of testing whether new, potential moral laws are correct or not (or right or wrong)—the principle of universality. How well does this work? Let's try to formulate some pros and cons.

What's good about the deontological approach to ethics?

- *It is rational*: It's based on the idea that rational humans can use logic to explain the *why* behind their actions.

- *The principle of universality produces universal moral guidelines*: These guidelines allow us to make clear moral judgments.

- *All people are treated as moral equals*: This gives us an ethical framework to combat discrimination.

What's not so good about the deontological approach to ethics?

- *Sometimes no single rule can fully characterize an action*: Example: I'm stealing food to feed my starving children. Although there is an ethical rule against stealing, there's also an ethical rule that you should protect your children. In this case, these two rules are in conflict.

- *Deontological arguments don't give us a way to resolve a conflict between two or more moral rules*: Kant's absolutist position on rules results in the idea that the deontological approach doesn't tell us which rules are more important than others. Given the example about stealing food for your starving children, there's nothing we've seen in the deontological discussion on how to resolve this conflict of rules.

- *Deontological theories (particularly Kant's) don't allow any exceptions to the moral rules*: This makes them difficult to apply in the real world, where we often need to bend the rules to avoid bad consequences. (But remember, deontological theory doesn't care about consequences; it cares about the act and the rule that the act embodies[9].)

If deontological theory is flawed, is there another way to think about these ethical situations and reason about how to apply moral rules to solve them?

---

[9]Quinn, pp. 66–67.

Consequentialism (Teleological Theories)

There's another way to think about these ethical situations and reason about them. In addition to thinking about the act, we can also think about the *consequences* of the act. This is known as a *teleological theory*. Teleological theories derive their name from the Greek word *telos*, meaning "end" or "goal."

Teleological theories give priority to the good over the right and evaluate actions by the goal or consequences that they produce, hence the name *consequentialism*. A consequentialist focuses only on the consequences of an act to determine whether the act is good or bad[10].

The classic form of consequentialism is called *utilitarianism* and was developed by Jeremy Bentham (1748-1832) and John Stuart Mill (1806-1873), two British philosophers. Utilitarianism is based on the *principle of utility*, which says that an action is morally good or right to the extent that it increases the total happiness (or utility) of the affected parties. The action is morally wrong if it decreases the total happiness. Thus *utility* is the tendency of an action to produce happiness (or prevent unhappiness) for an individual or a group of individuals or a community[11]. An action might increase utility for some people and decrease it for others. This is where Mill's aphorism *the greatest good for the greatest number* comes from.

According to utilitarianism, we must have a way to calculate the increase or decrease of happiness. This means we also need some common metric for how to measure happiness and we need to be able to calculate the total happiness or unhappiness of an action. This leads us to two variations on utilitarianism.

Act utilitarianism is the theory that an act is good if its net effect (over all the affected people) is to produce more happiness than unhappiness. Act utilitarians apply the principle of utility to individual acts and all the morally significant people that they affect.

For example, say the local county is considering replacing a stretch of very curvy highway with a straight stretch. We need to consider whether this is a good idea or not. In order to do this we must figure out who is affected by this new construction (who are the stakeholders) and what effect will the construction have on them (what is the cost). Say that in order to construct the highway, the county must take possession of 100 homes that the highway will cut through. Thus, these property holders are stakeholders. The homeowners will be compensated for their property. Also, say about 5,000 cars drive on the highway every day; these drivers are also stakeholders because the new road may make their commutes shorter and they'll thus have to buy less gas. More broadly, the county is a stakeholder because it will have to maintain the road over a certain period, say 20 years, so there will be a cost for maintenance. Even more broadly, there will be some kind of an environmental impact because of the new road, and that must be calculated as well. If we use money as the measure of utility, then we can attempt to calculate the utility of building the road. Say that the homeowners are compensated with $20 million. On the other hand, say that the car drivers incur a savings of about $2 each or $10,000 per workday for using the road, there are 250 workdays a year, and the road will last for 20 years. It costs the county $12 million to build the road and the environmental cost to animal species of lost habitat is calculated to be about $1 million. So the total costs for the highway are about $33 million and the benefit to the drivers is about $50 million. Clearly the road should be built, and the action is good.

While this example of act utilitarianism seems to work, there are several problems with it. We've not taken into account the unhappiness of the homeowners because some or all of them might not want to sell their homes. The impact on neighborhoods that may be divided by the new road is another cost. The cost of maintenance over 20 years to the county is another, but the value of having fewer accidents on a straight road is a benefit, and so on[12]. So, it seems for act utilitarianism we need to take into account more things than just the costs involved in the proximate action. It doesn't seem practical to perform this type of calculation on every ethical decision we have to make. Act utilitarianism also doesn't take into account people's innate sense of duty or obligation and how they take these into account when making ethical decisions. It also forces us to reduce all ethical decisions to a positive or negative outcome—in our example, dollars. Finally, act utilitarianism leads us down the path to the *problem of moral luck*. This is the

---

[10]Spinello, p. 27–28.
[11]Quinn, pp. 67-68.
[12]Quinn, p. 69.

problem where, when faced with an ethical decision, you don't have complete control over all the factors that determine the ethical goodness or badness of an action. The example Quinn uses for moral luck is of a dutiful nephew who sends his bedridden aunt a bouquet of flowers, only to discover that she is allergic to one of the flower species in the bouquet and ends up even sicker. Because the consequences for the aunt were very negative, the action is morally bad, but the nephew's intentions were good[13]. Finally, it seems like an awful lot of work to do a complete analysis of costs and benefits for every single action we propose that has an ethical component, so act utilitarianism appears to be quite a lot of work. What's the answer? Maybe we need to make some changes.

A variation of act utilitarianism is *rule utilitarianism*, which applies the principle of utility to general ethical rules instead of to individual actions. What we'll do here is make the utilitarian calculation, but for a general ethical rule rather than for individual actions. Simply put, "rule utilitarianism is the ethical theory that holds we ought to adopt those moral rules which, if followed by everyone, will lead to the greatest increase in happiness[14]." There's that *greatest good for the greatest number* thing again. Let's look at an example.

A computer worm is a self-contained computer program that exploits a security vulnerability, usually in operating system software, to release a payload that will normally do harm to an infected system and also to reproduce itself so it can propagate to other systems. On 11 August 2003, a worm called Blaster was released into the Internet. Blaster exploited a buffer overflow vulnerability in the remote procedure call (RPC) subsystem in the Windows XP and Windows 2000 operating systems in order to access the system, release its payload, and propagate. Microsoft had patched this vulnerability back in July 2003, but not all Windows users had applied the patch. In roughly four days, Blaster infected over 423,000 computers[15].

On 18 August 2003 a new worm, called Welchia, was released that exploited the same RPC vulnerability as the Blaster worm. However, when Welchia installed itself on a target system, instead of doing anything harmful it first looked for and deleted the Blaster worm if it was on the target system, downloaded the Microsoft patch for the RPC vulnerability, installed it, and rebooted the target system. All copies of Welchia deleted themselves on 1 January 2004. The Welchia worm did all its work without the permission of the target system owner. In the computer security community, a worm like Welchia is known as an *anti-worm* or *helper worm*. The ethical question we have is: was the action of the person who released the Welchia worm ethically good or bad? If bad, what might they have done instead? Let's analyze this ethical problem from a rule utilitarian perspective.

In order to analyze this ethical problem, we must create an appropriate ethical rule and then decide whether its universal adoption would increase the utility of all the stakeholders. We first need a rule: "If a harmful computer worm is infecting the Internet, and I can write a helpful worm that automatically removes the harmful worm from infected computers and shields them from future attacks, then I should write and release the helpful worm[16]." What would be the benefits? Well, clearly, every Windows user who had not already updated their computer with the Microsoft patch would benefit because Welchia deletes Blaster, installs the patch, and shields their computer from any further attacks by Blaster. A clear win.

What about harms? First of all, if everyone followed this rule, then every time there was a new malicious worm released, there would be a flood of helper worms also released. This would probably slow down or clog network traffic. Also, how could network or system administrators figure out the difference between malicious worms and helper worms? All they would see is a worm attempting to attack systems. So, the release of all the helper worms would reduce the benefit of using the Internet and other networks attached to it. Secondly, what if some of the helper worms contained bugs? Not all helpful programmers are perfect, so there is a high probability that some of the helper worms would damage the target systems. This would decrease the usefulness of the individual computer systems and harm their owners. Finally, the plethora of helper worms would create a large increase in the amount of work for network and system administrators, which would require overtime, or would cause them to not get other tasks finished, or both.

---

[13]Quinn, p. 72.
[14]Quinn, p. 72.
[15]https://en.wikipedia.org/wiki/Blaster_(computer_worm)
[16]Quinn, p. 73.

The harm caused by the ethical rule that allows the release of the helper worms seems to decrease the happiness or utility on the Internet rather than increase it. So, this ethical rule should not be created, and the actions of the person who released the Welchia worm are ethically wrong.

It seems like rule utilitarianism keeps the good parts of act utilitarianism but makes the overall calculation of ethical costs and benefits easier. Because we use this theory on ethical rules, we also don't have to recalculate the costs and benefits for every act. We're also free to choose which rule we'll enforce that can get us out of ethical dilemmas. Finally, it can eliminate the problem of moral luck. Rule utilitarianism seems like it could be the way to go. Except for one problem.

In both forms of utilitarianism there is the problem that there can be an *unequal distribution of good consequences* across all of the stakeholders. This problem arises because utilitarianism only cares about the total amount of increase in happiness, not how it's distributed across all the stakeholders. For example, suppose acting one way results in everyone getting 100 units of happiness, but acting a different way results in half the stakeholders getting 201 units of happiness each. According to the utilitarian calculation, we should choose the second option because that will result in more total happiness, regardless of the fact that in the second option half the stakeholders get nothing. This doesn't seem fair[17].

John Rawls (1921–2002) tried to fix this problem by proposing two *principles of justice*. These principles say that when making ethical decisions, social and economic inequalities are acceptable if they meet the following two conditions: (1) Every person in society should have an equal chance to rise to a higher level of social or economic standing, and (2) "social and economic inequalities must be justified. The only way to justify a social or economic inequality is to show that its overall effect is to provide the most benefit to the least advantaged.[18] " This second condition is known as the *difference principle*. It's the difference principle that provides the justification for social policies like a graduated income tax, where those with more income pay higher taxes, and those with less income are entitled to more benefits from society. The two principles of justice are meant to ensure an overall level playing field when making ethical decisions.

Ethical Drivers

In all ethical systems there are a set of constraints and rules that help guide any ethical discussion. Discussing ethical issues in computing and software development is no different. We'll look briefly in this section at two of these ethical drivers and how they relate to ethical problems in software development.

Legal Drivers

In all ethical discussions we must remember to consider the law because laws constrain our actions and also guide us down ethical paths that society has decided are acceptable behavior. These kind of legal drivers can include laws, including federal, state, and local, and government regulations (which are really interpretations of how the laws should be enforced). These laws govern areas like intellectual property, health and safety issues, privacy issues, and data protection.

Professional Drivers

Every profession has a set of ethical drivers that describe how members of the profession are expected to behave. Software development is no different. The two professional societies of computing, the *Association for Computing Machinery* (ACM) and the *IEEE Computer Society* (IEEE-CS), have each developed and published codes of conduct for their members. Every software developer should adhere to these codes of

---

[17]Quinn, p. 75.
[18]Quinn, p. 79.

conduct. The two codes of ethics, the *ACM Code of Ethics and Professional Conduct*[19] and the *ACM/IEEE-CS Software Engineering Code of Ethics*[20] are both included at the end of this chapter. I'll let the ACM/IEEE-CS code's preamble finish off this section. I've highlighted (italicized) particularly relevant sections.

Preamble to the ACM/IEEE-CS Software Engineering Code of Ethics

Computers have a central and growing role in commerce, industry, government, medicine, education, entertainment and society at large. Software engineers are those who contribute by direct participation or by teaching, to the analysis, specification, design, development, certification, maintenance and testing of software systems. *Because of their roles in developing software systems, software engineers have significant opportunities to do good or cause harm, to enable others to do good or cause harm, or to influence others to do good or cause harm. To ensure, as much as possible, that their efforts will be used for good, software engineers must commit themselves to making software engineering a beneficial and respected profession.* In accordance with that commitment, software engineers shall adhere to the following Code of Ethics and Professional Practice.

The Code contains eight Principles related to the behavior of and decisions made by professional software engineers, including practitioners, educators, managers, supervisors and policy makers, as well as trainees and students of the profession. *The Principles identify the ethically responsible relationships in which individuals, groups, and organizations participate and the primary obligations within these relationships.* The Clauses of each Principle are illustrations of some of the obligations included in these relationships. *These obligations are founded in the software engineer's humanity, in special care owed to people affected by the work of software engineers, and in the unique elements of the practice of software engineering. The Code prescribes these as obligations of anyone claiming to be or aspiring to be a software engineer.*

It is not intended that the individual parts of the Code be used in isolation to justify errors of omission or commission. The list of Principles and Clauses is not exhaustive. The Clauses should not be read as separating the acceptable from the unacceptable in professional conduct in all practical situations. *The Code is not a simple ethical algorithm that generates ethical decisions.* In some situations, standards may be in tension with each other or with standards from other sources. These situations require the software engineer to use ethical judgment to act in a manner that is most consistent with the spirit of the Code of Ethics and Professional Practice, given the circumstances.

Ethical tensions can best be addressed by thoughtful consideration of fundamental principles, rather than blind reliance on detailed regulations. These Principles should influence software engineers to consider broadly who is affected by their work; to examine if they and their colleagues are treating other human beings with due respect; to consider how the public, if reasonably well informed, would view their decisions; to analyze how the least empowered will be affected by their decisions; and to consider whether their acts would be judged worthy of the ideal professional working as a software engineer. In all these judgments concern for the health, safety and welfare of the public is primary; that is, the "Public Interest" is central to this Code.

The dynamic and demanding context of software engineering requires a code that is adaptable and relevant to new situations as they occur. However, even in this generality, the Code provides support for software engineers and managers of software engineers who need to take positive action in a specific case by documenting the ethical stance of the profession. *The Code provides an ethical foundation to which individuals within teams and the team as a whole can appeal. The Code helps to define those actions that are ethically improper to request of a software engineer or teams of software engineers.*

The Code is not simply for adjudicating the nature of questionable acts; it also has an important educational function. As this Code expresses the consensus of the profession on ethical issues, it is a means to educate both the public and aspiring professionals about the ethical obligations of all software engineers.

---

[19]ACM. 1992. *ACM Code of Ethics and Professional Conduct.* New York, NY: ACM. www.acm.org, retrieved August 18, 2017.
[20]ACM/IEEE-CS. *Software Engineering Code of Ethics and Professional Practice.* New York, NY: Association for Computing Machinery, www.acm.org (1999).

Ethical Discussion and Decision Making

Given all the theories we've looked at, how do you actually make a decision when faced with an ethical problem? Here's one process that can be followed. Divide the process into two parts: identifying and describing the problem, and then analyzing the problem and coming to a decision. Naturally, you can alter the steps here and do them in a different order. Change the process to one that fits your particular ethical situation and interests. Here are the steps:

Identifying and Describing the Problem

1. Write down the statement of the ethical problem. This will help to clarify what exactly you're talking about.

2. List the risks, problems, and possible consequences.

3. List all the stakeholders. This will include you and anyone else involved in the ethical situation and anyone involved in the consequences of the decision.

4. Identify all the basic ethical issues in each case. Try to establish the rights and wrongs of the situation and figure out what ethical rules might be involved.

5. Identify any legal issues. This includes intellectual property issues and health and safety issues.

6. List possible actions if the problem is more complex than a simple yes/no.

Analyzing the Problem

1. What are your first impressions or reactions to these issues? What does your *moral intuition* say?

2. Identify the responsibilities of the decision maker. This involves things like reporting ethical problems if you're an employee and what your responsibilities might be as a manager.

3. Identify the rights of the stakeholders.

4. Consider the consequences of the action options on the stakeholders. Analyze the consequences, risks, benefits, harms, and costs for each action considered.

5. Find the sections of the SE Code and the ACM code that pertain to the problem and the actions. This will help you with the ethical rules and in laying out the situation so you can consider alternatives.

6. Consider the deontological and utilitarian approaches to the problem. You'll need to have the ethical rules you've considered in front of you, as well as the sections of the SE and ACM codes of ethics. Then run through our examples here of other ethical situations and then follow those examples for your own situation.

7. Do the ethical theories point to one course of action? If more than one, which one should take precedence? List the different courses of action and then, if necessary, try to prioritize them. This will help you think about different courses of action.

8. Which of the potential actions do you think is the right one? Pick it. If you're using a utilitarian approach, you might consider picking a metric and seeing if you can measure the effects of the decision.

9. If there are several ethically acceptable options, pick one. Reflect on your decision.

Case Studies

This section will present four short case studies that illustrate the types of ethical problems you might encounter as a software developer. These case studies will cover ethical situations involving intellectual property, privacy issues, system safety issues, and conflicts of interest. Your job is to analyze each case study, identify the ethical issues, and propose a course of action. Be aware that there may not be one "right" answer to the particular ethical problem.

#1 Copying Software

Jane Hudson teaches mathematics at an inner city high school in Chicago. Like many rural and inner city high schools, Jane's has very little money to spend on computers or computer software. Although her students do very well and have even placed in a statewide math competition, many of her students come to high school woefully underprepared for high school mathematics, so Jane and her colleagues spend quite a bit of time on remedial work. Recently, a local company has offered to donate 24 iMacs to Jane's high school. It's been decided that a dozen of these computers will be used to create a mathematics computer lab specifically to help the students with remedial work in pre-algebra, algebra, geometry, and trigonometry. Jane wants to use a software program called MathTutor for the computer lab, but a site-wide license for the titles she wants is around $5,000—money that her school just doesn't have. The high school already has one copy of MathTutor, and there's no copy protection on the program. Jane's department chair has suggested that they just make copies of the program for the new computers. Jane doesn't think this is a good idea, but she's desperate to use the new computers to help her students. What should Jane do? What are the ethical issues here? (See ACM Code 1.5 and 2.3; SE Code 2.02.)

#2 Who's Computer Is It?

At Massive Corporation, you're a software development manager. A developer on one of your software projects is out sick. Another developer asks that you copy all the files from the sick developer's computer to his computer so he can do some important work. What should you do? What are the ethical issues here? (See ACM Code 1.7, 2.8, and 3.3.)

#3 How Much Testing Is Enough?

You're the project manager for a development team that's in the final stages of a project to create software that uses radiation therapy to destroy cancerous tumors. Once set up by an operator, the software controls the intensity, duration, and direction of the radiation. Because this is a new piece of software in a new product, there have been a series of problems and delays. The program is in the middle stages of system testing, and the routine testing that's been done so far has all gone well, with very few software defects found. Your project manager wants to cut the rest of the testing short in order to meet the (updated) software delivery deadline. This will mean just doing the routine testing and not doing the stress testing that's scheduled. You are trying to decide whether to ship the software on time and then continue the testing afterwards, shipping patches for any defects found. What are the ethical issues here? (You should look up the Therac-25 problem as a similar instance of a case like this at https://en.wikipedia.org/wiki/Therac-25.) (See ACM Code 1.1, 1.2, 2.1, and 3.4; SE Code 1.03, 1.04, 3.06, and 3.10.)

#4 How Much Should You Tell?

You're a principal in the J2MD computer software consulting company. One of your clients, the City of Charleston, South Carolina, wants your company to evaluate a set of proposals for a new administrative computing system and provide a recommendation to the city on which proposal to accept. The contract for the new system would be worth several million dollars to the winning company. Your spouse works for LowCountry Computing, one of the bidding companies, and she's the project manager in charge of writing their proposal to the city. You have seen early copies of her proposal and judge it to be excellent. Should you tell the project manager in the City of Charleston about your spouse's employment at LowCountry Computing? If so, when, and how much else should you reveal? (See ACM Code 1.3 and 2.5; SE Code Principle 4, 4.05, and 4.06.)

The Last Word on Ethics?

Every software development professional will encounter ethical problems during the course of their career. How you handle those ethical situations will say a lot about your professional behavior and moral character. To wrap up this discussion of professional practice, let's look at one more list of fundamental ethical principles that you should carry with you throughout your career. The original list comes largely from Quinn, and has been modified[21]:

1. *Be impartial*: You will have some amount of loyalty to your company, but you also must have loyalty to society as a whole and to yourself. Make sure you remember that.

2. *Disclose information that others ought to have*: Don't hide information from people who need to know it. Don't be deceptive or deliberately misleading. Make sure you disclose any conflicts of interest.

3. *Respect the rights of others*: This includes intellectual property rights, civil rights, and other property rights. Don't steal intellectual property or misuse others property (for example, by denying access to systems, networks, or services, or by breaking into other systems).

4. *Treat others justly*: Don't discriminate against others for attributes unrelated to their job. Make sure that others receive fair wages and benefits and credit for work done.

5. *Take responsibility for your own actions and inactions*: Take responsibility for everything you do—or don't do—whether good or bad.

6. *Take responsibility for the actions of those you supervise*: The old saying "The buck stops here" applies to you as a manager as well. This also includes making sure you communicate effectively with your employees.

---

[21]Quinn, pp. 383–384.

7. *Maintain your integrity*: Deliver on your commitments. Be loyal to your employer (as long as they also operate in an ethical manner). Don't ask someone to do anything you wouldn't do yourself.

8. *Continually improve your abilities*: Software development and the computer industry as a whole are in a constant state of flux. Tools and languages you used in college will be obsolete five years later. Make sure you're a life-long learner.

9. *Share your knowledge, expertise, and values*: The more experience you acquire in your profession, the more you're obligated to share your knowledge and expertise with your co-workers and subordinates. You should also set an example for others by living these values.

References

ACM. 1992. *ACM Code of Ethics and Professional Conduct*. New York, NY: ACM. www.acm.org, retrieved August 18, 2017.

ACM/IEEE-CS. 1999. *Software Engineering Code of Ethics and Professional Practice*. New York, NY: Association for Computing Machinery, www.acm.org.

Baase, Sara. *A Gift of Fire*, 2nd Edition. (Upper Saddle River, NJ: Prentice-Hall, 2003.)

Quinn, Michael J. *Ethics for the Information Age*. (Boston: Addison-Wesley, 2005.)

Spinello, Richard A. *Case Studies in Information and Computer Ethics*. (Upper Saddle River, NJ: Prentice-Hall, 1997.)

Spinello, Richard A., and Herman T. Tavani. *Readings in CyberEthics*, 2nd Edition. (Sudbury, MA: Jones and Bartlett Publishers, 2004.)

The ACM Code of Ethics and Professional Conduct

Adopted by ACM Council 10/16/92.

Preamble

Commitment to ethical professional conduct is expected of every member (voting members, associate members, and student members) of the Association for Computing Machinery (ACM).

This Code, consisting of 24 imperatives formulated as statements of personal responsibility, identifies the elements of such a commitment. It contains many, but not all, issues professionals are likely to face. Section 1 outlines fundamental ethical considerations, while Section 2 addresses additional, more specific considerations of professional conduct. Statements in Section 3 pertain more specifically to individuals who have a leadership role, whether in the workplace or in a volunteer capacity such as with organizations like ACM. Principles involving compliance with this Code are given in Section 4.

The Code shall be supplemented by a set of Guidelines, which provide explanation to assist members in dealing with the various issues contained in the Code. It is expected that the Guidelines will be changed more frequently than the Code.

The Code and its supplemented Guidelines are intended to serve as a basis for ethical decision making in the conduct of professional work. Secondarily, they may serve as a basis for judging the merit of a formal complaint pertaining to violation of professional ethical standards.

It should be noted that although computing is not mentioned in the imperatives of Section 1, the Code is concerned with how these fundamental imperatives apply to one's conduct as a computing professional. These imperatives are expressed in a general form to emphasize that ethical principles which apply to computer ethics are derived from more general ethical principles.

It is understood that some words and phrases in a code of ethics are subject to varying interpretations, and that any ethical principle may conflict with other ethical principles in specific situations. Questions related to ethical conflicts can best be answered by thoughtful consideration of fundamental principles, rather than reliance on detailed regulations.

Contents & Guidelines

1. GENERAL MORAL IMPERATIVES

As an ACM member I will . . .

1.1 Contribute to society and human well-being

This principle concerning the quality of life of all people affirms an obligation to protect fundamental human rights and to respect the diversity of all cultures. An essential aim of computing professionals is to minimize negative consequences of computing systems, including threats to health and safety. When designing or implementing systems, computing professionals must attempt to ensure that the products of their efforts will be used in socially responsible ways, will meet social needs, and will avoid harmful effects to health and welfare.

In addition to a safe social environment, human well-being includes a safe natural environment. Therefore, computing professionals who design and develop systems must be alert to, and make others aware of, any potential damage to the local or global environment.

1.2 Avoid harm to others

"Harm" means injury or negative consequences, such as undesirable loss of information, loss of property, property damage, or unwanted environmental impacts. This principle prohibits use of computing technology in ways that result in harm to any of the following: users, the general public, employees, or employers. Harmful actions include intentional destruction or modification of files and programs leading to serious loss of resources or unnecessary expenditure of human resources such as the time and effort required to purge systems of "computer viruses."

Well-intended actions, including those that accomplish assigned duties, may lead to harm unexpectedly. In such an event the responsible person or persons are obligated to undo or mitigate the negative consequences as much as possible. One way to avoid unintentional harm is to carefully consider potential impacts on all those affected by decisions made during design and implementation.

To minimize the possibility of indirectly harming others, computing professionals must minimize malfunctions by following generally accepted standards for system design and testing. Furthermore, it is often necessary to assess the social consequences of systems to project the likelihood of any serious harm to others. If system features are misrepresented to users, coworkers, or supervisors, the individual computing professional is responsible for any resulting injury.

In the work environment the computing professional has the additional obligation to report any signs of system dangers that might result in serious personal or social damage. If one's superiors do not act to curtail or mitigate such dangers, it may be necessary to "blow the whistle" to help correct the problem or reduce the risk. However, capricious or misguided reporting of violations can, itself, be harmful. Before reporting violations, all relevant aspects of the incident must be thoroughly assessed. In particular, the assessment of risk and responsibility must be credible. It is suggested that advice be sought from other computing professionals. See principle 2.5 regarding thorough evaluations.

1.3 Be honest and trustworthy

Honesty is an essential component of trust. Without trust an organization cannot function effectively. The honest computing professional will not make deliberately false or deceptive claims about a system or system design, but will instead provide full disclosure of all pertinent system limitations and problems.

A computer professional has a duty to be honest about his or her own qualifications, and about any circumstances that might lead to conflicts of interest.

Membership in volunteer organizations such as ACM may at times place individuals in situations where their statements or actions could be interpreted as carrying the "weight" of a larger group of professionals. An ACM member will exercise care to not misrepresent ACM or positions and policies of ACM or any ACM units.

1.4 Be fair and take action not to discriminate

The values of equality, tolerance, respect for others, and the principles of equal justice govern this imperative. Discrimination on the basis of race, sex, religion, age, disability, national origin, or other such factors is an explicit violation of ACM policy and will not be tolerated.

Inequities between different groups of people may result from the use or misuse of information and technology. In a fair society, all individuals would have equal opportunity to participate in, or benefit from, the use of computer resources regardless of race, sex, religion, age, disability, national origin or other such similar factors. However, these ideals do not justify unauthorized use of computer resources nor do they provide an adequate basis for violation of any other ethical imperatives of this code.

1.5 Honor property rights including copyrights and patent

Violation of copyrights, patents, trade secrets and the terms of license agreements is prohibited by law in most circumstances. Even when software is not so protected, such violations are contrary to professional behavior. Copies of software should be made only with proper authorization. Unauthorized duplication of materials must not be condoned.

1.6 Give proper credit for intellectual property

Computing professionals are obligated to protect the integrity of intellectual property. Specifically, one must not take credit for other's ideas or work, even in cases where the work has not been explicitly protected by copyright, patent, etc.

1.7 Respect the privacy of others

Computing and communication technology enables the collection and exchange of personal information on a scale unprecedented in the history of civilization. Thus there is increased potential for violating the privacy of individuals and groups. It is the responsibility of professionals to maintain the privacy and integrity of data describing individuals. This includes taking precautions to ensure the accuracy of data, as well as protecting it from unauthorized access or accidental disclosure to inappropriate individuals. Furthermore, procedures must be established to allow individuals to review their records and correct inaccuracies.

This imperative implies that only the necessary amount of personal information be collected in a system, that retention and disposal periods for that information be clearly defined and enforced, and that personal information gathered for a specific purpose not be used for other purposes without consent of the individual(s). These principles apply to electronic communications, including electronic mail, and prohibit procedures that capture or monitor electronic user data, including messages, without the permission of users or bona fide authorization related to system operation and maintenance. User data observed during the normal duties of system operation and maintenance must be treated with strictest confidentiality, except in cases where it is evidence for the violation of law, organizational regulations, or this Code. In these cases, the nature or contents of that information must be disclosed only to proper authorities.

1.8 Honor confidentiality

The principle of honesty extends to issues of confidentiality of information whenever one has made an explicit promise to honor confidentiality or, implicitly, when private information not directly related to the performance of one's duties becomes available. The ethical concern is to respect all obligations of confidentiality to employers, clients, and users unless discharged from such obligations by requirements of the law or other principles of this Code.

2. MORE SPECIFIC PROFESSIONAL RESPONSIBILITIES

As an ACM computing professional I will . . .

2.1 Strive to achieve the highest quality, effectiveness and dignity in both the process and products of professional work

Excellence is perhaps the most important obligation of a professional. The computing professional must strive to achieve quality and to be cognizant of the serious negative consequences that may result from poor quality in a system.

2.2 Acquire and maintain professional competence

Excellence depends on individuals who take responsibility for acquiring and maintaining professional competence. A professional must participate in setting standards for appropriate levels of competence, and strive to achieve those standards. Upgrading technical knowledge and competence can be achieved in several ways: doing independent study; attending seminars, conferences, or courses; and being involved in professional organizations.

2.3 Know and respect existing laws pertaining to professional work

ACM members must obey existing local, state, province, national, and international laws unless there is a compelling ethical basis not to do so. Policies and procedures of the organizations in which one participates must also be obeyed. But compliance must be balanced with the recognition that sometimes existing laws and rules may be immoral or inappropriate and, therefore, must be challenged. Violation of a law or regulation may be ethical when that law or rule has inadequate moral basis or when it conflicts with another law judged to be more important. If one decides to violate a law or rule because it is viewed as unethical, or for any other reason, one must fully accept responsibility for one's actions and for the consequences.

2.4 Accept and provide appropriate professional review

Quality professional work, especially in the computing profession, depends on professional reviewing and critiquing. Whenever appropriate, individual members should seek and utilize peer review as well as provide critical review of the work of others.

2.5 Give comprehensive and thorough evaluations of computer systems and their impacts, including analysis of possible risks

Computer professionals must strive to be perceptive, thorough, and objective when evaluating, recommending, and presenting system descriptions and alternatives. Computer professionals are in a position of special trust, and therefore have a special responsibility to provide objective, credible evaluations to employers, clients, users, and the public. When providing evaluations the professional must also identify any relevant conflicts of interest, as stated in imperative 1.3.

As noted in the discussion of principle 1.2 on avoiding harm, any signs of danger from systems must be reported to those who have opportunity and/or responsibility to resolve them. See the guidelines for imperative 1.2 for more details concerning harm, including the reporting of professional violations.

2.6 Honor contracts, agreements, and assigned responsibilities

Honoring one's commitments is a matter of integrity and honesty. For the computer professional this includes ensuring that system elements perform as intended. Also, when one contracts for work with another party, one has an obligation to keep that party properly informed about progress toward completing that work.

A computing professional has a responsibility to request a change in any assignment that he or she feels cannot be completed as defined. Only after serious consideration and with full disclosure of risks and concerns to the employer or client, should one accept the assignment. The major underlying principle here is the obligation to accept personal accountability for professional work. On some occasions other ethical principles may take greater priority.

A judgment that a specific assignment should not be performed may not be accepted. Having clearly identified one's concerns and reasons for that judgment, but failing to procure a change in that assignment, one may yet be obligated, by contract or by law, to proceed as directed. The computing professional's ethical judgment should be the final guide in deciding whether or not to proceed. Regardless of the decision, one must accept the responsibility for the consequences.

However, performing assignments "against one's own judgment" does not relieve the professional of responsibility for any negative consequences.

2.7 Improve public understanding of computing and its consequences

Computing professionals have a responsibility to share technical knowledge with the public by encouraging understanding of computing, including the impacts of computer systems and their limitations. This imperative implies an obligation to counter any false views related to computing.

2.8 Access computing and communication resources only when authorized to do so

Theft or destruction of tangible and electronic property is prohibited by imperative 1.2 - "Avoid harm to others." Trespassing and unauthorized use of a computer or communication system is addressed by this imperative. Trespassing includes accessing communication networks and computer systems, or accounts and/or files associated with those systems, without explicit authorization to do so. Individuals and organizations have the right to restrict access to their systems so long as they do not violate the discrimination principle (see 1.4). No one should enter or use another's computer system, software, or data files without permission. One must always have appropriate approval before using system resources, including communication ports, file space, other system peripherals, and computer time.

3. ORGANIZATIONAL LEADERSHIP IMPERATIVES

As an ACM member and an organizational leader, I will . . .

BACKGROUND NOTE: This section draws extensively from the draft IFIP Code of Ethics, especially its sections on organizational ethics and international concerns. The ethical obligations of organizations tend to be neglected in most codes of professional conduct, perhaps because these codes are written from the perspective of the individual member. This dilemma is addressed by stating these imperatives from the perspective of the organizational leader. In this context "leader" is viewed as any organizational member who has leadership or educational responsibilities. These imperatives generally may apply to organizations as well as their leaders. In this context "organizations" are corporations, government agencies, and other "employers," as well as volunteer professional organizations.

3.1 Articulate social responsibilities of members of an organizational unit and encourage full acceptance of those responsibilities

Because organizations of all kinds have impacts on the public, they must accept responsibilities to society. Organizational procedures and attitudes oriented toward quality and the welfare of society will reduce harm to members of the public, thereby serving public interest and fulfilling social responsibility. Therefore, organizational leaders must encourage full participation in meeting social responsibilities as well as quality performance.

3.2 Manage personnel and resources to design and build information systems that enhance the quality of working life

Organizational leaders are responsible for ensuring that computer systems enhance, not degrade, the quality of working life. When implementing a computer system, organizations must consider the personal and professional development, physical safety, and human dignity of all workers. Appropriate human-computer ergonomic standards should be considered in system design and in the workplace.

3.3 Acknowledge and support proper and authorized uses of an organization's computing and communication resources

Because computer systems can become tools to harm as well as to benefit an organization, the leadership has the responsibility to clearly define appropriate and inappropriate uses of organizational computing resources. While the number and scope of such rules should be minimal, they should be fully enforced when established.

3.4 Ensure that users and those who will be affected by a system have their needs clearly articulated during the assessment and design of requirements; later the system must be validated to meet requirements

Current system users, potential users and other persons whose lives may be affected by a system must have their needs assessed and incorporated in the statement of requirements. System validation should ensure compliance with those requirements.

3.5 Articulate and support policies that protect the dignity of users and others affected by a computing system

Designing or implementing systems that deliberately or inadvertently demean individuals or groups is ethically unacceptable. Computer professionals who are in decision making positions should verify that systems are designed and implemented to protect personal privacy and enhance personal dignity.

3.6 Create opportunities for members of the organization to learn the principles and limitations of computer systems

This complements the imperative on public understanding (2.7). Educational opportunities are essential to facilitate optimal participation of all organizational members. Opportunities must be available to all members to help them improve their knowledge and skills in computing, including courses that familiarize them with the consequences and limitations of particular types of systems. In particular, professionals must be made aware of the dangers of building systems around oversimplified models, the improbability of anticipating and designing for every possible operating condition, and other issues related to the complexity of this profession.

4. COMPLIANCE WITH THE CODE

As an ACM member I will . . .

4.1 Uphold and promote the principles of this Code

The future of the computing profession depends on both technical and ethical excellence. Not only is it important for ACM computing professionals to adhere to the principles expressed in this Code, each member should encourage and support adherence by other members.

4.2 Treat violations of this code as inconsistent with membership in the ACM

Adherence of professionals to a code of ethics is largely a voluntary matter. However, if a member does not follow this code by engaging in gross misconduct, membership in ACM may be terminated.

This Code and the supplemental Guidelines were developed by the Task Force for the Revision of the ACM Code of Ethics and Professional Conduct: Ronald E. Anderson, Chair, Gerald Engel, Donald Gotterbarn, Grace C. Hertlein, Alex Hoffman, Bruce Jawer, Deborah G. Johnson, Doris K. Lidtke, Joyce Currie Little, Dianne Martin, Donn B. Parker, Judith A. Perrolle, and Richard S. Rosenberg. The Task Force was organized by ACM/SIGCAS and funding was provided by the ACM SIG Discretionary Fund. This Code and the supplemental Guidelines were adopted by the ACM Council on October 16, 1992.

This Code may be published without permission as long as it is not changed in any way and it carries the copyright notice. Copyright ©1997, Association for Computing Machinery, Inc.

The ACM/IEEE-CS Software Engineering Code of Ethics

PREAMBLE

[See the section "Professional Drivers" earlier in this chapter for the Preamble to the Code of Ethics.]

PRINCIPLES

Principle 1 PUBLIC: Software engineers shall act consistently with the public interest. In particular, software engineers shall, as appropriate:

1.01. Accept full responsibility for their own work.

1.02. Moderate the interests of the software engineer, the employer, the client and the users with the public good.

1.03. Approve software only if they have a well-founded belief that it is safe, meets specifications, passes appropriate tests, and does not diminish quality of life, diminish privacy or harm the environment. The ultimate effect of the work should be to the public good.

1.04. Disclose to appropriate persons or authorities any actual or potential danger to the user, the public, or the environment, that they reasonably believe to be associated with software or related documents.

1.05. Cooperate in efforts to address matters of grave public concern caused by software, its installation, maintenance, support or documentation.

1.06. Be fair and avoid deception in all statements, particularly public ones, concerning software or related documents, methods and tools.

1.07. Consider issues of physical disabilities, allocation of resources, economic disadvantage and other factors that can diminish access to the benefits of software.

1.08. Be encouraged to volunteer professional skills to good causes and to contribute to public education concerning the discipline.

Principle 2 CLIENT AND EMPLOYER: Software engineers shall act in a manner that is in the best interests of their client and employer, consistent with the public interest. In particular, software engineers shall, as appropriate:

2.01. Provide service in their areas of competence, being honest and forthright about any limitations of their experience and education.

2.02. Not knowingly use software that is obtained or retained either illegally or unethically.

2.03. Use the property of a client or employer only in ways properly authorized, and with the client's or employer's knowledge and consent.

2.04. Ensure that any document upon which they rely has been approved, when required, by someone authorized to approve it.

2.05. Keep private any confidential information gained in their professional work, where such confidentiality is consistent with the public interest and consistent with the law.

2.06. Identify, document, collect evidence and report to the client or the employer promptly if, in their opinion, a project is likely to fail, to prove too expensive, to violate intellectual property law, or otherwise to be problematic.

2.07. Identify, document, and report significant issues of social concern, of which they are aware, in software or related documents, to the employer or the client.

2.08. Accept no outside work detrimental to the work they perform for their primary employer.

2.09. Promote no interest adverse to their employer or client, unless a higher ethical concern is being compromised; in that case, inform the employer or another appropriate authority of the ethical concern.

Principle 3 PRODUCT: Software engineers shall ensure that their products and related modifications meet the highest professional standards possible. In particular, software engineers shall, as appropriate:

3.01. Strive for high quality, acceptable cost, and a reasonable schedule, ensuring significant tradeoffs are clear to and accepted by the employer and the client, and are available for consideration by the user and the public.

3.02. Ensure proper and achievable goals and objectives for any project on which they work or propose.

3.03. Identify, define and address ethical, economic, cultural, legal and environmental issues related to work projects.

3.04. Ensure that they are qualified for any project on which they work or propose to work, by an appropriate combination of education, training, and experience,.

3.05. Ensure that an appropriate method is used for any project on which they work or propose to work.

3.06. Work to follow professional standards, when available, that are most appropriate for the task at hand, departing from these only when ethically or technically justified.

3.07. Strive to fully understand the specifications for software on which they work.

3.08. Ensure that specifications for software on which they work have been well documented, satisfy the users' requirements and have the appropriate approvals.

3.09. Ensure realistic quantitative estimates of cost, scheduling, personnel, quality and outcomes on any project on which they work or propose to work and provide an uncertainty assessment of these estimates.

3.10. Ensure adequate testing, debugging, and review of software and related documents on which they work.

3.11. Ensure adequate documentation, including significant problems discovered and solutions adopted, for any project on which they work.

3.12. Work to develop software and related documents that respect the privacy of those who will be affected by that software.

3.13. Be careful to use only accurate data derived by ethical and lawful means, and use it only in ways properly authorized.

3.14. Maintain the integrity of data, being sensitive to outdated or flawed occurrences.

3.15 Treat all forms of software maintenance with the same professionalism as new development.

Principle 4 JUDGMENT: Software engineers shall maintain integrity and independence in their professional judgment. In particular, software engineers shall, as appropriate:

4.01. Temper all technical judgments by the need to support and maintain human values.

4.02 Only endorse documents either prepared under their supervision or within their areas of competence and with which they are in agreement.

4.03. Maintain professional objectivity with respect to any software or related documents they are asked to evaluate.

4.04. Not engage in deceptive financial practices such as bribery, double billing, or other improper financial practices.

4.05. Disclose to all concerned parties those conflicts of interest that cannot reasonably be avoided or escaped.

4.06. Refuse to participate, as members or advisors, in a private, governmental or professional body concerned with software related issues, in which they, their employers or their clients have undisclosed potential conflicts of interest.

Principle 5 MANAGEMENT: Software engineering managers and leaders shall subscribe to and promote an ethical approach to the management of software development and maintenance. In particular, those managing or leading software engineers shall, as appropriate:

5.01 Ensure good management for any project on which they work, including effective procedures for promotion of quality and reduction of risk.

5.02. Ensure that software engineers are informed of standards before being held to them.

5.03. Ensure that software engineers know the employer's policies and procedures for protecting passwords, files and information that is confidential to the employer or confidential to others.

5.04. Assign work only after taking into account appropriate contributions of education and experience tempered with a desire to further that education and experience.

5.05. Ensure realistic quantitative estimates of cost, scheduling, personnel, quality and outcomes on any project on which they work or propose to work, and provide an uncertainty assessment of these estimates.

5.06. Attract potential software engineers only by full and accurate description of the conditions of employment.

5.07. Offer fair and just remuneration.

5.08. Not unjustly prevent someone from taking a position for which that person is suitably qualified.

5.09. Ensure that there is a fair agreement concerning ownership of any software, processes, research, writing, or other intellectual property to which a software engineer has contributed.

5.10. Provide for due process in hearing charges of violation of an employer's policy or of this Code.

5.11. Not ask a software engineer to do anything inconsistent with this Code.

5.12. Not punish anyone for expressing ethical concerns about a project.

Principle 6 PROFESSION: Software engineers shall advance the integrity and reputation of the profession consistent with the public interest. In particular, software engineers shall, as appropriate:

6.01. Help develop an organizational environment favorable to acting ethically.

6.02. Promote public knowledge of software engineering.

6.03. Extend software engineering knowledge by appropriate participation in professional organizations, meetings and publications.

6.04. Support, as members of a profession, other software engineers striving to follow this Code.

6.05. Not promote their own interest at the expense of the profession, client or employer.

6.06. Obey all laws governing their work, unless, in exceptional circumstances, such compliance is inconsistent with the public interest.

6.07. Be accurate in stating the characteristics of software on which they work, avoiding not only false claims but also claims that might reasonably be supposed to be speculative, vacuous, deceptive, misleading, or doubtful.

6.08. Take responsibility for detecting, correcting, and reporting errors in software and associated documents on which they work.

6.09. Ensure that clients, employers, and supervisors know of the software engineer's commitment to this Code of ethics, and the subsequent ramifications of such commitment.

6.10. Avoid associations with businesses and organizations that are in conflict with this code.

6.11. Recognize that violations of this Code are inconsistent with being a professional software engineer.

6.12. Express concerns to the people involved when significant violations of this Code are detected unless this is impossible, counter-productive, or dangerous.

6.13. Report significant violations of this Code to appropriate authorities when it is clear that consultation with people involved in these significant violations is impossible, counter-productive or dangerous.

Principle 7 COLLEAGUES: Software engineers shall be fair to and supportive of their colleagues. In particular, software engineers shall, as appropriate:

7.01. Encourage colleagues to adhere to this Code.

7.02. Assist colleagues in professional development.

7.03. Credit fully the work of others and refrain from taking undue credit.

7.04. Review the work of others in an objective, candid, and properly-documented way.

7.05. Give a fair hearing to the opinions, concerns, or complaints of a colleague.

7.06. Assist colleagues in being fully aware of current standard work practices including policies and procedures for protecting passwords, files and other confidential information, and security measures in general.

7.07. Not unfairly intervene in the career of any colleague; however, concern for the employer, the client or public interest may compel software engineers, in good faith, to question the competence of a colleague.

7.08. In situations outside of their own areas of competence, call upon the opinions of other professionals who have competence in that area.

Principle 8 SELF: Software engineers shall participate in lifelong learning regarding the practice of their profession and shall promote an ethical approach to the practice of the profession. In particular, software engineers shall continually endeavor to:

8.01. Further their knowledge of developments in the analysis, specification, design, development, maintenance and testing of software and related documents, together with the management of the development process.

8.02. Improve their ability to create safe, reliable, and useful quality software at reasonable cost and within a reasonable time.

8.03. Improve their ability to produce accurate, informative, and well-written documentation.

8.04. Improve their understanding of the software and related documents on which they work and of the environment in which they will be used.

8.05. Improve their knowledge of relevant standards and the law governing the software and related documents on which they work.

8.06 Improve their knowledge of this Code, its interpretation, and its application to their work.

8.07 Not give unfair treatment to anyone because of any irrelevant prejudices.

8.08 Not influence others to undertake any action that involves a breach of this Code.

8.09. Recognize that personal violations of this Code are inconsistent with being a professional software engineer.

This Code was developed by the IEEE-CS/ACM joint task force on Software Engineering Ethics and Professional Practices (SEEPP):

Executive Committee: Donald Gotterbarn (Chair), Keith Miller, and Simon Rogerson;

Members: Steve Barber, Peter Barnes, Ilene Burnstein, Michael Davis, Amr El-Kadi, N. Ben Fairweather, Milton Fulghum, N. Jayaram, Tom Jewett, Mark Kanko, Ernie Kallman, Duncan Langford, Joyce Currie Little, Ed Mechler, Manuel J. Norman, Douglas Phillips, Peter Ron Prinzivalli, Patrick Sullivan, John Weckert, Vivian Weil, S. Weisband and Laurie Honour Werth.

■ ■ ■

CHAPTER 19

Wrapping It all Up

All programmers are optimists. Perhaps this modern sorcery especially attracts those who believe in happy endings and fairy godmothers. Perhaps the hundreds of nitty frustrations drive away all but those who habitually focus on the end goal. Perhaps it is merely that computers are young, programmers are younger, and the young are always optimists.

—Frederick Brooks, Jr.[1]

It's the only job I can think of where I get to be both an engineer and an artist. There's an incredible, rigorous, technical element to it, which I like because you have to do very precise thinking. On the other hand, it has a wildly creative side where the boundaries of imagination are the only real limitation.

—Andy Hertzfeld

Reading Alex E. Bell's[2] and Mark Guzdial's[3] "Viewpoint" columns in the August 2008 issue of *Communications of the ACM*, I was struck by the synergy of the two articles. One is a cautionary tale about the tools to use in professional software development, and the other is, at least in part, a cautionary tale about language and syntax use in teaching programming. This got me to thinking about all the silver bullets we've tried in both development and education, and why most of them don't matter to real software development. This seems like an appropriate way to wrap up this extended discussion on software development.

What Have You Learned?

As I've said more than once in this book, software development is hard. I don't think that everyone can do it, and of those who can, I think few do it extremely well all the time. That, of course, is the attraction. Nobody really wants to work on easy problems. The challenge is to work on something you've never done before, something you might not even know if you can solve. That's what has you coming back to creating software again and again.

---

[1]Brooks, F. P. *The Mythical Man-Month : Essays on Software Engineering*, Silver Anniversary Edition. (Boston, MA: Addison-Wesley, 1995.)
[2]Bell, A. E. *Software Development Amidst the Whiz of Silver Bullets*, Communications of the ACM, 51, 8, 22–24 (August 2008).
[3]Guzdial, M. *Paving the Way for Computational Thinking*, Communications of the ACM, 51, 8, 25–27 (August 2008).

© John F. Dooley 2017
J. F. Dooley, *Software Development, Design and Coding*, https://doi.org/10.1007/978-1-4842-3153-1_19

Software development is one of the most creative things a human can do. Out of nothing, one takes a problem, wrestles with it, explores it, pokes at it, rips it apart, puts it back in a different form, comes up with that bit of inspiration that leads to a solution, and then converts it into an artifact that others can use effortlessly. Having others use your program to solve their problems is just the coolest thing.

Writing software is a humbling experience. It's so hard to get software right and so easy to get it wrong. In writing software, I've learned to embrace failure. Failure is an exciting and frustrating part of the process. From failure, you learn about yourself: you learn how you approach problems, you learn the types of mistakes you're prone to make, and you learn how to work around them. Failure teaches you perseverance because you just have to keep working until the program does.

Small teams build most software, and they build the best software. Small, highly motivated, and empowered teams are the most productive. Small teams also tend to use a slimmed-down development process. Unless you work for a large company that's desperate to be at SEI Capability Maturity Model Level 5[4], your processes can be very sparse. Detailed problem descriptions (most recently in the form of user stories), brainstorming design sessions, simple configuration management, peer code reviews, and a separate testing team take care of everything necessary to create almost defect-free code. Process flexibility, communication, and common ownership are the keys to project success.

A lot of really good software gets written, tested, and shipped every year—much more than the alleged "failure" numbers would have one believe.[5] The key issues dividing plan-driven development and agile development are the recognition of the constant changes in requirements and the idea that the end goal is always working software. The best thing about agile development is that it recognizes these facts and builds refactoring into its simple process.

Simple tools are the most effective. Simple tools allow you to cut to the heart of a problem and examine it closely with nothing in your way. They allow you to take it out, hold it in your hands, turn it over, and poke at it quickly and easily. Simple tools also allow you to join them together to do more complicated things. I'll just point you to Stephen Jenkins's article on "Old School" programming.[6] He's said it much better than I could.

Coding, debugging, and unit testing are at least as important as design. Experience gives a good programmer a deep sense of design and a wealth of patterns to draw on; experience gives a great programmer a deep, intimate knowledge of the programming language that is their tool. It's this deep, intimate knowledge that produces beautiful code.

The process of debugging a long, complex program is an immensely rewarding endeavor. Isolating a problem, uncovering your mistakes, building debugging scaffolding, hypothesizing a solution, reworking a design, finally identifying the error, and then creating a correct fix gives one such a rush of elation and satisfaction that it's at times nearly overwhelming.

What to Do Next?

Now that you've read all about software development and maybe tried some of the examples, what do you do next? How do you become a better software developer? Well, here are some suggestions:

- *Write code, write lots of code:* Experience helps a lot. Programming is a craft that requires practice and constant reinforcement. It's very likely that you'll need to learn a whole new set of tools and programming languages every five years or so. Having written lots of code will make that task easier.

---

[4]Paulk, M. C. *The Capability Maturity Model: Guidelines for Improving the Software Process*. (Reading, MA: Addison-Wesley, 1995.)

[5]Glass, R. "The Standish Report: Does It Really Describe a Software Crisis?" *Communications of the ACM*, 49, 8, 15–16 (August 2006).

[6]Jenkins, S. B. "Musings of an 'Old-School' Programmer," *Communications of the ACM*, 49, 5, 124–126 (May 2006).

- *Learn simple tools:* Simple tools give you flexibility. They also help you learn the fundamental skills that you can then take to more complicated IDEs. And when those IDEs get replaced—as they will—you can fall back on the simple tools till you learn the new IDE.

- *Read about problem solving and design:* People have been solving problems for several thousand years now and have been designing things for nearly that long. Writings in other areas can communicate common problem-solving strategies that also work for software development. Don't ignore Polya's *How to Solve It* book. It was written to solve math problems, but it translates very, very well to software[7]. Also don't ignore the classics in the computer science literature, like Dijkstra's *Structured Programming* book[8], Brooks's classic *The Mythical Man-Month*[9], Bentley's *Programming Pearls*[10], McConnell's *Rapid Development*[11,] and Beck's *Extreme Programming Explained*[12].

- *Read about programming and read about programmers:* There's a plethora of literature on programming. A number of books have been mentioned throughout this book. Two that bear repeating are Hunt and Thomas's *The Pragmatic Programmer*[13] and McConnell's *Code Complete 2*[14]. It's also a great idea to see how other programmers work. There's a developing literature on how great programmers think, work, and generally write great code. Two notable books are Lammer's *Programmers At Work*[15] and Oram and Wilson's *Beautiful Code*[16].

- *Talk to other programmers:* Books are an okay way to gather information, but talking to your peers can't be beat. A side-effect of pair programming is that you get to see how someone else works, how they approach problems, and how they code, debug, and write tests. Code review meetings are a great way to learn how others work. Code reviews also reinforce Gerald Weinberg's idea of *egoless programming*[17]. Once you get over the idea that you "own" the code in a software product (your employer owns it—read some of those documents you had to sign on the first day of work), you gain the ability to look at your code and the code of your co-workers objectively and you can learn from it.

- *Join the ACM and the IEEE-CS:* The Association for Computing Machinery (ACM) at `www.acm.org` and the IEEE Computer Society (IEEE-CS) at `www.computer.org` are the two main professional organizations for computer scientists. Their journals contain a wealth of information about all things related to computers and computing, their conferences are worth attending, and they have free online books and courses for members. You won't regret joining one or both of them.

---

[7]Polya, G. *How To Solve It: A New Aspect of Mathematical Method*, 2nd Edition. (Princeton, NJ: Princeton University Press, 1957.)

[8]Dahl, O. J., E. Dijkstra, et al. *Structured Programming*. (London, UK: Academic Press, 1972.)

[9]Brooks, 1995.

[10]Bentley, J. *Programming Pearls*, 2nd Edition. (Reading, MA: Addison-Wesley, 2000.)

[11]McConnell, S. *Rapid Development: Taming Wild Software Schedules*. (Redmond, WA: Microsoft Press, 1996.)

[12]Beck, K. *Extreme Programming Explained: Embrace Change*. (Boston, MA: Addison-Wesley, 2006.)

[13]Hunt, A. and D. Thomas. *The Pragmatic Programmer: From Journeyman to Master*. (Boston, MA: Addison-Wesley, 2000.)

[14]McConnell, S. *Code Complete 2*. (Redmond, WA: Microsoft Press, 2004.)

[15]Lammers, S. *Programmers At Work*. (Redmond, WA: Microsoft Press, 1986.)

[16]Oram, A. and G. Wilson, Eds. *Beautiful Code: Leading Programmers Explain How They Think*. (Sebastopol, CA: O'Reilly Media, 2007.)

[17]Weinberg, G. M. *The Psychology of Computer Programming, Silver Anniversary Edition*. (New York, NY: Dorset House, 1988.)

- *Be humble:* The following quote from Dijkstra says it all. Software development is hard. Programs are very complex, and programs of any size are extremely hard to understand completely. Besides being one of the most creative things that humans have ever done, computer software is one of the most complex. Be humble. Work hard. Have fun!

The competent programmer is fully aware of the strictly limited size of his own skull; therefore he approaches the programming task in full humility . . .

—Edsger Dijkstra[18]

And lastly, I couldn't resist a quote that had both the words *magic* and *computer* in it:

The magic of myth and legend has come true in our time. One types the correct incantation on a keyboard, and a display screen comes to life, showing things that never were nor could be. . . . The computer resembles the magic of legend in this respect, too. If one character, one pause, of the incantation is not strictly in proper form, the magic doesn't work. Human beings are not accustomed to being perfect, and few areas of human activity demand it. Adjusting to the requirement for perfection is, I think, the most difficult part of learning to program.

—Frederick Brooks

References

Beck, K. *Extreme Programming Explained: Embrace Change.* (Boston, MA: Addison-Wesley, 2006.)

Bell, A. E. "Software Development Amidst the Whiz of Silver Bullets," *Communications of the ACM*, 51, 8, 22–24 (August 2008).

Bentley, J. *Programming Pearls*, 2nd Edition. (Reading, MA: Addison-Wesley, 2000.)

Brooks, F. P. *The Mythical Man-Month : Essays on Software Engineering*, Silver Anniversary Edition. (Boston, MA: Addison-Wesley, 1995.)

Dahl, O. J., E. Dijkstra, et al. *Structured Programming.* (London, UK: Academic Press, 1972.)

Dijkstra, E. "The Humble Programmer," *CACM* 15(10): 859-866 (1972).

Glass, R. "The Standish Report: Does It Really Describe a Software Crisis?" *Communications of the ACM*, 49, 8, 15–16 (August 2006).

Guzdial, M. "Paving the Way for Computational Thinking," *Communications of the ACM*, 51, 8, 25–27 (August 2008).

Hunt, A. and D. Thomas. *The Pragmatic Programmer: From Journeyman to Master.* (Boston, MA: Addison-Wesley, 2000.)

Jenkins, S. B. "Musings of an 'Old-School' Programmer," *Communications of the ACM*, 49, 5, 124–126 (May 2006).

Lammers, S. *Programmers At Work.* (Redmond, WA: Microsoft Press, 1986.)

McConnell, S. *Rapid Development: Taming Wild Software Schedules.* (Redmond, WA: Microsoft Press, 1996.)

McConnell, S. *Code Complete 2.* (Redmond, WA: Microsoft Press, 2004.)

Oram, A. and G. Wilson, Eds. *Beautiful Code: Leading Programmers Explain How They Think.* (Sebastopol, CA: O'Reilly Media, Inc, 2007.)

Paulk, M. C. *The Capability Maturity Model: Guidelines for Improving the Software Process.* (Reading, MA: Addison-Wesley, 1995.)

---

[18]Dijkstra, E. "The Humble Programmer," *CACM* 15(10): 859-866 (1972).

Polya, G. *How To Solve It: A New Aspect of Mathematical Method*, 2nd Edition. (Princeton, NJ: Princeton University Press, 1957.)

Weinberg, G. M. *The Psychology of Computer Programming*, Silver Anniversary Edition. (New York, NY: Dorset House, 1988.)

Index

© John F. Dooley 2017
J. F. Dooley, *Software Development, Design and Coding*, https://doi.org/10.1007/978-1-4842-3153-1

Get the eBook for only $5!

Why limit yourself?

With most of our titles available in both PDF and ePUB format, you can access your content wherever and however you wish—on your PC, phone, tablet, or reader.

Since you've purchased this print book, we are happy to offer you the eBook for just $5.

To learn more, go to http://www.apress.com/companion or contact support@apress.com.

Apress®

Lightning Source UK Ltd.
Milton Keynes UK
UKHW051351010721
386464UK00004B/77